The Fate of Translation

Studies on Themes and Motifs in Literature

Horst S. Daemmrich
General Editor

Vol. 82

PETER LANG
New York • Washington, D.C./Baltimore • Bern
Frankfurt am Main • Berlin • Brussels • Vienna • Oxford

Robert Eisenhauer

The Fate of Translation

PETER LANG
New York • Washington, D.C./Baltimore • Bern
Frankfurt am Main • Berlin • Brussels • Vienna • Oxford

Library of Congress Cataloging-in-Publication Data
Eisenhauer, Robert G.
The fate of translation / Robert Eisenhauer.
p. cm. — (Studies on themes and motifs in literature; vol. 82)
Includes bibliographical references and index.
1. Literature, Modern—History and criticism. 2. Translating and interpreting.
I. Title. II. Series: Studies on themes and motifs in literature; v. 82.
PN710.E398   809'03—dc22   2005020640
ISBN 0-8204-6343-4
ISSN 1056-3970

Bibliographic information published by **Die Deutsche Bibliothek**.
Die Deutsche Bibliothek lists this publication in the "Deutsche
Nationalbibliografie"; detailed bibliographic data is available
on the Internet at http://dnb.ddb.de/.

The paper in this book meets the guidelines for permanence and durability
of the Committee on Production Guidelines for Book Longevity
of the Council of Library Resources.

© 2006 Peter Lang Publishing, Inc., New York
275 Seventh Avenue, 28th Floor, New York, NY 10001
www.peterlangusa.com

Printed in Germany

Contents

Illustrations

Preliminaries: *Translation on the* Carreteras

A voice from out the Future cries,
'On! on!'—but o'er the Past
(Dim gulf!) my spirit lies
Mute, motionless, aghast!
　　　　　　Edgar A. Poe

Books like *The Fate of Translation* have been written before by critics better known or, indeed, famous. As with anyone working in the field, I have the sense that I am under the ominous pressure of names: Goethe, Hölderlin, and Benjamin, much-discussed "brands" in the translation "industry," but also those of Abraham Cowley, William Taylor, Padgett Powell, and Matthew Barney, less familiar to many readers. Those who owe allegiance to a certain "school" of criticism and are used to seeing strong conclusions drawn from analytical *partis pris* will, perhaps, be disappointed. If I had to mention guiding principles, it would be Bakhtin's "surprisingness" and Manfred Frank's "Unhintergehbarkeit" (not easily translated into *Norte-American*ese, but roughly equivalent to "not-capable-of-being-gotten-behind-the-back-of") in matters of individuality and taste. This in no way scants the essential *aperçu* that "people are not integral" (Jackson Maclow). Jean-Luc Nancy's notion of a resensing through the poetic text has influenced my readings in numerous ways. The fate of translation is inseparable in practical terms from translators laboring in the trenches or within a cavern-like space—whose activities have either been lauded, taken for granted, or dismissed by scholar-critics with one or more pet hermeneutic aversions. Hölderlin's admonition notwithstanding, *habent sua fata literati litteratoresque*—this one included.

What makes *The Fate of Translation* different from preceding efforts is an attempt to construct partial narratives of translation and to discern the "full fan-experience" across a broad spectrum of European enactments, as well as through some of its peculiar native innings, most notable among them belonging to Poe in the 19th century and, equally salient, though certainly not (yet) a household name, to the performance art of Matt Barney at the end of the 20th and beginning of the 21st. The reception of the precursor-text and its translation, so it seems, is inseparable from the otherness of that which has displaced the ancient word or *logos* and just now crossed the threshold of the lyceum. At the point where the going gets either fate-fullest or simply weird, as Hunter Thompson used to say, or where inhuman eyes and ears confront us, as our shadows or doubles, we meet Poe and Barney.

Two critics who have also influenced my perspective on translation are Erich Heller and Hugh Kenner, both of whom allude in passing to the poetic efforts of Abraham Cowley. Since I discuss Kenner at some length in one of the essays, I will focus briefly on remarks made by Heller in his classic *The Disinherited Mind*. Heller's text places Cowley as a kind of simian figure in the midst of a literary-historical sequence beginning with the Zwingli–Luther debate on the literality of the sacramental host and ending with Faust puzzling over the correct translation of the word *Logos* on Easter Sunday: "*Logos* into word, word into deed, dog into devil—the scene is set for the hazard of modern poetry."[1] Briefly stated, the relevance of Cowley and Faust to our (post)modern precariousness would be that they, like Zwingli, are no longer willing to accept the authority of the literal word—as truth made self-evidently present or dogmatic certainty. Nothing is acceptable to Faust, and *tout est permi*; the literal *Logos* is no longer at the transsubstantiated center, but can only be displaced, exiled, and/or reprojected outward—in the direction of untrained or canine ears. Realizing that Pindar is too obscure to be presentable, Cowley assumes the brooding burden of re-presenting him, of making the Greek perspicuous to post-Renaissance minds inured to rational thought and hence of turning gold into lead, mythic flesh into prosaic bread, and metaphysical wine into the 17th-century equivalent of bottled water. Thus is it is Cowley who, precisely because of his "ungainliness" (*an sich*) is, *unhintergehbar for us*, in our humming state of repercussive art-lessness at the dawn of the 21st century—we who find ourselves deprived of Dionysian presence and therefore subject all the more to the hysterias of "fandom," a devil's menagerie of sometimes miniature or monstrous poodles.

We can, however, "air things out" a bit, abandoning the stuffiness of the study for the open road and what Wordsworth calls "broad highway appearances." The image of roads taken and not taken hounds translation. We have placed the Spanish word "*carreteras*" at the head of this preface because it tracks more closely than "roads" the Latin noun *carrus*, a cart or wagon, and because it suggests the Latin American universe that is, at the dawn of the century, closing in or opening up all around us who, apparently, are merely taking up space in "El Norte." The Anglo-Saxon inheritance of the United States will undergo a Latinate sea-change equivalent, perhaps, to that of the early 16th century. It will be carried out, however, not by doctors, lawyers, and prelates, but by the common people, the *campesinos* from a vast, boundaryless elsewhere who now trim our hedges. We have no choice but to accept the fact that we are living through one of those "epochal transitions" Lacan speaks of, when the relation between signifier and signified is fundamentally altered; we as a people are being translated to a different place, even as these words are being written. The *Plattenglisch* ground beneath our feet has shifted, whether we are aware of it or not, and we are already part Guatemalan, Mexican, or Cuban in our pedestrianism.

Equally, we are being pulled toward the Orient, as the East is stretched toward us. In the film *Lost in Translation,* the actors watch Fellini's *La Dolce Vita* in a Tokyo hotel-room. Murakami's latest novel bears the name of a major figure of 20th-century European fiction: the central character, if that word can even be meaningfully applied here, is named "Kafka." Postmodernism encourages hybridizations of the strangest sort, and the movement of a butterfly's wing in Tokyo seems to generate big gusts, if not hurricanes, in New York. The intense care that Nabokov lavishes on the accurate translation of "Die Verwandlung" projects a priceless philological allure, but our versions of the classics seem to belong in the bargain basement—more willing to engage in the labyrinthine errors and dead-end antics of avant-garde experimentation. Or they are homelier, ungainlier, and intended for a mutant reading public—the ever shifting, perennially fickle fan-base. Perhaps the freedom to be aberrant, experimentally grotesque *and* comedically arabesque, is the best we can hope for. Zukofsky's modernist, metapoetic *Catullus* is at the antipodes from Nabokovian rigor; it is bold in its strategy of "making it new," sophisticated, despite its egregious unschooledness, and exciting, as barbaric things sometimes are, the equivalent in some respects of Cowley's Pindar and *Finnegan's Wake.* The wheels of Fancy here are definitely set free. Much different from the Zukofsky is Armand Schwerner's multi-decade *Tablets* project, a translation of possible or virtual hieroglyphs from a Near East of the mind, whose signs reflect a care (*Sorge*) which can only "mean" us, in our state of precarious enigmahood. These projects, in turn, hearken back to the notorious *Ossian,* praised by many Romantics, and crucial, I think, to Hölderlin's Chiron-inspired project, emitting a radioactive, if bogus "Northern enchantment," whose simulacrous lugubriousness celebrates its triumph in a postmodernism where one is supposed to be enthusiastic about replicas and copies of all sorts, and feeding off someone else's cerebrospinal fluid seems a not entirely implausible, if also melancholy, hobby. We are becoming inured to rescaled, rewired, or juiced-up monsters of publicity, radiant and otherwise, that only yesterday played obscure twi-night doubleheaders somewhere down on the Rio Grande. No doubt, many similar "full fan-experiences" with crepuscular creatures, half-owls or half-horses, lie ahead.

Literary historians can look back to the threefold model proposed by Goethe in the *West-Östlicher Divan,* when it was still possible to think of literature as the province of poetry exclusively, of the epic, the lyric, and the dramatic. A translator might a) reproduce a poetic text as prose, b) substitute his or her *Sinn* for the meaning of the original, or c) translate literally. Metapoesis, or hyperbolically exceeding the language of the original, would be a strategy suggested by b), but it seems likely that Goethe had Wieland and his own Pindar translations in mind rather than the low-flying exercises of Cowley. With Cowley, sandwiched between Zwingli and Faust, not only a foreign *Sinn* emerges from the metapoetic barrel, but new thoughts, images, and entire "cool" passages not found in the *Ur*-text. These are the product of something we might label "enthusiastic clarification," a procedure still not fully understood, even if we compare it, say, with Baudrillard's "ecstasy of communication." To render the obscure "perspicuous" by a Muse of clarification requires a language different, sometimes worse but also, in isolated instances, not "better" than the original, but richer and stranger, like an isotope carefully nurtured in the physics lab.

The motive of clarification, though with different *modi operandi*, haunts Dryden and Wordsworth in their attempt to make Vergil speak modern English. When not translating Pindar literally, Goethe's goddess is "Fantasie," from which comes the word "fan" and a *soft* drink, products of 19th-century consensus. What is framed as a brilliantly facetious take on an Olympian ode (intended for Charlotte v. Stein) addresses issues of translation and metapoesis suggesting how we, wearing team jerseys in our derivative storming and stressing, become fans or fanatics instead of aspiring poet laureates. The problematics of multiculturalism confronts us in the texts of Padgett Powell and Günter Grass, where, between "the other truth" of seacoast dialect and the "no-man's-land" of history, translation (transliteration) goes on a Gullah, Kashubian, Polish, or German holiday from which there is no returning home to an unmediated *logos*. The rendering of names in Grass's novels continues to stir lively debates on the politics of translation, just as strident today as they were before the Wall fell, while Powell's *Edisto*, putting a Poe-like, Southern accent on "multi-culturalism," causes us to rethink, from the ground up, our sense of polyphonic discourse.

We are left desiring that elusive quality Pater found in Hellenic antiquity and in Romantic art, comparing it to a "Holy Grail"—going so far as to travel on potholed *carreteras* through the Greek islands in our quest. But a postmodern skepticism/cynicism also colors our nostalgia. We go to the Aegean and farther east, or south of the border, or back to Hölderlin in search of own version of a chiaroscuro "full fan-experience."

This and my other books are a compendium of that which may truly be said to be *unhintergehbar*, my own eclectic taste, as an enthused and sometimes impassioned reader of ancient as well as contemporary literature.

1. Wordsworth and the Goethean Intertext

...the wheels of thy bold Coach pass quick and free;
And all's an open Road to Thee....
　　　　Abraham Cowley, "The Muse"

Wisdom and Spirit of the universe!
Thou soul that art the Eternity of Thought!...
...thus from my first dawn
Of childhood didst Thou intertwine for me
The passions that build up our human Soul,
Not with the mean & vulgar works of Man,
But with high objects, with eternal things
With life & nature, purifying thus
The elements of feeling & of thought
And sanctifying, by such discipline,
Both pain & fear, until we recognize
A grandeur in the beatings of the heart.
　　　　Prelude (1805), I, 428–441

...The noise of wood and water, and the mist
Which on the line of each of those two Roads
Advanced in such indisputable shapes,
All these were spectacles and sounds by which
I often would repair and thence would drink,
As at a fountain....
　　　　Prelude (1805), I, 380–385

Vorspiel

The pack of Hecate barks. Three times the hollow valley echoes with a mournful
sound. The ground trembles. The earth shakes.
　　　　Seneca, *Oedipus.*

This essay revisits ground familiar to some Wordsworth scholars, examining texts by Wordsworth in the light of "Der Wandrer" (1774) one of Goethe's better known, ode-like lyrics in dialogue form, translated in 1798 by William Taylor of Norwich. Refocusing the perspective somewhat, I argue that Goethean *Andacht* (itself a Germanicized version of Latin *pietas*, and thus easily translated back into English as "piety," but altered yet again, significantly, by Wordworth into "natural piety"), the obsession or fascination with the genius-like mediation of an infant at a scene or site of aesthetic, sexual, political, or commercial intercourse, and the proximity of the poor to a locale connected with, but also disjoined from the cultural past are not only determinants of Wordsworth's poetic logic during the between 1797 and 1805, but also serve, in much expanded and intensified form. as guide- or mileposts on the way to a far larger imaginative restructuring of the fallen state of England's body politic. "Body," in this case, is the operative word—in the sense that Wordsworth's imagination, more than, say, that of Keats or Shelley, both controls and is controlled by a world of continual dis- and reincarnation,[1] of entity emptied and recharged, where thought is projected as striving to achieve corporeality, as an assembly-line of persons or person-like forces, through prosopopoeia. In this world of vagrant imagination, Wordsworth, shaken equally by the excesses of the French Revolution and reactionary politics at home, stages a Goethean reascent to one or more polemical or pre-historic springs (*Ur-sprünge*, both springs and leaps of the mind) for legitimating inspiration—in what becomes a belated effort to reimagine and resuscitate the nation's heart, not according to that which "once was reality," but according to that which the redemptive "I" of Wordsworth would make of it, a counter-historicism or, with apologies to Buber, an "encounter-historicism" of I/eye, ear, and other. Thus the importance of the monastic suppression as a pivotal moment in the psychohistory of the History-Subject established in the absolute Fichtean equivalence of "I" and "Not-I"—one that Wordsworth both appropriates and appreciates, in the sense that he adds programmatic value to it. Last, but hardly least, we are confronted in the Goethean *Ur*-scene with a situation of inscription and effacement which will not be unfamiliar to readers of de Man.

In the *Drei Abhandlungen* of 1905 Freud posits a startling reality behind or underlying the fantasies of his patients, encapsulating the "original insight":

> Es scheint mir sehr wohl möglich, daß alles, was uns heute in der Analyse als Phantasie erzählt wird, die Kinderverführung, die Entzündung der Sexualerregung an der Beobachtung des elterlichen Verkehrs, die Kastrationsdrohung—oder vielmehr die Kastration,—einmal Realität war.[2]

> [It appears to me <to be> quite likely possible, that everything, which is told to us today in the analysis of fantasy, the seduction of children, the incitement to sexual arousal in the observation of parental intercourse, the threat of castration—or, rather, castration,—was once reality.]

Immediately after this quote, Laplanche and Pontalis add parenthetically "...(was tatsächliche oder faktische Realität war, wäre demnach *psychische* Realitat geworden)...." ["...(what was actual or factual reality, according to this <Freud's insight> became psychic reality)."] before allowing Freud to continue: "...und daß das phantasierende Kind einfach Lücken der individuellen Wahrheit mit prähistorischer Wahrheit ausgefüllt hat" ["...and that the fantasy-producing child has simply filled out gaps of individual truth with prehistoric truth"] (*U*, 37). Scarcely a page later, the authors mention how Freud describes a case in which the paranoia of a female patient is triggered by a certain poking or ticking sound—"ein Pochen oder Ticken"—like that of a camera shutter or watch, whose noise is traced either to the sound of the parent's lovemaking or the fear the supervening child has that it might reveal itself *to* the parents in its nocturnal comings and goings. All it takes is a random "provocation" or accident to unleash the neurotic patient's fear of self-revealing crepitation.

Laplanche and Pontalis define originary fantasy thus:

> Die Urphantasie—die jenseits der Geschichte des Subjekts liegt, jedoch innerhalb der Geschichte; die Diskurs und symbolische Kette ist, jedoch geprägt vom Imaginären; Struktur zwar, aber aufgebaut aus zufälligen Elementen—ist zunächst einmal Phantasie und als solche durch bestimmte Züge gekennzeichnet, die sie nur schwer einem reinen transzendentalen Schema angleichen lassen, obschon sie der Erfahrung deren Bedingungen der Möglichkeit liefert. (*U*, 39)

> [The originary fantasy—which lies on the other side of the history of the subject, nevertheless within the history; which is discourse and symbolic chain, nonetheless traversed by the imaginary; <a> structure, indeed, but built up from coincidental elements—is from the outset fantasy and as such characterized by specific traits, which only allow themselves with difficulty to be compared to a purely transcendental scheme, although it <fantasy> supplies <us with a> possibility of the experience of those specificities.]

Therefore, as much as one might want to leave the subject within his or her own story or fantasy, there is nonetheless another history "on the other side" of the neurotic subject or patient, i.e., in a "discourse and symbolic chain" composed partly of imaginary elements and partly of purely random ones, which can rise to the level of a transcendental scheme or pattern only "with difficulty." Thus, even if we wanted to, we could not extract ourselves from the originary scene or escape the piling-up of fortuitous, "prehistoric" triggering mechanisms. There is something in originary fantasy that always pulls us down out of transcendence to "its level" or that prevents the evolution of a distinct or detached theory apart from the trepidation unleashed by the scene itself in its particulars, a scene that no one else, perhaps, could or should see, one whose repetitious instancing prevents our ascent to sublimer heights, that "haunts" us and resists psychic integration.[3] Nowhere is the affect associated with an originary scene asserted more forcefully that in "Nutting," whose title, as others have noted, suggests a pun on the common English word for the absence of something, a Lear-like word of nihilation, after Wordsworth notes how he, on piratic impulse, has torn a branch from one of the trees, taken perversely puerile delight in the act of mutilation (which at some point would involve a cracking sound or crepitation made when the branch actually was broken off), and then been observed by a spy- or warden-like heaven which seems reconfigured from the vertical to the horizontal, from the celestial to the level of a door being unexpectedly opened. Thus the scene of perpetration, of dream-like molestation as well as mutilation, is usurped by a king-like self, becoming uniquely *his* before a spectating, noiseless audience of trees:

> Ere from the mutilated bower I turned
> Exulting, rich beyond the wealth of kings,
> I felt a sense of pain when I beheld
> The silent trees, and saw the intruding sky....[4]

The guilt is then assuaged by a "Maiden"—or would be so assuaged, if the address to her were not framed by a hortatory subjunctive, i.e., a wish:

> Then, dearest Maiden, move along these shades
> In gentleness of heart: with gentle hand
> Touch—for there is a spirit in the woods. (54–56)

Whether the unnamed Maiden is not herself a shade, remains conjecture on the reader's part; her presence seems as shadowy as the Pan-like or "agrest" figure said to haunt the woods. Her touch remains, however, as a more substantial aspect of her being—a tactility which will resurface in the figure of Margaret at the well, another kind of sylvan spirit in a different neck of the woods. However, as late as 1842, in a "Prelude" prefixed to "Poems chiefly of Early and Late Years," the poet will resample the mutilated branch episode, making it an emblem of false projection, placing it in proximity to a Voice singing arias of communion with the humble outdoors:

> ...why should hope to me
> Be wanting that sometimes, where fancied ills
> Harass the mind and strip from off the bowers
> Of private life their natural pleasantness,
> A Voice...
> Lodged within compass of the humblest sights,
> The cheerful intercourse with wood and field...
> Will not be heard in vain? (*PW* 421, 34–37, 39–42)

Even more pertinent, however, is the question asked at the conclusion of Book I of *The Prelude*[5]:

> ...need I dread from thee
> Harsh judgments, if I am so loth to quit
> Those recollected hours that have the charm
> Of visionary things, and lovely forms
> And sweet sensations that throw back our life
> And almost make our Infancy itself

A visible scene, on which the sun is shining? (657–663)

Let me suggest how a passage from Book VII of *The Prelude*, where Wordsworth, by framing "the broad high-way appearance" in terms that would be understandable to "Strangers of all ages," describes his impressions of a London street, can be situated in the context of the foregoing psychoanalytical remarks and what Laplanche elsewhere calls the "implantation of fantasy" (*TSS*, 8)—the process of making a scene "his" or "yours" as opposed to "mine." When we get to the "comers and goers" it all begins to sound like Whitman:

> Shall I give way,
> Copying the impression of the memory,
> Though things remembered idly do half seem
> The work of Fancy, shall I, as the mood
> Inclines me, here describe, for pastime's sake
> Some portion of that motley imagery,
> A vivid pleasure of my youth, and, now
> Among the lonely places that I love
> A frequent day-dream for my riper mind?
> The broad high-way appearance, as it strikes
> On Strangers of all ages, the quick dance
> Of colours, lights and forms, the Babel din
> The endless stream of men, and moving things,
> From hour to hour the illimitable walk
> Still among streets with cloud and sky above,
> The wealth, the bustle and the eagerness,
> The glittering Chariots with their pamper'd Steeds,
> Stalls, Barrows, Porters; midway in the Street
> The Scavenger, who begs with hat in hand,
> The labouring Hackney Coaches, the rash speed
> Of Coaches travelling far, whirl'd on with horn
> Loud blowing, and the sturdy Drayman's Team,
> Ascending from some Alley of the Thames
> And striking right across the crowded Strand
> Till the fore Horse veer round with punctual skill:
> Here there and everywhere a weary throng
> The Comers and the Goers face to face,
> Face after face; the string of dazzling Wares,
> Shop after shop, with Symbols, blazon'd Names,
> And all the Tradesman's honours overhead;
> Here, fronts of houses, like a title-page
> With letters huge inscribed from top to toe;
> Station'd above the door, like guardian Saints,
> There, allegoric shapes, female or male;
> Or physiognomies of real men,
> Land-Warriors, Kings, or Admirals of the Sea,
> Boyle, Shakspear, Newton, or the attractive head

Of some Scotch doctor, famous in his day. (*P*, VII, 145–183)

I have quoted at length because it seems obvious that Wordsworth, while disgusted by many of the uglier, vulgar aspects of London life, cannot leave behind the "motley imagery" of this particular "discourse and symbolic chain," or the window it affords on the movement (a multifaceted rumbling, jostling, and knocking-about registered by parataxis rather than logical subordination) of humanity and things humanly connected within a confined and narrow space—a space much like a room, a country path, a river, or a river-bed. We might say that it is the traffic of Fancy, the embedded *Verkehr*, that interests Wordsworth, as Brooklyn Ferry would later interest the American bard, and that it is this which lends the scene its whole or integral vividness and, for the moment, its randomly sampled pleasure. Choosing to linger with Fancy means that Wordsworth allies himself, at least for the moment, with the freewheeling Muse of an Abraham Cowley, for example, who bids him harness "Phansie," Judgment, and Wit in order to put her vehicle onto an uncontested highway: "...the wheels of thy bold Coach pass quick and free;/ And all's an open Road to Thee...." And we will assume that the psychosexual sense of fancy or Fancy's traffic is one that "should not be missed" in a close reading of Wordsworth, either here in Book VII of *The Prelude* or anywhere else, for that matter, that Wordsworth's originary scene is one of *intercourse* within narrow boundaries preceded by the rhetorical question "Shall I give way?" which, as we recall, was asked by the archetypal traveler[6] on another road in the pre-history of ancient Greece—whose brigand-like waylaying of a royal personage whom he murders and subsequent quest for knowledge concerning his own crime initiates the tragic scenario underlying the earliest psychoanalytical insights. In the context of England's highways, however, "Shall I give way?" has an even more specific reference—which is that of yielding to the governmental and postal pressure of the king on *his* highway. Failure to make room for the royal business and equipage means the commission of a serious act of civil disobedience or *lèse-majesté* on the part of the supervening *subject*—one, however, that is far more dire *at the time*, in a symbolic sense, since it involves an entire suite of counter-revolutionary phobias and cross-Channel guilts associated with the decade of the 1790s. It was not for nothing that they buried the hearts of murderers and highwaymen, with a stake through them, beneath the crossroads of England, just as they placed gibbets on the limits of every city and village— as a warning to the fancifully seditious or randomly homicidal.[7] Wordsworth's "Shall I give way?" carries this rebellious burden as a subtext, especially in the final lines quoted above, which deal with the title-like house fronts of prominent and/or titled personages, while phrasing his own anxiety at yielding to the temptations of what he considers to be be mere memory bits or bytes, the data of purely visual recall (Fancy as opposed to the higher faculty of Imagination, a distinction developed by Wordsworth in the 1815 Preface to *Poems*).[8] His "giving way" to the clangor and "Babel din" of urban experience is our 21st-century gain, however, since we no longer share the critical anxieties of a Romantic subject, but do possess an unabated, perhaps infantile, thirst for the auditory and the visual, scenography, and even originary scenes—to the extent that this survey-like passage and others like it may claim to represent an essential component of the overall aesthetic merit in the major Wordsworth, suggesting a movement in the direction of realism and a revolution in the poetic language[9] of versifiers to come, programmatic voices such as Whitman and even Baudelaire.[10] Such a *seeming* recuperation of, or "giving way to" superficial experience, sensory certainty, and the "tyranny of the eye"[11] in *The Prelude* goes against the grain or taste of recent critical interpretation, but it fits very well what De Quincey calls "The Literature of Power," by virtue of its impressionistic quality, its search- or spotlighting of the vast panorama of London traffic, by which it—and by this I mean the poetic imagination—acquires a kind of rebounding neural power over the field that it scans. And part of such merit lies in Wordsworth's waylaying power or in the assertion of a fantastic, vividly totalizing[12] force over what constitutes the urban panorama—Cowley's "great and murmuring hive"— up to and including the way it signs itself "with Symbols" and "blazon'd names" suggesting a feudal or heraldic order yet present, vestigially, vagrantly, with worldly idols in place of saints—for the purpose, as it were, of providing a subjective ego with exquisite pleasure and pain—on the fronts of houses. We shall return to these fronts or faces of houses presently.

The passage just quoted mirrors the larger totalization which is Book VII, whose all-inclusiveness calls generic distinctions (between romance and pastoral, for example) into question and renders problematic the division between "high" and "low" subject matter, creating a "zone of contact" where the country gentleman[13] and city-dweller knock against each other for position in the high road of a text whose subjective, confessional focus, as in *The Excursion*, is the growth and development of the "Mind of Man," a region haunted by "My Mind," where the king can be obviated without being slain, and the noise of his and every other equipage hushed:

> A vivid pleasure of my youth, and, now
> Among the lonely places that I love

A frequent day-dream for my riper mind.

As if to reproject regicidal source material without the anxiety attendant upon an actual murder of the king, the poet takes a question from *Julius Caesar*, II, i, 285–286—"Dwell I but in the suburbs of your good pleasure?"— transposing the thought to the precincts and traffic of the "up close and personal," of *his* mind: "...yet all this/ Pass'd not beyond the suburbs of the mind" in lines 506–507. Book VII, then, is crucial to an understanding of how the creative process operates when Wordsworth examines the status of *his* scene or story with respect to traditional genres and the burden of the past. In terms of a poetic practice close to the realism of prose, Wordsworth is Nietzsche's disoriented or "modern man," who does not know what road he is on or who is on many roads, imaginatively and intertextually speaking, while at the same time thinking he knows in an Oedipal sense the position (*oide pou*) he finds himself in, in terms of that which is randomly vivid *to him*: looking for paratactic clues to the unity of all being, i.e. engaged in what Heidegger would term an existential hermeneutics. This makes the poet modern, like us, in that the lostness or the sense of the "country gentleman displaced" serves as an occasion for the registering of strange sights, whose feudal showiness may be contrasted with the more furtive blazonings of the human heart and its invisible privacies and privations—all this on the margins of the aesthetic and/or viatic implications of the skating question: "Shall I give way?"[14] In other words, "Shall I give way" is but a part of the larger context of scene-making and stealing on the contested street of anterior figuration, in which the razzle-dazzle of high station visible in Homeric or Vergilian "chariots" and their "steeds"—19th-century equivalents of chrome-plating and vanity effects on automobiles—gives way to "allegoric shapes."

We have to reckon also with the controversial insight of Marjorie Levinson that Wordsworth rewrites the pastoral scene, particularly in "Tintern Abbey," in order to further a "hortatory political discourse about the French and the Industrial Revolutions."[15] Thus the pastoral mode, an "under-" or "other" song of the urban predicament coordinate with elegy and epitaph, furthers ironic representation of post-traumatic "source material." The timeless *rus* functions as an inverted mirror of the hectic *urbs* and vice versa. While remaining ethically distinct spheres, they are aesthetically congruent—with the "iam summa procul villarum culmina fumant" of the first *Eclogue* serving as template (the 1850 text of *The Prelude* reveals the explicit debt to Vergil, inasmuch as "distance" made the sight of smoke rising from London "ruralized," i.e., the river-front factories were peasant huts pouring fireplace smoke into the air over Cumberland).

When Wordsworth encounters that busy street in London—head on, so to speak—he is also tracing a deictic itinerary down a country lane in Somerset (a name which puts a plain Anglo-Saxon front on its more poetic geographical designation in Latin as *aestiva regio* or "summery region"); when we see the heraldic fronts of the great London houses, we are looking, by means of a kind of telepathy or television, through a satiric or countersatiric lens, into a different time and space, equally the now of the West country, with its exquisite ruined abbeys and monasteries, *and* its polymorphously legended prehistoric past,[16] recalled in allusions to buried bones, barrows, mounds, and stone circles, and heard, at times, as a kind of magisterial voice. What I will call Wordsworth's "pastoral coding"[17] of reference thus requires a fairly energetic hermeneutic *Eingriff* to disengage what *seems* from what *is*, a subtler, not entirely tangential substance in which both Goethe and Shakespeare, among others, play primary roles. Even the most sedulous hermeneut may find such an effort daunting, if not impossible, at times, inasmuch as the language of Wordsworth skews objective reference for a representation in which the signifier receives subjective grounding, and signs point the way to a deixis of one or more cross-referential prime/primal time psycho-histories. In terms of Heideggerian thought, this means that ontology, the abstract discourse of being, finds itself displaced by the ontic, a discourse of the self retracing steps (*pas*) of being on the basis of a hermeneutic confrontation with the Not-I.[18] Subjectivity, in its sublimating accents and ascents, is crossed with or stages its uncanny rendezvous with substance in haunted spots of time. Pastoral irony is but one of the stylistic modes employed in the major texts.

Thus the importance of Wordsworth's Stendahl-like mirror dawdling down the busy London street and the deictic necessity of that which it finally sees, as "not just one," that which is *here*:

> Here, fronts of houses, like a title-page
> With letters huge inscribed from top to toe;
> Station'd above the door, like guardian Saints...

but also *there*:

> There, allegoric shapes, female or male;
> Or physiognomies of real men,
> Land-Warriors, Kings, or Admirals of the Sea,
> Boyle, Shakspear, Newton, or the attractive head
> Of some Scotch doctor, famous in his day....

It does not take great hermeneutic acumen to note that the huge letters inscribed on the fronts of the private houses occupy a place once reserved on the portals or tympanums of cathedrals for the faces of saints. These letters are like the beginnings of books, not just any books, but illuminated manuscripts of the Middle Ages, which usually have wonderfully large, highly decorative initials on their first pages. In short, Wordsworth here epitomizes the Protestant revolution in terms of the displacement of one kind of sign, which is il-literate and sculptural, that of the guardian saint, by another, represented by the literality of the printed word used to decorate the private edifices made possible, in their elevation before the partly admiring, partly threatened eye/I, by commerce. In the consciousness of such displacement the ontic perspective of the poet is forged as one looking up from below to the thread of the Reformation and the threat of history. On the second beat of the observing heart, its diastole, as it were, in the "there" moment, we see the physiognomies or faces of real men, placed in the verse according to no particular chronological order, Boyle, Shakespeare, Newton, juxtaposed with the nameless head of "some Scotch doctor famous in his day," but presumably unrecognizable in the present, whose name has, precisely, been effaced due to the obliterating flow of time, whose former stateliness has become, on the one hand, something like a nameless statistic to the indifferent cosmos, but also, in a deictic counter-turn, uniquely meaningful to the Oedipal observer *ab extra*, from "out-of-town." Thus, obliquely, by out-of-historical-sequence implication, Wordsworth, still remaining on the street in a place of literal and visual subjugation, points to a different, nihilating power whose is effect is clearly visible, but whose uncanny origin is obscure or hidden. I am suggesting that the power of imaginative *displacement* or rearrangement asserted here is counter-historical or meta-historical, i.e. hermeneutic, saying to the reader, in effect, like the tragic figure arriving in Thebes who has just solved the riddle of the Sphinx: "I am the first to see the signs history has laid in my path on this crowded London street; my viewpoint is sufficiently primary to see history only as it is significant or signifies *to me* who sees "not just one."[19] Yet— and this is my underlying argument—that which is meta-historical in Wordsworth is not one of White's post-Hegelian rhetorical tropes, synecdoche, irony, or metonymy, nor even Lacoue-Labarthe's chiasmus—it is viatic and broad, in the same de- or reincarnationist sense that organic nature resembles a Taoist or Goethean "way," requiring one who can read or thinks he can read hermeneutic signs of a nativity involving antiquity's displacement. In the most obvious sense, Wordsworth takes on the psychic work of making himself an aboriginal "out-of-towner" to entropic histories, a sublimative or negentropic process springing from an afflicted childhood and the traumatic experience of revolution and relationship across the Channel, one involving transgression and a turning of face on several fronts.

The omission of the abbey itself in "Tintern Abbey" can thus be seen not as a flaw or fault of reference, but rather as part of a strategy of oblique representation in which Wordsworth, by a "strange rendezvous" of the mind, is laying the phantasmagoric, para-phenomenological groundwork for a later, ultimate structure of transplantation, which is that of the Gothic cathedral to which the *Prelude* was to be but the ante-chapel. Alternately, the omission of the building and grounds of "Tintern Abbey" is one which has its reasons, having to do with the unrespresentability both of a primal scene and of a time in national and personal history too painful to be recalled, perhaps, except as a side-story to the writing of a life as of that which has already expired, an ascent of the Wye, under the cliffs of Symonds Yat,[20] serving as prelude to yet another farewell, the exhortation to Dorothy. *Reculer pour mieux sauter*. The model for the poetic imagination asserting or reasserting its power is one of give and take or give *in order to* take again, reappropriate or reshape, at some later, more tranquil time things that cannot be mentioned in their affect-laden immediacy. The visual serves an allegoric purpose (Spenser and Sidney are never entirely far from the pictorializing frame)—what you get is both the same and more than what you see, on the country path or city street—and an educative, moral-intellectual, or quietly creeping (satiric-ironic) one, especially with respect to the symbolic coding of color. In other words, the function of the visible, in the case of Book VII, as well as the invisible, in the case of the abbey, is to get at something else, something that can be disposed or disposed of, hidden or sought reflexively, and thus "held up," suspended and preserved, in something like but almost casually different from the Hegelian sense of "*aufgehoben*," for purposes of delayed and ultimately architectonic insertion or reimplantation, a process which is seen as motivated by and empowering the poetic imagination. But Hegel takes us too far toward a dialectic in which sensory certainty is sublated; we have to move a step backward, toward Kantian hypotyposis and subreption, to understand what Wordsworth is about.

It is at this point that we are halted in our critical itinerary by the words of de Man:

> ...the miracle of Wordsworth's figural diction is that, by stating its own precariousness so to speak face to face, without aesthetic evasion, it recovers the totality of the phenomenal world of sky and earth and thus, in a deeper sense than any color or melody could achieve, recovers the aesthetic in the process of its refusal.[21]

The aesthetic is thus both sacrificed and saved in the totalizing affirmation of "colours unknown to man." The confrontational deixis of Wordsworth, with its ontic frame made explicit on the London street as a "here" sometimes opposed to, but at times also inseparable from, a "there," challenges the primacy of aesthetic experience and thus confronts the viability of poetry (of itself) with respect to a thoroughgoing barbarism little interested in miracles of diction. But what would be the status of Wordsworth's Kantian para-phenomenology with respect to the thinkers who see the barbarians always arriving at the gates, the writers of philosophic epitaphs for art, Hegel and Heidegger? What is the deixis of nihilation but the signature of effacement in one or more modes of (de-) representation, signaling an end also of history/historicism and a beginning of what we may call the hermeneutic counter-turn, which at once saves and savors aesthetic experience in somewhat the same way that the raw, among aborigines, is mythically preserved and digested as the cooked?

An initiating premise of this essay is that at least one *Ur-Szene* or original scene is located in the viatic aperture of Wordsworth, as exemplified by the ego's confrontation with strangers or strange reminders of mortality and the Other on a public road, for example, in *The Two-Part Prelude* where a child loses his guide and comes upon a scene of ancient executions:

> I remember well
> ('Tis of an early season that I speak,
> The twilight of rememberable life),
> While I was yet an urchin...
> ...some mischance
> Disjoined me from my comrade, and, through fear
> Dismounting, down the rough and stony moor
> I led my horse, and stumbling on, at length
> Came to a bottom where in former times
> A man, the murderer of his wife, was hung
> In irons. Mouldered was the gibbet-mast;
> The bones were gone, the iron and the wood;
> Only a long green ridge of turf remained
> Whose shape was like a grave.
> (*Two-Part Prelude*, I, 296–313)

What remains is not so much the substance of the man—not even his bones are present—but a bottoming substance seen at the time and recalled later to be of another effacing kind, or the color of turfy substantiality, shaped *like* a grave. Another involves the legend of Peter Grimes, the notorious sorcerer-like murderer of his apprentices, a ghostly apparition forgotten and then suddenly remembered in "The Barberry Tree." The final appearance of the gibbet is the most famous; in lines 205–302 of Book XI of the 1805 *Prelude*, the boy who has lost his way can still read the letters of the hanged man's name on the carved memorial, but—it seems—cannot, as the older Wordsworth writing his autobiography, bring himself to pronounce or inscribe them in the text. The name is not blotted out for *him*, the originary experiencer, but it is obliterated for *us*, his readers, who are not permitted to see the nakedness of every thing (it) or every body (me, him, her). As Philippe Lacoue-Labarthe reminds us, autobiography is always *allothanatography*, a description of the death of the other *"sub specie mortis"* (Reik).[22] The deficit of the name, for all of its clarity to the initial viewer, is the blank space into which the lesson of the text obtrudes, into which we as readers...fall into or fall in with, as if taking our own first step toward Wordsworthian knowledge. What remains is the phenomenon of the encounter *qua* phenomenon, a shining forth or theorization (a *Lichtung* of the uncanny)—a pure or chastening deixis—on the highway of representation, at the crossroads of subject, *subjectum*, and substance, *hypostasis*, in hermeneutic, totalizing apostasy from the chronological facticity of history, of historicism *per se*.

Such thanatopses are secluded from other spots of time, those that involve springing and welling "themselves" or, perhaps, that emblematic well of wells, classical culture, with whose Goethean waters Wordsworth repeatedly, even obsessively, slakes a mimetic thirst between 1795 and 1815. This scene is exemplified on multiple occasions in *The Excursion* and, more blatantly, in "Hart Leap Well." Before approaching that source, I would stress once more the vividness, both concrete and psychic, of a primal scene—"I should need/ Colours and words that are unknown to man/ To paint the visionary dreariness...." (*Two-Part Prelude*, I, 320–322)—stumbled onto or into by the speaker: indices of a quality most like that of a dream dreamed by one "upon whom nothing is lost," as Henry James says *à propros* of a certain kind of reader. Whether half-fancied or not, Wordsworth in Book VII of the 1805 *Prelude* conjures up an urban totalization, which we, as readers in this age of copies and photographic reproduction, take delight in, thereby satisfying at least one prescription for poetic art. At the same time, however, the *urbs*, via pastoral coding[23] or moding, is positioned so as to take its part in the greater *rus* of the Wordsworthian imagination, a totalization of epic proportions with an Albion-like super-subject (a Borderer and Wanderer beyond the reach of centralized, state power—one who travels a different road or who contests the highway) as its invisible hero.[24] The pastoral mode exerts an irresistible pressure on Wordsworth's texts in the period 1795–1815—from the *Lyrical Ballads* to *The Excursion*—equal in force if not in lethal effect to that of the enclosure movement on the peasantry of England, enabling him to put things into the mouths of third persons, shepherds and the like, beyond the power of stately espionage, that may not be spoken overtly.

However, since it is two centuries later, and we are resampling *Ur-*

springs, why should we leave another ground, *Grund* or *Boden* out of the symbolic chain or stream of modern consciousness? In the essay of 1935–1936 (with a *Nachwort* or afterword written, z. *T.*, or "in part," at some later time) entitled "Der Ursprung des Kunstwerks," Heidegger locates the source of our contemporary, that is to say, *Western* groundlessness in the translation of the Greek word ὑποκείμενον into the Latin as *substantia* and of συμβεβηκός into *accidens*:

> Vielmehr verbirgt sich hinter der anscheinend wörtlichen und somit bewahrenden Übersetzung ein Übersetzen griechischer Erfahrung in eine andere Denkungsart. Das römische Denken ubernimmt die griechischen Wörter ohne die entsprechende gleichursprüngliche Erfahrung dessen, was sie sagen, ohne das griechische Wort. Die Bodenlosigkeit des abendländischen Denkens beginnt mit diesem Übersetzen.[25]

> [Behind the apparently literal and thus faithful translation there conceals itself, moreover, a translation of Greek experience into another mode of thought. Roman thought takes over the Greek words without the corresponding originary experience of that which they say, without the Greek words. The groundlessness of occidental thinking begins with this translation.]

Something or everything gets lost in the translation, just as something is saved, by means of art or the work of art, as its truth brought "ans Licht" or into the light, a truth "for us." The root of συμβεβηκός, *symbaino*, means to stand with the feet together, but also to stand to the side of, or assist, to happen, or to fall in with—casually, we might say, or as it "just so" happens. No matter how problematic the metaphysical argument, Heidegger explains it with now notorious reference to the peasant shoes of Van Gogh and a poetic text about falling water, not the ruined spring that is the wanderer's destination in Goethe, who develops an entirely different and highly complex problematic of cultural transference and decay,[26] but one by C. F. Meyer with the final lines "Und jede nimmt und gibt zugleich/Und strömt und ruht" ("And each <stream of water> takes and gives at once/And flows and rests") describing the effortless and harmonious movement of water borne by gravity down a Roman fountain. The essay as formulated in the mid-1930s goes on to discuss the truth of art in the light of that which is "canny" or *geheuer* and that which, in its counter-turn (*das Gegenwendige*), is "uncanny," monstrous or *Ungeheuer* (*H*, 43). Indeed, Heidegger agrees with Hegel at this point that truth only comes into evidence through the "originary struggle" or polemic of a dialectical process involving a certain delay or refusal (*Verweigern*) on the part of the truth to show itself. Up until this point truth is uncanny or "unheard of" (*un-geheuer*). It is not until the afterword, composed, perhaps, in more tranquil retrospect, that Heidegger makes an entirely different claim—not against Hegel, but in order to hold both occidental (Hesperian) groundlessness and Hegel's epitaph on the pastness of art "at bay" or in abeyance—for the centrality of art experienced as it is dying or in terms of the qualitative dimensions of its own demise. Experience turns out to be, in Heidegger's own *post-scriptum*, the postulated source or spring of the work of art, a spring which nonetheless turns out to be the element wherein art dies, whose epitaph it takes centuries to write:

> Das Erlebnis ist nicht nur für den Kunstgenuß, sondern ebenso für das Kunstschaffen die maßgebende Quelle. Alles ist Erlebnis. Doch vielleicht ist das Erlebnis das Element, in dem die Kunst stirbt. Das Sterben geht so langsam vor sich, daß es einige Jahrhunderte braucht.[27]

> [Experience is, not only for the enjoyment of art, but also for the creation of art, the source which provides the measure. But experience is also perhaps the element in which art dies. Dying proceeds so slowly, that it takes several centuries.]

Wordsworth's mapping of self as an Albion-like subject in confrontation with the other, the weird and the uncanny, with present and former bodies occupying the "pre-industrialized" space of an England both open and cavernous or crypt-like can be seen through the optic of one or more Freudian *Ur*-springs and Heidegger's notion of experience as the place where art writes its epitaph, whose final- or fatality is nonetheless delayed, deferred, or dispersed as the subject rereads or reprojects experience as substance. It is my argument that Wordsworth assigns himself the task of returning literature to an originary ground of pleasure and pain read *across* time, a vividness awakened in the cross-Channel, (*übersetzt*) Subject who resembles/rewrites Albion, perfidious and faithful alike, accompanied at transferential crossings by, i.e., always "falling in with" *das Ewig-Weibliche*. So here too, we are confronted by spectacles that get in the way of the ego: of obliteration, of the ob-vious and of two-faced or doubly turned ob-viation—the vagrants one meets on the road, that which presents itself as an obstacle to our passage and its surpassing, a yonder of art in which art repeatedly seeks and meets its own deferred end, obviously or not so obviously, in the epitaph. The "Gegenwendigkeit" that Heidegger speaks of, partly in the Freudian sense of an uncanniness in which one finds the Other "at home," has its meaning for the future of art, up to and including Adorno's "against the comb." It is suggested, beneath or to one side of, the asking of Wordsworth's Janus-faced question, "Shall I give way?" and, even more, in the *Essays upon Epitaphs*, especially those not published in his lifetime, where Wordsworth writes, "Language, if it do not uphold, and feed, and leave in quiet, like the power of gravitation or the air we breathe, is a counter-spirit unremittingly and noiselessly at work, to subvert, lay waste, to vitiate, and to dissolve."[28] The loss and the gain involved in translating classical culture into a contemporary, ballad-like stage or scene is represented (in terms of a shift of cultural paradigm) by Goethe in the 1774 text entitled "Der Wandrer," which I have discussed elsewhere[29] as a transgression or *stepping-over* of Vergilian *pietas* (*Andacht*) and the ruins of antiquity on the way to the projection of a new definition of procreative genius—infantility brought to wondrous speech beneath the inwoven subsumption of the golden bough ("der goldne Zweig"), as an impoverished humanity *enjoys* its dwellings over the graves of deceased ancestors and, perversely or ironically, prospers. The emblematic nature of such a dialogue between the exigent Now and the submerged Past (*gesunkenes Kulturgut*)— another initiatic *Ursprung* of the modern condition of groundlessness, there where the great It or Id of antiquity is sited—is discussed by Northrop Frye, when he describes the Romantic hierarchy that displaces the topocosm of the classical age and the Renaissance. Above are located outer space and the green world of nature, a world out of synch with the Industrial Age:

> Below, in the only place left for any *locus amoenus*, is the buried original form of society now concealed under the historical layers of civilization.[30]

Far from writing a nostalgia-laden epitaph for classical culture, Goethe, an inveterate and usually solitary wanderer waking and dreaming along the borders of rivers, lakes, and springs in roughly the same epoch as Rousseau, draws allegorical insight from the effacing of the past, together with its inscriptions, and their displacement by a maternal/infantile power at the heart or breast of nature—a power alternately provoked and tapped into. In other words, Goethe's originary scene is precisely lacking in the sense of imperilment[31] that affects the hysterical patient who hears the ticking of a clock or the clicking of a camera shutter. *Pietas*, the respect which ought to be shown by the children of contemporary civilization toward their Greek, Roman, and German grandfathers, is haply and happily negated/preserved (*aufgehoben*) in the image of the infant as genius and of Man as an impoverished squatter dwelling, parasitically, in the ruins of the ancient bath; the speaker registers neither guilt at what he has seen nor fear of being discovered because the spring is a pleasant place—*his*, i.e. the ego's, *locus amoenus,* a place that must be visited and then walked away from. In essential modification of Frye's threefold topocosm, we have antiquity buried under successive layers of civilization, but bearing strange, sometimes creepy, organic fruit. The traditional valences of romance and pastoral, of *entropic annihilation*, where the sublunary subject glimpses signs of his own passing and that of others, either Hartman's "halted traveler" perspective or the pastoral "et in Arcadia ego" are reversed through the universal urge to preserve a grub-like, embryonic self, an *effacing through organic surreption,*[32] where the fecund present in effect erases romance, pastoral, and epic, together with the inscriptions of the past, including epitaphs, to the lyrical benefit of a genius-like infant or impoverished subject on intimate terms with a balladic "Eternal Feminine":

> I look'd for universal things, perused
> The common countenance of earth and heaven:
> And, turning the mind in upon itself,
> Pored, watch'd, expected, listen'd: spread my thoughts
> And spread them with a wider creeping....(*Prelude* 1805, III, 110–114)

A Goethean mutation of effacing, different in tone, gender, and symbolic weighting from an epitaphic or epigrammatic *siste viator* moment, allows Wordsworth, as if drinking from wellsprings of the incursive imagination, to summon up pre-, extra-, or counter-historical powers, to rewrite his own autobiography (ever in the expostulatory mode of "Shall I give way?") as a series of "breaks" or "firsts" (the music of the id replayed "as if for the first time") from the perspective of the observer "*ab extra*" and of the infant closely, observed "*ab ovo*": dramatic dreams or dialogues, emblematically "original" vignettes where squalid habitations are built up on the edge of a still-open grave or on top of the palimpsest-like layering of previous epochs:

> Bless'd the infant Babe
> (For with my best conjectures I would trace
> The progress of our Being) blest the Babe,
> Nursed in his Mother's arms, the Babe who sleeps
> Upon his Mother's breast, who when his soul
> Claims manifest kindred with an earthly soul
> Doth gather passion from his Mother's eye...
> From this beloved presence, there exists
> A virtue which irradiates and exalts
> All objects through intercourse of sense. (*Prelude*, 1799)

"Der Wandrer," through its English translation by William Taylor of Norwich (1765–1836), becomes something more than an influence: its maternal paradigm serves repeatedly as a matrix of poetic thinking and translation in such texts as *The Excursion* (and its version of 1797–1798 "The Ruined Cottage,"[33] where an inwrapping or inweaving on the part of nature, since it cannot slow a general trend toward civilizational decay accelerated by encroaching state power and the Industrial Age, tempers or mitigates epitaph-like *sic transits* at certain junctions or crossroads of pastoral thought. Nowhere is the encroachment more in evidence than on the noisy roads of England—roads that formerly, in a pre-history before the Industrial Age, were paths or footpaths, where one, if he were a boy like Wordsworth, could lie concealed, listen for "knocks," or get lost on "illimitable walks."[34] It is the passage of traffic "outside the door," the interruption of the trance, which most irritated both the poet and his sister at Rydal Mount, perhaps because their home in Grasmere, Dove Cottage, had been situated on the main Ambleside-Keswick highway and thus exposed to the unending din of cart and carriage traffic. Such fascination with entrancement is shared by Coleridge, but surfaces also with some frequency in lines where a project of Keatsian noise-abatement reaches residential intensity:

> The leaves stir not,
> They all are steady as the cloudless sky;
> How deep the Quiet: all is motionless,
> As if the life of the vast world was hushed
> Into a breathless dream.[35]

On the other hand—one hesitates to say "dialectically"—it is Wordsworth's housemate De Quincey who wonderfully describes the English road as a place where the systole and diastole of a great and superhuman heart may be discerned, and where the royal mail-coach's posthorn creates in teamsters an instantaneously palpable terror:

> No dignity is perfect which does not ally itself at some point with the mysterious. The connexion of the mail with the state and with the executive government—a connexion obvious, but yet not strictly defined—gave to the whole mail establishment an official grandeur which did us service on the roads, and invested us with seasonable terrors...Look at that long line of carts and carters ahead, audaciously usurping the very crest of the road. Ah! traitors, they do not hear us as yet; but, as soon as the dreadful blast of our horn reaches them with proclamation of our approach, see with what frenzy of trepidation they fly to their horses' heads, and deprecate our wrath by the precipitation of their crane-neck quarterings. Treason they feel to be their crime, each individual carter feels himself under the ban of confiscation and attainder; his blood is attainted through six generations; and nothing is wanting but the headsman and his axe, the block and the sawdust, to close up the vista of his horrors. What! shall it be within benefit of clergy to delay the king's passage on the high road?—to interrupt the great respirations, ebb and flood, systole and diastole, of the national intercourse?....[36]

Proximate to the carter's anxiety lies the discipline-like fear of the guillotine and its bed of primal sawdust, a scene Wordsworth would naturally have conjured up for himself on numerous occasions during the 1790s and, on the second psychic beat, and even more naturally, wished to expunge from memory. We can only suggest that "national intercourse" carries a more intimate meaning for Wordsworth, as the instance of a potentially lethal governmental other and an antitype of the sort of heartbeat observed or imagined in the "allegoric shape" of maternal, material nature.[37] Simply put, the excursive moment enables an equally threatened and desiring ego to avoid the highway, so that it need not ask the politico-aesthetic question, "Shall I give way?" In terms of Wordsworth's career, a lifelong quest for both diversion and excursion, "national intercourse" may or may not connote the sexual traffic of elders or the threat of castration (though Bromwich refers to psychological trauma); the word "intercourse" takes on a more vivid suggestiveness *for us*, because we live in the knowledge Freud gives us—which may be more important to an understanding of scenes of the origin where implantation asserts its "wider creeping," a power so lowly and grounded as to be irresistible, through the counter-turn, or *Gegenwendigkeit* of organic surreption.

"Something Ails It Now": Translation/Transference in "Hart-Leap Well"

'...fletere si nequeo superos/Acheronta movebo....' Venus, speaking to her father Jupiter in *Aeneid*, VII, used by Freud as his motto in *The Interpretation of Dreams*

> Die Raup umspinnt den goldnen Zweig
> Zum Winterhaus für ihre Brut;
> Und du flickst zwischen der Vergangenheit
> Erhabne Trümmer
> Für deine Bedürfniss
> Eine Hütte, o Mensch
> Genießest über Gräbern—[38]

[The golden bud with webs the grub surrounds, / To form a winter dwelling for her offspring:/ And thou, O Man, between antiquity's/ Sublimest remnants patchest up a cot—/Art happy among tombs. (Taylor translation)]

In Taylor's rendering, which appeared in the *Monthly Magazine* of August, 1798 (Volume XXXV, 120–21), Goethe's verses

> Die Raup umspinnt den goldnen Zweig.
> Zum Winterhaus für ihre Brut...

become:

> The golden bud with webs the grub surrounds,
> To form a winter dwelling for her offspring....[39]

The choice of "grub" is not only metrically preferable to "butterfly;" the literal translation of "Raup" or *Raupe*; it also places an ideological edge on the text, referring, obliquely, perhaps, to the derogatory term for those native parasites or professional scribblers on "Grub Street," but more obviously to the commonest form of insect or insect larva—a term rather more descriptive of flies than of butterflies—resistant to the onslaught of frost in wintertime. Thus, in addition to the ruins of the classical bath described (or, rather, projected) by Goethe, ruins in a sense represented in the elided forms of words such as "Wandrer," "Raup," and "goldnen" suggesting one or more thefts at odds with cultural/filial piety, Taylor insists upon a commonness even more out of keeping with the pretensions of epic's rhetoric and aureate imagery. The choice of "grub" radicalizes anew Goethe's somewhat startling notion that the homeless can *enjoy* huts over the graves of the dead; the revolutionary slant of Taylor's diction reinforces the aspirations of the lower classes in the place of the *Raupe* or butterfly, whose organic insistence itself concretizes and displaces Vergil's "croceo fetu" in Book 6 of the *Aeneid*. Such a strategy—not an annihilative "rhetoricide" mirroring robberies and regicides near and far, but a strategic insistence on commonplace diction which squares with the theory invoked in the preface to *Lyrical Ballads*—is abetted by the choice of "bud" instead of "branch" for *Zweig*—so that the golden bough now vanishes entirely in the version of Taylor, concealed not only by the larva of the butterfly, but also by the translator in the monosyllabic percussions of "bud" and "grub," which foment local resistance to the chill of history's long winter. Thus the rhetoric and imagery of Vergil, filtered through Goethe, are suspended and preserved (partially) by an English off-spring twice removed, preparing, on his island of extra-continental, Protestant groundlessness, a new, lowlier, humbler seeding of translation, a kind of *sermo* at once dour and *humilior*.

This, however, is only the Taylorized dimension. Wordsworth's "primary" take on history represents an exponential broadening and widening of the way traveled by Goethe to the spring and explored by Taylor in his strategy of translation. The lowliness, as hut, vagrant, cup, ruin, or well, is still and always "there," a scene for ideological or post-ideological stealing and reimplantation, but the hermeneutic turning of Wordsworth's thought after the crucial, critical experience of France involves the empowering effects of something more than a translation of *pietas* (Goethean *Andacht*) into a word with anti-hegemonic implication, *fides*, translated literally as "faith" (just as *pietas* gives us piety, but means much more), yet carries the lexicological burden of "loyalty," as in *fides militum*, loyalty of (Roman and/or Christian) soldiers, and loyalty to the (Roman and/or French) republic. As Thompson makes clear (*WB, 5)*, the doctrine of justification by religious faith alone is among the most radical ideas of the 18th century and is at all times in conflict with state-sponsored *pietas*. Wordsworthian *fides* or faith, closely allied also with the *virtus* of Prudentius and the French revolution, resurfacing in various contexts as "frankness" or "franchise," motivates organic effacement, providing the text with a counter-historical, pastoral undersong. Thus, when the signs of paternal faith are effaced in the Goethe/Taylor "Wandrer," the absenting of the sign or signature of antiquity and paternity serves as an energizing trope for Wordsworth's representation of an ego's counter-turn or turning of face away from history and historicism toward the harboring emptiness of dreams and the resurgent empowerment of obliterating, subjective deixis.

The 1798 *Lyrical Ballads* deepen and extend the project of effacement through a "revolution" in poetic language. "Hart-Leap Well"(1800), with a pun on hart/heart placed too obviously in the title to be ignored, continues the in-scening of a subject "before" and "after" the experience of history, while it points up the entangled status of pastoral and romance carried over from Book VII of *The Prelude*. In Part I the knight Sir Walter slays the deer after it has leapt three times, leaving it at the foot of the fountain or well. The hart leaps in "Hart-Leap Well," but, as soon as it does so, or rather on the third jump, it is shot "stone-dead." The knight resolves to build a kind of shelter or pilgrim's cottage to memorialize the occasion. His almost casual hubris, in violation of some deeper, unstated law of nature, triggers a correspondent, post-traumatic curse forever spoiling the spot of ground upon which the well is situated. In Part II, the curse takes full effect, leaving his wayside mansion in ruins. What is surprising about "Hart-Leap Well" is not that it take its formal cues from the *Lyrical Ballads*, utilizing the familiar ABAB rhyme-scheme, nor that it tells the story of a knight who might belong to the world of Spenserian Romance. There are knights and noblemen in the ballad tradition as well; one thinks of Sir Patrick Spence, for example. But it is the virtue-*less* structure erected by Sir Walter on the spot where he slew the hart that is out of keeping with the loftier ethical aspirations of romance, those befitting a King Arthur or a Red-Cross Knight; it is what Shakespeare in a sonnet calls a "chronicle of wasted time," about "mean and vulgar" wayfarers and equivocal modes of behavior, rural temptation and the furthering of unheroic erotic exploits, a house not of worship, but of beds and bowers of bliss for anyone who happens to be "on the road"—an inn for persons, including himself, who do not wish to be public, but private, in the rudimentary assignations of a Merrymount *ménage*:

'I'll build a pleasure-house upon this spot,

> And a small arbour, made for rural joy;
> 'Twill be the traveller's shed, the pilgrim's cot,
> A place of love for damsels that are coy.' (*PW*, 201)

Unmindful of the ethical cost, Sir Walter, like Kubla Khan or Ozymandias, thinks he is building for eternity:

> 'Till the foundations of the mountains fail,
> My mansion with its arbour shall endure....' (*PW*, 201)

Part II awakens us from this pleasurable dream; it might be an evocation of a sight seen along the road from Hawes to Richmond, except that what catches the traveling speaker's eye are the "three pillars of rude stone," all that is left of Sir Walter's pleasure-house—tripodal signs not of just *any* ruins, but of classically rude or rudely classical ruins, where the fountain once stood, and of things that speak to us in oracular voice—in legends and riddles spun forth from the dark ages surrounding enlightened antiquity, in tri-vial threes, such as witches or knocks on a door or the leaps of harts—to menace pleasure palaces and hollow crowns. So blasted and desolate is the location that it seems spring itself is forbidden to visit, as if "Nature here were willing to decay." Soon the traveler meets a shepherd who tells him the story of how the fountain was "jolly" in the old days, while "something ails it now: the spot is curst" (*PW*, 202). Hartman supplies the biographical context (*WP*, 142) for Wordsworth's version of the tale: his return to Grasmere and Dove Cottage, the "trance-state" that the legend induces in him when he hears about it on his homeward journey.[40]

With precisely this subjective background in mind, it is possible, however, to read "Hart-Leap Well" in terms of a pastoral "undersong" suggested on several different levels: first, as biblical allegory, with Part I as Eden or a state antedating the knowledge of good and evil, and Part II as fallen history, the descent from the original scene of a primal Adamic surrogate and his pleasure-partner "Eve" to the guilty present. Second, in terms of contemporary ideas, if not of ideology, it is interesting to interpret the "before" and "after" as a telescoped and pastoralized version of one or more revolutions, loosely representing both the Protestant Henry VIII, famous for polygamous appetite, murderous impulse, and monastic suppression, and to the French Revolution, with Sir Walter representing a profligate aristocracy and the shepherd-interlocutor pair embodying the psychoanalytical situation of a chastened super-Subject England or Albion, which has come or is always coming back, not so much to the comforts of home, but to a ruined place of neurosis-like ailments, a waste land left behind by the cavorting delinquency of a Sir Walter-like id and the sadomasochistic rhythm of economic exploitation and war, to which spring, a release from inhibition and anxiety, may just as easily not return. We will take it that here, in the "before" and "after" of "Hart-Leap Well" (but even more in Coleridge's version of the pleasure palace), is an early unintended evoking of the situation of *Bodenlosigkeit* alluded to by Heidegger in his "Postscript" to the essay on the origin of the work of art: the past, with all it represents concerning pleasure's abode in the house of art, is untranslatable; the function of art has been negated or disfigured by the anxious and/or painfully guilty self-consciousness of modernity. For Wordsworth, on the other hand, in the heterocosmic and mediatory position of borderer and wanderer, it is a matter of taking the necessary dispositional or totalizing steps to arrive, projectively, at a "realm" where spring—contrary to the flux or current of historical time—can be allowed, figuratively speaking or as if in a self-imposed trance, to happen once again, where regreening can assume its rightful or virtuous place as an end-state of being, or rather as a totalization capable of assimilating hart-leaping to hart-expiring, death to life and life to death. And, in order to evoke that primal season, to engender it, as it were, a reinvigorating female presence, with or without accompanying infant, and/or the suggestion of such a presence "much to be desired," is indispensable.Thus the importance of the story of Margaret and her relics, a wooden bowl and bench, or, rather, of the bestowing of relic-like status upon the commonest of objects, tools and household implements.[41] It is here that the disembodying imagination veers away fom the primal scene suggested by "Der Wandrer" and toward a medievalism mediated by Tintern, Yarrow, and a hundred other ruined abbeys—many of which claim to be in possession, or to have assimilated the supernatural powers, of relics from the tomb, i.e., the bones of saints. One hastens to add that the imaginative use to which such relics are put by Wordsworth is a profoundly secular and deictic one, revolving more or less ambiguously and equivocally around something that we might call "hope" or the "analogy of hope" (in Coleridge's phrase) a Pandora-like residuum of what was, and "faith," a word with political as well as religious overtones, caught up in its own historical negation; in the absence both of communion and community, the *via naturaliter negativa* is secular and unpious, while claiming for itself the ability to mediate on behalf of numinous, apocalyptic powers and to return in the epiphanies of Book XII of *The Prelude*, to the ultimate *Ur*-scene, where among the undifferentiated masses, a *single* Briton, both here *and* there, in the Now of the present and in the Then of the past, dressed in wolf-skin attire appropriate to the state of nature (both of Rome and Britain), stands out in the reverie of a solitary mental promenader on the broad High Street of time:

> I had a reverie and saw the past,
> Saw multitudes of men, and here and there,
> A single Briton in his wolf-skin vest
> With shield and stone-axe, stride across the Wold....
> (*P*, 227, 320–323)

Close upon his heels there follows a scene of human sacrifice, conned, no doubt, from Caesar's *Commentaries*, where aboriginal Druids "stand in" for Jacobins, and the wicker "man" filled with "living men" substitutes for the wheeled vehicles used to cart victims of the Terror toward the guillotine:

> It is the sacrificial Altar, fed
> With living men, how deep the groans, the voice
> Of those in the gigantic wicker thrills
> Throughout the region far and near; pervades
> The monumental hillocks; and the pomp
> Is for both worlds, the living and the dead. (*P*, 227, 331–336)

Who but Wordsworth, fresh from France, would have used the word "thrills" as an intransitive verb, meaning "to quiver" or "vibrate," but carrying also the connotation of a noise that pierces or bores into the landscape to the extent that the hills themselves are said to be magically thrilled, i.e., "alive" to the sound of human sacrifice, that is to say, haunted by ancient echoes? We, on the other hand, who are unfamiliar with such diction, inured to more pedestrian kinds of sad music, summon up thoughts of a "thrill" ride or thrilling movie, such as "Night of the Living Dead," noting that scenes of originary gruesomeness excite the nervous system in ways of which the Romantics, and especially Wordsworth, have made us only too aware. From Margaret's bowl to the wicker of the primeval Britons, the use of reliquary devices intones the secular subtext of Wordsworth's verse, which is to project primal scenes, of one sort or another, into *this* present of poetic speaking, and to deflect time's arrow so that it might become an ouroboros, representing history as *saecular* or cyclical in its cataclysmic repetition and nature as subversively matriarchal.

Pomp Enough for Two Worlds: Return to the *Ur*-Spring

> All our ancient boundaries and landmarks-are pulled up by the roots and all the ties
> and bonds of human society in our English horizon totally destroyed and extirpated.
> Alas for pity.   John Lilburne, 1649

It seems that the issue of intertextuality—of dialogical translation from Goethean and pastoral sources—"comes to a head" in Book I of *The*

Excursion, itself entitled "The Wanderer," where the story of Margaret and the ruined cottage (originally written in the late 1790s) is resited or inwoven.[42] It affords an ultimate view of ruins adjacent to a spring or of ruins where once stood an edifice whose purpose was to allay the thirst of vagabonds and itinerant "passengers" journeying through pastoral time and space (or to afford other kinds of pleasure, as in "Hart-Leap Well").[43] Reading the Book of Nature in Part I, Wordsworth's herdsman relies on nothing but his senses and heart to carry him ever upward to a sublimer version of....himself. His being, his existence, has been taken over by a correspondent power through what is termed "intercourse," a designation applied repeatedly in *The Prelude* drafts of 1799 to the manner in which the senses, especially that of sight, seize and are seized upon by nature:

> A Herdsman on the lonely mountain-tops,
> Such intercourse was his, and in this sort
> Was his existence oftentimes *possessed*.
> O then how beautiful, how bright, appeared
> The written promise! Early had he learned
> To reverence the volume that displays
> The mystery, the life which cannot die:
> But in the mountains did he *feel* his faith.
> All things, responsive to the writing, there
> Breathed immortality, revolving life,
> Annd greatness still revolving: infinite:
> There littleness was not: the least of things
> Seemed infinite: and there his spirit shaped
> Her prospects, nor did he believe—he *saw*.
> What wonder if his being thus became
> Sublime and comprehensive.   (*PW* 759, 219–234)

Reverence for the book of nature, a *volumen* whose pages are rolled into a completed text over the entire course of human history, can be seen here as a Wordsworthian version of Goethean *Andacht* or Vergilian *pietas*—whose inscription or epitaph is effaced by time and the footsteps of strangers. The seasonal and/or epochal revolutions of nature, footed on no ground other than subjective vision, culminate in the seizure of a comprehensive faith, a literal grab for unreflective, vivid power through unmediated sentience— expressed by the three italicized verbs "*possessed...feel...saw*"—on the part of the Shepherd, whose journey to tranquillity and sublime composure is supposed to mirror that of Wordsworth. No matter how dilapidated, or precisely because of its sorry state of decay, the well, an *Ur*-spring liberated from the burden of history and escaping the censorship of ego and super-ego, haunts poetic and nostalgic consciousness and must be returned to again and again; each time it is mentioned, there is more literary-historical traffic beneath or on the margins of the literal text than appears on its surface. The pastoral coding, however, persists, as does a Goethean sense of retracing a past which is at once historical *Wahrheit* and allegorical *Dichtung*, where other wanderers off the beaten path, like lost sheep, have stepped over the *pietas* owing to their fathers and grandfathers, trespassed upon sacred ground, and been tempted to "o'erleap" or jump upward, off the earth, entering another enchanted realm beyond the symbolically broken wall :

> He rose
> And ere our lively greeting into peace
> Had settled, 'Tis,' said I, 'a burning day:
> My lips are parched with thirst, but you, it seems,
> Have somewhere found relief.' He, at the word,
> Pointing towards a sweet-briar, bade me climb
> The fence where that aspiring shrub looked out
> Upon the public way. It was a plot
> Of garden ground run wild, its matted weeds
> Marked with the steps of those whom, as they passed,
> The goose-berry trees...
> Had tempted to o'erleap the broken wall...
> My thirst I slaked....   (446–463, *PW*, 762–763)

The "aspiring shrub" may or may not echo the remote "grub" that Taylor uses to translate the caterpillar's nest in the Goethean *Ur*-text; it sounds even more (strangely and against all likelihood) like a reminiscence of the "Gesträuch" (nondescript bushes) that Goethe's wanderer must struggle through to get to the spring where he converses with "woman" (*Frau*).[44] The wooden bowl, whatever its more exotic connotation as a Grail-like gratification, functions on the literal level as a Theocritean stage-prop. But, as in the 1777 "Wanderer," a text everywhere alert to its own historical belatedness, Wordsworth's composite, palimpsest "Wanderer" is laden with multiple nostalgias, the speaker is acutely aware of his own pastoral mode of speech and circumstances, even as he notes the effacing activity of time:

> I yet was standing, freely to respire,
> And cool my temples in the fanning air,
> Thus did he speak. 'I see around me here
> Things which you cannot see: we die, my Friend,
> Nor we alone, but that which each man loved
> And prized in his particular nook of earth
> Dies with him, or is changed: and very soon
> Even of the good is no memorial left.
> —The Poets in their elegies and songs
> Lamenting the departed, call the groves,

> They call upon the hills and steams to mourn,
> And senseless rocks, nor idly: for they speak,
> In these their invocations, with a voice
> Obedient to the strong creative power
> Of human passion.　　　　(*PW*, 763, 467–481)

Death's nihilation here is total and totalizing, the inverse of the poet's panoramic view of the "triumph" of London commercial and stately traffic in *The Prelude*. Its effacing activity wipes out the memorials of the good and the bad alike. But the process of memorialization is engaged at almost exactly the same moment that the memorials are negated; echoing the poets "in their elegies and songs"—pastoral lyrics—who once invoked the woodland Muses to sing of that which outlasts mortality, the "I" of the Wanderer expresses a sympathy between the I's eye and the waters it surveys. At this point, if not earlier and later, it is a Shakespearean sonnet, that ghost-writes this passage, if not the whole of Margaret's story, along with a Goethean *Ur*-text touched (up) by Taylor:

> When in the sessions of sweet silent thought
> I summon up remembrance of things past,
> I sigh the lack of many a thing I sought:
> And with old woes new wail my my dear time's waste...[45]

Wordsworth conjures the thought without the woe (repeated five times in the sonnet), but with the passion in a more tranquil or tranquillized state:

> 　　　　Sympathies there are
> More tranquil, yet perhaps of kindred birth,
> That steal upon the meditative mind,
> And grow with thought. Beside yon spring I stood,
> And eyed its waters till we seemed to feel
> One sadness, they and I. For them a bond
> Of brotherhood is broken: time has been
> When, every day, the touch of human hand
> Dislodged the natural sleep that binds them up
> In mortal stillness: and they ministered
> To human comfort. Stooping down to drink,
> Upon the slimy foot-stone I espied
> The useless fragment of a wooden bowl,
> Green with the moss of years and subject only
> To the soft handling of the elements:
> There let it lie—how foolish are such thoughts!
> Forgive them:—never—never did my steps
> Approach this door but she who dwelt within
> A daughter's welcome gave me, and I loved her
> As my own child. Oh, Sir: the good die first,
> And they whose hearts are dry as summer dust

> Burn to the socket. Many a passenger
> Hath blessed poor Margaret for her gentle looks
> When she upheld the cool refreshment drawn
> From that forsaken spring: and no one came
> But he was welcome....' (*PW*, 763, 481–506)

Left purposely vague in terms of historical reference, the description of the spring privileges a pastoral coding which allows the Wanderer to utter a famous epitaph-like statement or epigram on the longevity of the those who are good and those whose hearts are "dry as summer dust"—one that goes on to lead an independent, extra-textual life of its own, reinscribing itself as the epigraph to Shelley's *Alastor* and finding the first half of its thought resampled in the later 20th century in a popular song entitled "Only the good die young." The fact that Shelley turns the thought against its author proves de Man's (and Rousseau's) point about the treachery of language or points us along the precarious road that leads from history to meta-history, a realm of fabulation turned toward the other as an "Oh sir" or Reader who has yet to be. As soon as the text draws a moral from the tale told by a fictional character *within* it and allows that character to advertise a moral as the tropological truth of *his* story, the statement becomes suspect and even more subject to the aleatory play of disfiguration, deconstructing what may have been thought as its original deixis. Indeed, when examined coolly and rationally, the Wanderer's gnomic utterance can only claim for itself the value of unassailable truth in *his* never-never land, by virtue of the fact that good people can and do live on into old age, both now and in Wordsworth's time, while those "whose hearts are dry as dust" sometimes die prematurely. Randomness always, or nearly always, wins. What is given out as a universal moral truth or folk wisdom in fact applies only *locally* in its firstness or deixis as the contextualized speech of one character; it is the truth of *this* Margaret as opposed to another, seen from the Wanderer's perspective; it is the specious generalization whose veracity ought only to be tested against the facts of *this* recalcitrant reality and at the level of the narrative sympathy required by a *particular* case, taking priority in its circumstances over all the others that might disprove its nonce verisimilitude. In a return to the *Ur*-spring of Margaret, the logic of the heart is given priority over the standards of proof that might be required by a rational mind; the pomp or pretension of a concrete universal is replaced by the humility of the fabled or entranced particular. And it is this kernel of irrationality—of a half-foolish thought which sounds an exceptionally solemn note of fraternity and solidarity with those who are less fortunate—that renders the tune, in its truncated translation, as well as the specious thought, both catchy and subject to misprision.[46]

What seems to belong to a bygone era of sympathy and sympathetic magic, along with a "prehistoric" Margaret, is the notion of brotherhood itself, equally (we think) or ambivalently connected with England's monastic past and the hotly contested ideals of the French Revolution. The text itself seems based or built upon a dialectic of fusing or melting, seen in the joining of Margaret, as a spiritual presence, with the water, and refusing, reflected in the forsaken nature of the present spring. Equally, "burning to the socket," brings to mind a candle-like life evilly prolonged by gradually burning down to the holder, suggesting a refutation or refusal of Macbeth's famous metaphor on the brevity of life. The objective correlative for the effaced ideal of fraternity is the fragmentary wooden bowl itself, now rendered useless by the "soft touch" of a thoroughly feminized nature. The primal nature of the scene is reflected even more in the sentence beginning with the balladic or fairy-tale-like "...time has been," where the inanimate waters are said to have ministered to human needs—awakened to vivid function through Margaret's miraculous touch. Indeed, she has roused the waters out of their elemental sleep, practicing a kind of innocent witchcraft in "dislodging" them from their grave-like "mortal stillness." To approach the fragmentary bowl via its stepping-stone, however, is to tread a slippery ground like ice or glass, moving toward deeper fantasies, as in a dream or daydream of prehistory. The bowl, a morsel-like fragment of the Wanderer's *temps retrouvé* (whose literal inauguration is Shakespeare's "remembrance of things past" in the line just cited) has been almost reabsorbed by nature through the green of its mossy covering. Its regression, under the trance-like thought of poetry's session, would just about be complete, were it not for its remembrance and memorialization by the Wanderer who, with the stranger as his interlocutor, characterizes his own mode of recall, half experience and half imagination, as "foolish thoughts" or meandering fantasies, stops three times in his delivery, as indicated by dashes—as if to work toward some new version of "halted analysand" motivation, a threefold systole or interruption of subjectivity within the heart of the Wanderer's discourse and just before the epigram on the good who die first.

Margaret, in an earlier, pastoral incarnation, served as resident *genius loci*, half pagan spirit, half saint of the spring; her aquarian task was that of proferring bowls of water to "passengers" in vehicles who traveled along the nearby road, a function altogether in keeping with the function of religious sister- and brotherhoods of the Middle Ages. The "siste viator" of the halted traveler, reflected in the text of "the Wanderer's" speech, introduces a "dark backward and abysm of time" lost (even now) to active historical memory, a forsaken ground of pilgrim-like sympathy and brotherhood—either invisible or too obliquely described to be identified certainly with mythical, monastic, or revolutionary praxis, but also accentuated in such a way as to render deictically vivid an ethical principle lodged in the unity of nature, the "elegies and songs" of poets, and the philanthropy of the heathen/Christian "saint" whom Margaret both re-presents and "de-presents," if such a word can be used to describe the vanishing of a person into the discourse of another's memorializing memory. Her ruined hut, we will suggest, together with the forsaken spring, is a much translated, thickly overgrown projection of a ruined monastery, the home of England and the super-subject Albion, who once dwelt on monastic grounds, as if in a grand or grandfatherly edifice. Dove Cottage and Rydal Mount participate in this quest for an originary, undiluted, and undisturbed heterocosm, whose scene is suggested on the margins of the Gothic cathedral that *The Prelude* and *The Excursion* are supposed to become part of. We may liken it too to the Western artistic heritage, built on the ruins of the past, in danger of collapsing into the grave-pit, or being hurried along in that direction by Hegel, and equivocally "rescued" by Heidegger in the infinite delaying strategy of his *postscriptum* on experience. We take it that the principle of fraternal benevolence and sympathy (represented by the Church as purveyor of the Celtic legend of Arthur) is inferred beneath or remains invisible behind the veil of the pastoral conceit or secularized relic that is the wooden bowl of Margaret (as Joseph Campbell shows, the Holy "Grail" itself in the *L'Estoire del Saint Graal* or Vulgate Cycle was in any case not a chalice, but a dish, bowl, or *escuele*). Thus the bowl, while it bears the outward stamp of pastoral simplicity, casts an even longer shadow of Romantic or Grail-legend allusiveness, suggesting an optic looking toward Celtic and Roman times: *Et in Arcadia Arturus*. England, with a vivid classical and prehistoric past, *is* Italy as seen through the Hesperian optic; Glastonbury is the Cumae of the insular, ponent West, if one chooses to enchant history, as Wordsworth does. But organic effacement in the case of Wordsworth takes on a role not assigned to it in the Goethean *Ur*-text: that of an obliquely seditious critique of the status quo, one in league or aligned with the obliteration of epitaphs and the cyclical resurgence of spring, whose green robes do not cancel or suspend death, but render its shock less shocking or dampen its noise with the power of vivid surreptition. Meanwhile, what seems to be "mere" memory cannot resist a tropological procedure in which the speaker continually adverts toward the other with notations of its own subjective truths, trance- or dream-like dicta superior or at least external to the actual record of history, "wie es eigentlich war."

However, in terms of the time and space of modernity, an aftermath that we and Wordsworth share, we look back upon Margaret much as we would look back on the holiness once attached to a defunct pagan demigod, such as Pan, *Lieblingsgott* of both Baudelaire and Shelley, also associated with shepherds and noontime epiphany, or to the relics of the English past associated with a principle of charitable works towards "all comers," namely, the dissolved monasteries. In the history of the early Church, it was an urban Christianity that came to the pagan *rus*, planting legends of the saints and even of Christ's immediate family (Blake's song, "And did those feet in ancient time..." brings to poetic expression the tantalizingly undecidable, counter-historical, apocryphal core of Arthurian romance and runs it like a battering ram against the "dark Satanic Mills" of Industrial Age England) in the local habitation of local deities, much as the Romans came to Bath and named it Aquae Sulis, after the Celtic "Sul." Glastonbury most famous of these. What seems to have interested Wordsworth is the counter-historical, quasi-mythic status of this unfortunate woman, a *quondam genius loci* if there ever was one, her ability to be imagined out of time, or in ambivalent topocosms, the twilit or bordering sadness of her emblematic story.[47] When Margaret, the spirit of a generous *natura naturans*, drops catastrophically into history it is to find herself subject to an entropic decay and disorder which might easily unleash melancholy, were it not for the Wanderer's carefully chosen words of consolation.[48] This pastoral projection cannot, however, conceal the underlying "excursion," a residual polemical "undersong" coded by "plumes," the "spear" in "spear-grass," and "dominion." Just as in the street-scene of *Prelude*, Book VI, it is Being which is being unveiled once more as a "passing show":

> 'She sleeps in the calm earth, and peace is here.
> I well remember that those very plumes,
> Those weeds, and the high spear-grass of that wall,
> By mist and silent rain-drops silvered o'er
> As once I passed, into my heart conveyed
> So still an image of tranquillity,
> So calm and still, and looked so beautiful
> Amid the uneasy thoughts which filled my mind,
> That what we feel of sorrow and despair
> From ruin and from change, and all the grief
> That passing shows of Being leave behind
> Apppeared an idle dream, that could maintain,
> Nowhere, dominion o'er the enlightened spirit:
> Whose meditative sympathies repose
> Upon the breast of Faith. I turned away,
> And walked along my road in happiness.' (941–956; *PW*, 602)

According to the leap ahead or prolepsis involved in the thinking-through of organic effacement, the pompous plumage of pride, which might otherwise be worn by persons in political or military authority, has already been transformed into common "weeds." Spears are not carried for purposes of military conquest, but, as leaves of grass, reprojected on a rung far less elevated with respect to human affairs and "eternized" in residual cosmic status. The implication that "my road" is not a kingly or national highway stems from the crucial or critical allusion to contestation in line 953, where the autonomous, enlightened subject proclaims its utopian difference—in an unassailable, yet ubiquitous "Nowhere"—from grief, but also from hierarchical sources of grievous unenlightenment. The infant-ego, a "mesocosm" unto itself, cannot assert its preeminence as default *rex quondam futurusque* except by relying or leaning upon the maternal breast of an upper-case "Faith," a designation vague and, perhaps, anachronistic enough to encompass both the medieval and the contemporary, the surpassed revolutionary *fides* of a child-sacrificing Lucius Junius Brutus and the unexpressed truth of an emancipatory political ideology to come.

Nor is the Arthurian subtext and the shadowy presence of Shakespeare's sonnet the only aside to this description of what an "ordinary" wanderer-at-the-*Ur*-spring can project as being "our there." Another relic of sessions past, of the quasi-saintly *genius loci* of the spring, appears—a bench, where, we may infer, Margaret, while living in desolation and squalor, plunged back into the past, on the lookout for spirits of the dead, roaming abroad:

> On this old bench
> For hours she sate: and evermore her eye
> Was busy in the distance, shaping things
> That made her heart beat quick. (*PW*, 769, 879–881)

We can only recall the famous epigram about the good dying first and the Wanderer's recollection, "A daughter's welcome gave me, and I loved her/ As my own child." The connection between the beating of the heart, or its quickening, the "shaping vision" off into the distance, graves, and shepherds is made for us by De Quincey, writing about one of the saddest moments in the history of the Wordsworths, the death of their little daughter Kate, aged four, in 1812. What he sees at a distance is her phantom, that which Herodotus called a *phasma anthropou*, like the ghosts in Shakespeare and the spirits of dead warriors haunting the pages of Macpherson's *Ossian*, the shadow or spectre of a human being; the telling of what he sees or thinks he sees, vividly, no doubt, with haunted eye, after lying upon her grave, begins with a mythic paradigm of an Aurora-like spirit coming from the East, always a figure, or perhaps *the* figure, of poetry's illumination, and ends with something like a phenomenology of spirits:

—I had always viewed her as an impersonation of the dawn and the spirit of infancy; and this abstraction seated in her person, together with the visionary sort of connexion which, even in her parting hours, she assumed with the summer sun, by timing her immersion into the cloud of death with the rising and setting of that fountain of life—these combined impressions recoiled so violently into a contrast or polar antithesis in the image of death that each exalted and brightened the other. I returned hastily to Grasmere; stretched myself every night, for more than two months running, upon her grave; in fact, often passed the night upon her grave; not (as may readily be supposed) in any parade of grief; on the contrary, in that quite valley of simple shepherds, I was secure enough from observation until morning light began to return; but in mere intensity of sick, frantic yearning after neighborhood in to the darling of my heart....in many solitary fields, at a considerable elevation above the level of the valleys—fields which, in the local dialect, are called 'intacks'—my eye was haunted at times, in broad noonday (oftener, however, in the afternoon), with a facility, but at times also with a necessity, for weaving out of a few simple elements, a perfect picture of little Kate in the attitude and onward motion of walking. I resorted constantly to these 'intacks,' as places where I was little liable to disturbance; and usually I saw her at the opposite side of the field, which might sometimes be at a distance of a mile, generally not so much. (*TDQ*, 510–511)

"...in many solitary fields, at a considerable elevation above the level of the valleys...in broad noonday...places where I was little liable to disturbance....": by sleeping with death and waking to ghostly vision, De Quincey sets up the prime or primal time for viewing a scene of wish-fulfillment; a "spirit of infancy" feminizing the paradigm of a demiurgic Pan haunting fields at midday. "Shaping things in the distance," especially the televised spirits of the dead, by means of a "haunted eye" tracks also the text of "The Two April Mornings," where the speaker sees "yet now" the buried schoolmaster, whose epitaph was written in "Matthew," with "a bough of wilding in his hand." De Quincey's remarks reflect back upon Wordsworth's larger anthropomorphic ambition to "flesh out" nature or give mythic shape to natural phenomena. As Langan points out, (*RV* (268), the vision of dead persons with botanical specimens in their hands is both meditatively ironic and macabre, since the purpose of such botanizing was to preserve health and ensure longevity. Can anyone, other than impoverished squatters—Wordworth included—be "happy among tombs"?

A partial or excursive answer may be found in Book VII, entitled "A Churchyard in the Mountains," where the imagery of natural inwrapping or inweaving in *effect* trumps the epitaph. It is civilization which, with the famously brief candle of *Macbeth* an echoing intertext, prides itself on badges of merit and hierarchies of status:

> So fails, so languishes, grows dim, and dies...
> All that this World is proud of. From their spheres
> The stars of human glory are cast down...

> Their virtue, service, happiness, and state
> Expire; and nature's pleasant robe of green,
> Humanity's appointed shroud, enwraps
> Their monuments and their memory.   (*PW*, 680, VII, 976–999;)

Wordsworth enfolds both Goethean pleasure *and* usurpatory motivation in the epilogue to this paradigmatically elegiac text, tuning or turning the motivation of "Der Wandrer" and its translation against the vainglorious pretensions of the human star system, going so far as to place the noun "state" next to the verb "expire." Moreover, within the color-coding of these verses, verdant nature—occupying in Frye's Romantic topocosm a middle zone between outer space and the palimpsest of previous civilizations—is seen in a feminine light, wearing a "robe of green" that is pleasant or gives pleasure to those who behold her, as opposed to what we may infer to be the more unpleasant sensations aroused by autumnal shades symbolizing stately power on the wane and/or women of ill repute, i.e., reds and/or purples. Thus, what may on the surface seem to be yet another Wordsworthian *sic transit*, in fact turns out to be a deep transformation of the regenerative scenario suggested by Goethe and reinforced in Taylor's translation, where genius no longer rises from the breast of nature, and the wanderer no longer walks over the pious inscriptions of the past, but where nature's silent greening slides or creeps in to bury the *state*-liness of the *status quo* and, in effect, effaces the sin of Pride. In part, this is a lesson drawn from the Middle Ages, bearing not its inflection but its ecclesiastical echo made strange, just as it is also one observed through the prism of revolutionary disappointment and whose emphasis upon verdancy may be transferred or applied to a pleasant *ground* now lost beneath successive stages of history: the notion of England as an Albion-like super-subject whose happy and prosperous childhood was spent in the proximity of springs, great houses, and/or monasteries. Thus, in "The Churchyard in the Mountains," Wordsworth converts the annihilative or entropic epitaph into a text utilizing the vivid sensory imagery of organic effacement, rescanning it, rhetorically, as a pleasant fecundity enclosing death in a shroud of green— in effect, masking death beneath a veil of regeneration, erasing it or its civilizational (dis)content, and promoting the green robe of a Primavera-like nature to a mythically transcendent status.[49] In order to return to a sexual scene both sublime and vivid in the imagination, the *Ur*-spring of poetic renewal, to pass beyond the trauma of 1790, Wordsworth implants the gender-specific matrix or template of Goethe's "Wandrer," as mediated/mutilated by its English translator. Such organicism need not become an obstacle to advanced critical thinking or theoretical insight— since the originary scene, either repressed or expressed, cannot be "present" but only re-presented in terms of that which has already vanished. It is but an element in the critical construction of a meaning or meanings from the absentings of the text (shadowed ever by a mind *above*, over the ruins of a Tintern-like past, or on the second story at Rydal Mount) whose deference to silence—a *disciplina* of fear and/or pleasure at the crossroads or at many junctions of personal/Albionic non-being, where the traffic (intercourse) was once at its densest and most hotly contested—is matched only by its ability to detect the din of inanimate noises. It is in a shroud-, cocoon- or grubby weave that the great leveling and nihilation that is death can be perceived, owing to organic surreption, as but an element in nature's impersonal, greening, casually sinister seductiveness. It is this half-sermonic, half-elegiac invention, "humanity's appointed shroud," which enfolds the high and mighty who once presided over the state, making them objectively equal to the lowest of the hut-dwellers, to grubs, snakes, newts, and lizards, creatures haunting the *Grund* of Britain. This is not a pastoral annihilation echoing Marvell's annihilation of everything to a "green thought in a green shade," but an organic effacement with political or, perhaps, cosmic ramifications, an end not of the individual, but of contemporary institutions and hierarchies: "All that this World is proud of."

When we arrive in Book X of *The Prelude* at Wordsworth's epitaph for his schoolmaster, unrelated to the more famous translator, Rev. William Taylor, M. A., of Hawkshead Grammar School, who dies, sadly, in 1786 at the age of 32, a not insignificant number with respect to *The Prelude* itself, it is to find him on the unfamiliar ground of Leven's Estuary in Lancashire—a traveler moving easily over smooth and level sands, much as he did when he retreated from the uproar of skating to a "silent bay" and "glassy plain" in the 1799 *Ur*-text of *The Prelude* entitled "Influence of Natural Objects in calling forth and strengthening the Imagination in Boyhood and Early Youth," and much like the passenger in a boat on a lake or in a coach on the King's Road—recalling how it was his own larval self, a schoolboy apprentice in distant hills, who "began to spin" instead of sing— as if it took hard, silent, feminine labor to make the fibers of poetic cloth—verses eight years before under schoolmaster Taylor's "command" :

> And when I saw the turf that cover'd him,
> After the lapse of full eight years, those words,
> With sound of voice, and countenance of the Man,
> Came back upon me; so that some few tears
> Fell from me in my own despite. And now,
> Thus travelling smoothly o'er the level Sands,
> I thought with pleasure of the Verses, graven
> Upon his Tombstone, saying to myself
> He loved the Poets, and if now alive,

> Would have loved me, as one not destitute
> Of promise, nor belying the kind hope
> Which he had form'd, when I at his command,
> Began to spin, at first, my toilsome Songs. (*P*, 191; 502–514)

This is yet another recapitulation/translation of "Der Wandrer," with the spinning poet—Goethe's "umspinnt" will be heard at some level of unconscious crepitation beyond literal translation—stealing the larval scenography of Cumae. The recollection of self in these smoother places serves as both an invitation to (day)dreaming and an erasure of painful memory. The pleasure afforded the ego is of a piece with the unconscious pleasure of the infant and of the impoverished who thrive at the lip of antiquity's grave or dwell amid its turf-covered ruins. The speaker can look back with pleasure only now, in the act of writing, upon that hard gestational labor which brought the domesticated poetic spinner into public being. The melancholy affect of the epitaph is displaced in the reflected delight which its verses give one who *thinks* about them after an interval of eight years in which the toil and experiential labor have gone elsewhere. The sequence—teacher—budding poet—poetic man—death of teacher— teacher recollected—generates an eternizing pattern "up" and "over" allothanatography: a vegetative principle akin to that of nature when it greenly obscures stately "stars" or transforms them into a funereal statistic in a world whose more important task is not that of mourning (like bucolic poets) but of regreening. The verses of Gray on Taylor's tombstone, once read in the past, go uncited by Wordsworth, as the death of the parent-like teacher launches the verse and life of his "off-spring," the pupa-like pupil/spinner nourished by "the kind hope/ Which he had form'd." Such hope, a perverse joy at grave's edge, outlives the one who originally had it.

The climactic "Siste viator" moment in "The Churchyard among the Mountains" is written on no grave-stone as epitaph, but can be cited everywhere and in everything; its energy is that of vernal rejuvenation:

> From you have I been absent in the spring,
> When proud-pied April dress'd in all his trim
> Hath put a spirit of youth in every thing. (Sonnet 98, *SS*, 118)

Thus the importance of a statement like the following:

> The advantages of an education such as that which Wordsworth had received in nature lay...in the face that the 'vital' was constantly being turned back to the 'organic' and rewedded to it. (*WHH*, 88–89)

Goethean *Genuß* or genially juvenile delight is translated in the first drafts of *The Prelude* as "pure organic pleasure": the fantasy of a primary or primal scene involving the "I," the "you," and the "It." The wishes and desires orbiting the primal scene, patricide and incestuous marriage, go unalluded to except through wholly projective poetic means. And, among the most *original* of Wordsworth's strategies—a positioning of the eye of the speaking subject at or near the source where nature takes anthropo- or theomorphic form—is what seems on first glance to be the eroticizing of Mother Nature, but is recognized *ab initio* and *ab extra* by the apperceptive subject as a pleasurable "accomplishment" of its own imagination or, if you will, as a Kantian *fantasy* whose ground, existing only in the mind, can be incorporated into the larger, ungrounded yet sacred space of a discipline:

> And those who have undergone his influence, and followed this difficult way, are like people who have passed through some initiation, a *disciplina arcani*, by submitting to which they become able constantly to distinguish in art, speech, feeling, manner that which is organic, animated, expressive from that which is only conventional, derivative, inexpressive.[50]

In other words, that which is vivid can be distinguished from that which is dead and/or deadening and thus hope-less.

In the prehistory of childhood, Wordsworth had experienced one or more weddings "out where the waves are," among "unfathered vapors," and

> ...held unconscious intercourse
> With the eternal beauty drinking in
> A pure organic pleasure from the lines
> Of curling mist or from the smooth expanse
> Of waters coloured by the clouds of heaven.[51]

As Beer notes, "The term 'organic' (unusual in Wordsworth's writing) is crucial here, suggesting a direct influx of power from nature to the very roots of the primary being" (*WHH*, 89). Space and time, abstract philosophical categories, are thus seen, in the "indisputable shapes" of the literary absolute, to become Primavera-like; they involve the speaker's primary being in intimations that are, precisely, intimate in terms of their hallucinatory intensity and subtle suggestiveness. Where the mist curls and seems to form lines (verses in the air), the id both is and is not, drinking in that which, though only the vaguest shadow of a self, is active and actual to the subject; the waters of the lake not only mirror the iridescence of the sky, but also suggest Praxitelean possibilities, a flaring and spellbinding "out there," on the lake, or the allures of a legendary and unseen, mother-like Aphrodite who might subtend the thoughts and prayers of a Wordsworth who, in Aeneas-like fashion, has "with living nature hath been intimate"

(*Prelude* V, 612). Or, to change the myth to an even earlier paradigm familiar to every English schoolchild: what seems to be seen "out there"— both less and more—is a woman formed out of the air above the water, an enchanted lady of the lake beckoning to an Arthurian "grub" or shrub, a Lake poet still in school. In other words, all of these mimetic possibilities exist in part, while none is allowed to exist wholly, because the level of infantile anxiety is too great or because the ground where they might have stood and been named has been dissolved by secular modernity and the Industrial Age; autobiography, legend, erotic coding, history, genre, et al. blur in a single prosopopoetic hallucination or—to combine Wordsworth's phraseology—into "a thousand fatherless mists." Because the ego alone is used as a psychological standard, Arthurian enchantment cannot be separated from other varieties of seduction. The deterritorialized fantasy of the post-Kantian subject plays itself out in "living colors," as it were, becoming comprehensively aware that smooth space, exemplified by an expanse of water or glassy surface of sand, as in a Faustian dream, can afford glimpses of the pre-historic, beauteous, tantalizingly sexual yet curiously desexualized truth of the Sibyl, of the "Eternal Feminine."

Siste Dominator: Housing, Householding, Liberality, Literariness

> The wind is now the organist—a clank
> (We know not whence) ministers for a bell
> To mark some change of service. As the swell
> Of music reached its height, and even when sank
> The notes, in prelude, ROSLIN! to a blank
> Of silence, how it thrilled thy sumptuous roof,
> Pillars, and arches—not in vain time-proof,
> Though Christian rites be wanting!
> Wordsworth, *Yarrow Revisited*

Amid the ruins of history and the "still, sad music" of one's fellow human beings, in the absence of fideistic certainty, psychological injuries done to the self in its pre-history acquire sacred status, as stated in the 1799 drafts that were to become *The Prelude*, by being elaborated through successive poetic acts that might well be part of monastic *disciplina* if they were not so subjectively displaced, i.e., made subject to one or more originary (psychosexual) spaces and scenes:

> ...sanctifying by such discipline
> Both pain & fear....

Wordsworth not only seeks a translation of that monastic ideal, which, after all, finds itself latent also in the notion of the university; he envisions its incorporation into his own being, or, as Laplanche says in the context of Da Vinci, he "implants" it in the space between a clank, "the ghostly language of the antient earth," and the larger blank of history forced, like a restive schoolboy, into silence. In the great arena of the "Intimations Ode," it is a younger, Magus- or Druid-like self that is said to move in a ponent or westward direction: "The Youth, who daily farther from the east/ Must travel, still is Nature's Priest...." But the self seeking sanctification—a cure in one or more senses—of the past comes to resemble a house, castle, or temple, one which has undergone immemorial shocks and renovations, whose passageways and rooms reflect insightful moments in a life. It thus takes on a capacity for the storage of psychic energy, functioning much like a kind of voltaic cell or battery. As Pater remarks, "in the airy building of the brain a special day or hour even, comes to have for him a personal identity, a spirit or angel given to it, by which, for its exceptional insight, or the happy light upon it, it has a presence in one's history, and acts there, as a separate power or accomplishment."[52] It is the underlying analogy between the ego and the "separate power" of a domicile, a house or even a cathedral, which makes the text a palimpsest, as Levinson suggests (*ML*, 34–35). Tintern, Grasmere, and Rydal Mount point also to the possibilities of surmounting previous injuries and guilts, of secluded nesting and procreation, of telling or riddling, equally a process of cathartic ridding, on a second story, where the flight "upstairs" problematically mirrors ascents out of precarious passes and/or routes in previous life-experience. Then there is the Grail-like vision of the ecclesiastical, but also casual structure of the "whole" poetic work, projected to be like a Gothic church. If Wordsworth's imagination is totalizing, or "like a realm," as Hartman suggests, then the surveillance of the despotic "I" or eye becomes more than supreme espionage; its force of imagination must identify itself with a noon of emancipation at odds with the midnight fears aroused by terrestrial potentates. As a chilling line from the "Intimations Ode" indicates, Wordsworth in his impoverished youth, understands that danger comes in the form of an equally uninspiring and imprisoning house or nation:

> Shades of the prison-house begin to close
> Upon the growing Boy....

If the vagrants dwell in "houseless woods" in "Tintern Abbey," their homelessness, on the one hand, delivers them from various forms of stately espionage and legal imprisonment, such as the work-house, permitting them a level of enviable, de-viant, or secluded liberation, and, on the other, illustrates on a more symbolic level, the transcendental homelessness of Albion, a Super-Subject deprived of its spiritual center or nervous system, of which Tintern Abbey once formed a part. Dove Cottage, on the other hand, where Wordsworth and his sister live for seven years and which De Quincey occupies in 1808–1809, was "...a little domain which he...himself apostrophized as the 'lowest stair in that magnificent temple' forming the north-eastern boundary of Grasmere" (*TDQ*, 504). Nature has not yet assumed the role of living Baudelairean temple, but its fostering femininity, and above all, its capacious lap, provide a store of pleasure for the usurping infant or infant-like mind. The speaker of the ode seizes upon the prison-house image and turns it around: the homely nurse becomes an unbeauteous, warden-like Muse ministering to her "inmate" Man, teaching him to forget the gaudier housings of an imperial "palace, whence he came," a domicile that seems to be located in heaven, though a heaven that sounds as if it might once have been on earth, in a previous era when the inmate and his Rights were sheltered in a place now reserved for Emperors and/or Kings:

> Earth fills her lap with pleasures of her own;
> Yearnings she hath in her own natural kind,
> And, even with something of a mother's mind,
> And no unworthy aim,
>   The homely nurse doth all she can
> To make her foster-child, her inmate, Man,
> Forget the glories he hath known,
>   And that imperial palace whence he came.....

Scenes of dislodging, often with the sense of upland houses being abandoned for valley dwellings, are a significant feature of the pastoral landscape of *The Prelude* (a poem of the poet's thirty-second year, when he attained the same age as the schoolmaster Taylor at his death) at the beginning of Book VI; we have come to expect from Wordsworth's preoccupation with pastoral coding that such departures will take the form of bucolic farewells and be informed by the recollection of schisms and seclusions past. The projected "I" of the speaker, a displaced king both itself and not-itself, is representative of the "flock" of the realm which "troops" together at the false lure of the Fowler; the woods and the cloisters reflect the self's past and England's past, reprojected or estranged in pastoral terms. Woodland departure is autumnally coded, in terms of a dominant hue, to reflect upon the season in which the alternative nation of nature finds itself, at a distance of little more than twenty miles from Hawkshead grammar school. It is a crocus-like, Hesperian shade of yellow, but not red, a color befitting soldierly uniforms and ecclesiastical pomp, that other, down-country realm of fallen history and falsely fair alluring:

> The leaves were yellow when to Furness Fells,
> The haunt of shepherds, and to cottage life
> I bade adieu; and, one among the Flock
> Who by that season are conven'd, like birds
> Trooping together at the Fowler's lure,
> Went back to Granta's cloisters; not so fond,
> Or eager, though as gay and undepress'd
> In spirit, as when I thence had taken flight
> A few short months before. I turn'd my face
> Without repining from the mountain pomp
> Of Autumn, and its beauty enter'd in
> With calmer Lakes, and louder Streams; and You,
> Frank-hearted Maids of rocky Cumberland.... (VI, 1–13; *P*, 85)

In one of the most closely argued passages of his Wordsworth monograph, Professor Hartman analyzes in detail the six variants on the opening of Book VI between 1804 and 1850, focusing on the delicate transformations that take place in the depiction of seasonal change. Premising his discussion on the notion that "the passage of one season to another as from one state of being to another is thought of as a gentle transfer of energies" (*WP*, 203), he notes the shifts in diction, tone, and syntax that make such a transfer more vivid for the poet over the course of several decades, not least of which is an experiment in two variants using the more poetically significant "gold" as a modifier, once with "mountains clothed in golden robes of fire," another with "golden ferns." These choices, in turn, point to a larger conclusion, namely, that the text concerns itself with a complex strategy of intellectual and emotional purgation, on the one hand, a cleansing of some grosser sense of *power*, on the other of some equally coarse *idea* (Hartman's italics). Just what these unrefined and leaden constructs are the critic does not say, but one infers that they are in some way connected with the clumsiness of artificial rhetoric, as opposed to vivid and immediate apprehension, or with notions of violent transition, would be the case of autumn were represented, say, by melancholic images of a Keatsian fullness portending death.[53] In one of the few concessions to the organic in his entire study, Hartman writes:

> 'Clothed in the sunshine of the withering fern.' In this image we have the culminating of all the revisions, which is (1) the purging of artificial in favor of natural contrasts and (2) the depiction, related to this, of a perfectly easy, organic transition mixing death and birth, and so diminishing the idea of change as discontinuity.
>
> (*WP*, 206–207)

In the context of our previous discussion of "Der Wandrer" and the organic surreption of the golden bough, one can interpret the fabric that covers the dying fern somewhat differently: that the sunshine-cloth, while as stunningly vivid as Hartman suggests, is something more, that it bears the trace not only of previous variants (a movement from mythic "gold" to the spontaneous fragility of ungilded sunlight), but also the entire burden of the inweaving/effacing dynamic applied by Goethe to the pious memorials of previous cultural epochs, including antiquity's golden bough, and their replacement by the genius-infant and the self-renewing generosity of maternal nature. It is the truth of organic effacement that the *via naturaliter negativa* is always, and from the origin, a *via naturaliter positiva*— something Hartman is keenly aware of, at least here, if only in the alchemical sense of a refined thing being produced from dross, of life springing from inanimate matter. The intertwining of the energies of life and death is a central feature of Goethean thought, as is that of the unity of substance, be it living or luminous. The fact that Hartman interprets the beginning of Book VI, through the six variants, as a quest for a more sancitified or purged power[54] on the part of Wordsworth therefore seems inextricably linked with organic surreption. This is a suspicion that further reading of the return to "Granta's cloisters" will confirm.

We will hazard a few remarks, at first in divergence from Hartman's analysis, then returning to his notion of purgation at yet another crossing or crossroads where literariness is employed to counteract the deadening literality of historical events, in this case, those that took place in France in the early 1790s. Reading beyond the place where Hartman stops, we find that the first "you" addressed by this greater, pastorally accentuated "I" is not a singular, but a feminine plural—as if the "Maids of rocky Cumberland," through choices of diction and context, could be envisaged as *genii loci* frequenting the rocky outcroppings of their native locale. The qualification "rocky" makes us look backward, "one more time," as it were, beyond the syntactical break of the semi-colon, to the lakes and streams, conjuring up a mirage-like vision of pastoral space inhabited by feminine spirits like Margaret. What the speaker has turned his face from is "the mountain pomp/Of Autumn," where he had "enter'd in" only "a few short months before." Despite the bar of the semi-colon, the Maids, whom he must also "quit" after a few weeks of falling-in with them, of "mirth" and "revelry," complete or round out the second part of a single thought beginning with the change of season. Through the actions of turning and quitting the traveler is seen, in this case, not halting, but moving downward, out of the zone of mirth and frank-hearted pleasure, and back...to school...one among a flock of convening, juvenile "animals" being attracted by a hunter with a false "lure." The Cumberland maids might be modern-day equivalents of pastoral nymphs or shepherdesses, eligible brides for pleasure-seeking ego- or faun-like spirits haunting the lakes and streams as the water plays thrilling music for a larger, seemingly more substantial regional landscape. But this is a lure too. The landscape, unfortunately, is either going, because it is autumn, or already gone, since stately powers now rule in the place of divine *numina*; the pastoral personae are projections or stage-props of a mind self-consciously inventing ways, literary and otherwise, to abandon or silence its past. But the fact that the speaker says "you" only after the semi-colon, a distinct and more fully elaborated third "beat" after the *piano* of the (re)collected lakes and the *forte* of the untamed or unrepressed streams, gives the parting its special sorrow. The "threeness" is not so much *tri-vial*, a three-roaded epistrophe to the invocation of seasonal change and wandering, as a deictic "here-" and "thereness," in the sense that the maids are a sexualized, yet distant "you" which has already become an "it"; they occupy the pleasurable space of an objectified, now (ac-)quitted past and are themselves a kind of cross(ing) or crossroads where conflated, conflicted times and spaces intersect *as the face of the subject is turned*. Before psychoanalysts there were schoolmasters, shepherds, poets, and maids:

> Projection is the cross psychoanalysts have to bear; the cross is a transference that cannot be resolved.[55]

If the autumnal season energizes the turning of face, like the changing of the leaves' color, then the maids are an equally powerful motivating force. The accumulated energies of the season are "saved" for this dynamic, ambivalent instance of frank-heartedness and reflected back upon the landscape and numinous spirits (of the past) inhabiting it. The stubborn semi-colon, then, may be seen as the graphic sign of the semi-ness or halvedness of past and present being, of pastoral and autobiography—of a doubleness of heart readable on countless other occasions in *The Prelude*.

And what of the maids themselves whom Wordsworth now leaves behind? Their English hearts, on the one hand, are in the right place, because they are frank, *franc*, free or open; on the other, however, those hearts seem curiously displaced, since "frank" is an adjective etymologically related to the proper noun and adjective denoting the quite un-English territory occupied by the Franks toward the end or autumn of the Roman empire. In place of "stout-" or "true-hearted," duller choices which might have been expected in a lesser (and less conflicted) poet, we have "frank-hearted," and are thus permitted to read a deterritorialization at odds with Cumberland's native ground; but, even more in the sound of the word itself, its "frank-o-phonic" materiality, associated psychologically with a much more personal *etymon* or root, one that replicates, re-implants, or replays the tracks of memory associated with a scene of cross-Channel transgression. The rocky ground has not so much been stolen from beneath the feet of the *numina* as dematerialized and made a function of the *franchise* or liberality of the freely associating political/poetical subject experiencing what is now a dis-pleasured or sublimated groundlessness (*Bodenlosigkeit*), a doubleness in time, the de-presencing of the Eternal Feminine:

> **frank** adj. [ME. fr/ OF *franc*. fr/ ML: *francus*. fr/ LL *Francus*. n., Frank] **1**. *obs*. **a:** free from bondage or restraint **b:** free of charge or other conditions: UNCONDITIONAL. **2**. archaic: LIBERAL, GENEROUS, PROFUSE **3**. obs **a:** superior in quality or strength **b:** LUXURIANT, RANK, VIGOROUS **4**. **a:** marked by free unrestrained willing expression of facts, opinions, or feelings without reticence, inhibition or concealment.

> **frank** *n cap* [ME *Frank, Franc*, partly fr. OE *Franca*: partly fr. OF *Franca*: fr. LL *Francus*, of Gmc origin: akin to OHG *Franko* Frank, OE *Franca*] **1:** a member of the West Germanic peoples entering the Roman provinces in A. D. 253....
> Webster's *Third International Dictionary* , 902–903

The presence of "frank" as a modifier placed before "hearted" reminds us also of the word "franchise," in the sense of liberty, later used in *Ecclesiastical Sonnets* (Part III, x), "Obligations of Civil to Religious Liberty":

> Ungrateful Country, if thus e'er forget
> The sons who for thy civil rights have bled!
> How like a Roman, Sidney bowed his head.
> ...Nor yet
> (Grave this within thy heart!) if spiritual things
> Be lost, through apathy, or scorn, or fear,
> Shalt thou thy humbler franchises support
> However hardly won or justly dear:
> What came from heaven to heaven by nature clings,
> And, if dissevered thence, its course is short. (*PW*, 348).

The indeterminate "What" at the end of the sonnet is only very remotely connected to the "Ungrateful Country" apostrophized in the first line; that "What," however, is doomed to a short life by its separation from "nature." A synonym-like, if not exactly synonymous word, not found in the dictionary but in a good thesaurus, is "Arcadian." "Frank" is thus a better *pastoral* choice than "stout" or "true," both because it expresses liberation from a manifold repressed or hidden scene, a frank- or lower-case *"franchise"* allied in thought if not in fact with the loudness of Cumberland maids—an emancipatory bridging or abridgement of space Wordsworth may not have been aware of at the time of writing, but with explicit reverberations in Rousseau[56]—and because it invokes pastoral coding in order to reproject the maid, in a sense, backward to a state of literary rather than literal virginity or maidenhood, undoing experiential guilt through a cathartic act of imagination. Likewise, the projection back in time, to school-days, seeks to expunge the guilt associated with the all-too personal history of the French Revolution. Unlike the changing of seasons, or the enforced silence of the prison-like school to which the speaker must return, the maids are allowed, by implication, to be bucolically boisterous, like the streams. Thus a scene of turning one's face, even if it explicitly refers to the innocent return of an adolescent to school, may not be able to resist leaning on the episode later in life, echoing the farewell to Annette Vallon and the poet's underlying consternation at never being able to let go...of a certain feminine sound. Thus it is subjectivity, through the very language used to describe its amphibious turnings, that becomes Janus-faced. These remarks on the doubleness of the word "frank" and its ability to carry a significance *of* something, distinct from its meaning *to* the subject of enunciation, suggest Laplanche's notion of the split imago:

> Resolving, analyzing , and dissolving means slipping a knife in somewhere, and it is not possible to slip a kinife in if there are no tracks, no cleavage planes. A hollow transference is a hollow which fits into another hollow. The enigmatic messages of childhood are reactivated, investigated and worked through thanks to the situation itself as it facilitates the return of the enigmatic and secondary revision...but it is only when a split appears in the heart of the transferential imagos or scenes, only when it is possible to slip in the knife, that full transference can evolve into hollow transference and be worked through. (*NF*, 161)

"Hollow" is the word Wordsworth uses to describe the world of lies, of pomp, show, and stateliness, as he works throught the manifold stages of an epochal exit from that toward which his face had been turned in France. And it should be remembered that it is Alexander Pope who in a certain sense inaugurates this splitting of thought and rhetorical duplicity by identifying the word "romantic" with that image of a past which yet lingers or haunts, the hollowed-out trunk of a tree.

It is significant, on the other hand, that Hartman's argument concerning the gradual transformation of season and purgation, while pursued with great rigor, never directs itself at the conclusion of the literal text of Book VI (lines 9–13), as it stood in 1805, those lines where the speaker says his

Amyntas- or Corydon-like good-bye to lakes, streams, and "frank-hearted Cumberland maids." As Hartman has said elsewhere, one of Wordsworth's favorite—some might say obsessive—routines is the farewell to nature. In a certain sense, the power and the idea, no matter how purified or sanctified in the clothing assigned to autumn, seem channeled toward the moment at which the speaker turns his face away and toward the registering of *elemental* quaintness, quietness, loudness, or frankness, all of which sound like layerings or projections of another scene entirely, one that is embedded in well-hidden, *Ur*-subjective experience. By leaving these lines undiscussed, Hartman omits or chooses to ignore the dialectic of trauma and to pursue the traces of a difference that is engendered beyond or "on the other side of" the literal or literary history of the successive variants. On another level, however, this line of explication is not taken far enough (at least in the early book), because what is being purged in the alembicated variants is the very word "golden" that begins to intrude itself in MS B and then undergoes successive stages of alteration leading up to the final version of 1850, where, just as in 1805, it is nowhere to be found, when we have the line: "Clothed in the sunshine of the withering fern," which, as Hartman suggests, mutes the glare of noon with insight into the vegetative ground of transience, which distances Thanatos from Eros, while embedding them in a single figure. The process of revision, by which goldenness vanishes, again suggests the "Der Wandrer," where the golden bough of antiquity, part of the scenography of an emblematic "Ur-spring" of cultural transference, suffers an organic inweaving by the grub and is thus alienated, the vagrants' hut is perched on the grave's edge, and the infant asserts a genius-like power. In the word "withering" is contained a tale of every body and of every body's gradual disembodiment. Wordsworth, as we have seen, reenergizes and radicalizes this primal scene, applying it, *mutatis mutandis*, to himself and significant others, snatching pleasure from the wasting and nihilation he observes around him.

It is England itself, however, that is revealed as the greater haunted house, to which all the ruined cottages and unroofed transepts pay hushed or clanking homage, and in which Albion, the implicit super-Subject, yet dwells. Wordsworth, with an imagination vivid enough to seem like a realm, is, in a sense, recuperating the monasteries, from *The Prelude* to "Yarrow Revisited" to the *Ecclesiastical Sonnets*, in order to energize their liminality, ensconcing his own visionary transcendence, as it were, on the upper story of a Rydal Mount of the mind. What De Quincey calls the literature of power thus overrides the literature of knowledge, especially with respect to "Tintern Abbey" and the controversial avoidance of any explicit reference to the abbey itself. Such reference might have banished

Wordsworth to a kind of satiric low-country or kept him at the level of a historical relativity over which the deer-like mind rebounds, as if surmounting a broken wall of dilapidated time. The face turns away from that reality to address Dorothy, as a female presence in need of reinvigoration, so that *her* mind, equally *his* mind, can become a "dwelling-place/For all sweet sounds and harmonies," of a counter-factual or heterocosmic, optative sublime.

But this house, any house, is a place both of pleasure and of pain. It is not as if the wish for an enduring euphony could become realized, either in pre- or recorded history. It remains a fantasy or figment of the haunted poetic consciousness. Equally, the entropic parable of Margaret and her cottage reveals the disembodying force of Thanatos, just as the quest for imaginative vigor never entirely departs from the lower ground of a sadomasochism implicated in the anterior quest for knowledge (see *TSS*, 16–17). Goethe's image of the peasant squatter's house situated in precarious proximity to the grave-pit, in the midst of classical ruins, the ruins of art as a source of innocent pleasure, is controlling; Wordsworth likewise envisions a house built at the edge or upon the grave itself, as it says in a text of 1799 entitled "A Poet's Epitaph." Not surprisingly, it begins with an address to one on the broad highway of public life, toward the front, where polemical power is exercised—on his way to becoming a Statist-ic:

> Art thou a Statist in the van
> Of public conflicts trained and bred?
> —First learn to love one living man;
> *Then* may'st thou think upon the dead.... (*PW*, 380, 1–4)

And then moves to a question as to the identity of the private man dressed in homelier shades of brown, who expresses a pastoral music more beautiful than that of nature itself, and dies in doing so. He is without status—state-and/or homeless:

> But who is He, with modest looks,
> And clad in homely russet brown?
> He murmurs near the running brooks,
> A music sweeter than their own...
>
> —Come hither in thy hour of strength;
> Come, weak as is a breaking wave!
> Here stretch thy body at full length;
> Or build thy house upon this grave. (*PW*, 380, 37–40,
>   57–60)

Post Post-Scriptum: "Semblances of a Realm" and the Re-Sensing of History

Die Gesänge des Ossian besonders sind wahrhaftige Centaurengesänge....
Friedrich Hölderlin, notes to Pindaric fragment "Das Belebende"
[*The songs of Ossian, especially, are true centaur-songs....*]

'*Here we are again yesterday.*' J. Grimaldi

What is significant is not that the essay[57] on Goethe and Wordsworth discusses texts ("The Danish Boy" and "Der Erlkönig") exhibiting remarkable affinities and differences, but that the text of "Der Wandrer" (illustrating the lowest level in Frye's post-Renaissance topocosm, that of the buried "original form of society now concealed under the historical layers of civilization"), is excommunicated by hermeneutic *Vorgriff* from critical discussion, *as if it never existed.* The so-called "Taylorized Goethe" (*FR*, 280), a key Romantic *Ur*-text and an archetype for Wordsworth's reaccentuation of pastoral coding through organic effacement and civilizational decay,[58] becomes a taboo subject. By shifting the focus to "The Danish Boy" and "The Erl-King," in particular, Hartman takes on the meta-Herderian task of applying an historicist imagination to the age of historicism (*WG*, 181). Echoing E. R. Curtius, the founder of modern *Topos-Forschung*, the critic suggests, it is one of the highest functions of comparative literature: "to study the relation between the historical development of a culture and its ideology" (*WG*, 181). Hartman's perception of that relation, however, seems biased from the outset against *this* organicist topos, i.e., against a Goethean reading that is other than ghost-like or "psycho-kleptic," one that might be capable of evoking one or more primal scenes and for this reason predisposed to read the "historical development" from the perspective of a Janus-like turnabout at the crossroads, where death and life, Eros and Thanatos, cannot be clearly distinguished, where they occupy the same bed, where the imago is yet in the process of being split. This in turn suggests a scene *other* than the one where the traveler halts at an epitaph; it conjures up noontime hallucinations of the middle distance, as described by De Quincey after the death of "little Kate" Wordsworth. An anti-organicist bias means that the original text of "Der Wandrer" and its translation by Taylor, especially, the *effaced* inscription and the grubby inwrapping or inweaving of the golden bough, will be ignored or read obliquely, just as the infant and the impoverished dwelling are elided in favor of the hauntings of an ethereal *genius loci*. Hartman privileges legible inscriptions and epitaph-writing (spun out to one extent or another from the expostulation-reply duo of

Hegel–Heidegger, and post-metaphysical, post-organicist Derrida–de Man), seeming to foreclose in advance a reading of Wordsworth via Goethe *and* Freud, via *Ur*-fantastic displacements of the "primal" scene of one or more antiquities, a wellspring of nativity with countless half-embodied off-spring. The refusal of sensory certainty and of the symbolic, while it might do justice to the owl of Minerva and philosophic insight, relegates the critic to a zone of abstraction rather than of deictic concreteness, where substance and psychological content might impinge upon representation,[59] as they do, for example, with rare and hitherto uncharted force, in the post-Hegelian atmospheres, "cooked" signifiers, and "deep" surfaces of Henry James.

Hartman takes as his own critical *Ur*-spring in the Wordsworth–Goethe essay what is called the "Northern Enchantment," a body of folklore, literary fabulation purporting to be authentic (*Ossian*), and myth informing their respective texts. This curiously amorphous, partly apocryphal, yet enticing literary-historical "body" of texts, an enchanting and educational *corpus* unto itself, then serves as a jumping-off place for the discovery of a ground or site of haunting where the dead and the living share dusky half-lives or half-deaths. And no place is better suited for this than the horizontality of the grave with the vertical stele of the grave-stone and legible epitaph placed over it. With this perpendicular construct in place, an equally perspicuous, triangular historicist model[60] is privileged over that of a literary-psychological deixis involving at some level the unsublatable exigency of sublimation, with its own dialectic of "master" and "slave"— lacking, precisely, the third or transcendental component which might "balance the books," comparatively speaking, and bring about a "bottom line" of stasis or equilibrium between competing egos or egotistical sublimes. In other words, the second model, lacking both an inscription and a stone upon which to write it, represents the interminable or abyssal stepping over of *pietas* through organic effacement and (this is Wordsworth's unique contribution) the hysteria of the phantasmagoric, illimitable symbolic sign, both canceling and preserving aisthesis:

Topos 1 Hartman's *Ur*-spring→   Northern enchantment
              Erlkönig   Danish Boy

Topos 2 Goethean *Ur*-spring→   Enchantment of antiquity/inweaving of Golden
                                        Bough

Goethe "Der Wandrer"→   WW residual deictic inscription 1
                  "   "   "   2
                  "   "   "   3 et al.

Transgression of *pietas*→ death/ impeachment of fallen *status quo* through organic effacement

↓
answerable to antiquity (*pietas* or Oedipal antithesis)
and
to Freud (as discourse and symbolic chain→
transferential hollowing-out, deixis of the "romantic")

What reasons can be adduced for Hartman's disenchantment with the "Taylorized Goethe"? While occasioned by what it takes to be a certain insularity of focus or inattention to literary history, it can be seen, in part, as the symptom of a larger anti-organicism dating from the early days of structuralism and continuing on into postmodernism. No doubt there was and still is some justification for this. Early 20th-century notions of organic form, derived from Goethe and Coleridge, could scarcely do justice to what Wordsworth envisages as "organic pleasure"—something morphologically distinct from the genial unity of Goethean "Genuß"—and its ability to energize   poetic discourse as a zone of   troubling interference situated between beggar and bourgeois, public road and private edifice, Eros and Thanatos—a *via naturaliter negativa*, as Hartman suggests, but also the suggestion of a negative dialectic. Logocentric metaphors that once spoke of the "whole" or "integral" work of art, assigning it some "overarching" telic purpose elaborated by an Author/Creator could not account for a decentering deconstructive "Furie des Verschwindens" exhibited at the heart of the Romantic text, especially in the fragment, or speakers attempting to balance entropic political and personal forces with negentropic vision. What Lukács thought of and advertised as a reinauguration of Goethean aesthetics missed the kernel of a crucial negativity to be found in the *Xenien*, for example, if not in "Der Wandrer," and thus could only invite the castigatory jibes of Adorno. There is, moreover, the whole issue of vision, of seeing "what actually takes place," of a certain embarrassment occasioned by primal scenes examined a little too closely, of too literal a tyranny of the Freudian eye. But what if organic effacement made something *like* a post-ideological case—in the absence of or due to the anxiety caused by revolutionary ideology, from Jacobinism to Fourierism to postmodernism—for evanescence and ephemerality and for something labeled by a younger generation of critics as "radical pastoral"?[61] *Reculer pour mieux sauter.* Bolstered by closer readings of Goethe and invigorated by the return to Freud, critics gain new insight into Wordsworth's "psychological trauma," as discussed by Bromwich[62] and by Hartman in a recent essay entitled "Trauma within the limits of literature."[63] Organic metaphors, linked to the fate of the body and of bodies, are something more than an ideological superstructure. They refer to or represent residual plasma or somatic substance, *illo tempore* or in the *hic et nunc*. If surreption is given equal footing with the *memento mori*, if pastoral pleasure is placed in the context of parasitic dispersion and withering, if the vicissitudes of "et in Arcadia ego" inform the literary absolute, the organic need not remain an object of vilification in the lyceum.

"Strange Changes of Service": From History to Residual Heterocosm

Wordsworth returns to the sonnet form in his middle years to elaborate a poetic version or rescanning of the pre- and post-Reformation millennium, using Bede's *Ecclesiastical History of England* as a source. On the one hand, the vastness of *The Ecclesiastical Sonnets*, written in the second or third heyday of historicism, argues for the notion that Wordsworth is asserting a totalizing power over something like a realm, the history and pre-history of Great Britain, through what is arguably one of the most disciplined forms in poetry. The fact that he chooses the sonnet rather than a vehicle more suited to historical epic, such as blank verse, is not so surprising, given the fact that he would have none other than Milton and his younger self to contend with as sublime precursors. But arguments specifically focused on "organic wholeness" would be out of place and anachronistic here, given the fact that the sonnet is a Renaissance importation from Italy, closely allied to song, mathematical in its detachment, severe in its theoretical art. The sonnet's "answerable style" seems ideally suited to address itself to matters of life and death, in terms of civilized discontents and ecclesiastical substance, because of an inherent tension between tight, highly organized structure and the chaos of conflicting emotions it is asked to express. It can be suggested that another kind of organicist dynamic is at work here, that it is the *disciplina* of the sonnet, occupying a psychic territory or space coextensive with the late medieval *decline* of monastic discipline over pain and pleasure, which attracts Wordsworth to the form. Such disciplined control would serve as a counterweight to various autumns and wanings, some, no doubt, quite contemporary. The sentimentalized, melodramatic, "modern" uses to which the sonnet is being put in the early 19th century, uses out of keeping with the originary sense of detachment and mastery just alluded to, make the form a blunter instrument, unable to register entropy, organic surreption, and cultural withering. The sonnet provides a means for Wordsworth, on the other hand, to reproject a sense of temperamental (egoistic) superiority, psychomachic *virtus*, and power[64]—in tune with a bygone era of unsurpassed stylistic control in which poets are engaged in a dialectic or dialogue with secular, i.e., 16th-century, social, and religious upheaval and are reacting to it via an utterly sublime or sublimated language—upon the broad expanse of the past, in order to control and rehistoricize it on his own terms, but also to chasten the sonneteering excesses of his own epoch. Thus is focused the intelligence of a sequestered mind engaged, with critical precision, in castigating the *mores* of its own era and in cathedralizing autobiography via a form of disembodying reenchantment, converting a precious relic of England's aesthetic past into a riddle-like admonition to the present, an enigmatic harbinger of the future.

The sonnet, in particular, is built in or amid the ruins of the Middle Ages in its late autumn, in living memory of the monastic suppression, when the literal ground not only of faith, but of society, in general, is stolen from beneath the feet of the displaced peasants and Arthurian legend rendered ideologically obsolete by Tudor opportunism. It is the epoch in which huge numbers, if not a majority, of Englishman are turned, as if by malign sorcery, into vagrants, displaced peasants showing up in urban centers, most notably, London. In the sonnet's different ambition, in the devastating regularity of its meter and rhyme, the self, in effect, can be construed, meditatively, as a ruined Gothic edifice in the same way that Margaret and the ruined cottage are seemingly interchangeable; time present may be felt as equivalent with the lowest ebb in the natural cycle, and a waning, crepuscular or Hesperian face may be put on organicism. The leafless trees, the unroofed transepts of England's great monasteries, and the speaker's own advanced age become *one* overarching yet unroofed thought:

> That time of year thou mayst in me behold
> When yellow leaves, or one, or few, do hang
> Upon these boughs which shake against the cold.
> Bare ruin'd choirs, where late the sweet birds sang,
> In me thou see'st the twilight of such day
> As after sunset fadeth in the west,
> Which by and by black night doth take away,
> Death's second self, that seals up all in rest.
> In me thou see'st the glowing of such fire
> That on the ashes of his youth doth lie,
> As the death-bed whereon it must expire
> Consum'd with that which it was nourish'd by.
> This thou perceiv'st, which makes thy love more strong,
> To love that well which thou must leave ere long.   Sonnet 73 (*SS*, 93)

Wordsworth's take on "bare ruin'd choirs" is a lyric not only of organic surreption, but of political and religious, i.e., ideological, displacement, reflected in a realignment (a literal translation) of the palette traditionally associated with those in positions of lofty clerical or regal eminence, down the organic scale, to a restored state of nature *unmolested* and imagery traditionally associated with melancholia and the tracts of Levellers: grubby creatures of the *Grund*, brambles, lizards, newts, owls and foxes. It begins with a threefold clause on invasive power—with the word "no" resounding like an organ-note of nihilation in three *Lear*-like verses:

Dissolution of the Monasteries

Threats come which no submission may assuage,
No sacrifice avert, no power dispute:
The tapers shall be quenched, the belfries mute,
And, 'mid their choirs unroofed by selfish rage,
The warbling wren shall find a leafy cage;
The gadding bramble hang her purple fruit;
And the green lizard and the gilded newt
Lead unmolested lives, and die of age.
The owl of evening and the woodland fox
For their abode the shrines of Waltham choose:
Proud Glastonbury can no more refuse
To stoop her head before these desperate shocks—
She whose high pomp displaced, as story tells,
Arimathean Joseph's wattled cells.   Sonnet XXI (*PW*, 341)

What is clearly missing is the self-dramatized "I" whose voice of meditation was so insistent in Shakespeare's sonnet and, of course, the ineffably sweet music of the terminal, rhyming syllables. That egoistical instance, the issue or issuance of the "I," recedes behind a panoramic scene of monastic dissolution (where Waltham and Glastonbury are given their literal historical due, which may be something other than fully realized, vivid poetic force) suggesting another kind of *reculer pour mieux sauter*, in which it is the problematized "I" that is now concealed beneath and made subservient to the literal text of English history, so that the directorial, totalizing, second-story "I" may set the scene the way it wants to—despite "desperate shocks" from the outside, on the greater Keswick-Ambleside highway of history—in a gradual progress towards an organic power which now becomes overtly or phenomenologically para-sitic upon worldy power.

What is not missing therefore—in the first two lines of the text, at any rate—is a clear reference to power and its disputation. The fact that certain powers cannot be resisted is not forgotten or elided after the Shakespearean allusion to "choirs unroofed by selfish rage" as put down or beneath the "undersong" of organic effacement. Here it is not Hegel's owl of Minerva, perceiving only philosophic shades of gray, that presides, but a melancholic "owl of evening" equal to the "woodland fox" in taking up its *residence* in the ruins of the monastery. Their abode is marked by signs of an even more chastened, undisturbed, in- or non-human tranquillity, where the gilding appears on the lowliest of animals rather than on the vestments of status-seeking prelates. The first line, however, tells a different story or points to a moral before the story of "high pomp displaced" can begin: how a threat "comes" that cannot be placated by any act of subservience or moving aside, how one power supervenes upon another by means of overtures which cannnot be refused on the broad highway of history. The rhythm of political and religious displacement, while in operation from the first to the last verse, is undercut and overmastered by the obliterating, effacing action of the alternative state of nature. The text suggests an ominous equation between the way in which Henry VIII, in another regime of terror, appropriated monastic territory and that by which the "wattled cells" of the supposedly original Christian on the island, Joseph of Arimathea, were forced to give way to the monasteries themselves, in their "high pomp." In a different time and space, with a wholly different political and experiential gilding. Shelley will expand upon this theme at some length in the thisworldly parade of *The Triumph of Life*, where cells will take on a totally different and more sinister meaning, in terms of the sad music of humanity. For Wordsworth, the "wattled cells" of Joseph Arimathea suggest an insect-like virtue and simplicity at odds with the ecclesiastical finery of the later Church (he is also apt to refer to shorter texts as "cells" in the projectively architectonic or "organic" totality of his *oeuvre*). The only residence where power cannot be contested, where the ego is secure, is one that lies off the road, one that is also unmolested in the sense of being, so to speak, "wattled," waddled and/or swaddled in the branches torn from trees—no longer the prison cell to which youth might have been prematurely, penally confined but a little domain unto itself, secluded, insular, seditious, a Rydal priory that would remain a romantic riddle to passersby. The great mistake of the monasteries was that they were not secluded enough, that they did not follow the vow of poverty sufficiently, that they succumbed to the noise of dynastic upheaval. Their displacement is not a matter of *Schein* or appearance, even as the surreptitious invasion of the monastery by wild animals, a thought of the transience of every form of "high pomp," is something more than subreption or pathetic fallacy.

The notion of literature as a means of transcending the flux of time and taste, as a kind of writing "for eternity," the aesthetic equivalent of Bede's *History*, must have appealed to Wordsworth's doubly turned, counter-historical imagination. The contestation of power suggests another one of those ascents to the sublime described in De Quincey's essay entitled "The Literature of Knowledge and the Literature of Power, where it is not Shakespeare, but Chaucer and Ovid who are seen as paragons of the kind of writing that will outlast the time in which it was written:

At this hour, one thousand eight hundred years since their creation, the Pagan tales of Ovid, never equalled on this earth for the gaiety of their movement and the capricious graces of their narrative, are read by all Christendom. This man's people and their monuments are dust: but he is alove: he has survived them, as he told us that he had it in his commission to do, by a thousand years: 'and *shall* a thousand more.' (*TDQ*, 1104)

And what Ovid points to, in his deixis, is Greece, or, rather, the romance of Greece filtered through Roman eyes. But De Quincey feels compelled at this point to return to metaphors of nature that reflect upon the transience of the lesser kind of literature:

All the Literature of Knowledge builds only ground-nests, that are swept away by floods, or confounded by the plough; but the Literature of Power builds nests in aerial altitudes of temples sacred from violation, or of forests inaccessible to fraud. The knowledge literature, like the fashion of this world, passeth away...But all literature properly so called—literature κατ᾽ ᾽εξοχην—for the very same reason that it is so much more durable than the Literature of Knowledge, is...more intense and electrically searching in its impressions. The directions in which the tragedy of this planet has trained our human feelings to play, and the combinations into which the poetry of this planet has thrown our human passions of love and hatred, of admiration and contempt, exercise a power for good or bad over human life that cannot be contemplated, when stretching through many generations, without a sentiment allied to awe....Dim by their origination, these emotions yet arise in him and mould him through life, like forgotten incidents of his childhood. (*TDQ*, 1104–1105)

If the primal or primary scenes of childhood mould Wordsworth in a similar way, then the full knowledge of the scene itself will have been forgotten or elided for the sake of what Pater calls an "accomplishment," a posterior awe or fearfulness recollected in tranquillity. What we then have is another vindication of the scenario of effacement in Goethe's "Wandrer" and of organic surreption. The rhythm by which knowledge is forsaken for power is one with the confrontational energy of the question "Shall I give way?" on a crowded street in London. If the poet gives way to fancy, random impressions, or stateliness, it amounts to a dampening of the pulse that springs "eternal" from the originary scene, a submission to the traffic that leads to the fronts of great houses and the characters inscribed there, forms expropriated or displaced from the portals of Gothic churches:

> Here, fronts of houses, like a title-page
> With letters huge inscribed from top to toe;
> Station'd above the door, like guardian Saints,
> There, allegoric shapes, female or male;
> Or physiognomies of real men.

On the other hand, Taylor's grub and bud, resistant to the chill of winters, political and otherwise, project an organic cosmos which is revolutionary in a cultural and political sense in terms of pastoral coding: antiquity, together with its inscriptions, is always being effaced or erased; the grounded green lizard, gilded newt, or displaced peasant can intrude upon and ultimately parasitize the mansions and realms of the powerful. Their surreptitious negativity of the *Grund*, whose overtures (spring, the color green, et al.) cannot be refused, is absolute in this world, surpassing even the dictatorship of money; it is an ultimatum which Wordsworth seeks neither to ally himself with nor to distance himself from in the sonnet on the dissolution of the monasteries. The verses, matter-of-factly, "point things out." In the cosmos of *The Ecclesiastical Sonnets* the entropy of history is not balanced by nature's negentropy; it is surpassed by it, or taken to an entirely different, in- or non-human level, at the *Grund* or ground level of ruined monasteries occupied by lizards or at the "aerial altitudes of temples sacred from violation," where the notion of cultural decay is transformed into something "richer" and "stranger," something heterocosmically *ungeheuer* or uncanny in the sense of its subverted cellular- or insularity, half privacy, half privation, something unsublatably romantic, i.e. Greek. Pater's characterization of Coleridge can be applied, *mutatis mutandis*, to a Wordsworth who asks in each precarious situation "Shall I give way?", who counters the confrontational language of man with the language of a man confronted by nature, who hears the wind playing deictic organ-notes in unroofed choirs where an uncanny, phobic clank takes the place of "a bell/ To mark some change of service." He

> ...represents that inexhaustible discontent, languor, and home-sickness, that endless regret, the chords of which ring all through our modern literature. It is to the romantic element in literature that those qualities belong. One day, perhaps, we may come to forget the distant horizon, with full knowledge of the situation, to be content with 'what is here and now'; and herein is the essence of classical feeling. But by us of the present moment, certainly—by us for whom the Greek spirit, with its engaging naturalness, simple, chastened, debonair, τρυφῆς [delicate], ἀβρό-τατος [softest], χλιδῆς [charming], χαρίτων [of graces], ἱμέρου [of desire], πόθου πατήρ [of longing, the father] is itself the Sangrail of an endless pilgrimage, Coleridge...may be reckoned one of the constituent elements of our life.
>
> (*WP*, 104)

Thus we glimpse fleeting moments of a stubbornly "matter-of-fact" virtue, gauging aesthetic value by the ironic *sermo humilis* of pastoral creeping and/or crepitation—whose irrepressible deixis is continually resensed in (dis)embodiments of an *Ur*-scene or Goethean wellspring, the Eternal

Feminine, genial effacement, and the state of nature, signs of a Rousseau-inspired, republican *fides*.

In what might otherwise be interpreted as an evocation of cosmic balance, the text projects a deixis without idea or *logos*, where there is no genius-like human infant, where a different owl of evening communicates a legacy of egalitarian metamorphosis—no longer the owl of Minervan (Roman) wisdom, but of Athena-like, i.e., Greek transformation, the *hypokeimenon* which, as Heidegger notes, translates badly into Latin as *substantia*. Ultimately, Wordsworth's ascent to satiric power restages and resites scenes of childhood within *his* mesocosm/topocosm—i.e. an ontic heterocosm. It is a splitting of the imago of the Eternal Feminine and of gold/gilding which renders the oft-repeated, never-to-be-completed turning of the face necessary—a procedure and intellectual posture whose romance is the hollowing-out of transference. At the same time, Wordsworth's systoles and diastoles, in the oscillation of that which is seen and felt *organically*, in and beneath pastoral coding, cannot be reduced to the heartbeats or hollowness projected on just *any* traveler. Infant art, gifted with powers of strange and vivid speech, from everywhere and nowhere, from the highways and byways, turns deictically toward *this* and away from *that*, and in the elusiveness of its quest for the numinous (already, both *now* and *then*) anticipates the next great writer of *its* epitaph.

We conclude with a schema representing some of the matters under discussion. It will be criticized, justly no doubt, for the religious implications of its axes, but it should be clear by now (especially after reading the sonnet on Glastonbury) that these are not a surreptitious argument for some sort of Wordsworthian orthodoxy, no matter how much the superficial details of autobiography may cast him in the light of one or the other religious institution. What Wordsworth means by hope and faith is both the same as and utterly different from what Paul means by them in his letter to the Hebrews:

Residual Deixis (Fides Virtusque)
Heterocosmic Phenomenalization/ Haunting

```
    O          "Broad High-way Appearances"=urban/pastoral topocosm
E F   U        London street in The Prelude
V     N        initiatic haunting by phasmas/fantasy of ghosts/little Kate/
I T S S        Danish Boy/ Lucy
D H E E        gibbets/ beggars/ vagrants/ discharged soldier
E I E E        ghost of schoolmaster with bough of wilding
N N N N        pomp of medieval Church and stately powers
C G &          gilded newts/ three rude pillars/ Margaret's cup and bench
E S
```

SUBSTANCE OF THINGS HOPED FOR[65]

As the philosopher Jean-Luc Nancy suggests, hope, "today more than ever," is the *virtus* of thought, that which remains when we are confronted by a symptomatic powerlessness on the part of thought itself in a world of increasing harshness and brutality.[66] The substance of Wordsworthian "things hoped for" lies expressed in a few subversive lines from "Inscriptions supposed to be found in and near a Hermit's Cell" (1818). Not surprisingly, the metaphorical vehicle of transitoriness mirrors almost exactly the spears of grass silvered by the rain near Margaret's ruined cottage. Hope, at the beginning of life's day or later on, is a thing both beautiful and dangerous, strung out like beads of water to mark the spider's web at a pass or impasse where the going gets fear-laden and anxious:

> Hopes what are they? Beads of morning
> Strung on slender blades of grass
> Or a spider's web adorning
> In a strait and treacherous pass.   (*PW*, 430, 1–4)

We place a similarly Goethean but also self-reflexive insight, suggestive of many a primal deixis and prefixed to the volume entitled "Poems chiefly of Early and Late Years" (a text written twenty-four years later) in the context of that other, earlier "Prelude" cited at the beginning of this study:

> ...and, as even the wish
> Has virtue in it, why should hope to me
> Be wanting that sometimes, where fancied ills
> Harass the mind and strip from off the bowers
> Of private life their natural pleasantness,
> A Voice...
> Lodged within compass of the humblest sights,
> The cheerful intercourse with wood and field...
> Will not be heard in vain?   (*PW* 421, 33–37; 39–42)

We read these verses now with the amplifying, connected, and completing thought following them—a voice addressing itself, in Rousseauistic contrariety, to the negativity of current history—to the increasingly less pastoral, less natural, less simple, less chaste, less debonair, less fraternal Industrial Age England of the 1840s (and *a fortiori* to us who live in a seemingly parallel age) and to the hope that the libretto-like book, transfomed into a dialectically positioned, pastoral "strain" or musical note, may win auditors at one fleeting time or another, as if caught on the wind:

> ...And in these days

When unforeseen distress spreads far and wide,
Among a People mournfully cast down,
Or into anger roused by venal words
In recklessness flung out to overturn
The judgment, and divert the general heart
From mutual good—some strain of thine, my Book!
Caught at propitious intervals, may win
Listeners.... (*PW* 538, 42–50)

Nonetheless, the final thing that must be said of *The Ecclesiastical Sonnets* is that—despite their topical subject matter and valorization of organic effacement and parasitism—they cannot be joined to the Gothic edifice Wordsworth thought he was building. Their totalization, filtered through a sonnet sequence that sits on or *over* history, on its second floor or upper story, as it were, no longer exhibits that relationship of language to itself which takes on exemplary ontic force in Book VII, where the stately show parades its chariots down the London street and the question "Shall I give way?" still resonates at the crossroads of lived being and substance, always in a "strait and dangerous pass." Wordsworth, in a sense, is no longer living that "large" in terms of a history experienced confrontationally, a primary scene to be made *his own* in the danger and narrow straits of its alternately pleasurable and disconcerting traffic. Nor are his characters, in the sense of both letters and persons, large. In concretizing the monastic impetus toward fraternity, equality, and liberty, in giving it a name "Waltham, Glastonbury," Wordsworth sacrifices the passion of a heterocosmic vision which, by preserving a state of anonymity or giving its characters, like saints or angels, only hauntingly intimate first names, "Margaret," "Matthew," et al., makes the totalization both deictic and romantic, in the sense Pater applies to it, both distinctively historicized and intensely personal, i.e., major verse. This is something Goethe seems to have sensed instinctively when in 1777 he made his scene of cultural inscription and effacement a dialogue between an indeterminate "Wandrer" and an even more nondescript, residual Eternal Feminine known only as "Frau."

If as Heringman suggests, an aesthetic principle is being tested in Wordsworth's poetry against a "recalcitrant reality," is it possible to say that an ethical or philosophical axiom is also seeking vindication through what may be thought of as a contrapuntalism or controversion on the part of the poetic word? If one is de Man, heterocosmic representation collapses under the pressure of the undecidable, treacherous nature of language. Organic effacement seems only too willing to play its role here. But there is another "face" to organic effacement, one that moves ahead by means of its oppositional turning or *Gegenwendigkeit*, which is that of a truth revealed by what Pater calls Romantic art; it finds its inscription in the displacement of the Muses, in signs and speeches of beggars or squatters, exiled from monastic grounds for reasons loosely connected to the Protestant revolution, dispossessed by the enclosure movement, exploited by the Industrial Revolution. To say that such a hermeneutic counterturn is negated is to participate in the cognitive lie of the bourgeois that the vagrant is not his double, that a state of homelessness does not constitute a *mene tekel* for him or her. The lesson of Wordsworth's turning of face is one of deixis, not sublation; it is to situate both the sign and its humble or pompous wearer on the broad highway of experience, to see allegoric shapes on the fronts of houses, allegories not of reading, but of substance, as that which is lived on and in thoroughfares and narrower alleyways. Whatever else one may say about the verse, it seems clear that the entirety of the *oeuvre*, from *The Lyrical Ballads* to "The Ecclesiastal Sonnets" is directed against the blindly narcissistic stateliness of those "rich beyond the wealth of kings," who are always willing, like Pentheus, to pretend that the laws of nature do not apply to them, that the planet can be treated like the branch in "Nutting," as so much matter or material for casual mutilation, that the colors can be scraped off nature through a process of universally deadening acquisition.

Wordsworth thus thinks through a para-phenomenology in which the *Geist* of history is replaced by the "deixis" of experience, something both less than a religion and more than an aesthetics, premised by and on intimate terms with natural metamorphosis, that most Goethean of thoughts. This "ersatz" construct may justly be termed a phenomenalization of historicism, where the action of the supernatural, relics, and haunting, in their valor and valence, take the place of the labor of the historically determined *Begriff*. At its core is an indestructible kernel of Rousseauist ideology, equally active in Goethe, projecting geographic particulars and linear history in terms of the cyclicality of a universal State of Nature existing before and after history. The "Taylorizing" of Goethe, far from being a matter of literary curiosity or insular interest, ought to be seen as belonging to the *ens* or substance of that which is represented by Wordsworth as being covertly operative and, in all times and places, i.e., counter-historically, valid: a necessary hope torturing him and us in the ruins of what was and in the residual, counterturned heterocosm.

2. The Numinous, the Noumenal, and Wordsworthian Deixis

On the same spot in summer, at thrush-hour, I
As the last light falls, have heard that full
Shadow-shimmered and deep-glinting liquidity, and
Again will, but not now.
> Robert Penn Warren, "Sunset Walk in Thaw-Time in Vermont"

In an essay devoted, in part, to Alexander Pope, Thomas De Quincey asserts that literature, far from being a unified endeavor, can be divided into two distinct fields, each with its own reason for existence:

> There is first the Literature of *Knowledge*: and secondly the Literature of *Power*. The function of the first is—to *teach*; of the second is—to *move*. The first speaks to the mere discursive understanding; the second speaks ultimately...to the higher understanding or reason, but always *through* the affections of pleasure and sympathy. Remotely, it may travel towards an object seated in what Lord Bacon calls *dry* light; but, proximately, it does and must operate...on and through that *humid* light which clothes itself in the mists and glittering iris of human passions, desires, and genial emotions...Besides which, there is a rarer thing than truth, namely *power* or deep sympathy with truth...What you owe to Milton is not any knowledge...what you owe is *power*, that is, exercise and expansion to your own latent capacity of sympathy with the infinite, where every pulse and each separate influx is a step upwards....[1]

Since it functions, locally, nearly, or "humidly," before ascending to a higher, drier realm of reason, the Literature of Power—and here De Quincey seems to be referring to Wordsworth beneath the explicit mention of Milton as its representative—must have at least a nerve for affect or be impassioned in some way in order to achieve a profounder "sympathy with truth," one that exists on a plane parallel to "sympathy with the infinite." Where could a source of power embedded in the self-as-wonder, yet allied with infinite truth be found? The answer lay not only in nature, but in nature qualified as being *unschooled*—making us sense that De Quincey had a passage such as this in mind—a *pas* of ascent or climbing—when he wrote that the Literature of Power is felt rather than taught:

> ...that a work of mine,
> Proceeding from the depth of untaught things,
> Enduring and creative might become
> A power like one of Nature's.[2]

In other words, if we had to consider what such a power "like one of Nature's" would be, we might do worse than to call it not only an affective, but also an *effective* presence. And this is the term Henri Bergson uses to define the Latin word *numen* (based on the verb *nuo, nuere*, to nod) in the context of the "genius," an extra-scholastic tutelary spirit presiding over place or person:

> Are we to consider as a god the personal genius or daemon of a particular individual? The Roman genius was *numen*, not *deus*; it has neither shape nor name; it was very near to that mere 'effective presence' which we have seen to be the primitive and essential element of divinity.[3]

But such an effective presence may or may not rest easily in one place; it may be transferable, moving from presence to absence, revealing itself by what is "not there" or hollowed out. Its power seems often to be or reside in motion; so primitive is it that it may be everywhere and nowhere at once. In one of the most famous of passages alluding to *numen*, Anchises recognizes in the sign sent by heaven a power which will be transferred from him to his son: "Vestrum hoc augurium, vestroque in numine Troia est" (*Aeneid* II, 703). *Numen* therefore is what poets and oracles take to be the deixis of the cosmos, or as the will of God, made legible in the book of nature, yet requiring no teaching. At the same time, however, when used by wizards and witches, it takes the form of another kind of power or craft, a power, like melancholy, strongly allied with night rather than day, capable of being employed either for good or for ill. The devolution of power from Aeneas to Ascanius—made emphatic in the reiterated possessive adjective *vestrum...vestro*—is unambiguously fitting and made to seem inevitable in epic circumstances; what I am calling the counter-turn of deixis in Wordsworth, who writes, more or less fabulously, with Vergil as his companion and precursor-guide.[4] In a far more secular and secular age than Dante's, the invocation of sorcery-like effects is a good deal more problematic, because possession and augury have themselves become ambivalently effective in their "presencing" and thus require another kind of (art-less) poetic representation and translation, a re-sensing of devotion in a time and space deprived of the feeling for poetic art, when the no doubt personally painful question must be raised, by Wordsworth himself, "What is a poet?" But the sense of England as another Hesperia is vivid from the beginning, as in "The Female Vagrant," whose first two lines begin far from the bookshelf, i.e., on the river's edge:

> By Derwent's side my father's cottage stood,
> (The Woman thus her artless story told)....

but whose text then leads through a labyrinthine series of hyper-balladic dislocations and traumatic voyagings to these lines of Hesperian storm and stress, untimely ripped from the womb of Latinity:

> Our hopes such harvest of affliction reap,
> That we the mercy of the waves should rue.
> We reached the western world, a poor devoted crew.[5]

To be unschooled, one must first to go to school. The pressures of Wordsworth's education are at all times evident in the poetic text, even when the imagery takes him far beyond the classroom, or when the subject matter is at its most colorfully folkloristic.[6]

In Wordsworth, the transfer of numinous gifts is often delayed, deferred, or occulted. The nod of *numen*—or what seems like *numen*, inasmuch as antiquity was "then" and this is the disenchanted "now," at least after 1793, is thus fluid and fluctuating—as we know from the Witches' Scene in *Macbeth*—it cannot be definitively bestowed for long upon any one person or thing, though there are countless places, such as Hart-Leap Well and Margaret's cottage, which, though fallen into ruin, seem to have been struck by divine agency: either tainted by emblems of unholy profligacy or held spellbound by the saintly abjection of a bygone era. An anxiety concerning power insists upon the text through features of landscape or characters revealed within those features. *Numen's* currently empowered address is "home" in the fells and rivers of the Lake District, but the poet's uncertainty as to his own augural gifts—or, rather, the desire to communicate thoughts of futurity in a deixis perspicuous to his readers—means that *numen*, if it is still seen as effectual, will be re-presented dramatically, i.e., through the discourse of the other, in the form of a third person, like the Female Vagrant, or in the inarticulate burrings of the Idiot Boy.[7] Thus, when we encounter witchcraft in "Goody Blake and Harry Gill," from *The Lyrical Ballads*, it will *not* be in the form of a summoning of familiar spirits, as in a text by Horace, where the witch Canidia invokes the spirits of the night and of Diana, goddess of virgins, of the moon, and of witchcraft who rule over a silence in which occult things become sacred:

> '...o rebus meis
> non infideles arbitrae,
> Nox et Diana quae silentium regis
> arcana cum fient sacra,
> nunc, nunc, adeste, nunc in hostiles domos
> iram atque numen vertite. '[8]

['...O not unfaithful witnesses/ to my affairs,Night and Diana, <you> who rule the silence/ when the arcana become sacred,/ now, now, be present, now turn rage and numen/ against hostile houses.']

Wordsworth will place the invocation of *numen* in another space or archetypographic scene, one with unmistakable sociosemiotic implication, where Goody Blake, a "poor woman" who "dwelt alone," trespasses upon the hedge of her neighbor in order to steal firewood, is caught, and then brings down the wrath of God upon him and his hostile house:

> She pray'd, her wither'd hand uprearing,
> While Harry held her by the arm—
> 'God! who art never out of hearing,
> 'O may he never more be warm!'
> The cold, cold moon above her head,
> Thus on her knees did Goody pray,
> Young Harry heard what she had said,
> And icy-cold he turned away.
>
> He went complaining all the morrow...
>
> 'Twas in vain, a useless matter,
> And blankets were about him pinn'd;
> Yet still his jaws and teeth they clatter,
> Like a loose casement in the wind.
> And Harry's flesh it fell away.... (*LB*, 54, 97–117)

The landowner suffers a "harvest" of disembodying affliction which can only be due to the imprecation of Goody. At the same time, the text cannot omit the moon's presence as a witness to the scene, either because it is the symptomatic sign of a haunting by the "witch Poesy," in the country of romance, or, more likely, because Diana is the helpmate of witches everywhere, and it is the continuity of *numen* or something "like" it, from pagan centuries into the Christian age, as the counterturn of supernatural agency against secular schooling, that is being stressed. But we note in passing that for the Wordsworth of *The Lyrical Ballads* numinous action, in the form of a spell or curse, is frequently associated with traumatic hypothermia, a lowering of physical temperature—eerily reminiscent, in a "Gothic" key, perhaps—of the poet's habitually detached matter-of-factness, a retreat from fever-like, participatory cathexis to a cooler psychological dispassion and sublime or insular tranquillity. This is Wordsworth's somewhat unexpected counterturn against the classical tradition itself, inasmuch as Horace associates Canidia with the most famous witch of mythology, Medea, whose malign arts make the flesh boil or burn—often, as with her brother Apsyrtus, after being butchered. In the case of Harry Gill and, even more blatantly in the case of the Danish Boy,[9] a Canidia-like female emanation takes lethal control of the other. In the case of Harry Gill, who is hardly innocent, the words "pinn'd," "jaws," and "teeth," assert the grisly, Medea-like power of *numen* to anatomize the corpse or corporeality of man *as specimen*, seeing in him nothing but an assemblage of elemental, unschooled, relic-like parts. *Numen* thus participates in a surgical procedure, like vivisection, where the supreme power of God, and of the living over the dead, is projected, where the underdog who is Goody Blake is given liberty to pursue what property law considers a bad or illegal course of action and to rise up against an oppressive social system, turning its unneighborly embodiment into a charnel emblem, a collection of cadaverous parts. And, if we need to be reminded, there is no suggestion here of a Salem-like trial for the witch of the withered hand. Her divinely assisted assault on property rights is left— "meant" in a deictic sense—to stand, character- or type-like, as a monitory emblem for those in similarly penurious situations. Goody Blake thus becomes a law unto herself, allied with a force higher than human jurisprudence. At the same time, and this is a feature which may well have appealed to the balladeer, she cannot be regarded as an outlaw, because she has invoked supernatural assistance. The "long arm" of the law, unlike the once apprehending grip of Harry Gill, is unable to reach the perpetrator who escapes over a supernatural border. The distance between earthly and celestial jurisprudence could not be greater. It is *numen*, a god- or witch-like power that asserts itself in the contrast between dark and light, night and day, sickness and health, power and powerlessness, vivisectionist and corpse on the operating table. The cold that overpowers complaining Harry Gill corresponds, on one level of symbolism, to the chilling of social relations in the unfraternal landscape of Industrial Age England, a symptomatic instance of "imaginative elaboration" described by Geoffrey Hartman in his analysis of the post-traumatic stress of Holocaust survivors:

> In our time, the imaginative burden is aggravated by the fact that many families were decimated in the Holocaust, so that the injury suffered becomes an injury to memory itself, to the very possibility of recollection. Remembrance, especially by the immediate descendants, turns in a void as it tries to recover individual details about the life and death of those who disappeared. A *cold* trauma, so to say, may result: not only an immediate, overwhelming affright at that void and the defensive, emotional deadening that may follow, but also a chill brought on by the absence of what facilitates normal sympathetic identification and the working-through of loss. A process of imaginative elaboration, or the filling of a lacuna, may also take place in the collective memory and explain why, over the long run, legend consolidates as historical fact. Here too 'Men make their own history.' Real suffering and humiliation as well as vague terrors are delimited, or a defeat is turned into a celebration. For mankind to lose its fear of the gods, Hesiod said, it had to give them a definite shape—even, we might add, free itself from them by an inventive, form-giving power.[10]

Hartman is almost certainly referring to De Quincey's "Literature of Power" with the phrase "inventive, form-giving power." The imaginative elaboration of a scene, especially a scene of witchcraft, relocates the hermeneutic or gnomic value of deixis (made perspicuous in the Blind Beggar episode of *The Prelude*), confronting us with a cynosure-like *memento mori* of clattering jaws and teeth or the comedic refrains punctuating the long night of "The Idiot Boy." Day-lit terrors, on the other hand, teach, perhaps, too much. History and historical memory, in their decibel-level or shock-value, the charnel pageantry of snow-covered corpses spilling out of freight-cars, put the deixis of "eternal forms divine" into near-total eclipse.[11] But there is a salvific counterturn to such scenes of utter desolation, a resurfacing or resensing of that which can be or ought to be salvaged from personal and historical holocaust, from *Goody* Blake to the lunar sunshine of "The Idiot Boy" to the thoroughly diabolical and pandemic *numina* of Auschwitz, through a form of revelation which does not sear in its *apo-kalypsis* or unobscuring, but burns with a colder, reflected, and nocturnal light, freeing *us* from fear, and thus turned outward and away from the merely factual recollection of historical terrors.

Applied in the context of song or ballad, *numen* may involve a personal transaction where the verses, turned themselves, ask that the turbulence of a spell be mimetically counteracted. Thus it is not surprising to find Proserpina or Persephone invoked, who rules over Hades for six months of the year.[12] The *carmina* become, in effect, anti-tunes, whose object is to implore a counterturning or unspinning of magical effect already set in motion by the "bad" or merely worse witch:

> Iam iam efficaci do manus scientiae,
> supplex et oro regna per Proserpinae,
> per et Dianae non movenda numina,
> per atque libros carminum valentium
> refixa caelo devocare sidera,
> Canidia, parce vocibus tandem sacris,
> citumque retro solve, solve turbinam.
>
> (*HF*, 161, Epode 17, 1–7)

[Already, already, I give hands to the powerful knowledge,/ As a suppliant, and I pray by the realm of Proserpina,/ And by the not-to-be-moved *numina* of Diana,/ And by the books of strong songs/ Which call down the fixed stars from the skies/ Canidia, finally, save the sacred voices/ And quickly set the wheel to moving in reverse.]

According to one commentator, the actual device employed by the witches of Horace's day for deploying numinous spells was a device similar to that used from prehistorical times to the present by Australian aborigines:

The magic wheel is probably a bull-roarer: a flat piece of wood whirled by a long cord. The artificial thunder thus produced, says Jane Harrison (*Themis*, p. 64), 'possesses in a high degree the quality of uncanniness. Heard in the open sunlight it sends a shudder through even modern nerves.' The magic spell is broken by reversing the direction of the whirl.[13]

The notion of dark forces moving with the wind suggests the numinous force of the wild "witch Poesy," born and active in the night and operative in the poetic effort to reach a transcendent altitude:

> ...Visionary Power
> Attends upon the motions of the winds
> Embodied in the mystery of words.
> There darkness makes abode, and all the host
> Of shadowy things do work their changes there,
> As in a mansion like their proper home;
> Even forms and substances are circumfus'd
> By that transparent veil with light divine;
> And through the turnings intricate of Verse,
> Present themselves as objects recogniz'd,
> In flashes, and with a glory scarcely known. (*Prelude* 1805,
> 84, V, 619–629)

Turning around, circumfusing, turbulences of wind and water: these are potential deixes of a numinous effect. But the phenomenal in Wordsworth is often transformed into something else, less visible and sometimes scarcely audible or entirely silent. The visionary power turns sooner or later to the eidetic, not the realm of Platonic forms, but to objects that are not truly revealed until we re-cognize them by ad-verting *to* them...in the umbilical "turnings intricate" of poetic language. The lines do not say that truth can be discovered, dialectically, by winnowing predicates and avoiding shadowy objects (as with Plato's cave analogy), but rather that the objects themselves can become the focus of loftier poetic interest—once the veil of appearance is lifted, and a higher, colder light is poured around them. Out of the darkness of mystery light proceeds, which would be like the light of day were it not subject to bursts of fulgurant insight. In Book VI, the Platonic forms will be described as playthings of confined schoolboy study, "wild ideal pageantry.../ Debarr'd from Nature's living images" (*Prelude* 1805, VI, 309, 313). The forms must break out of scholarly confinement, onto the road, and into the wild in order to make a stronger song.

Numen, like the bemusement of the Muse, is an unmoved mover over which the poet has incomplete and temporary control. It is at once a flickering something and a shadowy, intangible "no-thing," that "comes and goes," whose fluctuation in and for the human subject suggests not the stasis of knowledge, but the dwindling and resurgence of effective power. The place to look for such intermittent sources of supernatural coerciveness would therefore be those cataracts and waterfalls which seem always to cast a spell upon the poet who observes them, whose presence is at once illuminating and threatening to vision, whose "stationary blast" he would adapt, though scarcely harness, to fit a cogent mental purpose. In the Literature of Power, that purpose is to move rather than to teach. Yet, when we arrive in Gondo Gorge, in Book VI of *The Prelude*, the emphasis is placed upon the unmoving appearance of the falling water, a unity of Light and Dark suggesting the absolute oneness of all phenomena, "Characters of the great Apocalypse,/ The types and symbols of Eternity," which may overwhelm even the most powerful mind with their sublimity. That is one sort of insight or deixis, experienced when the act itself, passing over the crest of the Alps, is past, and Wordsworth is left with nothing but a melancholy sleep not far from the deafening roar of the gorge. As Rudolf Dirk Schier suggests, the dialogue with nature fades away in Book VI, and the sense of being in the presence of something numinous gradually, over the course of three narrative episodes, abates—to be replaced by a sense of anxiety, inaccomplishment, or brooding guilt.[14] This distancing or chastening effect is at a remove from power or the concern with power that De Quincey alludes to in the aforementioned essay. It suggests, as Irwin demonstrates, not so much a freeing from fear (phobic anxieties associated with primal scenes of force or forcing) as a dizzying vision of contraries merging (as sexual or polar opposites) in the abyss:

> Having transgressed a natural limit to confront within the poem a primal scene of imagination/insemination (the overflowing of the imagination/the Nile's fertilizing of the Egyptian plain), Wordsworth descends into a womblike chasm in the Gondo Gorge passage and is given a prefiguration of the merging of opposites in the absolute...
>
> In the passage on the imagination, Wordsworth balances the opening image of the Power rising 'from the mind's abyss/Like an unfathered vapor' against the concluding image of the Nile rising to 'fertilize the whole Egyptian plain,' and in the latter instance as in the former, the origin of the rising is a vapor from the abyss; the river is poured from the 'fount of Abyssinian clouds.' Besides evoking, in the image of the rising of a river, the roots of the words 'origin' (L. *origo, originis* from *orior*, 'to rise') and 'source' (L. *surgere*, 'to rise'; literally, a spring or fountain, the starting point of a stream), Wordsworth plays on the etymological relationship of the words 'abyss' and 'Abyssinia' and on the classical tradition of treating Abyssinia—the mysterious source of the Nile, the unexplored lower region of the classical world—as if it were literally an abyss.[15]

The level of word-play involved in turning "abyss" and "Abyssinia" into mirror-like tropes suggests a Wordsworth in flight from the notion of a numinous power residing in words taken out of context—their "abracadabra effect"—and much more interested in the dislocating or disseminative power of a poetic intelligence used to bend etymology and literalness to the will or performative specifications of the one on whom the *numen* of Troy or Abyssinia is bestowed: "*vestrum* hoc augurium." Thus *numen* becomes less a matter of being "out there," and more an autonomous power situated in the *arbitrium* of the self-empowered poet.

The scene of unneighborly privation and numinous vengeance in "Goody Blake and Harry Gill" has as its complement and comedic antithesis another text from *The Lyrical Ballads*, "The Idiot Boy," which mirrors, in a number of respects, both more and less "forcefully," the night-inspired, moonily romantic or supernatural anatomy observed there, but also suggests a "dumb and dumber take" on the Lacanian *fort/da* paradigm. Both ballads are concerned with "mothers" of the night, poor, in the case of Goody Blake, or hysterically anxious, in the case of Johnny Foy's mother, Betty. Nowhere in Wordsworth is there such an overwhelming textual connection made between women (Betty cares not only for her boy, but also for the sickly Susan Gill), physical and/or supernatural "force," and the image of the stationary cataract or waterfall. While it happens that a waterfall in the Lake District of England is also known as a "force," there is no guarantee that a punning play upon native idiom affects the meaning of the poetic text. Yet, when we read the word, we may be compelled to look below the immediate context to subtextual resonances (of numinous disturbance or turbulence) affecting the utterance in its performative (self-referential) implication.[16] As Hartman suggests, "The Idiot Boy" is "...full of joyfully unrepressed 'turns' or tautologies."[17] By "turns" are meant the repeated, almost comedic routines of speech, such as Johnny's constant "burr...burr" with his lips, the sign that he is cold, even though he does not recognize himself as such,[18] and the "Or...Or...Ors" commencing each of Betty Foy's anxious expostulations concerning her straying son. At the same time, another purpose is scanned in Wordsworth's commentary, which is that of a balladic attempt at tempering, or, rather, emphasizing the "eternally recurrent " nature of things, which serves as a potential source or resource of poetic inspiration. Wordsworth, who admits in the letters to feeling "glee" at his creation, is left in the position of one who laughs at his own jokes, leading Hartman to the conclusion that there is too abundant a release of (psychic) energy on the part of the self-indulgent storyteller (*WP*, 150). What no commentator has observed up to this point, so far as I am able to discern, is that "Goody Blake and Harry Blake" involves the chilling and wasting-away of Harry *Gill*, by the "bad" witch who is *Goody* Blake, while, in addtion to the happy return of a prodigal son, "The Idiot Boy" includes as includes as a side-effect the miraculous cure of Betty's friend Susan *Gale*, whose name connects with the force or fury of the wind (a little like the comic actress of the 1950s who called herself "Gale Storm"), but can also be seen as a near anagram of "glee," the very emotion Wordsworth says he has while composing the poetic text (J. B. Owen cites Wordsworth's words in *LB*, 143)—one that is completed in a single "go" and almost entirely without correction :

> 'Alas! what is become of them?
> 'These fears can never be endured,
> 'I'll to the wood.'—These words scarce said,
> Did Susan rise up from her bed,
> As if by magic cured.
>
> Away she posts up hill and down,
> And to the wood at length is come,
> She spies her friends, she shouts a greeting;
> Oh me! it is a merry meeting,
> As ever was in Christendom. (*LB*, 100, 432–441)

The piling-up of G's and L's—an alphabetic troping of the steam-like water-vapor released into the air by the violence of the cataract (one that Wordsworth uses as a metaphor or symbol of poetic imagination)—suggests a turning of supernatural force and lexical fate into arbitrary typographic glee—a transfer of energy from trauma to unrepressed license. Susan's sudden "reading" of the situation with Betty and Johnny, a hermeneutics of the fearing heart rather than of the intrepid head, expressed in the panic-stricken words "I'll to the woods," occurs in the moment immediately before she sees her friends; in effect, the sympathy of Susan begins her healing by means other than a talking-cure or a cure which is "all talk," like that of the village doctor who is, in effect, the real idiot of the poem—he who lacks, precisely, the sense to be sensitive to the plight of another. Extracurricular sympathy, that is, begins in Susan's "*fort*," her excursive thought or animadversion *toward* the woods and precedes her curative glee, mirroring the joy of Wordsworth who suggests to a correspondent that human beings can be taught to have feelings where none exist at present, thereby making the world a better and more moral place in which to live (*LB*, 144). Again, the motivation of innervation, of providing or restoring feelings where only numbness now prevails, is similar to that of "Goody Blake and Harry Gill," since it focuses on a lack of sympathy between neighbors (due to the concept of private property) and its pathological, supernatural consequences. The reunion of the caring trio of mother, idiot son, and Susan Gale is depicted as a scene of maternal/filial good cheer recuperating, if only for a gleeful, echoing moment, as if onstage in some theatre at a Bartholomew Fair of the mind, a merrier, older, now vanished England, a scene from which phobia, anxiety, and fear have been banished in the "*da*" or dada of scopic *jouissance*, and Betty is free to lose herself in a bout of celebratory, Falstaffian drinking.

Why put an idiot at center stage? As Bewell points out, the 18th century had made idiots into subjects of serious philosophical study, privileging them as representatives of the state of uncorrupted nature from which modern civilization has wandered and decayed. This is not only the ideology of Rousseau and his time; it is also the perspective of Baudelaire, Emerson, Whitman, and others. But, as Bewell makes abundantly clear, the chilled or "chillin'" nature boy who is Johnny Foy has no extraordinary insight to share either with his mother or with readers. He is the unideal or atypical experimental subject in the poem. If Wordsworth is having fun with Betty Foy, the *Sturm und Drang*, and Bürger's *Lenore* (available in Taylor's translation), he is also casting a satirical light on scientific investigation, thus "debunking" (*WPS*, 333) the tendency of 18th-century *philosophes* to turn living nature, including wild children and idiots, into anatomical specimens. If he is projecting a counter-case or counter-argument against Enlightenment optimism and "Gothic" romance, these lines can be taken, in fact, as some of the funniest in *The Lyrical Ballads*:

> 'Oh saints! what is become of him?
> 'Perhaps he's climbed into an oak,
> 'Where he will stay till he is dead;
> 'Or sadly he has been misled,
> 'And joined the wandering gypsey-folk.

> 'Or him that wicked pony's carried
> 'To the dark cave, the goblins' hall,
> 'Or in the castle he's pursuing,
> 'Among the ghosts, his own undoing;
> 'Or playing with the waterfall.'   (*LB*, 93, 232–241)

"Playing with the waterfall" remains to be translated, if that is possible, from Wordsworth's gleeful reprojection of numinous effect. "Waterfall-play," if taken seriously, means pursuing one's private or privative undoing among marginal types like the gypsies, or in the neighborhood of goblins and ghosts inhabiting antecedent odes and romances. It is the truant occupation of Wordsworth in the *Lyrical Ballads*, a *poein* or doing in the secluded interest of that which needs to be undone—phobic fear and anxiety concerning poverty, military service, revolutionary guilt, and so on. Sane or whole people would be advised against toying with the potentially *numen*-ridden force that is the waterfall, but it is not Johnny who does so. His actual nocturnal exploits are an unwritten, excursive blank; we can only diagnose the "hyper" or hyperbolic windings of Betty's language, as it sympathetically, affect-fully explores, with more than a little poetic license and no doubt occasioning much glee on the part of Wordsworth as he wrote it, the uncanny or alien recesses of maternal trepidation. And, to be sure, Wordsworth's mirror-like or narcissistic self-indulgence is reflected in all the places that Johnny *might* have been—the waterfalls that the real Wordsworth visits for poetic inspiration—and in the hyperbolic anxiety of his maternal other, Betty Foy. The vocation of poet partakes of idiot, mother, and *wyrd*, weird spirits, fate, the supernatural. But in these case Wordsworth's ego is split and spilt; he sees himself in comedic form straddling both worlds, that of poetic lunacy and that of phobic projection. Thus the tautological "Or...or...ors" amount to something. They are deixes of fear, the stuttering, idiot-like mental state of Betty *Foy*—in translation (assisted by *The American Heritage Dictionary of the English Language*), Betty *Faith*, if we choose the Norman French, or the rarer meaning, a variation on the French *voie*, chiefly found in Scots dialect, first attested in 1496 but occurring also in the 17th-century diary of Pepys, a gift or "parting entertainment" given by or to one who is setting out on a journey? We would not be forcing matters too much to characterize the simple ballad as an allegory or riddle of the familiar/familial *numina* of poetry, counterturned away from or against romance toward the comedic in an effort to *gift* the self with the antidote of laughter and thus escape fatality of another kind, a neurosis concerning not only poetry, but the filial relationship with a dead mother, "...tracing the maternal passion in many of its more subtle windings,"[19] windings no doubt as intensely intricate and diverse as poetry itself. On the one hand, it is an allegory of Foy or *Foi*, of faith, losing its subject or subjecthood, where the errant subject, like a Parzival or some other knight wandering away from a Round Table of beneficent female presences, can climb into the temporary shelter of a hollow oak, as a dryad or homeless persons have been known to do, go to the caves of gypsies (read...witches) and sojourn with the ghosts—playing with the waterfall and thus be a gleeful way of parting or heterocosmic, *out-of-this-world* partying (to the world the poet remains an unpatent, jejune blank), while being still in it. The Idiot Boy, like Lucy, is both dead and not dead; he is certainly "dead" to his mother for most of the text, just as they are to him in the "dream-time" of the night's long-winding, umbilical passage. On the one hand, this is the balladic equivalent of the nightmare of a secular civilization deprived of the female impersonation of faith and become patently, pedantically idiotic; on the other, it is the poet saying, in effect, to himself, "here is the antidote to the ailment of poetry's past, i.e., me." The erasure of subjecthood, which is what "playing with the waterfall," at least on one level of extracurricular excursiveness, means, can be seen as the analogue of Wordsworth's effort to expunge the record of his commitments across the Channel—not least in terms of the avenging and truly awesome *numina* of the British state.

However, the text's vociferousness collides with the waterfall's numinous ponderousness, validating Juvenal's assertion in *Satire 3* (152f) that penury is made more onerous by the fact that it makes the poor *seem* ridiculous. "Foy" rhymes with "boy," which rhymes with—what else—but "joy." We would be Enlightenment *idiots savants* to look for gnomic truth out of school, where meaning is either playing hooky or nocturnally truant. Betty Foy looks for her "poor dear [and lost] boy," interrogating saints whose beneficence is problematic, at best, while numinous agency has been converted into an admixture of ridicule and sympathetic affect:

> She looks again—her arms are up—
> She screams—she cannot move for joy;
> She darts as with a torrent's force,
> She almost has o'erturned the horse,
> And fast she holds her idiot boy. (*LB*, 98, 382–386)

> 'The cocks did crow to-whoo, to-whoo,
> 'And the sun did shine so cold.'
> —Thus answered Johnny in his glory,
> And that was all his travel's story. (460–463)

"*Voiçi Johnny!*" and we are primed and programmed, two centuries later, at least from the 1960s to the 1990s, for laughter. *Tout*—or *presque*—is *permis*. But, in this case, we are in for a let down: *here* at last is Johnny, who was thought to be *there*. Johnny Foy's "*da*" or dada has no monologue and no glory, just as the sun has no warmth—at the beginning of the day that ends the story or *his* story, the dawn where en-light-enment meets the "*fort*" of darkness and superstition. The enchantment of medieval, womby dream-time, when the moon might have been warm even if hearts were icy with pre-Enlightenment dread of witches, goblins, and numinous spirits, at least for Johnny, is over. Comedy surrounds him, but he is not laughing, despite the fact that the ancient fears of the night have been banished in the pleonastic merriment of the moment. "She darts with a torrent's force." The last two words can be taken as a hendiadys and tautology only if the sense of force as a waterfall is "forced." In mangled form, the line could have read, "She darts as with a force's torrent," and the sense, at least for Lake District ears, would have been preserved. Saying the same thing twice is not a deixis, except of the narrative mentality required to bring synonomous or nearly synonomous words into stutter-like collusion in the first place. Yet the direness of the act of darting is undercut in the altogether slapstick collision of the next verse, the most hilarious evacuation or puncturing of the Romantic sublime in the text, where the "force" of Betty, the "good" witch, almost overturns the horse Johnny is riding upon—his or her night-mare—a comedic turn worthy of the circus of Philip Astley, the "Billy Buttons" of the late 18th century. The forceful glee of the maternal is thus harnessed to a physical action whose dynamism overturns or counterturns nocturnal hysteria, a psychologized or internalized *numen*. At the same time, it shows Betty's spectral or supernatural mightiness, a momentary power of action equivalent to witchcraft, but in an altogether different key and of a singular, dart-like velocity. The frantic action that might have suggested a witch's known power over animals and ended in tragedy, at least for the horse, turns out to be farcical because the waterfall, where Johnny was thought to have lingered, has its force reprojected as a pratfall; what in another context is an unchanging, static source of sublime wonder is refigured through the maternal vehicle as something kinetic and humorously finite, a somapoetic joke. The moon cannot appear, because it is now day, the day of the prodigal's return and of the end of romantic projection. As Hartman (*WP*, 298) indicates, the cold sunshine shows the "...economy and density of the repressed imagination." However, as Bewell suggests,

> The paradox that Johnny's body can feel and express painful coolness [by making a repeated 'burring' sound with his lips] while he remains unconscious of it... indicates that language, in its primal form, precedes consciousness. Belonging to the somatic rather than the intellectual sphere of life, the first language, even if Johnny and Betty are unaware of it, is one of the body, the 'burring of lips' in mute response to the cold. (*WPS*, 334)

But we need to be reminded, precisely at the point where language precedes consciousness, that the *Ur*-language also has a clearly somatic impact upon Susan Gale, precisely as a "cure for that which ails her," as an antidote, that her healing via the medicine of joy, preceded by the moment in which she takes to the woods out of sympathy, represents the antithesis of Harry Gill's chilled wasting-away, and that "the intellectual sphere of life" (aka medical science in its idiot-boy phase) could, as it were, care less about any of the uncanniness here depicted: either Johnny's homecoming or Susan's "miracle cure." The "somapoetic," the comedic aversion of tragedy on multiple levels and the keen diagnosing of ailment, is that which operates in a different theatre of faith. Susan Gale's "miracle cure" is another instance of the counter-case against clinical detachment, a means of showing how a sympathetic innervation or becoming sensitive to the plight of the other can achieve numinous or *numen*-like effects.

Another instance of a numinous disturbance or turbulence affecting the speaker's point of view, one that involves a force "like" that of waterfalls or cataracts and blindness, is found in an episode of *The Prelude* where "...power is purchased by terror, and terror assaults the possibility of perception or insight,"[20] the Blind Beggar episode in Book VII. Here, the effects of the numinous are sensed in the presence of a

> ...blind Beggar, who with upright face,
> Stood propp'd against a Wall, upon his Chest
> Wearing a written paper, to explain
> The story of Man and who he was.
> My mind did at this spectacle turn around
> As with the might of waters, and it seemed
> To me that in this Label was a type,
> Or emblem, of the utmost that we know,
> Both of ourselves and of the universe.... (*Prelude* 1805, VII, 612–620)

As Celeste Langan has shown (*RV*, 53–57) the beggar represents in emblematic terms, at least since Rousseau, a possible devolutionary omega for the bourgeois as type, whose phobic alpha is primitive man in the cave—the middle-class returned to that which it fears most: a state of natural deprivation, erasure, or homelessness, where one's address is "The Oak Tree" or "Somewhere" on Main Street. As Hartman suggests, the shocking thing about the blind beggar is that his appearance and the paper he wears are of one piece; there is no contrast between his physiognomy and the sign he wears (*WP*, 241); this "being of one piece" is not a Rohrschach of some psychological state which lends itself to deeper insight or scrutiny. The label and the face, taken together, amount to a blank—or a blankness equivalent to that of idiocy or the unknown doings of Johnny while he is away on his horse. They beggar our knowledge and intelligence. The fact that the beggar is blind provides deixis only of the weirdly woeful state of human ignorance; the blind man is not other than ourselves at the crossroads, confronted by an inscrutable universe and destiny. As Wordsworth feels his mind swung round by the spectacle, he is caught up in the overpowering force of something beyond his control and power of vision, something akin to the confusion set loose by Canidia's imprecation or Goody Blake's curse, except that the turbulence in this case brings around a kind of Socratic insight—"to know that we do not know is to know oneself and the other"—rather than lethal somatic effect. His turning around is meant also to have a deictic effect upon the reader, different from school-knowledge—in effect, engaging the reader's mind in the motive or motivation of a sympathetic turbulence. Far from being an invitation to solipsism, as Hartman opines, Wordsworth's counterturning of *numen* allows a tragic insight into the human condition—whether as beggar (in a state of savageness suggested by the teachings of Rousseau) or philosophical blind-man far removed from the optimistic aura surrounding the Enlightenment's privileged clinical specimen, William Saunderson[21]— to move from an epistemological horizon to the cavernous space of an insight into the ignorance or forgetfulness of being. Like the counter-case Johnny Foy, *this* blind man on *this* street delivers a different and equally exigent, extracurricular truth concerning existence, a lesson in unschooled reading and innervation. In a non-literal form, without the emblematic subtext and the written paper, such an enlistment of sympathy would be called mesmerism—all show and no deixis. At the same time, however, the blind beggar episode is one which, unlike the comedic peculiarities of the vaudevillian Foy family, cannot be displayed in a theatre or arcade of Bartholomew Fair where raillery and "good fun" are the order of the day. It is a monitory type which cannot be erased or laughed off the stage.

Stonehenge and the Voice of History

In the period of literary history before *The Lyrical Ballads*, a time we might well designate "B. W. E." or "Before the Wordsworth Era," it might still be possible to write a sonnet on Stonehenge, as Thomas Warton does below, which omits the subjective point of view, instead ticking off a sequence of conventional references, turning the first-hand experience of prehistory into a subject for polite tea-time musing. The literature of knowledge knows everything and hence is power-less, most of all in the way it can address a sublime object quite familiarly, across the table of Salisbury Plain and holding the bone-china of history between thumb and forefinger:

Sonnet. Written at Stonehenge.

'Thou noblest monument of Albion's isle,
Whether, by Merlin's aid, from Scythia's shore
To Amber's fatal plain Pendragon bore,
Huge frame of giant hands, the mighty pile,
T'entomb his Britons slain by Hengist's guile;
Or Druid priests, sprinkled with human gore,
Taught mid thy massy maze their mystic lore:
Or Danish chiefs, enrich'd with savage spoil,
To victory's idol vast, an unhewn shrine,
Rear'd the rude heap, or in they hallow'd ground

> Repose the kings of Brutus' genuine line;
> Or here those kings in solemn state were crown'd;
> Studious to trace thy wondrous origin,
> We muse on many an ancient tale renown'd.' (quoted in *LEP*, 121)

But, as Diderot remarks, ruins refer not so much to the past as to us. What Wordsworth would not essay is anything in the Warton "vein"—instead saving the subject matter and jettisoning the style. Wordsworth is not interested in "musing" on anything. For him, poetry has an entirely different ground, an utterly primal or primitive reason for being, one allied to self-scrutiny and to Lawrentian themes, such as sex, birth, and death. Thus the prehistoric tombs and landmarks situated around England signify, among other things, possible constructions of the originary *"femme fatale,"* the sacred mother; they are *omphaloi* or navels of the earth, something numinous, attractive and terrifying at once—to be alternately fascinated and repulsed by, to be traveled to and gotten away from almost as quickly.

As for the monolithic circle of Stonehenge, it is "modern" in a monstrous way that both Wordsworth and Poe can identify with in terms of a well-illustrated, ponderous undecidability or tediousness. The literature of power may know something, but it also registers a certain futility by breaking the vessels of previous research, revealing that it does not know through an art of studious negation: a frustration with the kind of traditional scholarship that would be mocked more savagely by Poe in any number of fictional contexts:

> In regard to the history of these extraordinary monuments, there is little of any definite nature. The earliest account of them occurs in Nennius, who lived in the eighth century. He says there were erected by the Britons to commemorate a massacre which took place at the spot. The Historicial Triads of the Welch refer their origin to the same cause. Camden calls the structure *insana*, but says nothing about it entitled to notice. Modern authors have been profuse in speculation, but no more. The general opinion seems to be in favor of a Druidical Temple. The Rev. James Ingram supposes it to have been 'a heathen burial-place.' Borlase remarks that 'the work of Stonehenge must have been that of a great and powerful nation, not of a limited community of priests; the grandeur of the design, the distance of the materials, the tediousness with which all such massive works are necessarily attended, all show that such designs were the fruits of peace and religion.' Bryant, whose authority we regard as superior to any, discredits the Druidical theory altogether.[22]

That is to say, because Stonehenge, like the barrow, is of uncertain origin and function, it "lends" itself to a hermeneutics of the self or to a deixis that can write whatever it wishes to at the site or in the siting of its enigmatic reality. The prehistoric invites not only touristic excursions, but also an excursiveness on the part of the writer, be he Poe or Wordsworth. Ancient monoliths sticking up out of the earth, often arranged in circles, like those in Somerset or the Lake District, Saxon forts, and the like are thus open to excursive projection or reconstruction furthered by the fact that commentaries, as is in Poe's text, are often accompanied by illustrations. When the figure of Stonehenge is coupled with a descriptive or poetic text, the possibility of an even more problematic intertext arises, one that both looks askance at history and makes it more vivid than it actually is by virtue of an excursivity, through a process of hearing something *prepositioned* with respect to recorded facts—the elaboration of which both confronts eternal issues of life and death and steers to one side of it, a picto-graphic text of the self posed at the threshold or on the border of prehistoric monuments and thus, at all times, in varying lights and shades, edging in on autobiographical representation. Stonehenge, in the uncanny perception of the author of *The Prelude*, is more than a piece of Druidic furniture; it conjures up the primal source or scene of religion, something which, in its liminal terror is like a gigantic mouth. Into it proceed the sacrificial victims, emitting groans that are heard in the qualifying "how deep" and in the marvelous verb "thrills," which penetrates the landscape far and wide. Nor is the experience distant; the spectacle involves and is *for* us, the living, who feed what Robert Frost describes as the waterfall or cataract of death, and are directed to listen to the pervasive voice of prehistory:

> It is the sacrificial Altar, fed
> With living men, how deep the groans, the voice
> Of those in the gigantic wicker thrills
> Throughout the region far and near; pervades
> The monumental hillocks; and the pomp
> Is for both worlds, the living and the dead.   (*Prelude* 1805, 227, 331–
> 336)

The prepositioned parade is also counterturned against the subject. Frost's words cannot help but suggest also that unfortunate character who dwells, paradigmatically, in these two worlds, the "devoted" Margaret of *The Ruined Cottage* and *The Excursion*. Her sacrifice, to male domination and marriage, seems an echo-like answer to the immolation performed in at Stonehenge and in the wicker-men of Celtic fame. At the same time, it reprojects inhuman horror and despair into vignettes of a uniquely maternal power of care, half Christian and half-pagan (in her function as spirit or sprite of the well ministering to the thirsty need of wayfarers):

> ...virtue thus
> Sets forth and magnifies herself; thus feeds
> A calm, a beautiful, and silent fire....

Silencing Apocalypse

In the two texts from the *Lyrical Ballads* discussed above, the contrast between dark and light, sympathy and antipathy, could not be clearer. In a sense, such a physical and moral contrast is the same as the difference between the dark letter or character and the light or white page: it is *typo*graphic. "Making light" of nocturnal terror concerning the other as a marginal or supernatural type (gypsies, witches, goblins et al.) is involved in the comedic pratfall with which "The Idiot Boy" ends. Glee serves as an antidote to psychic ills and the privations inflicted upon the underprivileged. In the Gondo Gorge sequence, however, what begins as a dialogue with nature and certainty concerning types of eternity and apocalyptic characters ends, if not in monological uncertainty, at least in discomfort as to the timing and strategy of vision. In the Blind Beggar episode, the contrasts become blurred yet again, as Hartman suggests, and we, turned as by a cataract or turbine, are forced to read differently or "quasi-apocalyptically" (*WP*, 242)—on a less perspicuous page or on one that is "all one thing," where face and sign constitute an undifferentiated, monitory whole. Finally, in *The Recluse*, what was once the *numen* of Diana, the goddess of tri-vial crossroads and the moon, is filtered through an interposed matrix or lattice-work of language which seems to translate it from the realm of unmediated, numinous *effect* into the key of a grammatical restlessness or discontent. These varying apertures through which the numinous alternately conceals and reveals itself suggest not only the epistemological terrain of Plato's allegory of the cave, where the noumenal, a realm of eternal forms, will be portrayed, but also the cavernous and cliff-like spaces, the charm and counter-charm, of pastoral.

In the version of the cave found in the *Republic* (515a, 2–3), there are shadows of men, who carry artifacts resembling real objects, moving across the walls behind the prisoners. Some of the shadows are speaking and some are silent. But there is no guarantee that any of the objects is truly what it seems to be or that the speeches refer to real existences. Some of the shadows claim to be able to interpret the oracular noises made by the objects (515b10). But one hermeneutic speech has no greater claim to validity than any another. They may be linking an unreal object or person, such as a god, with a real predicate, such as angry or beautiful, and thus be lying. As Seth Benardete suggests, while none of the shadows can be philosophically vindicated, Socrates does not dismiss the analytical tool of language or the relevance of the predicates used in the speeches. It is not a matter of denying linguistic access to the truth (*aletheia*), as the pre-Socratics do in their claim to immediate knowledge, but rather of employing language dialectically, through a process of *muthologein*, argumentative speeches, in order to arrive at the certainty that we can only know that we do not know. This is what is described as Socrates' "second sailing," alluded to not only in *The Republic*, but also in *Phaedo* at 99d, when he has, so he says, given up his noetic quest for "realities" of true being:

> The second sailing of Socrates starts precisely from the arbitrariness of speeches in the cave, and the realization that it is possible to examine the predicates without the subjects. The predicates are forms of the good, and the good is not hypothetical. The pre-Socratic philosopher, however, rushes past the speeches of the city and claims to know directly the true originals from which the artifacts have been copied. He believes it is easy to discriminate between Zeus and man, for man is not himself a question. The pre-Socratic is like Oedipus: he knows that the solution to the riddle is man but not that the solution is enigmatic. Both the pre-Socratic philosopher and the Socratic philosopher begin in the same way. There is no disagreement between them about the need to distinguish between nature and convention and that this involves a general denial of any reality to the highest beings of the city. To make a cut between these subjects and their predicates is common to both the pre-Socratic and Socratic philosopher, but the former dismisses the predicates as so much babble—their inappropriateness to their subjects is self-evident.[23]
> ... the ascent from the cave must begin with the attempt to recover the beings that are in truth before the descent can become possible. The turnaround to face the cave must follow the turnaround away from the cave. This double turn Socrates calls on occasion *muthologein* or the speaking of myth (*Republic* 376d9; *Phaedo* 61e2). It is his name for the unavoidable impurity of dialectic (*Theaetetus* 196d7–197a4).
>
> (*SSS*, 175)

Is the numinous what Wordsworth salvages from the phenomenal world, even as he acknowledges the precariousness of his own vision? The deixis Wordsworth is attempting in *The Prelude* and other texts prior to *The Excursion* seems Socratic only in the doubt or skepticism it would sow concerning the justification of existence (existents), including the prevalent social order and its claim to represent a state of ultimate good. "The good is not hypothetical." It is the stuff of dreams, of hope, however anxious, and of faith. *Numen*, as seen in the Goody Blake ballad, overturns the status quo and is thus in league with a reenergized ethical sensorium, with revolutionary art and thinking. In "The Idiot Boy" the rationalistic premises of the 18th century are turned on their clinical ear; Wordsworth receives a premium of primal pleasure from the inversion or excursion into humor, and the priority of language, as Bewell suggests, surfaces in the ability of Johnny to say how he is cold (by burring), even before he knows what cold is. The answers supplied in *The Excursion* attempt to supplement revolutionary hope with another kind of coldness, derived from the cold fire of the moon and the unconsumed vegetative deixis confronting Moses. This has as its effect the projection of virtuous power, the foundation of a

Kantian law for or unto the self.

We may say, with a certain reluctance due to the baldness of formulation, that *numen* (from the Latin *nuo/nuere*, to nod) is a nodding-yes to which Wordsworth more often than not, in effect, says no. It is this antithetical movement which suggests a counterturn that is as forceful as that which Heidegger terms *das Gegenwendige* (that which turns against us or toward us, in order to remind us of being, the uncanny in art).[24] Thus the numinous yes, via a deictic counterturn, is pressed into the service of a negativity or of something resembling, in aesthetic terms, the negative sublime, enabling the mind to think through its own transcendence of guilt and facticity. The numinous thus serves the noumenal or provides a deictic phenomenology of "true being," of the noumenal, in terms of a mediated auguration (taking of auspices) from or recommencement of nature, inspired by the privileging of the unspoiled natural subject in Rousseau and a resensing or reaccentuation of the *vestrum* in Aeneas' address to Ascanius: *vestrum hoc augurium.* Nature thus finds itself turned mediately, by means of an extremely "liberal" view of poetic arbitrariness, including puns and a matrix of prepositional phrases, in the direction of Wordsworth's speakers or protagonists, just as his deixis is inflected toward the reader.

> Like power abides
> In man's celestial spirit; virtue thus
> Sets forth and magnifies herself; thus feeds
> A calm, a beautiful, and silent fire....

Such a strategy of counterturning (approximating *das Gegenwendige* of art), in divergence from *numen* considered purely as sorcery, as in Horace, and toward the reader ("für uns"), so as to "gift" the other with consciousness of a reflexive power, is followed, though on different religious and dramatic terms, later on in the century by Walt Whitman, among others.

Duncan Wu suggests that there is a "numinous silence" in Wordsworth's Cambridge Sonnets, (*NM*, 357) one that fits the mythic paradigm of Orpheus as well as the scenario of Horace's Epode 17, where Canidia invokes a power whose effect or rule operates noiselessly, one that will ultimately be turned against her; in Hades, to be sure, a queen rules for half the year whose name, Persephone, implies the destruction of sound, the annihilation of the cataract's roar. Indeed, to read the numinous and noumenal against the backdrop or undercurrent of one or more primal scenes is to be reminded of a flight from sound, from the *Pochen* or *Ticken* that threatens the neurotic patient, because—in the darkened, Hades-like psychic landscape—these might have alerted the parents to the presence of the child. But the child is father to the man. The babble or incoherence of shadowy speakers in Plato's cave, their *muthologein*, may or may not be akin to the kind of stuttering with which we are acquainted at the level of ballad-making and/or critical inquiry.[25] We do know that it is the propensity of waterfalls and idiots to say the same thing over and over again. In "The Idiot Boy" healing is taken as a matter of "pure" surprise, a victory of the psychic counter-case or excursive spell over dogma, which ceaselessly reiterates its rationalizings, *and* skepticism. This is accompanied by a gleeful release of affect, one which spills or pours over into comedy and exorcizes somapoetic demons. Language, even out of the mouths of babes, precedes consciousness. It is a sound out of nature in Gondo Gorge that keeps Wordsworth awake at night—"...deafened and stunned/ By noise of waters, making innocent Sleep/ Lie melancholy among weary bones" (*Prelude* 1805, VI, 578–580)—projecting a trance-like state by the figure of a premature death or graveyard of the mind. *Numen*, on the other hand, requires silence and a colder, lunar fire for its elaboration. When dawn comes there is an end to nightmares and an awakening to the larger, more vividly expansive dream of day. A different or deferred deixis lies beyond the grave-like confinement of the chasm, on the open road, turned toward "broad high-way appearances" only so as to be counterturned away from them, in encounters with un-Socratic, but nonetheless uncannily sophisticated outsiders. Undoing and isolation are here allied against eidetic "ultimate knowledge"; the poetic anatomist of the present, obedient to the pastoral imperative of movement and skeptical about Midas-like acquisitiveness, refuses to be possessed by numinous spells or mesmerized by excessive reverence for maternal objects. Thus the genial, stronger song.

"In lack of worthier explanation": Vegetative Deixis, Caverns, Cave-Dwellers

We will take it as our second thesis that *numen*, as discovered in nature, will be a subset of the noumenal, i.e., a sign of subjective powers, except in *The Lyrical Ballads*, where it is closely linked to case histories and counter-cases, i.e., the example-like, yet extracurricular "records" of marginal individuals who would normally fall beyond the scope of moral sympathy—thus supplying for Wordsworth, a measure of indirect therapeutic alleviation (*lesmosuné*) from personal guilt and trauma associated with one or more primal scenes. The glee occasioned by "The Idiot Boy" can be taken as an indication of this personal or "personalist" strain. The primal scene, we might say, since it cannot "present" itself but is nonetheless felt unconsciously as turbulence or as a repressed force, finds itself translated and/or hydraulically transferred in the morbidly animated, entrancing, and, at times, merry scenery of idiots, old women, and beggars. Figures and tropes from "Goody Blake" and "The Idiot Boy" reappear in later texts, but with more solemn, mantic, or gnomic intonation, through deictic inscription, which means a shift in point of view from the classical model of *numen*, as an effective presence, to a totalizing, encyclopedic code, in which the elements of an aesthetic psychology based on Rousseau and Kant, are (pre)positioned across or obliquely with respect to the text, even when it alludes to the Bible. Similarly, in the first verses of *The Excursion*, based on *An Evening Walk* (1793) and *The Ruined Cottage* (1798), the pleasure of one who reposes in a swaddling softness is delayed or put off altogether:

> 'Twas summer, and the sun had mounted high:
> Southward the landscape indistinctly glared
> Through a pale stream; but all the northern downs,
> In clearest air ascending, showed far off
> A surface dappled o'er with shadows flung
> From brooding clouds; shadows that lay in spots
> Determined and unmoved, with steady beams
> Of bright and pleasant sunshine interposed;
> To him most pleasant who on soft cool moss
> Extends his careless limbs along the front
> Of some huge cave, whose rocky ceiling casts
> A twilight of its own, an ample shade,
> Where the wren warbles, while the dreaming man,
> Half-conscious of the soothing melody,
> With side-long eye looks out upon the scene,
> By power of that impending covert, thrown
> To finer distance. Mine was at that hour
> Far other lot, yet with good hope that soon
> Under a shade as grateful I should find
> Rest, and be welcomed there to livelier joy....'[26]

The interposing of sunlit areas of vision with shadier spots to the north is mediated by an interstitial barrage of remarkably articulated pre-positional phrases. This tortuously modified, winding rhetorical apparatus is a poetic device for the delivery of thought, a model instance of deixis by prepositioning.[27] The phrases themselves seem to be the only shadow-play or "show" referred to, reflecting an excessive intricacy of mediatory calculation on the part of one whose vision is "thrown," by power of the socket-like recess of the cave. This strategy, where the poet plays both infant and obstetrician, can be rather grotesquely overemphasized by running the phrases together into a single, stream-like current beginning with the remarkable verb "glared," which is something people and not landscapes are supposed to do—at the sight of anyone who is strange, guilty-looking, or embarrassingly out of place, like a child or a highwayman—and the adverbial modifier "indistinctly" showing the inadequacy of a vision confronted by too much light: *through* a pale stream...*with* shadows flung/ *From* brooding clouds... shadows that lay *in* spots...*with* steady beams of bright and pleasant sunshine interposed;/ *To* him most pleasant... *on* soft cool moss....along the front *of* some huge cave...*of* the soothing melody...*with* side-long eye looks out...*upon* the scene by power *of* that impending covert...thrown *to* finer distance...*at* that hour with good hope...*under* a shade *to* livelier joy..... The eidetic, *what* is seen, is made to derive from the logical or the grammatical, the language that is all about obliqueness of vision and a psychologically comforting *lesmosuné*[28] experienced at the mouth or entrance of the womb-like cave or *on its verge*. This is not so much a translation of mythic paradigms or cave imagery from a philosophical umbilicus as an entranced looking to the side or from side to side for (dis)embodiments of antecedent texts—something like a totalizing, yet displacing synthesis of Plato, Spenser, Kant, and Rousseau—with a coda seeming to distance the "my" from the "one" who was resting at the lip of the cave, both reverting to and turning its back on personal guilt or "encumbrance": "Mine was at that hour/ Far other lot, yet with good hope that soon/...I should find.../ Rest, and... livelier joy." The counterturn away from tuneful allusiveness (inherited notions of *numen*) toward the deixis of thought runs the gamut of prepositional unease and insufficient, deadening stasis—the only Now the text at present knows—exiting in an invitation to movement, the only form of knowledge that the Literature of Power understands. To move beyond is to find "livelier joy"—as if displacing present entrancement and moving away from the umbilical source—a maieutic as well as a hermeneutic process—were the means to such an end. The articulated phrases demonstrate, if they can be said to point out anything at all, the *deixis of an excess* or exigency, the capacity of language to offer a covert or shade with which to deal with the eidetic "too much" that is "out there," an intrusive though indistinct glare, serving as an encouragement to mediate or mediated vision, the necessity to filter visual "types" and "characters" of eternity and/or apocalypse through a dense and obstacle-like hedgework of prepositional phrasing—though not for pedagogical purpose, as in the Socratic path to philosophical knowledge (or doubt) through the analysis of predicates, but for the purpose of achieving a "finer distance," a throwing-off or to the side of vision as deliberate and strategic as Heideggerian distancing and de-distancing. At the same time, we remember that the speaker is in an Ulro- or fairy-tale-like state and only "half-conscious." An homunculus-like embryo-self, he is about to be born or reborn, from joylessness to "livelier joy." Later on, it will be by the light of the moon or Artemis, whose arrows, once loosened, "once upon a time," might bring either pain or release from the pain of childbirth. Now, it is the soothing effect of the birthing melody which must be abandoned for a different or "far other" lot. In the emphasis upon a birthing at the lip of the cave, Wordsworth's text takes up the fate of translation adumbrated in Goethe's "Der Wandrer," the mesocosmic topography of antecedent texts, inscriptions, epigraphs, et al. in their effacement, coupled with the necessity of thought, in modernity, to move elsewhere, to submit to displacement.

The ultimate effect of the prepositional hedgework is that of thrusting recrimination off to one side or of making a shadow-play out of guilty affect through obliqueness of vision, the "sidelong eye"—which one might interpret as an Augustinean variation on a Neoplatonic trope or even more as a take on the visual rhetoric of the *Phaedo*, where a direct glimpsing of the eternal, changeless forms of being is said to be as dangerous to the sight as staring at the sun after an eclipse. The reason for the eye's turning to the side or "tailing" need not be sought, however, above; it seems a direct response to the glare of the landscape and to a light which is not so much filtered through the pale or white stream as focused and made more intense by it. The speaker needs shade or the beneficent and colder fire of the moon, but can gain representational access to the experience of it only through the entranced byplay of prepositional phrases. In Wordsworth's text we have nothing but dampening obstacles or interpolations, where contrasts work upon poetic imagination to achieve a *countervisual* effect: that of a turning of the vision inward, to the cave of the soul, a mirror of the womb itself. The headlong, abyssally endangered Gondo Gorge episode, which looks outward but also down and up to scan the unfathered vapor of poetic imagination, has been chastened by the prepositioning of shade or shades.

We turn now to lines from Book IV of *The Excursion* which, by extracurricular demonstration, answer a favorite 18th-century academic question concerning the site and functioning of a metaphysical *Seelenorgan*:

> Within the soul a faculty abides,
> That with interpositions, which would hide
> And darken, so can deal that they become
> Contingencies of pomp: and serve to exalt
> Her native brightness. As the ample moon,
> In the deep stillness of a summer even
> Rising behind a thick and lofty grove,
> Burns, like an unconsuming fire of light,
> In the green trees; and, kindling on all sides
> Their leafy umbrage, turns the dusky veil
> Into a substance glorious as her own,
> Yea, with her own incorporated, by power

> Capacious and serene. Like power abides
> In man's celestial spirit; virtue thus
> Sets forth and magnifies herself; thus feeds
> A calm, a beautiful, and silent fire,
> From the encumbrances of mortal life,
> From error, disappointment—nay, from guilt;
> And sometimes, so relenting justice wills,
> From palpable oppressions of despair. (*Excursion*, IV, 1058–77)

The first interposition is that of the thick and lofty grove placed in front of the moon, and thus between the observer and the infinite cosmos—where the symbol of Diana's numinous power provides the deixis of higher illumination. In this situation a vivid contrast (as opposed to the blank uniformity of the blind beggar and his sign) is registered when the speaker gazes upward toward the sky—the chiaroscuro effect aids or assists deictic purpose. We have to do also with cold fire—this time occasioned not by supernatural agency, unleashed by the imprecation of of Goody Blake, not consuming a Harry Gill, but nonetheless burning in the green trees without consuming them. Hence we have Johnston's suggestion that the Mosaic figure is here controlling, one that I read, however, as the effacing of reference in favor of representation, a scene of natural pomp in which the veil of appearance is transformed into substance *for the subjective beholder* through vegetative deixis. But the natural pomp is also denatured in the sense that it dwells in the interiorized, privative construction of reality, not in goblins, fairies, or ghosts of the past, not in the garish vermilions and scarlets of autumn, which in other contexts remind him of street-walkers or redcoats, and certainly not in the regal pomp of prelates and dignitaries of state. The substance of numinous appearance is not a ground or *Grund* but the appearance itself in its colder shining, sheen or *Schein*.[29] These might or might not suggest shadows lit up by fires in a Platonic cave, but we must direct our attention to what the words say. We, on the way to our "birth to freedom," which is always elsewhere, away from the umbilical site, in excursion from it, must "deal" with interpositions which would, conditionally, obscure the soul, if they could. Our "dealing" faculty, our ability to make a deal or a great deal of the cold fire and "dusky veil," transforms the obstacle into something bright or transparent—a strategy or habit of mind certainly found in Rousseau.[30] Thus the perception of cold fire is a product of the power of reason enunciated in the Kantian sublime; we find our mental faculties overwhelmed but also exercised in the act of thinking of the scene as sublime. The agency of the numinous, something "out there," is counterturned yet again, back upon the perplexed or slowed subject as a naive charm or inborn brightness. Thus far, at least, there is no suggestion of a language that is other than visual: a contrastive play of embarrassing obstacle and insightful transparency. The appearance is all, and the character, as type or Type, is absent, as we move toward something "calm, beautiful, and silent," which is located not outside, on a board or face, but within—something that is no longer an image. There is no longer a looking beyond the self for types and characters, since these are indwelling, not as objective "forms" to be recognized again through anamnesis, but as intimations arrived at the end of time, the interposition of shading language, a turning from "broad highway appearances" to maieutic silence.

In the extended moon metaphor Rousseau and Kant (or, as Johnston reads, Platonic Ideas and the Burning Bush of the Old Testament,[31]) are silently prepositioned *scenographically* in a topocosm reminiscent of the Bible, of Vergilian pastoral, and of Spenserian romance, but in no way referring to them. The unconsuming fire, evidence of *something* supernatural, neither Christian nor pagan, receives its blessing in the name not of theology, but of a power and virtue first indicted, deictically, in the unconsuming fire, and then located in the spirit. The colder fire is a figure or trope of the interruptive, interpolative function of language, inducing consciousness on the part of the speaker of that which is "out of the glare," of the other or of daylight, preceding the bucolic awareness that he must move elsewhere to find joy. Wordsworth may, as Johnston suggests, perceive the "visible fabric of the world" as a "veil enabling the imagination to transfigure the accidents of mortal life to moral good" (*J*, 273), noting also the variant "embodied" for "incorporated" in line 1069: "Virtue in this sense denotes both strength and goodness, and carries its own validating power: by transforming 'the encumbrances of mortal life' into 'contingencies of pomp,' it operates imaginatively, supplying and receiving value simultaneously" (*J*, 274). His reading, however, elides the evident, if understated, connection between the prepositional thrusting-aside expressed by the line "From error, disappointment—nay from guilt" and the absolutely essential "accidents" of autobiography, a personal history of thought's birthing delivered by way of those same "broad highway appearances," in a tumultuous series of excursive episodes—readings of experience from Rousseau to the French Revolution and back again, via *The Prelude*, to earlier, brighter days of childhood. Pomp is more difficult to read, because it finds itself rejected on so many other occasions in Wordsworth, especially when seen as an attribute of temporal power or moral corruption. Etymologically, "pomp" derives from the Latin word, *pompa*, a parade; in *The Prelude*, evoking the human sacrifices of the prehistoric Celts, Wordsworth speaks of "pomp enough for both worlds," a spectacle "fit" for the living and the dead. We read it as a metaphor for the pageant of life, seen here in the cooler perspective of recollection, as in a silent movie, a series of "to" and "fro-ings," of light and dark interpositionings. The passage performs a transformative gesture, terrific in the silent displacements of its grammar; *numen*, Diana, and fire become accouterments of colder thought, a "like faculty" of spirit internalizing the parade, the "whole play" or excessively entrancing by-play by which we arrive at thought "in the first place," while still on the broad highway of appearances or lodged at the mouth of the cave, listening to the sweeter music of daytime, seeing filtered light, filtering Plato through pastoral.

The original choice of "embodied" makes the case for a reading of the text as an allegory of thinking's birth and/or rebirth in much the same way that Aeneas means it when he says that the wandered *numen* of Troy now belongs to Ascanius—not of anything numinous or noumenal dwelling outside our own perception of what is "ours." The encumbrance of mortal life is the weight of experience, from which mortals will be freed only by reflection upon their own faculty of representation or at death. Pomp and its contingencies are measured on a scale which is not physical but metaphysical, in terms of an unearthly, silent power wedded to the Kantian sublime. Negation of the physical serves as the affirmation of a silent deixis which, however, can only consist "in the writing" of prepositional phrases, their obstetric and taciturn by-play of entrancement, which brings thought to itself by means of a "sigetics": "The utterance of thought is a telling silence."[32] The Heideggerian *Erschweigen* of thought counterturns *numen* against itself; it is the *Gegenwendige* of an uncanny which knows only the obstetric art of producing doubt as to noumenal being, but certainty as to the faculty in us for perceiving what we take to be the noumenal. We could not dispense with the unconsuming *Schein*, however, even if we wanted to, since it points us elsewhere, either to other excursions, umbilical or sacrificial scenes, ot back inside our cavernous selves. What we are "presented with" is no longer the silence of *numen* in which we wait for something to happen, to "affect" either us or our intended victim, but a deictic thinking through nature, a thinking of the place of the "I" in nature, in its reflective counterturn to antiquity and history. What began as liquid light in the literature of power is thus transformed into the drier light of a reflection whose virtuous delineation, having transcended affect, is able to become both silently sublime and surprisingly unapocalyptic:

> ...virtue thus
> Sets forth and magnifies herself; thus feeds
> A calm, a beautiful, and silent fire....

—a revelation whose *Schein* can be made deictically "plain" only through the cooler, entrancing prepositionings of language.

3. "Radiant Monsters": The Full Fan-Experience from Cowley to Barney

The fashionable style remained chiefly with Cowley...
    Samuel Johnson

And travellers, now, within that valley,
    Through the encrimsoned windows see
Vast forms that move fantastically
    To a discordant melody,
While, like a ghastly rapid river,
    Through the pale door
A hideous throng rush out forever
And laugh—but smile no more.
        Poe, "The Haunted Palace"

Hugh Kenner's "historical comedy" *The Counterfeiters* (published in the early 1970s[1]) offers a number of thought-provoking perspectives on modernism, observing in its labyrinthine meditation the comings and goings of remarkable persons and things—from Buster Keaton to Vaucanson's Duck, from Cicero's use of the word *humanitas* to Andy Warhol's soup cans. The underlying assumption is that the rise of modernism entails a burgeoning uncertainty as to what determines authenticity, in a human being, say, as opposed to a robotic android, what defines a work of art as "art," and what makes "this" verse superior or inferior to "that." One of the more interesting of the aesthetic objects scrutinized is a small sample of the poetic output of Abraham Cowley, anthologized in the satirical collection compiled by Wyndham Lewis and Charles Lee in 1930, *The Stuffed Owl*. The 20th century, in general, was unkind to Cowley, especially his "translations" from the Greek. In her Penguin anthology of metaphysical verse, Dame Helen Gardner, for example, assesses the poet's versions of Pindar through a prism of literary-critical pique: "...a further misconception of the nature of his talents is seen in the so-called Pindaric Odes, the ungainly parents of much of the worst verse of the subsequent hundred years."[2] Kenner, succinctly judgmental, as usual, renders a similarly dismissive verdict as well on Cowley's bathos; it is "exquisitely ridiculous" (*TC*, 38) Cowley, he continues, is not so much the "last of the Metaphysicals" as the first of the Augustans—an "unread joke" after the time of Samuel Johnson, who sets a kind of precedent for negative judgment.[3] Kenner diagnoses the problem in Cowley's penchant for a clarity so clear that it ceases to be poetic: his conceits

...are not even conceits in Donne's sense at all. They are frantically logical developments of ideas a prose exposition could make perfectly acceptable...That is what comes of the Restoration emphasis on clarity; it leaves nothing whatever for the poet to do but strike a bardic posture and elevate his language. Language has only one function, to communicate information, and only one indispensable virtue, to be clear. Cowley is on all occasions a poet of absolute clarity.   (*TC*, 38)

One begins to perceive—almost against the will of the critic writing the words—that there may be a *kind* of virtue (allied with or related to clarity, in the sense of the Latin word *clarus*, meaning both clear *and* famous) which cannot be gainsaid, a *cogitandum* making Cowley worthy of his eventual memorialization in Poet's Corner and the effort of reevaluation being attempted in this essay. This virtue, I suggest, is that of a sometimes incandescent, often scintillating, surprise.[4] What makes this surprise—or ungainliness, as Dame Helen says—worth considering is its very prosaic gracelessness, its quality of being un-, or even dis-graced—one which therefore appeals to us in an age in which the arts are "no longer beautiful."

It is strange, just the same, that neither commentator pays attention to the critical tradition supporting Cowley's claim to spotty fame: the *somewhat* glowing words of Dryden, the judgment by Addison that his lyrics are works "of genius," the flattering imitations by a thirteen-year-old Alexander Pope. Cowley, as Gardner admits only sneeringly, was the chief instigator and one of many contributors to an entire "Pindar industry" or craze which lasts from the Restoration to the late Augustan age, reaching its zenith in Dryden's "Ode for St. Cecilia's Day" and culminating in Thomas Gray's "The Bard":

The *Pindarique Odes,* prefaced by paraphrases of Pindar's second Olympian and first Nemean odes, were introduced by Cowley with a little diffidence. He is afraid that even experienced readers will not understand them. Their voluble licence of metre may give the mistaken impression that they are easy to compose. The 'sweetness and numerosity' of the irregular lines may be overlooked by a disregard of the necessary cadences in pronunciation. He had little or no insight into Pindar's metrical schemes: his imitations of the "stile and manner" of his author follow no fixed system of prosody. The quality which he sought to reproduce was the "Enthusiastical manner" of Pindar, with its digressions and bold figures....[5]

It is curious that Kenner's otherwise perspicacious survey of humanoids and other fabulous fakes omits mention of Cowley's enthused Pindar imitations and the "stile and manner," bad or good, thus set loose upon the world of letters, a phenomenon said by Johnson to be akin to universal infection, i.e., the plague. The fashionable, "everyone is doing it now" aspect of Pindarism offers a paradigm for the discussion of latter-day specialists in robotics, pasticheurs, mannerists, parasites of enthusiasm, and the like—those who style themselves poets, photographers, performance artists, minimalists, and film-makers in the era of postmodernism. The question thus presents itself: is Cowley the first *littérateur* to make the medium (translation or what Johnson more modestly terms "paraphrasis") the message, and thus the first pop artist? What standards, if any, should be applied to the art of modifying mimicry and simulation of another, much more famous poet's style, through what others and I call "metapoesis"?[6]

Earlier in the century (ca. 1630) Ben Jonson, sympathetic to the royalist cause, writes an ode in rhyming couplets to Sir Lucius Cary and Sir Henry Morison, going so far as to label strophe as "Turn," antistrophe as "Counterturn," and epistrophe as "Stand." But Jonson at no time indicates that this is anything other than his own vehicle from the ground up, even if it is transparently mounted on the formal chassis of Pindar and Aeschylus. Pindarism, requiring a high level of education, can be said to begin its career as a poetic medium designed to communicate with the aristocratic cause or as the hobby-horse of one or more aristocratically minded, enthused *caballeros*. More problematic imitation[7] of the Pindaric style becomes "à la mode," however, at a time when debates are raging between "ancients" and "moderns," in the so-called Battle of the Books, concerning the status of literature in the vernacular languages, as opposed to the authority of Greek and Latin, and the role played by "free-wheeling" genius and fancy (or "Phansie," as Cowley spells it) on the open road of poetic inspiration, as opposed to slavish imitation, is being advocated. "Enthused" Pindar is thus coeval with the birth of modern literary criticism, and the underlying issues of license and restraint, of excess and its disciplining, are never far from either pursuit, either then or now. What the larger debate is really about is an assertion of the right of modern literature, a kind of 17th-century performance art, to be considered on its own strengths, to be fashionable, autonomous and, from one enthusiastic performance to another, ungainly and/or bad. For Cowley, a royalist, the prerogatives of the "Muse's Hannibal," i.e., himself, can be asserted boldly in the company of a select and aristocratic few who will be able to follow him across the rugged Alps of "strong"[8] diction and rhetoric. But translation and the aesthetic theories behind it have strange and sometimes ironic fortunes. It is known, if not well known, that enthusiasm is later given judicious treatment in the truly innovative, "pre-Romantic" aesthetics of Shaftesbury, a theorist of genius and famous Whig, from which stems the modern Labor Party of England.[9] It is thus that the art of rendering Pindar enthusiastically *seems* to track entrances and exits on the political scene of England, beginning in the rusticated milieu of exiled courtiers and Restoration intrigue (Cowley was employed as a counterrevolutionary spy when he was not living in Paris) and ending up coopted by a "liberal" or middle-class ideology whose philanthropic policies would require identification with those less fortunate ("feeling their pain") through something that came to be known as the welfare state. Even stranger fortunes await the word "enthusiasm" itself: throughout the later 17th and in the whole of the 18th century "enthusiastic" has clear and pejorative religious connotations pertaining to those outside the fold of the Anglican Church and thus automatically suspected of harboring unorthodox or even antinomian ideas.

We now read the final lines of one of Cowley's better jokes, a "translation" of Pindar's *First Nemean* ode, on Hercules' apotheosis:

> And that the grateful Gods, at last,
> The race of his laborious Virtue past,
> Heaven, which he sav'ed, should to him give;
> Where marry'd to eternal youth, he should for ever live;
> Drink nectar with the Gods, and all his senses please
> In their harmonious, golden palaces;
> Walk with ineffable delight
> Through the thick groves of never-withering light,
> And, as he walks, affright
> The Lyon and the Bear,
> Bull, Centaur, Scorpion, all the radiant monsters there.[10]

By importing exotic imagery and florid diction—"golden palaces," "thick groves of never-withering light," and so on—Cowley's imitation of the "enthusiastical" manner supplies with "absolute clarity" an alien content that was never present in the literal Greek. Imitation of the spirit is more important than violation of the letter; implied in the enthusiasm of the manner and mannerist is what we might describe either as bold falsification or blatant hybridization. By alluding to the constellations, Cowley may have thought that he would gain points with an audience that had not yet learned to make nice distinctions between astronomy and astrology. We, however, may admire and wonder at the last line, if we allow ourselves to become enchanted and child-like, because it has monsters in it and because they occupy telescopically verifiable outer space, which is where, at least since Galileo and Flash Gordon, we like to see our bug- and/or starry-eyed monsters, because they are less painful to contemplate and more easily frightened *there*, by a Greek super-hero, than *here* on earth, under our beds or on some distant continent. And we will readily concede also that Pindar, as Nietzsche suggests, intensifies the present—his and our own— transforming it into something monstrous and eternal[11] to compete with the "rich and strange" of a much-translated rival named Shakespeare. But we also find the last verse grippingly, if not absolutely, perspicuous in the sense that we live in an age of forgeries, monstrosities, and artificial illumination, of isotopes with half-lives measured in hundreds of thousands of years, neon lights, and nuclear power—which can and do threaten us with disease, death, and so on—so that "radiant monsters" seems scientifically up-to-date and filmable, ready to be projected on *our* screen, in a neighborhood theatre of the alternately shocked (schlocked) and awed 21st-century mind, where pleasure and pain take up their scintillating abode and we are little concerned with sweetess of diction or symmetry of "numbers." The original Greek has nothing in it to even faintly suggest "radiant monsters" or constellations for Hercules to stride through:

...αὐτὸν μὰν ἐν εἰρήνᾳ τὸν ἄπαντα χρόνον
ἐνσχερῷ
ἡσυχίαν καμάτων μεγάλων ποινὰν λαχόντ᾽ ἐξαίρετον
ὀλβίοις ἐν δώμασι· δεξάμενον θαλερὰν Ἥβαν ἄκοιτιν καὶ γάμον
δαίσαντα πὰρ Δὶ Κρονίδᾳ, σεμνὸν αἰνήσειν νόμον·[12]

These lines are rendered, literally, by T. K. Hubbard:

But he himself [70] will have allotted to him in peace, as an extraordinary reward for his great hardship, continuous peace for all time among the homes of the blessed. He will receive flourishing Hebe as his bride and celebrate the wedding-feast, and in the presence of Zeus the son of Cronus he will praise the sacred law.[13]

Thus, obeying his own metapoetic inspiration, a Muse of excessive clarification, Cowley creates an almost entirely asymmetrical, original text, which affects or simulates the Pindaric manner, summoning up mythic ghosts to reinforce the posture or pose of "Pindarizer." A Pindarizer is one who sets out to rise to the level or spirit of the Greek on a horse of his own imagination (from which he hopes not to fall), creating a simulacrum that exceeds the literal limits of the original text while glossing it meta-textually, creating a new text based on nothing but sedulous erudition, emulous audacity, and the wish to excite in the reader a certain derivative aura or haze of expectation as to what Pindar would have been like if he were not inimitably "mad." This is something altogether different from what passes for translation in the respectable academic world, but, as I will contend, it is altogether acceptable in the world of the postmodern avant-garde, which goes well beyond the limits set by Johnson:

His endeavour was, not to shew precisely what Pindar spoke, but his manner of speaking. He was much to his sentiments; nothing was required of him, but not to write as Pindar would not have written. (*PSA*)

To be a Pindar "paraphrast" one has to accept the sentimental *risk* of a

Pegasus ride, the danger involved in being seen as ridiculous by one's contemporaries or by later ages of criticism used to taking things, especially classical things, literally. The same holds true of his imitations of Anacreon:

> The Anacreon of Cowley, like the Homer of Pope, has admitted the decoration of some modern graces, by which he is undoubtedly made more amiable to common readers, and perhaps, if they would honestly declare their own preceptions, to far the greater part of those whom courtesy and ignorance are content to stile the Learned.
>
> *(PSA)*

"Modern graces": Johnson is as aware of the difference between ancient and modern as he is of the psychology of reader reception and scholarly pretension. When he speaks of making the Greeks "more amiable" to a contemporary audience, he brings to mind the pressure of consumers and markets. In a world familiar only with the gods of commerce and politics, we find the arts of readerly ingratiation applied everywhere other than in pursuit of poetic Fancy, on our video- and movie-house screens. Yet the perils of such an "amiability project" are something other than what Horace had warned against in the famous line about the waxen wings of anyone attempting to "do" or outdo Pindar ("Pindarum quisquis studet aemulari...."). The foolhardiness of *that* undertaking is known to all, Cowley included; the point would seem to be asserted—in defiance of literary orthodoxy and "the ancients"—that even at the risk of being seen as "exquisitely ridiculous," an ingratiating, even "cheeky" attempt must be made to clarify and amplify Pindar, who was thought to be obscure to the point of irrationality; the literary market-place must be given alternately inspired and clunky monsters, "my Pindaricks," in order to reinforce the notion of a modernity where the Graces are no longer present, a modernity *after* the Muses. This is not to gainsay what Kenner says about Cowley's badness on other occasions or even here, where "radiant monsters" seems anachronistically *outré* or over-the-top in the context of the rest of Pindar's poem. But what excites us today, as readers, is the rhetorical imposture or imposition of the phrase, a surprise that deserves to be seen (and anthologized, even) as belonging to the category of that which is mimetically vivid, as Greek art and the Baroque itself are vivid, and of a piece with the use of "monster" in fields quite other than translation, such as mathematics, where John Wallis in his *Treatise of Algebra* (1685) describes the fourth dimension as a "Monster in Nature, and less possible than a *Chimera*, or *Centaure*."[14] "All the radiant monsters there" might not be any less ungainly placed at the end of a treatise on algebra or astronomy, but the more important point would be that it makes, apparently without irony, casual allusion to and dwells comfortably within the context of the infantile state of 17th-century science. This is in keeping with certain other less memorable texts by Cowley, on gardening, for example, and, when one thinks about it, with Hesiod's *Works and Days* or Vergil's *Georgics*. The fact that its diction jars *against* mythology and even more gracelessly against the original text makes the phrase all the more scintillating in our reading of "the event."

One can read countless passages which have none of this quality, as T. S. Eliot does when he compares Cowley at his most prosaic and low-flying to a vivid passage in Dryden's *Mac Flecknoe*:

> The passage from Cowley is by no means despicable verse. But it is a commonplace description of commonly poetic objects. It has not the element of *surprise* [emphasis Eliot's] so essential to poetry, and this Dryden supplies.[15]

We can thus take Eliot's own judgment as to what constitutes an essential element of poetry, surprise, and apply it *a fortiori* in another context to the very poet he would scant by comparison to Dryden—the same Dryden who first praises Cowley rather slyly as the author who introduced the "Pindaric" style into English poetry at a rapid pace—"he indeed has brought it [Pindaric verse] as near perfection as was possible in so short a time"[16]— and then goes on to find "somewhat of the purity of English, somewhat of more equal thoughts, somewhat of sweetness in the Numbers, in one word, somewhat of a finer turn and more lyrical verse" (*BD*, 500) missing. Which qualities, no doubt, Dryden and others would supply at greater leisure in the decades following Cowley's death. But if Dryden is Eliot's exemplar, and the basis for such exemplarity lies in the essential element of surprise (this is Coleridge's verdict, too, in chapter 28 of *Biographia Literaria*, where he nonetheless joins the chorus of Cowley deprecators), it follows that at least some of Cowley, especially the Cowley flirting with Pindaric style on a very tricky, low-flying horse, is poetry of some artificial quality, indeed, and not merely "ungainly," bathetic, or a little too prosaically clear, as Kenner would have it. Merely to call Cowley "ridiculous," as he no doubt is from time to time, is to beg the question of translation seen wholly as a concretization of mimetic enthusiasm, of the ecstatic nature of communication in a post-Cowleyan world of multiple media and mixed or equivocal messages, of unknown or ignored originals and the pressure of the simulacrum in the otherworldly space and imagination. As Baudrillard suggests in a now classic essay entitled "The Ecstasy of Communication," we are nowadays more than a little "schizo" in our manufacturing zeal, our imitation of the real and enjoyment of the simulacrum:

> The schizo is bereft of every scene, open to everything in spite of himself, living in

the greatest confusion. He is himself obscene, the obscene prey of the world of obscenity. What characterizes him is less the loss of the real, the light years of estrangement from the real, the pathos of distance and radical separation, as is commonly said: but, every much to the contrary, the absolute proximity, the total instantaneity of things, the feeling of no defense, no retreat. It is the end of interiority and intimacy, the overexposure and transparence of the world which traverses him without obstacle. He can no longer produce the limits of his own being, can no longer play nor stage himself, can no longer produce himself as mirror. He is now only a pure screen, a switching center for the networks of influence.[17]

Though couched in other terms, a similar case is made by Kenner concerning the schizophrenia of modern culture from Cowley to Cage and Warhol: its inability to decide which signal is real and which "faux," when a recital consists solely in the opening and closing of a piano lid, when a painted soup can aspires to be nothing more than a painted soup can.

It is therefore to be expected that Cowley will anticipate our own epoch in terms or in a language that it will understand, to which it is receptive, to which at a certain limit of obscenity and badness, it can even become addicted. The words of one line in particular, from *The Muse*, another text modeled on Pindar, find themselves occurring in the title of a cult horror classic, *Liquid Sky* (1982), a film decorated by unsmiling "modern graces" if there ever was one, where aliens come from outer space looking for a heroin high, but are instead enticed (enthused, as it were) by chemical compounds released by the brain of earthlings during orgasm. This causes a number of unfortunate actors to have their skulls punctured by pipettes—a "brain drain" of a peculiarly fluid and odious sort, as Johnson might say— so that the aliens can artificially induce a sexual ecstasy which they themselves cannot feel "naturally," or without a simulacrum supplied by the mediumistic other. Cowley's speaker, on the other hand, bids his imagination soar to heights and depths where *no* physical being has ever ventured. Thus clarified, a Cavalier's "light years of estrangement" suggest themselves in the way the text employs imagery at a much *lower* altitude:

> Where never *Foot* of *Man*, or *Hoof* of *Beast*,
>   The passage prest,
>   Where never *Fish* did *fly*,
> And with short silver *wings* cut the low liquid *Sky*.[18]

As with "radiant monsters there," "low liquid *Sky*," constrasted with the etherial region to which Cowley's Muse takes him, surprises, not least because the sky is not really liquid, or rather because the sky *could* be liquid if we only allowed our imagination to cooperate in the enthused, derivative illusion that some fish have wings and thus can *fly*, if only for a second, rather than leap, fins flipping, through the nethermost reaches of the atmosphere. Kenner is right; this is not a conceit. It is a reasoned version of a conceit, or a conceit made to "fess up," showing the process of its making, which gives it a different kind of charm or allure—in the author's and reader's simultaneous knowledge that this is "only" a piece of verse, only a simulacrum, say, on the level of "professional" wrestling, where the spectators both know and do not know they are witnessing a sham spectacle. The enthusiasm with which one enters the arena, of the text, of the "good-guy-versus-bad-guy dream" is everything, or nearly everything, because on the other side lies the disillusioned realization that one is being had, that this is "all there is"—to exploit and be exploited—in the undertow of a marketplace purveying newer, sleeker, more glowingly prurient monsters to fans preprogrammed for consensus.

Another part of the charm of the line consists in the balance between clusters of four syllables each, "short silver wings" and "low liquid *Sky*," each with its own pleasing vocalic properties, the first heavy in sibilants, the second, about the water-like atmosphere, in alliterating l's, a "liquid" consonant. There is also the sequence of short i's followed by the long "y" in *Sky*, which makes the surprise of the line even more emphatic, if also transparently engineered for maximum effect upon the reader. The penultimate insult to Cowley's Pindaric pretensions is, of course, supplied by the unfortunate metaphor for heroin in our own time, i. e. "horse," a noun applied—we imagine—because of the chemically induced rush of riding on an unruly steed. The final one comes with the realization that Cowley is the alien with the pipette and that Pindar or the texts of Pindar are the "obscure" brain from which he is draining the enthusiasm or "high" of brighter, even more fantastic Pindaric simulacra.

Lexical Asides

Enthusiasm. 1609. late Latin *enthusiasmus*, Gr. ἐνθουσιασμός from ἐνθουσιάζειν, from ἐνθουσία, the fact of being possessed by a god. **1.** Possession by a god, supernatural inspiration, prophetic or poetic ecstasy—1807. b. Poetical fervour—1781. **2.** Fancied inspiration: a conceit of divine favour or communication. In 18th century often: ill-regulated religious emotion or speculation (*arch.*)—1660. **3.** Rapturous intensity of feeling on behalf of a person, cause, etc.: passionate eagerness in any pursuit. (The current sense) 1716. *Oxford Universal Dictionary*

Enthousiasm 1714. '...That there is a Power in Numbers, Harmony, Proportion and Beauty of every kind, which naturally captivates the Heart, and raises the Imagination to an Opinion, or Conceit of something *majestick* and *divine*!'
Shaftesbury, "Miscellaneous Reflections" in *Characteristicks*, vol. III

The related word, "enthusiast," means in the 18th century one who believed in miracles that did not actually take place, according to John Wesley. This pejorative was applied also to natural philosophers of the Renaissance, among them, Paracelsus, who, despite their potent herbalism and prescient approach to medicine, were thought to rely solely on astrology and other fanciful or fantastic sources of magical lore, such as alchemy. The enthusiast would be one who is in danger of being at some time or another taken for a liar, fake, swindle, or cheat. Mimetic enthusiasm exemplifies that which refuses to come under the regulation or rule of reason. Its delusional "works," often ungainly, cannot be canonized. Institutional regulations are challenged by the enthusiasm of the copyist, (dis-)simulator, and forger. A religious enthusiast is, in kind, if not in sacred or ecclesiastical degree, homologous with a secular one and deserves to be placed in the context of words such as "fan" and "fanatic":

> **Fan.** orig. U. S. 1889. (In earlier use *fann*). 1682. [abbrev. of FANATIC] An enthusiast (orig. a keen spectator of a sport, in early use esp. baseball). *Oxford Universal Dictionary*

> **Fanatic.** 1533. [ad. L. *fanaticus*, f. *fanum* temple...**A.** adj. **1.** Of an action or speech: Such as might result from possession by a deity or demon: frantic. Of a person: Frenzied—1660. **2.** Of persons, etc.: Affected by excessive and mistaken enthusiasm, esp. in religious matters. 1647...**B.** sb. **1.** A (religious) maniac—1806. **2.** A fanatic person; an unreasoning enthusiast; applied about 1650 to Nonconformists. *Oxford Universal Dictionary*

> **Fantastic.** Middle English. [ad. med. L. *fantasticus*, late L. *phantasticus*, a. Gr., φανταστικός, f. φαντάζειν, to make visible.... **a.** adj. **1.** Existing only in imagination, unequal (*Obs.*), perversely or irrationally imagined....**4**.... Now: Extravagantly fanciful, odd in behaviour. **5.** Arbitrarily devised. Now *rare.* 1658. **6.** Eccentric, quaint, or grotesque in design or conception 1616. *Oxford Universal Dictionary*

It is in the context of these definitions that we situate the fate of Ixion, who is the lineal ancestor of the centaur Chiron, as told in Pindar's *Second Pythian Ode* and paraphrased by Hamilton:

> The poem...goes back to relate in quick sketches the story of this man [Ixion] who first spilled kindred blood. When his new father-in-law came to collect the appropriate marriage-gifts, Ixion killed him, in order to marry the daughter without paying the expected price. Rather than punish this murderer, Zeus instead purified him and bore him up to Olympus. In effect, Zeus rewarded Ixion. But then, residing among the gods, Ixion planned yet another act of ingratitude, to make a sexual advance on Hera. Having discerned Ixion's intentions, the father of the gods created a 'sweet lie' (37)—a beautiful cloud fashioned in the form of the divine queen. Like his sister Coronis, Ixion fell into a deep 'delusion' (αὐάτον, 28)...he slept with a

phantasm of a goddess and fathered a monster named Kentauros. The child will grow up to mate with 'Magnesian mares,' and thereby engender an astonishing race, half-man, half-horse—the Centaurs (including Chiron). Now for this act, even though the transgression was entirely hallucinatory—the rape of a cloud—Zeus punishes Ixion, crucifying him upon a wheel that will spin forevermore in the darkness of the underworld. (*SD*, 67)

And, as Hamilton states, it is the fate of the Centaurs to be born "without the attendance of the Graces" (*SD*, 68) who should be present at the birth not only of intelligent beings, but of genuine art. The Centaurs, half-human, half-equine children of the phantasm, pedagogical "tools" of the Literature of Knowledge, displace the Muses precisely at the dawn of modern science and thus pronounce not the death of poetic art, but its mimetic "after-life." Those who listen to, or become enthused by them, produce replicas of poems, or, like Cowley, think in terms of an enlightening that only deepens the dusky fatedness of translation, producing in their (post)modernity not beauteous goddesses of dawn but only radiant monsters.

Disappearance of the Work of Art

Classical Model

| Artist/Author | Work of art | Reader/Beholder |

Cowleyan/Postmodernist Metapoesis

| [Artist/Author] | Text=Simulacrum parasitic upon Enthusiasm, Expectation, Publicity | Consensualist/ Fan |

In *Torquato Tasso*, at line 947, the dialogue indicates that, at the birth of Tasso's antagonist Antonio, "die Grazien sind leider ausgeblieben" ("the Graces were unfortunately missing"), a circumstance which makes him not only a person whose ear is deaf to the Muses, but also a stepchild of Kentauros embodying the modern erosion of poetic sensibility.

Pindaric Echoes: Imitation and Metapoesis in Goethe

Yet surely those verses are not without a just claim to praise; of which it may be said with truth, that no man but Cowley could have written them.
Johnson, *Preface*

Die Gesänge des Ossian besonders sind wahrhaftige Centaurengesänge, mit dem Stromgeist gesungen, und wie vom griechischen Chiron, der den Achill auch des Saitenspiel gelehrt.

[The songs of Ossian, especially, are true centaur-songs, sung with the spirit of the storm, and as if from the Greek Chiron, who also taught Achilles how to play on stringed instruments.]
Friedrich Hölderlin, note entitled "Das Belebende," to a Pindaric fragment

On September 15, 1780 Goethe sends to Charlotte von Stein an ode, "Meine Göttin," based briefly, solely in its opening strophe, on Pindar's *Second Olympian*.[19] In its depiction of the extramarital pursuit of "das ewig Weibliche," who, from the first to the last line is "only" an allegorical figure invented on the spot by the poet, delineated on this occasion as a foolish and coy daughter of Jove, Goethe's Muse at least equals the facetious daring of Cowley and the Cavalier poets. The only direct, literal translation (of *tina theon*, etc.) begins and ends in the first two lines, but Goethe assimilates the philosophic "spirit" of Pindar,[20] in terms of a vision of man as a "creature of a day," and allows it to color the whole of the text, as that from which an Olympian few, the "we alone" of the text, would gladly be exempt.[21] Where the Greek ode had praised water as the noblest of the four elements, this epinician directs its flattery elsewhere, to different, mythically and socially aberrant, even problematic fields, where the opposite of wisdom, namely, mutable, ever changing *ek-stasis*, with clearly erotic implications, is being praised and, after the first two lines, a Cowley-like Pegasus, as it were, boldly goes where no Pindar went before:

Welcher Unsterblichen	To which immortal
Soll der höchste Preis sein?	Shall the highest prize belong?
Mit niemand streit ich,	I argue with no one,
Aber ich geb ihn	But I give it
Der ewig beweglichen,	To the forever moving,
Immer neuen,	Forever new,
Seltsamen Tochter Jovis,	Strange daughter of Jove,
Seinem Schoßkinde,	His lapchild,
Der Phantasie.	Fantasy.
Denn ihr hat er	For to her he has
Alle Launen,	Allotted all the moods,
Die er sonst nur allein	Which he otherwise
Sich vorbehält,	Allows only
Zugestanden	To himself
Und hat seine Freude	And he derives joy
An der Törin.[22]	From the foolish girl.

The allusion to the "female fool" favored by father Jove suggests that the terrain of imitation is about to be altered. Something rather different begins to happen after verse three, and especially in the third strophe. Goethe, we may say, allows himself the privilege of becoming jovially enthused, filling the text with a cataract of sensuous images of a seemingly conventional, yet altogether ingenious or *seltsam* sort, writing better and more surprising verse than he had before. Fantasy, appropriately enough, dominates the fields she wanders through:

Sie mag rosenbekränzt	She likes to walk, rose-crowned,
Mit dem Lilienstengel	With a lily-stem, through
Blumentäler betreten,	Valleys of flowers,
Sommervögeln begleiten	To accompany summer-birds
Und leichtnährenden Tau	And to suck lightly nourishing
Mit Bienenlippen	Dew from blooming flowers
Von Blüten saugen;	With the lips of bees.
Oder sie mag	Or she likes
Mit fliegendem Haar	To rush in the wind
Und düsterm Blicke	With flying hair
Im Winde sausen	And gloomy look
Um Felsenwände,	Around cliff-walls,
Und tausendfärbig,	Or to shine down
Wie Morgen und Abend	On mortals
Immer wechselnd,	Like morning and evening,
Wie Mondesblicke,	Always changing,
Den Sterblichen scheinen.	Like glances from the moon.

As a sustained flight of genuine fancy, nothing could be farther from the "Pindarick" disease. Nothing, on the other hand, could be closer to the aristocratic spirit of Cowley and to the landscape of an idealized 18th-century pleasure-garden, of an English rather than French design. "Mondesblicke," followed immediately by "den Sterblichen," alluding to the Pindaric topos of the mortal ephemerid, would be more surprising if it were not anticipated by the image of flying hair and the constrasting look of gloom. In ten lines, Goethe gives us what is, *in nuce*, the silhouette of a romantic plot, a sentimental novel in miniature, which, in the last verse, will turn on and around the speaker's "I," giving voice to a wish for the companionship of Fantasy and Hope throughout life. Cowley might have handled it differently, and been less graceful in the process, but he would never have *organized* the imagery so strategically to fit the geometry or calculus of foolish seduction. Instead of being weighted with tragic melancholy, the final line of the strophe merely emphasizes the mutability of fantasy. The coquettish, ever changing glances of the moon appear as the logical outcome of that which has gone before; mortals, in their brief days and nights, are left in the position of passive spectators to what the goddess Fantasy has in store for them.

The following strophes picks up the theme of the ephemeral, in order to offer the surprising thesis that mortal man is married not to woman, but to the goddess Fancy or Fantasy, which remains with him in thick and thin—and is said to be, as in Cowley's invocation of Hercules' immortality, "unverwelklich," i.e., forever in bloom:

Laßt uns alle	Let us all
Den Vater preisen!	Praise the father!
Den alten, hohen,	The old, the lofty,
Der solch eine schöne,	Who has wished
Unverwelkliche Gattin	To place mortal human
Dem sterblichen	Beings in the company
Menschen	Of such a beautiful,
Gesellen mögen!	Never withering wife!
Denn uns allein	For to us alone
Hat er sie verbunden	He has bound her
Mit Himmelsband	With a heavenly tie
Und ihr geboten,	And bidden her,
In Freud und Elend	In joy and misery,
Als treue Gattin	As a true wife,
Nicht zu entweichen.	Not to flee.
Alle die andern	All the other
Armen Geschlechter	Poor races
Der kinderreichen,	Of the prolific,
Lebendigen Erde	Living earth
Wandeln und weiden	Pass their days and pasture
In dunkelm Genuß	In the dark pleasure
Und trüben Schmerzen	And gloomy pains
Des augenblicklichen	Of momentary
Beschränkten Lebens,	Circumscribed life,
Gebeugt vom Joche	Bent over by the yoke
Der Notdurft.	Of harsh necessity.

This aristocratic ideology is then further reinforced by the exclusivity of the next two words: "Uns aber," "To us, however"—leading to the ultimate surprise, as the speaker addresses the reader as "you," asking her to rejoice, i.e., become enthused about the prospect of celebrating Fantasy as the "matron of the house" precisely because of her indispensability to *us* who need her to be unwithering: a psychological take on Hercules' apotheosis and marriage to another daughter of Jove, i.e., Hebe, the Olympian cup-bearer, alluded to in *Nemean V* and Cowley's translation. The speaker, projected as genius- and/or Hercules-like, exempts himself from ordinary mortality, as he brings the source of his pleasure into the light:

Uns aber hat er	Upon us, however,

Seine gewandteste,	He has bestowed his most talented,
Verzärtelte Tochter,	Tenderest daughter,
Freut euch! gegönnt.	Rejoice!
Begegnet ihr lieblich,	Greet her lovingly,
Wie einer Geliebten!	Like a lover!
Laßt ihr die Würde	Grant her the dignity
Der Frauen im Haus!	Of matrons in the house!
Und daß die alte	And see to it that the old
Schwiegermutter Weisheit	Mother-in-law wisdom
Das zarte Seelchen	Does not insult
Ja nicht beleidge!	The tender little soul in any way!
Doch kenn ich ihre Schwester,	For I know her sister,
Die ältere, gesetztere,	The older, plumper,
Meine stille Freundin:	My quiet friend:
O daß die erst	O that she might only
Mit dem Lichte des Lebens	Turn away from me when
Sich von mir wende,	The light of life [goes out], she
Die edle Treiberin,	Who beats game into the open,
Trösterin Hoffnung!	The comforter who is Hope!

One wonders about the word "Treiberin," applied as an epithet describing Hope, as the sister of Fantasy—meaning a person of female gender assigned the task of beating hunted animals out into the open, especially if the "I" of the poem is seen in the role of amorous, receptive hunter. An escape clause to further *in flagrante* concretization is provided by the initiating trope of facetious celebration underlying the text, as a whole, that it concerns itself with "nothing but" a test-flight of allegorical strategies spun forth concerning fantasy, that the poetic atmosphere is one of distanced mediation or representation, not of immediate referentiality. Such an escape is rendered problematic, however, by the unsettling imperatives addressed to the "household," that Fantasy, a young and foolish girl, be taken as the mistress of the domestic economy of the speaker's mind, that Hope dwell with her sister in his consciousness until his dying day. Nowhere is enthusiasm or ecstasy mentioned explicitly, but they everywhere provide the emotional subtext—as that which the speaker would gladly preserve even into old age, a kind of bliss, whose name cannot be spoken of except in poetic terms, a principle allied to what, for lack of other words, must be called, in the "spirit" of Goethe, "das Ewig-Töchterliche," to that which is full of surprises for young and old alike, because it is not other than fantastic or, to be brief, a "full fan-experience":

Und hat seine Freude	And he derives joy
An der Törin.	From the foolish girl.

We have chosen not to quote the Greek, because Goethe is not Pindarizing on a paraphrastic horse—supplementing the mythological and rhetorical inventory of a Pindar text with his own surprises—but creating an entirely original, self-sufficient vehicle of praise and thinly veiled amorous errance, of Eros, which can be said to use Pindaric enthusiasm as a stimulant to the imagination—in a certain sense, like coffee or tea. Yet a Cowleyan note can be detected in the deity being celebrated: "die Phantasie," fantasy, a faculty closely related to Cowley's privileged Phansie or Fancy, a goddess, above all, of the open road. More significant, however, are the words of the letter accompanying "Meine Göttin," a text in which Goethe writes that he has become subject to fits of a disconcerting intensity, in which he imagines his horse (with the *élan* of a Cowleyan Pegasus) suddenly taking wing with him on it:

> ...ich sitze auf meinem Klepper und reite meine pflichtmäßige Station ab, auf einmal kriegt die Mähre unter mir eine herrliche Gestalt, unbezwingliche Lust und Flügel, und geht mit mir davon.[23]
> [...I am sitting on my nag and riding along my duty-prescribed station, <when> suddenly the mare beneath me assumes a majestic shape, unmasterable joy and wings, and takes off with me.]

It is no exaggeration to say that, coming both to and from Pindar, Goethe is obsessed with horses and horsemanship of the most wildly and widely diverse kind.[24] He too would be a master of horses, a horse-man. This is to say that the sessions or trances of translation, its transits and traversings, may be likened to rides of one sort or another, seeking an encounter with the strangeness of the other, born out of rapture, doomed to disappointment only in the aftermath of the act. The charioteer in Pindar is the *cybernos*, the charioteer, equally driver and driven, and the work of translation is no doubt a cybernetic work of steering one's way through a network of reef-like passages, a navigation of the text from its hazardous beginning to a problematic end, whose erotic component is not overlooked by Benjamin:

> It seems, then that Benjamin's translation is an allegory of the kernel of his philosophy of translation and language, and the allegorical figure of translation would be the figure of the erotic encounter. Eros as the figure of translation, but translation also as the figure of Eros. [25]

Equally, as Hamilton suggests, in the *térma* or goal-line of the track lies the radical *–trans*, "...denoting now the stone towards which one races, that which defines the passage as a passage" (*SD*, 305). Translation's restlessness knows no home or only a very equivocal one; its wanderlust is always toward the boundary-stone, a no-man's or no-woman's-land where

Fantasy alone rules the *Haushalt* (household). The Eros of cults, on the other hand, grows out of the Buñuelian obscurity of the beloved or adored object of group desire, where trysting encounters more often than not fail to take place. The cult and the occult merge not in the early Goethe, whose fantasies are limpid, but in the after-effects of Goethe-worship. The enthused translator who uses *Olympian 2* as his launching-pad may attempt to turn his duty-driven "nag" into a Pegasus. The occult allegories at play in the rhetoric of the "Treiberin" and in the domination of the household by a young girl begin, however, to take on a certain surreal quality in our fan-like, hyperbolic imagination, which is that of the profane incongruity of Goethe's horse suddenly sprouting wings with him still on it.

Down River: Taught by Half a Horse

A Translator, who cannot equal his original, is incapable of expressing its beauties.
James Macpherson, 1796 preface to *Ossian*

In his study of Pindar in translation, Professor Hamilton notes how the figure or "mythic paradigm" of Chiron exercises a controlling influence over Hölderlin's translation of Pindaric fragments. In terms of the overall ambition of rendering ancient Greek into contemporary German, Hamilton agrees that Hölderlin undertakes a project of "hyperbolic translation," in which the translator is free to exercise a new kind of license, "not by submitting to the writer's intended and then elicited intention, but by bringing his own personal vision to an understated text and creating the writer's intention."[26] The question would then be: how does this half-equine, half-human vision relate to an antecedent "Monster" in literature, one "less possible than a *Chimera*, or *Centaure*," Cowley's Pindar? Does the monstrous, in- or half-human provide a resource of translation for which the centaur, Achilles' teacher but taken allegorically as the incongruously halved, "model" teacher of humanity as a whole, serves as hyperbolic mediator? There is, to be sure, a suitable myth concerning the non-Olympian offspring of Magnesian mares and Kentauros:

ὁ δάμαν δ'ἐπεὶ φῆρες δάεν ρι-
πᾶν μελιηδέος οἴνου, ἐσσυμένως ἀπὸ
μὲν λευκὸν γάλα χερσὶ τράπεζαν ὤ-
θεον, αὐτόματοι δ'ἐξ ἀργυρέων κε-
ράτων πίνοντες ἐπλάζοντο.

Die männerbezwingende, nachdem
Gelernet die Centauren

Die Gewalt
Des honigsüßen Weines, plözlich trieben
Die weiße Milch mit Händen, den Tisch sie fort, von selber,
Und aus den silbernen Hörnern trinkend
Bethörten sie sich.

Der Begriff von den Centauren ist wohl der vom Geiste eines Stromes, so fern der Bahn und Gränze macht, mit Gewalt, auf der ursprünglich pfadlosen aufwärtswachsenden Erde.

Sein Bild ist deswegen an Stellen der Natur, wo das Gestade reich an Felsen und Grotten ist, besonderes an Orten, wo ursprünglich der Strom die Kette der Gebirge verlassen und ihre Richtung queer durchreißen mußte.

Centauren sind deswegen auch ursprünglich Lehrer der Naturwissenschaft, weil sich aus jenem Gesichtspuncte die Natur am besten einsehn läßt.

In solchen Gegenden mußt' ursprünglich der Strom umirren, eh' er sich eine Bahn riß. Dadurch bildeten sich, wie an Teichen, feuchte Wiesen und Höhlen in der Erde für säugende Thiere, und der Centauer war indessen wilder Hirte, dem Odyssäischen Cyklops gleich; die Gewässer suchten sehnend ihre Richtung. Je mehr sich aber von seinen beiden Ufern das troknere fester bildete, und Richtung gewann durch festwurzelnde Bäume, und Gesträuche und den Weinstok, destomehr mußt' auch der Strom, der seine Bewegung von der Gestalt des Ufers annahm, Richtung gewinnen, bis er, von seinem Ursprung an gedrängt, an einer Stelle durchbrach, wo die Berge, die ihn einschlossen, am leichtesten zusammenhiengen.

So lernten die Centauren die Gewalt des honigsüßen Weins, sie nahmen von dem festgebildeten, bäumereichen Ufer Bewegung und Richtung an, und warfen die weiße Milch und den Tisch mit Händen weg, die gestaltete Welle verdrängte sich, der Überfall des Waldes, mit den Stürmen und den sicheren Fürsten des Forsts regte das müßige Leben der Haide auf, das stagnirende Gewässer ward so lange zurückgestosen, vom jäheren Ufer, bis es Arme gewann, und so mit eigener Richtung, von selbst aus silbernen Hörnern trinkend, sich Bahn machte, eine Bestimmung annahm.

Die Gesänge des Ossian besonders sind wahrhaftige Centaurengesänge, mit dem Stromgeist gesungen, und wie vom griechischen Chiron, der den Achill auch des Saitenspiel gelehrt.[27]

[The concept of the Centaurs is most likely that of the spirit of a river, insofar as it makes a track and a boundary, with force, on the originally pathless, upward-growing earth. [The Centaur's] picture is therefore [found] in places of nature, where the coastline is rich in cliffs and grottoes, especially in places, where originally the river had to abandon the chain of mountains and had to cut across their direction transversely.

Centaurs are therefore also originally teachers of natural science, because one can best gain insight into nature from that viewpoint.

In such regions the river originally was forced to wander about, before it could make a track for itself. Thereby, moist meadows and caverns in the earth for mammals came into being, as [there are] next to ponds, and the Centaur was for the time being a wild shepherd, like the Odyssean Cyclops; the waters sought their direction with longing. The more the dry [land] formed itself from its two banks, however, and took its direction through firmly rooted trees, and bushes and the grapevine, the more the river, which took its motion from the shape of the bank, had to gain direction, until it, pushed away from its origin, broke through at a place where the mountains, which hemmed it in, were gathered together most easily.

Thus the Centaurs learned the power of the honeysweet wine; they took on motion and direction from the solidified, well-treed riverbank, and they threw away the white milk and the table with hands; the shaped wave [the pond] repressed itself; the attack of the forest, with the storms and the secure princes of the forest, stimulated the lazy life of the wilderness; the stagnant water was thrown back from the more abrupt bank for the amount of time it needed to grow arms, and thus with its own direction, drinking on its own from silver horns, it made a track for itself, took on a determination.

The songs of Ossian, especially, are true centaur-songs, sung with the spirit of the river, and as if from the Greek Chiron, who also taught Achilles how to play on stringed instruments.]

Is this commentary meant to be taken literally, symbolically, or in some other way? One errs by treating it either as allegory or as an encyclopedia entry. It is "all" or in an entirely hyperbolic, yet literal sense, a translation meant to elucidate, beyond what we take as philological rigor, "the concept" of the Centaurs—which is something different from what the Centaurs as demigods meant in mythology, to the Greeks themselves. At the same time, the passages where the shaped wave or pond "repressed itself," while the river, having displaced the Centaurs in Hölderlin's explication as the focus of the text, drinks from "silver horns" indicate a self-consciously naive mode of speaking somewhere between fairy-tale and myth—a metapoesis which, since it can no longer be mere information or translation, must "comment" on the original text (a mere five lines of Greek), elucidating it in a manner which, Hölderlin hopes, will re-present Pindar's text not as it might have been reflected upon by Greek thinkers, but as it may be thought by profane contemporaries who can no longer feel or think as the Greeks did. Present-day readers no doubt find it difficult to understand the elucidation, since the water takes on anthropomorphic qualities throughout the text, even as the Centaur is described as a "natural scientist" and compared to the Cyclops in Homer's *Odyssey*. The "subject" of the commentary turns out to be not only the mythical being that taught Achilles how to play the lyre, but the very point of view (*Gesichtspunkt*) that produced the songs in the first place *as a mythopoetic version of natural science*. For Hölderlin, rewriting mythology meta-poetically, the Greeks could not be more distant from us. That distance forces us to consider their mythology in the most *sobering* terms, yet our notion of sobriety is utterly different from theirs. Centaurs are teachers of the natural sciences because they find themselves in a landscape reminiscent of the island of Lemnos in Sophocles' *Philoctetes*—where grottoes and cliffs predominate, as on a coastline, or where rivers flow down to the sea. We know that the Centaurs are Philoctetes-like both in their isolation and in their accursedness—they are the offspring of Ixion, who attempted to rape Hera. For all the pedagogical, poetic, or scientific sense that the Centaurs make, they are traversed by irrational passion or sexual excess, a motivation which certainly shadows Hölderlin's text, thought it is nowhere brought to the surface as an unrepressed or explicit meaning. They make paths, with force, where none had been before, striating the earth's previously smooth or unlined surface. The rivers, likewise, move transversely across the mountains. Natural science is grotesque in the sense that it can be learned only in these places, where nature opens itself up to investigative scrutiny or "Einsicht," not where it is beautifully unblemished or unfurrowed. The Centaur-scientist's viewpoint, as an observer, is "built into" his own experiments; as the observer observed by Hölderlin, his viewpoint (*Gesichtspunkt*) is situated in the feminine, meadow-like, or moist nature whose tranquil surface he disrupts, precisely as the Centaurs disrupted the wedding of the Lapithae. But because natural science is grotesque, the two sides of the Centaur, the unbeauteous joining of human and horse, subsumes both the raw and the cooked, the coercion involved in furrowing nature (analogous to the Centaurs' attack upon the women at the wedding) and the rational activity of bringing nature under the concept or *Begriff* of science. The determination (*Bestimmung*) of the concept arises out of an incoherent, inchoate swamp of data. But the two things are grotesquely inseparable. One cannot have the science without the grotto, nor the reason without the wine, because it is in the cultivation of the grape that the Centaurs depart from their pre-rational condition as shepherds.

The "hymns" of *Ossian* are centaur-songs because they are both derivative or "doctrinaire" and based on a grotesque illusion; they are *modern* analogues of ancient monsters who, according to Pindar, were born without the presence of the Graces—products of a Centaur-like inebriation *and* rationalization (on the model or in the rhythm of a maddeningly mutant pleasure-pain syndrome) which owes its existence to readerly enthusiasm and receptivity. Not that Hölderlin disparages the Centaur-songs for this, despite the fact that the highest point of the Greeks is reached, for him, in utter sobriety. What the Greeks understood as sobriety might be inebriation for us. Indeed, Hölderlin's theory of translation is, perhaps, closest to what is being attempted, without critical reflection, in *Ossian*: the ambition to make the ancients say what they never said. *Ossian*, on the other hand, is unlike a Hölderlin translation because it feeds off the "full fan-experience" of the later 18th century. Hölderlin can only wish for fans in his own time, finding them only in a modernity which begins with World War I, continues into the grotesquerie of a Heidegger who makes Hölderlin say what he never said, and has its fruition in the great commentaries of the second half of the 20th century, most notably, in Szondi, de Man, Derrida, and Lacoue-

Labarthe. Conversely, the sobriety of Hölderlin appears from the outset to be the dialectical opposite of what Cowley calls the "enthusiastic" method, a derivative tapping-into the cranium of another to siphon off a fluid-like Pindaric "high." In terms of the labor of translation, a rigorous poetic logic and the rendering of Greek rhythms and vowel quantity into accentuated modern idiom, Hölderlin's *measure* exceeds the scintillating surprises of his English predecessor. Cowley, the brilliant, "Cavalier" amateur, rides a Pegasus of a different breed and color. But what if the two trajectories or transits of translation were, finally, from one point of view, at least, not the same thing, but indistinguishable in the night of cultural transition—from a world where art still occupies a central position to one where it claims, at best, an "eccentric" position with respect to mimetic economies—as enthusiasm or non-conforming unorthodoxy, something beyond the limits of institutional or canonical "piety." Cowley the poet who "belongs" in the prosaic, scientific 18th century, as Kenner suggests, Hölderlin the poet who seems to have written for a 20th century in which notions of the sacred and the natural cannot be recuperated ever, in anything like their original form:

> But the fact that the proper being of the Greeks should be lost, and consequently, inimitable (what the Nietzsche of *The Birth of Tragedy*, as we can see, will not have heard), does not in the least mean that we might imitate what remains to us of the Greeks—that is, their art, that by which they tend to be, in all impropriety and strangeness in relation to themselves, near to what is for us, still so distantly, proper. Greek art is inimitable, *because it is an art* and because the sobriety that it indicates to us is, or should be, nature for us. Our nature (sobriety) can no more take its bearing from their culture than our culture (sacred pathos) can take its bearings from their nature—which was never carried into effect.[28]

As Hamilton points out (*SD*, 306), there is a tension in Hölderlin's translations and commentaries on the Pindaric fragments which is focused on on the unsublatable struggle between competing interpretations (*Auslegungen*), in that which cannot come to completion or "into effect," something left "up in the air" (as reflected by Hölderlin's use of the verb *hängen*, to hang) and, in its very obstinacy and indeterminacy, left open to futurity. This relates, again, to the "*trans-*" of translation, that is, its capacity to be everywhere and nowhere, its movement to and fro between self and other, its navigation from the merely mortal to the supernaturally immortal or god-like:

> The in-between, of course, is precisely the space that is opened ·in the work of translation. The trans—moving in transit—is a movement from one place to the next, while itself occupying no place. Like the place on a moving train, it is always someplace but no place. Or like the flutter of bees. *Transe*, in French, is 'fear'

because it apprehends the *transitus* to come, the passage from this world to the next.

(*SD*, 305)

But the point of Chiron's pedagogy would seem to lie in the necessity of making things, rivers, poetry, history or time itself, *happen*, to bring things out of the stasis of a grotesque "hanging-about" and into the light—not, as Heidegger might (wrongly) say, to establish these things, which are in any case, poetic shadows or projections of being, as gnomically valid, but *exigently*, as a force which is both needful and worth striving for through an interminable process of turning outward and winding around, as if by arabesque translation. The *transe* is equally and, at all times, a passage to the future seen as the ultimate "full fan-experience" in terms of its desolation, etiolation, and elation, its enthusiasm and fickleness.

Cowley, in the knowledge that Pindar is "obscure," accepts even more fully and far more naively than Hölderlin, the notion that Greek art is inimitable; the original Greek can only be compensated for by a "supplement" of clarification. On the other hand, Greece for Hölderlin. must become—wholly, thoroughly, *durchaus* android-like and/or cybernetic, "more real than the real," without limit, even in, or precisely because of, its sobriety. The "monstrous" is accomplished with or through a clairvoyant, oracle-like attention to the "dark" literality or inscrutability of the other text, the text of the absent other. The sign of Chiron—a godlike, but also grotesque, half-horsed-, semi human mutancy—traverses him, as it also traverses us. A postmodernism like that of Matthew Barney does not even wish to achieve a sobriety which would antedate viniculture and thus culture itself, since it is, on the one hand, premeditatedly post-post-Romantic and only too aware of its cultural lateness, while, on the other, only too willing to engender a fan-base by filming in exotic locations and staging ever more "over the top," Grand Guignol versions of mythic and/or anatomical paradigms. It is all-too-attractively human and bestial at once—the saturated symbolism of a Runge crossed with the canny staginess of 60s happenings. The Centaurs, as Hölderlin sees them, are "people of the grotto." The homes of the Centaurs are cavernous spaces where the light of the past meets the darkness of the future, and the future encounters the obscure past. At one pole of grotesqueness in translation, we find words echoing not with their original force, but in a broken or fractured idiom which is sometimes more than a little difficult to understand, but which has the virtue of being everything other than facile. At a different pole of half-horsed grotesqueness, we find translation written as the Masque or masquerade of an Apollonian clarity, where enthusiasm flies high and pretends to echo a noise that was never actually heard. In order to bring things "down to our level," in a Centaur-like way, all the while leading up to the point where the art of harping can be taught to Achilles, the river has to cut through the mountains or traverse them, gaining direction between the banks on either side.

Nothing could be farther removed from the purity of Benjamin's notion of translation than the art of Pindarizing practiced downriver by Cowley and the netherworld leapings of mutant progeny from *Liquid Sky* onward, yet that which is "strong" in "radiant monsters shining there" also suggests an element of wishful thinking embedded in every future:

> It is the task of the translator to find that unique strategic place where the echo can be produced, in order to make audible and perceptible in the resonance that pure language that is intended by all languages. And it would be the task of the critic to reveal, in a strategic arrangement of echoes, the original tones as elements of a wishful thinking. (*ET*, 35)

How similar is this "strategic place" to the very point of view or look-out (*Gesichtspunkt*) which produced the Centaur-songs in the first place—songs which, according to Hölderlin, are to be seen as a mythopoetic version or translation of natural science? From what postmodern perspective should we consider these mutants whose progenitor was born in the absence of the Graces, but who also taught Achilles how to play the lyre?

Too Many Harps: Enthusiasm Nowadays

> 'Raise, ye bards of other times,' continued the great Fingal, 'raise high the praise of heroes: that my soul may settle on their fame; that the mind of Swaran may cease to be sad.' They lay in the heath of Mora. The dark winds rustled over the chiefs. A hundred voices, at once, arose; a hundred harps were strung. They sung of other times; the mighty chiefs of former years! When now shall I hear the bard? When rejoice at the fame of my fathers? The harp is not strung on Morven. The voice of music ascends not on Cona. Dead, with the mighty, is the bard. Fame is in the desert no more.' [29]

> In 1994, Barney began work on his epic *CREMASTER* cycle, a five-part film project accompanied by related sculptures, photographs, and drawings. Eschewing chronological order, Barney first produced *CREMASTER 4* (1994), followed by *CREMASTER 1* (1995), *CREMASTER 5* (1997), and *CREMASTER 2* (1999). *CREMASTER 3* was completed this year [2002]. [30]

The postmodern may be seen a zone of infamy, (wretched) *ekstasis*, or brilliant apocalypse (elaborating things to their final "sculptural" clarity) at a secular remove from sobriety and nature as it once was or was supposed to be: i.e., sacred ground. We now sample the Centaur's song at two or three removes of siphoned-off derivation. With the imperative of shocking the beholder/reader into thought or reflection, performance art takes up its abode in ecstatic nature, once or twice separated from what we thought nature was, in artifice with an ecological edge, or in an alternative physis (beyond genre and gender stereotypes), asserting that the distinction between natural and unnatural is itself odious. The concept or the reasoning behind the actual work of art, and thus elucidating it, asserts its ugly, or at least no longer beautiful, preeminence. For such an age, the boldness and badness of Cowley seems ideally suited. In the so-called "CREMASTER series," the avant-garde conceptual artist Matthew Barney films himself and not-so-famous or famous others, like Norman Mailer, playing leading parts in a number of splashy, culturally "marked" and marketed locations, such as the harness track in Saratoga Springs, Giant's Causeway in Northern Ireland, Fingal's Cave, on Staffa, an island in the Scottish Hebrides, the cabin of a dirigible, a football field, the Chrysler Building, and the Guggenheim Museum. More eclectic and set- or prop-driven than pornographic, these works make use of many of many of the same "over the top" (Grand Guignol) and silent-movie effects used by Kenneth Anger in such works as *Scorpio Rising* (1963), whose title and content finds an intriguing intertext in Cowley's "Bull, Centaur, Scorpion, all the radiant monsters there," and *The Inauguration of the Pleasure Dome* (1966), and by Jack Smith in *Flaming Creatures* (1961). Anger and Smith were legendary film-makers known throughout the avant-garde and gay communities. Anger's later film relies heavily on the symbolism of pre-Christian and pagan religion: thus the borrowings from ancient Egypt (actors costumed as androgynous pharaohs) and witchcraft (the pentagram). The title alone reflects Coleridge's text—or the overall iciness, in the sense of bejeweled hedonism, of the "Oriental" pleasures there depicted. Such precursor texts are fairly tame and R-rated, however, when contrasted with the serialized, much gamier conceptualizations of Barney, who deploys myth at the level of obscene mutancy, but claims that he is being "sculptural" rather than pornographic.The cremaster is a muscle whose operation allows the retraction or extension of the testes. It comes into play, especially, in cold temperatures or fear-inducing circumstances:

> The *CREMASTER* cycle takes as its point of conceptual departure the male cremaster muscle which controls testicular contractions in response to external stimuli. The cycle circulates around anatomical conditions of 'ascension' or 'descension' to metaphorically describe the evolution of form through biological, psychosexual, and morphological allusions. Barney's *CREMASTER* cycle is an intricately interrelated symbolic system: the locations, characters, prosthetic effects, costumes, and sets portray an ever-evolving organism that thrives through competition with itself. (*GM*)

What is interesting, on the one hand, is that Barney incorporates into his cinematic texts not only the hidden physiology of the virile member, but a "new myth" concerning the origin of the Isle of Man—"Man" itself becoming something like an ironic, "emptied signifier" motivating a series of films which name themselves after a portion of the male anatomy— suggesting a postmodern recycling rather than a translation of the "Northern enchantment," with echoes in early Romanticism and the *faux* epic *Ossian* (whose original language, never published in a literal version by the "translator" Macpherson, was supposedly Gaelic):

> *CREMASTER 4* is set on the Isle of Man—a topographical body punctured by orifices and passageways—where a feverish motorbike race traverses the landscape, a dandified, tap-dancing satyr writhes his way through a treacherous underwater canal, and three burly, ambigendered fairies picnic on a grassy knoll. Part vaudeville, part Victorian comedy of manners, and part road-movie, this film portrays sheer drive in its eternal struggle to surpass itself. (*GM*)

In their Wagnerian, masque-like totalization of art "in and out of the body," the *CREMASTERS* may be approaching the limits of possibility in terms of the disillusioning of the Western tradition.Their equivocal, androgynous cavorting moves in the direction of that which is abysmally or even absurdly satyr- or satirical, testifying to the exigency of the ungraced. As David Farrell Krell asks in the context of Heidegger's take on Nietzsche,

> Everything in the hero's sphere turns to tragedy, everyting in the demigod's sphere turns to satyr-play, and everything in God's sphere turns to...what ? 'world' perhaps.?[31]

The "I" of Barney, if not the *logos*, is "with" the flesh, and the full-fan experience is *like* religion because it *likes* Barney. Liking something or someone is to want to be just like them, becoming victimized either by the "full fan-experience" or the alternately ludicrous and tragic inability to recapture the past, the necessity to make it say what it never said. As with Cowley and Hölderlin, the disappointment or melancholy is built in, in terms of the negativity of a fickleness interlocking with every full fan-experience. In Barney, however, becomes a matter of erectile reflex, circulation (from site to site), and parasitic digestion. The so-called cremaster-response, at the level of the id, serves as the mimetic equivalent of the eternal return staged by a tap-dancing "demigod."

The Internet has provided Barney's fans with an ideal medium for the communication of derivative enthusiasm, their own "full fan-experience," a parasitism or para-websitism in some respects similar to the Pindar craze of the later 17th and early 18th centuries, making Baudrillard's notion of the "ecstasy of communication" all the more relevant: "The schizo is bereft of every scene, open to everything in spite of himself, living in the greatest confusion. He is himself obscene, the obscene prey of the world of obscenity." Barney, however, flips ecstasy over into the possible appropriation of every scene, "making it," as promiscuously as possible, with the Western tradition, pop as well as "square" culture.

It has been said that Barney's films reflect Wagnerian ambition, but I would suggest that an equally relevant "source" is the late Renaissance masque, a multi-media *Gesamtkunstwerk* involving music, painting, poetry, sculptural decor, and a sophisticated awareness of itself as theatrical diversion. The postmodern masque at the same time systematizes excess or delivers it to a region of androgynous, mythic otherness where the play of satyrs, in equivocal regalia, permits itself a deterritorialized freedom of expression. Another analogue, in addition to Wagner, masque, and *Ossian*, can be found in the Jacobean-era teachers of Artaud, practitioners of the theatre of cruelty, Webster, Tourneur, and Fletcher. Surprise itself returns in Barney to a Renaissance of unseemly and wondrous humors, becoming liquid on a cosmic scale, spilling over into vaseline Valhallas. While remaining conceptual and/or sculptural, especially in their preference for tableau-like set-pieces, the *CREMASTERS* are not devoid of reflective consciousness. An entire lugubrious cosmos or "System of Melancholy"— something that would have to be analyzed in terms of an evident world-weariness and enthusiasm for the monstrously excessive, whose roots can be traced back to Cowley, the Baroque, and Shaftesbury—lends itself only too well to parasitizing by mutant armies of fans, the Cremasterfanatics, who are like flying fish in that they find in anatomy the apparatus for fairly low-level excursions beyond the liquid medium. Barney becomes the *CREMASTER*-host or mother-ship for an invasion of the Internet by Cremasterfanatics, or he is a white whale in league with some unspeakable ancient evil, more out of Lovecraft than Melville. Instead of crying out, like Fingal, for the bards of other times to raise high the praise of heroes, Barney stimulates the need on the part of groupies to participate in the highness of faux bardolatry, to make slavishly imitative mini-myths in the cult spirit of the great anti-Fingal, the CREMASTER of Disaster, in some ways equal to Warhol, but—mysteriously and inexplicably—uninterested in selling out. In 2005 Barney is either the corpse of the avant-garde or the radiant monster of its future.

In *The New York Times* of Sunday, January 2, 2005, section 2, page 2 appears a note describing a website entitled cremasterfanatic.com, created by New York media entrepreneur Eric Doeringer to praise the much more famous conceptual artist Barney and his films. For such examples of fairly low-flying enthusiasm, a new field of academic study, designated "smegmatics," paralleling studies of films of the soapy rather than celluoid kind,[32] does not seem entirely inappropriate:

> Pearl filled baths
> The pigeons flap
> His cremaster relaxes.

This, we will say, is the almost exact 21st-centiury equivalent of Cowley's Pindarism. The noticer, Choire Sicha, asks in parting:

> Is Cremaster Fanatic the first Warholian Web site? Mr. Doeringer said: 'I prefer to think of...what's his name? Uh...Andy Kaufman. With the best of his work, all the wrestling stuff, you were really never sure if it was made up or what was really happening. Mr. Doeringer is perhaps the first artist to work in the medium of enthusiasm: 'I'm getting the full fan experience,' he said.[33]

Doeringer, like Cowley before him, coopts the cult of the angelic original, creating little obscene (in the sense of beyond the actual show or series, as staged in the *CREMASTER* series) echo-texts of their own. Their medium, as Sicha suggests, is enthusiasm. Their Internet domain is that examined by Kenner in his study of counterfeiting, the realm of the "never really sure," which again is different from the garishly costumed and semiotically ambiguous mythological commitments of Anger or Barney himself. And, since the word communication derives from a Latin word meaning to fortify or build walls, it seems that the ecstasy of communication, through an Internet without walls, requires a new word to deal with it. We are perhaps living in an age like that of Europe in the late 18th century or Napoleonic period, when the medieval walls surrounding cities were demolished or preserved, in part, as tourist attractions, as in York or Vienna, a word like dilapidation but without pejorative connotation—not "creative destruction," equivocal in its politics, but perhaps "consensualist appropriation." Where Barney and his fans take us is to a region where art is no longer privileged, beauteous, or "fine," and the walls of the museum have vanished or been coopted as props. Here there is no battle of the books or skirmishing between ancients and moderns, because past as well as present have become "fair game," and questions about "authentic" as opposed to "inauthentic" need no longer be asked. There is only the evanescent, addictive substance of the "full fan-experience," in the sense of a low-flying, alien siphoning-off of antecedent enchantment, as if from an earthling brain, the parasitizing of art's exquisite corpse. This is not so different from the situation in which an *Ossian* might capitalize on the stuff or *Stoff* of Celtic legend in the popular imagination, with much of literary Europe "tuning in" to ersatz harpings beyond the reach of philology and antiquated notions of originality and authority. The derivative quality of Cowley, Barney, and *Ossian*—that product of a centaur-like mind—seems to place Baumgarten's definition of art, as a kind of "lower knowledge" or *gnoseologia inferior*, in capital letters, as literary form become "sculptural" content. The proliferation of media "outlets" can only hasten a process of leveling in which fifteen minutes spent on "this" *Ossian*-like replica are seen as equivalent to the next fifteen minutes spent on "that." "Surprise me" may be a phrase still heard in casting and program development, yet translated into the language of ecstatic communication, it means "get me someone/something like...."

However, because the fate of translation, as we see it now, is to be delivered, especially in North America, to the "full fan-experience," it follows that the Kants to come will have to reckon with the logic not only of disinterested pleasure (*interesseloses Wohlgefallen*), but also of "interested displeasure" (or *"interessiertes Mißfallen,"* a concept not found in any Kantian critique), since the inevitable corollary of fifteen minutes' worth of adulation is a disaffection born in the sixteenth minute, and the heroes/heroines (whether Tasso or Cowley, DiMaggio or Christo and Jeanne-Claude) currently being lionized[34] fall prey tomorrow to the fickleness of the once adoring mob: "durch einen Hauch, in einem Augenblick" ("through a breath, in a moment"). A "Bronx cheer" has been for some time the *mene tekel* not only of the batter in a slump, but of yesterday's avant-garde. What Adorno once celebrated as the kernel of the ephemeral in modernism finds itself cooked in a Conceptualist *kitsch*en as spicier slices of the past.

What relevance do Cowley's virtuosity, his "radiant monsters" shining in post-Olympian space, and the Pindaric enthusiasm have to all of this? Do we need criteria to separate what is remarkable, surprising, and gracelessly ungainly—still in the domain of "You're never really sure"—from the glut of that which is surely deadening, "Reality" TV shows and the like? A positive answer requires that we have both the "ecstasy of communication" and critics like Samuel Johnson and High Kenner, if for nothing else than the discrimination of varying degrees of incertitude concerning the natural and the man-made and for the critical distance required to gain perspective on our postmodernist simulacra. We need to know why *Chevy Chase* is not the epic Addison thought it was and why *Liquid Sky* is both a bad film and a cult classic. The mass media, on the other hand, do not discriminate; they, like the pharmaceutical industry, foster group addiction to "products" designed to obviate surprise and alleviate the pain of being human. The addiction of the "full-fan experience," since it encapsulates and reproduces something which at least calls itself experience, is superior. Radiant monsters are rarely found in literature—something like finding the first reference to team sports in literary criticism, where the battle of the books, controversies between "substantial Divines or grave Philosophers," academic dog- or horse-men with sharp teeth—there where the human comes into contact with animal not on the way up but on the way down—is compared to a game of football played down on the street by adolescent "fans," but which is initiated by an entrepreneur who derives an unstated economic interest from the seemingly anarchic breaking of windows:

> ...finally 'by long worrying one another, they are grown out of breath, and have almost lost their Force of Biting—'So have I known a crafty *Glazier*, in time of Frost, to procure a *Foot-ball*, to draw into the street the emulous Chiefs of the Robust Youth. The tumid Bladder bounds at every kick, bursts the withstanding *Casements*, ...*Lanterns*, and all the brittle vitrous *Ware*. The Noise of Blows and Out-Crys fills the whole Neighborhood; and ruins of Glass cover the stony Pavements; till the bloated battering Engine, subdu'd by Force of Foot and Fist, and yielding up its Breath at many a fatal Cranny, becomes lank and harmless, sinks in its Flight, and can no longer uphold the Spirit of the contending Partys.[35]

As to what enthuses/inflates the humidly "human" as opposed to the inhuman, and the definition of a-not-yet-determined (*bestimmt*) *humanitas*, Nietzsche may be allowed to state a dissonant case concerning the "fog" of inherited, authoritative definitions propounded by pundits and pedagogues:

> Dieser Nebel von Meinungen und Gewöhnungen wächst und lebt fast unabhängig von den Menschen, die er einhüllt, in ihm liegt die ungeheure Wirkung allgemeiner Urteile über 'den Menschen', alle diese sich selber unbekannten Menschen glauben an das blutlose Abstraktum 'Mensch', das heißt an eine Fiktion; und jede Veränderung, die mit diesem Abstraktum vorgenommen word, durch die Urteile einzelner Mächtiger (wie Fürsten und Philosophen), wirkt außerordentlich und in unvernünftigem Maße auf die große Mehrzahl,—alles aus dem Grunde, daß jeder einzelne in dieser Mehrzahl kein wirkliches, ihm zugängliches und von ihm ergründetes *ego* der allgemeinen blassen Fiktion entgegenzustellen und sie damit zu vernichten vermag.[36]
>
> [This fog of opinions and habituations grows and lives almost independently of the human beings that it enshrouds; within it lies the uncanny impact of general judgments concerning 'the human'; all these human beings, who remain unknown to themselves, believe in the bloodless abstraction 'human being,' that is, in a fiction; and each change, which is undertaken with respect to this abstraction, through the judgments of individual potentates (such as princes and philosophers), has an extraordinary impact on the great majority—all of this having as its basis <the fact> that each individual in this majority has no actual *ego*, accessible to and founded by him <or her>, to oppose to the general, pale fiction and thereby to destroy it.]

In a zone of indeterminacy as to what constitutes the "bloodless abstraction" that we call "a human being," Nietzsche encounters the figure on the chasm wall at the end of *The Narrative of A. Gordon Pym.* The question posed by Kenner, as to the criteria needed to tell the copy from the "real thing," the mechanical duck from the quacking replica, can no longer be answered with anything like certainty, since the very distinction, as John Irwin suggests, is man-made and thus a matter of certainty as we, you, or I *like* it:

> ...Pym's and Peters' uncertainty about whether the markings are natural or man-made reflects a deeper uncertainty inherent in the very opposition between nature and art— a constitutive uncertainty that the markings in the chasm are intended to exhibit. Though the hieroglyphic figure on the wall evokes a language whose characters are necessarily natural shapes rather than arbitrary, man-made signs, the very fact that the hieroglyph in this case is the representation of a human figure tends to make the 'natural/man-made' distinction problematic. For it suggests, on the one hand, that since man is as naturally occurring an object as trees or rocks or rivers, his arbitrary designs, the traces of human movements, are just as much natural shapes as are leaves or fissures or erosions; and it suggests, on the other hand, that the concept of the 'natural,' as a function of the differential opposition 'natural/man-made,' is itself something man-made.[37]

In recent fiction, Haruki Murakami's *Wind-Up Bird Chronicle* suggests other ways in which the distinction between natural and unnatural may have outlived its usefulness; the narrator who at the beginning of the text observes birds in his backyard that seem like artificial birds "winding the spring of his neighborhood" becomes "Mr. Wind-Up Bird" at in the final chapter; states of ecstatic being, of lives reassembled out of genes, lives relived in other lives, lives programmed in advance by obscure forces beyond our control, no longer occasion wonder. Characters are screens for the projection of other texts or, as David Mitchell has the metafictional Luisa Ray, a mystery-writer whose name is shadowed by a Thornton Wilder novel, say, "lunatics are writers whose works write them."[38]

One likes to think that on a spaceship centuries from now, in a future for which the terms "art" and "human" have some more exquisite, exotic meaning because everyone is him- or herself and nanotechnically or neuromantically "other," both graceless and gratuitously engineered or "gifted," when "Fame is in the desert no more," astronauts will want words to describe the scintillating surprises they are hurtling toward in a "bold Coach" that makes the starship *Enterprise* look like an Edsel and discover, on what passes in that distant time for an Internet, the phrase of a half-horsed *caballero*: "all the radiant monsters there."

4. The Full Fan-Experience Revisited: From the Arabesque to Kafka on the Shore

> *...the huntsmen are up in America, and they are already past their first sleep in Persia....*
> Thomas Browne

> *That the chaos was harmonised, has been recited of old; but whence the different sounds arose, remained for a modern to discover....*
> Samuel Johnson, *Preface to Abraham Cowley*

> *She derived, however, great consolation, (during the tightening of the bowstring) from the reflection that much of the history remained still untold, and that the petulance of the brute of a husband had reaped for him a most righteous reward, in depriving him of many inconceivable adventures.*
> Edgar A. Poe, "The Thousand-and-Second Tale of Scheherazade"

> *'I long afflicted myself as to what those words meant, when I might easily have asked and found out.'*
> William Dean Howells on the terms "grotesque" and "arabesque"

In a series of seminars and lectures[1] the eminent novelist John Barth argues for an apparent correlation, among other things, between the Romantic theory of the arabesque, Oriental rugs, and chaos theory. The major sources for Barth's analysis of the Romantic arabesque are the theoretical writings of Friedrich Schlegel, together with his novel *Lucinde* (1799), where the word "chaos" occurs with some frequency, and the mathematics of Benoit Mandelbrot, who gave us fractal geometry in the late seventies.[2] Barth suggests that there are two meanings for arabesque: "in the oldest sense...the term refers to an Arabo-Oriental tradition of figuration that predates Islam" (*FF*, 311) and such a figural tradition is found in textiles: "...a main border or frame, secondary borders that may interpenetrate the main border, and a framed field with four corner elements and a central medallion with pendants top and bottom that to my eyes look quite a lot like Mandelbrot fractals" (*FF*, 312–313). In the newer sense introduced to literature by the German Romantics, "...the significant European appropriation from Arabo-Oriental literature and art history is not subject matter but design: 'arabesque' in the sense of elaborately and/or subtly *framed* design" (*FF*, 318). What is meant by this is the notion that fiction, seen by Schlegel as a "gebildetes künstliches Chaos" or "constructed artificial chaos," becomes delimited, infinitized on a macro- and microcosmic scale, through the Scheherazade-like process of finding a story within a story, or through an elevation in the level of abstractness applicable not only to Schlegel, but to every novel which draws its own narrative process into question or seeks actively to undermine it (Sterne and Jean Paul) by authorial intrusion or aberration. Schlegel cites *Tristram Shandy* and Diderot's *Jacques le fataliste* (smuggled out of France into Germany and translated, in part, by Schiller) as examples, but Barth is able to show how the practice of arabesque is equally relevant to *fin-de-20ème-siécle* meta-fiction. After making some remarks on Barth's text, the arabesque in Runge and some pertinent meta- or intertexts, most notably, those by Coover and Grass, we will briefly consider David Mitchell's *Ghostwritten* (whose title mutates to *Chaos* in the German-language edition), his recent and, to my mind, more aesthetically "pleasing" *Cloud Atlas*, and Haruki Murakami's *Kafka on the Shore* as meta-fictions in some ways measuring up to Schlegel's prescription of the "artificially constructed" chaos and in others diverging significantly from it.

Meta-fiction implies a text or collection of texts utilizing the technique of story within a story or frame within a frame (Romantic irony), as in *The Arabian Nights*. But there would also be a *meta* of meta-fiction, that which lies "beyond" the horizon of the text in the sense of events occurring in the "real" world where nature and civilizations interact, from one abstractly conceived "nation" to the next, where baseball cap, and all that it implies, encounters turban. Equally, the telling of *The Arabian Nights* prolongs itself by linking one story with the next, one exotic dream with another. Scheherazade's famous fictions have as their intended effect the preservation of the storyteller's own life beyond a single night into the dawn of a new day, followed by another night in which to tell yet another tale. If she told the same tale twice, she would likely not live long beyond the act of reiteration. Repetition of the same, in cooking, storytelling, or painting, is the one unpardonable sin.

Equally, beyond or behind the curtain of the arabesque, lies the unpredictable *terra incognita* of the Arab, *Arabia deserta*, of *The Arabian Nights* in one or more Western translations, for those without Arabic.[3] There, too, behind or beneath the textile surface, can be imagined the receptive, proprioceptive, or appropriative intelligence of a West whose poetry and/or wisdom begins in the East, that which our literature and religion inevitably look toward, if we believe (in) the Romantics. Mandelbrot's theory, on the other hand, while it shows remarkable tolerance for the chimeras of mathematics that made its own progress possible, is not a theory of fiction, but a mathematical attempt to account for nature "from the ground up," and for the history of real markets, from one level of scale or complexity to the next. But it is not at all certain that the universe "out there," in the uncannily natural/unnatural "world" beyond meta-fiction, obeys a fractal "logic" of repetitive structure rather than a principle of metamorphosis and unpredictability. Among the more egregious heresies that Mandelbrot believes he has eradicated by mathematical proof are the random or Brownian motion of molecules and the discontinuity of Riemann space.[4] Thus, to put things succinctly, Mandelbrot, if not the Scheherazade of the natural order of things—each equation limning a different chapter of the fractal epic—qualifies as a regulative instance amid the more controversial fictions of a mathematical Dodge City/Islamabad. If this is so, then an element of diegesis may play a role, even if it is only a subordinating or hierarchizing one.

Inscribed as the *meta* of Barth's arguments, which, to be fair, do not aim at encyclopedic completeness, but are intended as a provocation to thought and dialogue with students and readers, such as myself, are issues of the ground or *Grund*—many of which are treated on an altogether different philosophical basis in Foucault's *Les mots et les choses*—that transcend periodization: human nature and nurture, language and the unconscious, Orientalism, imperialism, and the perennial complications (old as Herodotus) of East–West relations, literary and otherwise—issues raised in the work of the late Edward Said. With amazing understatement, Barth calls the West's fascination with the East "...an impressive and ambivalent phenomenon" (*FF*, 319), noting the role played by trader-adventurers such as Marco Polo and Christopher Columbus (Cristóbal Colón). But Marco Polo is a Venetian, immersed in the labyrinthine, canal-like, or fractal logic of his time; Columbus is an Italian pirate/entrepreneur in the service of the Queen of Spain—one whose impact upon the indigenous peoples of the Caribbean, whom he called "Indians," was unequivocally catastrophic, whose economic rationalization has a name, slavery, an institution or ethical dysfunction that is also the undeniable subtext of the Scheherazade stories. Implicit within chaotic histories—more chaotic for those on the receiving end of advanced technology—lies the descent into a catastrophic negativity and unpredictabilty which mar the map, so to speak, of Western as well as Eastern enterprise:

'As you know, we live in a violent and chaotic world. And within this world, there are places that are still more violent, still more chaotic.'[5]

The actual shape or space of catastrophe, projected in real time, from cusp to swallow-tail, may be other than geometric, just as different universes, each with its own level of chaos and terror, may exist simultaneously and side by side.[6] Would Barth be willing to concede that Sterne, Diderot, Schlegel, to a certain degree, but above all Jean Paul, are *satirical* authors and hence interested in the art of provoking their readers to critical questions—in the best Enlightenment tradition—regarding themselves and the metaphysical certainties of the civilization in which they currently live?

To return things to a literary-philosophical level of complexity, the Romantic arabesque suggests absolute subjectivity, that which has been called, with some equivocation, no doubt, the "literary absolute" In the term "absolute" lies the notion of a dissolution of subject- and objectivity, not a dissolution into the Void, but a fusion of self and other in a landscape prodigiously and flagrantly filled—"teeming," as Barth says—not only with other *things*, animal, vegetable and mineral, but with other *beings*, some visible, some not. It is not as if one can limit or close off the arabesque, as Schlegel, Novalis, and others may have conceived of it, from the intrusion of the other, the universe "down here," wearing a sometimes Medusa-like visage, and the one that we think or believe is "out" or "up there," in a region populated by salamanders, nymphs, sylphs, fairies, and space aliens. Indeed, a Romantic painter like Philipp Otto Runge specifically alludes to the visual text as a "boundaryless illumination of the universe" and sets himself the uncanny task of "painting the invisible," something which was not at all uncommon in the Middle Ages or Renaissance, but which is revolutionary at the time (1809) because it omits reference to a Supreme Being, while incorporating a mélange of biblical and pagan "characters," including a female goddess entirely unlike the Mary of the New Testament and an infant who is more earthbound, still enshadowed "Holy Child" than baby Jesus, and is thus, in totalizing, secular displacement, not so much a-theistic as polymorphously, excessively, even egregiously, theistic.

That, as they say, was then, more than two hundred years ago, at a time of epochal shifts in philosophical and literary consciousness following a century of unparalleled advancement in human thought. That light coming out of obscurity has, in our time, been threatened by totalitarian eclipse and a return to sectarian darkness. Can critics, novelists, and poets speak meaningfully today in terms of a formalism in which Katherine Hayles's notion of the "denaturing of context" is taken as the primary criterion of aesthetic merit or does this artificially constructed chaos of textile and text somehow relate to that socially, economically, and religiously motivated "meta-" of meta-fiction, whose "arabesque" origin is double or Janus-faced: on the one hand, generated, much more equivocally than any Oriental carpet, in "finite areas surrounded by infinitely long borders" (*FF*, 316), i. e., spun forth *by women* in the bazaars of such historically constructed entities as Afghanistan and Pakistan and from the mullah's harangues of Iran, Saudi Arabia, and Iraq, while, on the other, produced in the alternately dream-like and nightmarish marketing proclivities of Europe from the 13th to the 20th century? Why should the opportunistically "rational" West be concerned with sectarian violence erupting in border zones between tribes still living (we think) in the Middle Ages, unless they project resentful, medallion-like figures of "piety and ruthlessness"[7] woven into the mercantile fabric of our infinitival, chaotically teeming, Hobbesian present—unless they have become part of the dream-like projection of that which is Other, posing a threat to national survival, and thus branded "evil," according to the demagogic *sermo* of political Scheherazades delivering their sound-bites (tuned to the frequency of political survival) for the insatiable satellite "feeds" of infotaining media? How large is the carpet and how many naked games and grounds of exploitation, past, present, and future, does this rug cover on the way from the 18th-century notion of a nation-state to the new globalism? Why should we wonder about the fractal quality of fiction and textiles unless it affects us "where we live," somewhere between the front door and the gas pump, between Wall Street and home plate, from *Misbehaving Markets: A Fractal View of Risk, Ruin, and Reward* (title of a recent work by Mandelbrot) to the drama played out on an artificially constructed, geometrically conceived field of (political) dreams? After discussing the piracy of peoples living along the northern coast of Africa and the inhospitability of *Arabia deserta*, Kant, following the best Enlightenment tradition, discusses the Pandora's box opened by the West's dream of economic expansion:

> But to this perfection [of an ideal world-state brought under the rule of law] compare the inhospitable actions of the civilized and especially of the commercial states of our part of the world. The injustice which they show to lands an people they visit (which is equivalent to conquering them) is carried by them to terrifying lengths. America, the lands inhabited by the Negro, the Spice Islands, the Cape, etc., were at the time of their discovery considered by these civilized intruders as lands without owners, for they counted the inhabitants as nothing. In East India (Hindustan), under the pretense of establishing economic undertakings they brought in foreign soldiers and used them to oppress the natives, excited widespread wars among the various states, spread famine, rebellion, perfidy, and the whole litany of evils which afflict mankind. [8]

If the postmodern is "disaffected" in its eschewing of "lived experience," as Jameson says it is, and if Barth takes us from fiction to metafiction, from nature to a Haylesian denaturing, we might want to examine how we arrived at such a state seemingly out of touch with the impassioned premises of *Naturphilosophie*, specifically and most prominently, that of the early Schelling, and the metaphysical projections of German (and American) Romantics. Does the fractal, as Barth applies it to Schlegel and the Oriental carpet, really *refer* to reality in the same way that Mandelbrot uses it to account for the smoothnesses and roughnesses of disparate, altogether *real* phenomena? Can it deal with the cross-border, discipline-melding traffic of ideas informing the Romantic arabesque, above all, in its refracted, fractional, fragmentary proximity to the satirical and the grotesque? The arabesque and the grotesque go "hand in hand," so to speak, in almost every major text of the period, especially those (as in Jean Paul) where fiction goes "over the top," into a zone not only of Scheherazade-like excess, holding entire *Lesezirkel* spellbound in tearful readership (an early version of the full fan-experience, "fleshed out" and vulgarized in the theatre of mesmerism), but of encyclopedic and emancipatory *satire* on its more or less equivocal path of criticizing the grotesque socioeconomic status quo.[9]

Thus a certain turbulence or dissonance becomes evident in the equivocal inscriptions of absolute subjectivity, precisely there where writing (*Schrift*), and picture (*Bild*) intersect, or where *Schrift* becomes poetic *Ton* (sound), on the grid of pain and pleasure, in the grotesque, the arabesque, and the hieroglyphic, and in the problematic claim of the citizen-subject to assert its revolutionary prerogative in a religious sense or with the sense of religious awe (and thus to gather a tribe of fans at, near, beside, or in front of the temple) in the dawn of a new philosophic art—when a sound, like a drum in the jungle or a guitar string, coming from who knows where, becomes audible. And such a *novel*, surprising, disruptive sound, tenor, or *tone* does not lack a paradigm—one found not in mathematics, but in that most "romantically" transcendent of arts, closely related to mathematics: music. It lies in the contest between Athena and Marsyas, a contest judged by the inventor of the lyre, Apollo, when the goddess, upon seeing the reflection of herself in the water while playing the flute, and the ungainly, grotesque manner in which her cheeks are distended in order to create a violent force of wind, throws the instrument away in disgust[10] The fate of the satyr turned flute-player who loses the contest is that of being skinned alive. Embedded in the satirical itself, as the critique of beauteous appearance, and the beginning of critical thought, is the strident surplus of a dissonant "word" or "sound" which goes grinning or grimacing to its own funereal flaying, whose music, in performance, is anything but harmonious or beautiful. As Nietzsche reminds us, one name for this raucous sound is "passion" (*Leidenschaft*). Has something like passion and the uncanny, ambiguously Dionysian figure of "The Natural" (title of a baseball novel by Bernard Malamud with Romantic overtones, though by no means a meta-fiction), as opposed to the inhuman, been omitted from the abstract and at times uneven field of aesthetico-political play? Then, in an altogether different epochal context, provided for us by Baudelaire,[11] can we disregard Poe's claim to represent the arabesque, in terms of a coolly malign Romanticism at the end-point or omega of terrific dissonance, in a collection (published at almost exactly the same moment, in the early 1840s, as Lane's expurgated, abridged, and extremely popular translation of *The Arabian Nights*, and the "official" rules of the equally popular game known as baseball entitled *Tales of the Grotesque and Arabesque*—to the extent that if Poe, Baudelaire's anti-bourgeois *sauvage* or *dandy*, had written a sports story it might have been called "The Un-" or "The Supernatural"?[12]

From the tone or tenor of that which is both natural and unnatural at once, and thus equivocal and uncanny in a Freudian sense, springs the excessive, terror-margined cohabitation of the arabesque, the grotesque, and the hieroglyphic—that which in all likelihood can be covered or converted to a rug-like surface only if passion (as *Liebe* and *Leidenschaft*, especially in Schlegel) is woven out of the denatured context. At the same time, the very notion of the arabesque "in the West," as made by Barth and the scholars he cites, may coincide very will both with the Romantics' program of a progressive universal poesy and with the Kantian project of a world brought under the rule of enlightened reason. For now (this is written in 2005), we are forced to read *with* Poe, if only for the appreciative "dose" of jaundiced acumen he brings to our estimation of the terms arabesque and grotesque.

Take as one pole of this satirical, saturated, satyr- or medley-like disturbance the claim of the Romantic ego to be supreme or godlike; assume as the other a descent into farce or sublimely delusion—the *torquato* aspect of *Torquato Tasso*, the *furioso* element of *Faust*, the insanity of the first-person narrator in Gogol's "arabesque" tale, *The Diary of a Madman*. Despite the fact that Schlegel's protagonist at one point in *Lucinde* praises sleep for its godlike passivity, aspiring, so the text says, to a state of intelligence equally meditative and vegetative, the aesthetic style suggested by this mystical disappearance of the self into the Void is just the opposite of the tendril-like, calligraphic projections of the arabesque. It is "greatness" (or "sublimity") seen in terms of sculptural stasis and "vegging out":

Gleich einem Weisen des Orients war ich ganz versunken in ein heiliges Hinbrüten und ruhiges Anschauen der ewigen Substanzen, vorzüglich der deinigen und der meinigen. Größe in Ruhe, sagen die Meister, sei der höchste Gegenstand der bildenden Kunst; und ohne es deutlich zu wollen oder mich unwürdig zu bemühen, bildete und dichtete ich auch meine ewigen Substanzen in diesem würdigen Stil.[13]

[Like a wiseman of the Orient I was completely absorbed in a holy meditation and tranquil intuition of the eternal substances, primarily of yours and of mine. The masters say that the highest goal of sculptural art is greatness in quietude, and without wishing it blatantly or to bestir myself in an unworthy manner, I sculpted and poetically expressed my eternal substances in this worthy style]

A dialectic of dignity and lack of dignity, derived at some ironic distance from Winckelmann and Schiller's "Anmut und Würde," but represented in terms of a self in anguished interior monologue about its own "style," even to the point of a certain schizophrenia, pervades Schlegel's text. Equally, there is the observation, made in an earlier generation of criticism, prior to the dawn of postmodernism, that in Novalis, along with Schlegel the most influential theorist of the fragment and literary "Unendlichkeit," "desire, religion, and cruelty"[14] are commingled, and that Romantic sadomasochism has its source in inordinate or grotesque desire—something that is "...im Guten wie im Schlechten kräftiger, wilder, kühner, ungeheurer... [...in the good as well as in the bad, stronger, wilder, bolder, uncannier....]," as the narrator says of his future (presumably reincarnated) life in Schlegel's *Lucinde* (*L*, 104). Thus the Romantic arabesque insinuates something more problematically self-referential and dramatizing than vegetative stasis or the disappearance into an Orientalized Void, something which will culminate in the last gasp of the new mythology, a Nietzschean "dawn" and a text calling itself *The Birth of Tragedy*. Poe, it seems, is a crucial figure, certainly larger than Friedrich Schlegel in his importance to *Weltliteratur*, but noteworthy in the context of the grotesque, the arabesque, and, especially, the hieroglyphic as a far more than merely transitional figure between the first generation of German Romanticism, Baudelaire, and the Dionysiac otherness of Nietzsche. In Poe, the arabesque and the grotesque become functions not of the "Far" Orientalism of the Persian rug, but of the "near" Orientalism of the Egyptian hieroglyphic, while both the grotesque and the arabesque are made subordinate to the "legitimation" of *literary* terror, a design not without relevance to the symptomatology of the present moment in East–West relations. Of course, the near and the far exist in some sort of unstable dynamic, but the critical step toward that synthesis should, I would suggest, only be taken after the privileging of the hieroglyphic sign in Romantic art—that which must, like every book, be *read* and not merely beheld—and the unreliability or undecidability of narration—posed, precisely, as a problem of articulation and hermeneutical subjectivity (*who* is speaking/interpreting)—is considered:

Und was ist jede schöne Mythologie anders als ein hieroglyphischer Ausdruck der umgebenden Natur in dieser Verklärung von Phantasie und Liebe?[15]
[And what is every beautiful mythology but a hieroglyphic expression of surrounding nature in this transfiguration of fantasy and love?]

Thus, even with Barth's "pure" definition of the two kinds of arabesque in mind, we are left with the question, what exactly is the meaning of "arabesque"? How seriously or lightly did the Romantics—should we—take it? In what sense is it "Arab" as opposed to or embedded in "the Oriental"? Or is it only the "Arab-like" or what we take, from our (post)-colonial perspective, to be, still, like an "Arab" in the thousand-and-one resensings of that tribal word? Is there not something, or a good deal, that is left "in the air," so to speak, in the equivocal "nature" of the "Arabesque," which allows it to be used, say, to define a certain literary text, like *Lucinde*, with its "artificially constructed chaos," but also to critique (rightly or wrongly) a specific text of hieroglyphic visual art, such as Runge's *The Times of Day*, which from the beginning generates, equivocally, for better and for worse, the enthusiasm of a more or less arabesque and thus more or less grotesque "full fan-experience"? And is not this equivocation a hallmark, specifically, of a textuality which aims in Novalis, Schlegel, and Runge at nothing less than the "boundaryless illumination of the universe," and is thus to a greater or lesser degree always equivocal in its generation/genre and nearly always revolutionary or emancipatory in its import?

Barth at one point acknowledges the duplicity of the "arabesque" in its problematic nearness to the related term "grotesque," a feature, above all, of Baroque art, but which has relevance to the all- or only too American Poe:

> Speaking of Edgar Poe's 1840 framed-tale collection called *Tales of the Grotesque and Arabesque*, and of the assumption by Poe critics that 'grotesque' refers to the comic stories and 'arabesque' to the serious ones, Thompson argues that for the German Romantics by whom Poe was influenced, 'each term has a double meaning, and each definition shares some properties of the other.' The two modes share a tendency to juxtapose disparate, even contradictory elements of humor and horror, illusion and realitiy, the realistic and the fantastic, the sublime and the vulgar.
>
> (*FF*, 288)

Nothing, that is, could be more equivocal than a "mode" which does nothing but juxtapose or mix one thing with another. And would not the borderless infinity and equivocal literariness of the word "arabesque" present us with something, at least in its crowd appeal, different from that which is mathematically verifiable and hence perspicuously, geometrically, or generically representable in or as nature? Something which, to quote a phrase by Margaret Fuller, the "monster" Muse of all things translatable in the 1840s, is luminous and equivocally mythic in its bold and unhallowed "crossing of the day," which both eradicates obscurity, in order to grab hold of us—our eyes wide-open and unblinking at the spectacle—and places flamboyant E(r)os, hieroglyphically, between the celestial lily and the yet obscured earthly "babe"? And would not this oscillating something, whose "Blick" is a seizing "Augenblick," read more like a text than a fractally mappable rug?[16]

New Mythology and Team Spirit: From *Cityoyen* to Fan

Oh say, can you see by the dawn's early light....?
Francis Scott Key, from "The National Anthem"

'...I get off here....' David Mitchell, *Ghostwritten*

Whether we wish to think in literary-historical terms are not, we are forced to confront a rupture between Novalis, Schlegel, and the "Scheherzades" of fiction, Sterne, Diderot, and Jean Paul, who may have used "arabesque" with one kind of literary equivocation in mind, and the next generation of writers who use "arabesque," even more loosely, in close proximity to the grotesque. These slippages in the meaning of the term from one generation of Romantics to the next, or subtle shifts of emphasis within Schlegel's own epoch, cannot be dealt with in the limited space allotted to Barth in a semester or two—in seminars where seed-like links between *Lucinde* and postmodern metafiction are proposed. A German critic of the generation preceding postmodernism, Ricarda Huch, somewhat more attuned to dissonance and equivocation on the part of contemporary critics, elucidated some specific nuances in texts dating from the postwar period gathered together under the title "Literaturgeschichte und Literatur-Kritik." Her discussion of the art-historical context is presented here as a supplement to Barth's examination of the theme in literature:

> Die Kunstkritiker, die nach Runges frühem Tode das Wort über ihn ergriffen, betonten alle, daß seine Kunst eine Kunst der Arabeske sei. In der modernen Literatur ist es nicht anders: viele Bücher gleichen reizenden Arabesken, denen nichts fehlt als der feste Kern, den sie umranken sollten. Zierat, Dekoration, was als krönender Schmuck aus dem Stamme herauswächst, ist selbstständig geworden und schwankt als ein befremdendes Wunder in der Luft. 'Und wie sollen wir die Weise nennen in der diese Bilder gedacht erscheinen?' Mit diesen Worten beschließt der Mystiker Görres seine begeisterte Besprechung des verstorbenen Malers. 'Sollen wir die Arabesken heißen? Wir würden ihm unrecht tun, indem wir, was tiefer Ernst und Sinn gebildet, vergleichen mit dem, was bloß aus spielendem Scherz einer heitern Phantastik hervorgegangen. Die Arabeske ist Waldblume in dem Zauberlande, die höhere Kunst aber windet Kränze aus den Blumen und kränzt damit die Götterbilder. Nennen wir sie lieber daher Hieroglyphik der Kunst, plastische Symbolik.'[17]
>
> [The art critics who spoke of Runge after his early death all emphasized that his art was an art of the arabesque. In modern literature things have not gone differently: many books are comparable to charming arabesques, in which nothing is missing except the solid center, which they ought to be framing with their foliage, adornment, decoration, that which grows out of the stem as <the> crowning jewel, has become independent and hovers in the air like an alienating wonder. 'And how are we to name the manner in which these images appear <to have been> thought?' With these words the mystic Görres closes his spirited discussion of the deceased painter. 'Ought we to call them arabesques? We would do him an injustice by comparing that which

was shaped by deep seriousness and meaning with that which proceeds merely from the playful levity of a jovial fantasy. The arabesque is a forest flower in wonderland, but higher art weaves crowns out of flowers and crowns the images of gods with them. Let us name them rather hieroglyphics of art, <an art of> plastic symbolism.']

"The manner" in which Runge's arabesques "appear to have been thought"—the pictorial equivalent of that which has been termed the "literary absolute," can be seen as asserting something rather different from the self-immolative strategies of postmodernism and the abstraction of the Oriental carpet. It is in the translation of the script or letter into a *Bild*, a hieroglyphic picture, glyph, or map, that Romantic literature continues to pose important questions to us in its unique and bold (de)sign. On or within this field of dreams and its *interpretation*, the human, *qua* figure, is both celebrated and transcended in a series of alphabetical notations, like so many X's and O's. Likewise, Runge's texts seem to be accompanied from the outset by a *Begeisterung* (a "haunting" by fervent admirers, such as Görres and Schellling) which has its "natural" (but also artificial, morose, and/or melancholic) efflorescence in séances, mesmerizings, and occult associations from the New World to India and beyond. Runge, above all, "lived" where *Schrift*, profane and holy at once, and *Bild* shared a unitary painterly and philosophical field, on a ground (*Grund*) one where one or more post-Enlightenment *jeux d'esprit* or intellectual athleticisms might begin in earnest.

Romanticism's interdisciplinary dream, represented in the fragments of Novalis and Schlegel, might have been to transcend or dissolve the boundaries of genre, so as to inaugurate the equivocal *satura* of the literary absolute; its Faustian or alchemical bargain was that of comprehending the unity of microcosm and macrocosm through an occult mathesis, a unity founded on number symbolism and theosophical algebra—a crown of human knowledge to be placed on the head of the imaged or imagined macrocosm. That is why Coleridge, upon reading Thomas Browne's enthusiastic recommendation of the number five as a "master" number for explaining the mysteries of the universe, exclaims, "Quincunxes in heaven above, quincunxes in earth below!" and why Novalis can write, "Echte Mathematik ist das eigentliche Element des Magiers" ["Genuine mathematics is the genuine element of the magician"].[18] In the Renaissance, when philology and natural science were regarded equally as "accomplishments" on the part of a scholar, alchemists, such as Böhme and Browne, thought it essential to *read* nature in terms of a hieroglyphic script or writing; experimentation, prior to modern mathematics, was primarily a *literary* pursuit; the "cabalistical" interpretation of the Bible, Homer, and Hesiod. Hebrew, Egyptian, and Greek letters were supposed to provide access to knowledge of nature (as Leibniz also proposes) in both its infinite and infinitesimal aspects—the same "great chain of being" that Mandelbrot maps with an altogether different degree of scientific rigor, though acknowledging its precursors in the fantastic/fanatical rescalings of Swift, among others. Romantic and Renaissance theosophists did not label their literal-geometrical chimeras fractal; in fragmentary texts they call upon "influences" to descend on a transmutational ladder from one element to the next, from one world to the other, *disposing* matter in a synthesis of the philosophical and philological imagination and *spelling* it anew. It is in this "natural supernaturalism," as Abrams terms it, that the German Romantics and many in the century before are born and bred. Translation begins where worlds collide, where writing imitates nature, as in primitive Chinese, Chaldean, and Egyptian hieroglyphs; "X" marks the chiastic spot on the operator's map before being "reflected" or translated into a circle:

> And if Egyptian philosophy may obtain, the scale of influences was thus disposed, and the genial spirits of both worlds do trace their way in ascending and descending pyramids, mystically apprehended in the letter 'X' and the open bill and straddling legs of a stork, which was imitated by that character.
>
> Of this figure Plato made choice to illustrate the motion of the soul, both of the world and man, while he delivereth that God divided the whole conjunction lengthwise, according to the figure of a Greek [chi] 'X' and then turning it about reflected it into a circle; by the circle implying the uniform motion of the first orb, and by the right-lines the planetical and various motions within it. [19]

The scriptural-geometrical operation of reflecting (drawing) or translating the Greek letter *chi*, X, into a circle demonstrates what we might today call the faculty of philosophical reflection. Browne goes on to elaborate what amounts to a primitive version of apperception and the Kantian *Ur-teil*. As in post-Kantian philosophy, be it that of Fichte or Schelling, this originary division is healed in the comprehensive *Wissenschaft* where a single substance uniting soul and matter is marked or demonstrated in its *Bild* (picture) or *Bildung* (construction, but also education) through a process of becoming figured which Browne calls the decussation:

> And this also with application unto the soul of man, which hath a double aspect: one right, whereby it beholdeth and body and objects without, another circular and reciprocal, whereby it beholdeth itself. The circle declaring the motion of the indivisible and simple, according to the divinity of its nature and returning into itself; the right lines respecting the motion pertaining unto sense and vegetation; and the central decussation the wondrous connection of the several faculties conjointly in one substance. (*GC*, 99)

Browne's central medallion, from which all the right lines radiate, is human substance—split into its constitutent parts a little more than a century before the Kantian *Ur-teil* and Novalis' "inneres Du." Conversely, in each of its mirror-like fracturings, in every angle and curve by which it is marked and remarked, Romanticism expands beyond itself, negating the medallion-like center, positing an eccentric space between sign and picture or a zone where the pictorial and scriptorial collide in their dissonance, a *satura*-like, saturated mathesis. It is not accidental that Hegel wishes to abandon the sensory orientation of the symbol for the abstractness of the verbal sign. Pater is not incorrect in his estimation that Browne should be compared to Jean Paul. and Montaigne. More than any other Romantic painter, Philipp Otto Runge would seem to be an ideal test-case for Barth's arguments concerning the arabesque and the Romantic quest for the artificially created simulacrum, the *Bild* or *Bildung* of chaos in its "fearful symmetry."[20] Equally, and perhaps even more justifiably, because we dealing with borders that border nothing (no thing) and arabesques that spin out into equivocal zones of decontextualization, we can observe in Runge the facet-like geometry of something different from the Mandelbrot fractal, yet resembling it in certain respects. On the one hand, the invisible world Runge paints is a symmetrical space with which Sir Thomas Browne would have been familiar: it is occupied equally by what we cannot see, seraphs and homunculi-like cherubs, and the goddess of the dawn, Aurora, a familiar figure in theosophy from Böhme onward, and what we can see, the light of the dawn. At the same time, it is a painting that is "absolutely modern," as Baudelaire might say, in the sense that it lends itself in its theosophical sincerity to immediate appropriation by Schelling, and, no doubt, more than a few philosophical rivals, becoming an object of wonder and provocation among the intelligentsia. Finally, as if to channel the aether at its most profane,[21] Runge's visual text places a certain religious iconography in the celestial space above the pagan/Christian spectacle of dawn and the emergent Super-Subject representing Aurora, Venus, and Mary. To be sure, this dawn is meant "for us," terrestrial beholders or fans-to-be "down here," either in a neo-Gothic "meta-church" or in some other kind of quasi-religious gathering-place designed for secular masses.

Equally, however, at one end of the denatured or supernatural scale of fandom, there is something fantastically modern and sincere in this particular text which to American eyes looks like the decussation or medallion of a sport combining sublime exaltation with pure terror, whose rules are codified in the same decade as some of our most arabesquely figured literature: i.e. Poe's *Tales of the Grotesque and Arabesque* and Lane's translation of *The Arabian Nights*. If nothing else, Poe teaches us, especially in his facetiously cruel "The Thousand-and-Second Tale of

Scheherazade," that Orientalism can be a subject of near and ambivalent American interest—an offshoot or equivocal branch of the *Begeisterung* that accompanies the translation of *The Arabian Nights* in the early 1840s. Thus, if Barth chooses to see Mandelbrot fractals in Persian rugs and Schlegel, we may be justified in seeing a baseball diamond in Runge's painting *"Der Morgen,"* a visual text "saturated," apparently, with philosophical significance derived in part from Böhme, and with Magian symbolism imported from what Germans call the "land of morning" ("das Morgenland").

An "all-American" spin is placed almost immediately on the arabesque, whose proximity to the grotesque, as its "lighter side," will be articulated in Poe's introduction to the aforementioned collection of tales. That is, a certain, if not the whole, later history of the American novel, up to and including such writers as Faulkner, Capote, Mailer, Updike, Cheever, Heller, Barth himself, Malamud, Pynchon, Salinger, and many others may be seen as an elaboration and refinement of the arabesque–grotesque distinction (especially as set forth by Poe, who is able to see terror encroaching from the edges and becoming the central medallion of his own fiction), in texts where the liberation of the citizen-subject from prior or "Old World" constraints of myth and manners is represented and problematized. However, it is not as if the arabesque, as "new mythology," could be limited to any one type of writing or any one art. It is not only a feature of the textile, but also of an art of three dimensions. Henry James subtly accentuates the conflicted or distressed sense of the arabesque, as a function of Oriental urban design and American recuperation, in *The Europeans*. By suggesting new architectural possibilities, the "Mahometan" element demarcates a boundary between Europe and the New World in the way each one "touches the sky." The arabesque (or "Mahometan," as Felix *Young* describes it) both situates and dislocates because he sees it *here*, i.e., in Boston, where the *coincidentia oppositorum* plays its games at home:

> 'It shows how extremes meet,' the young man rejoined. 'Instead of coming to the West we seem to have gone to the East. The way the sky touches the house-tops is just like Cairo; and the red and blue signboards remind one of Mahometan decoration.'[22]

Such a skyline is, without doubt, a perfect instance of a fractal object., just as James's storytelling is the *fons et origo* of the all-American "figure in the carpet." As always in James, however, the innovative, symmetrical, or asymmetrical *other*, in this case the arabesque or "Mahometan," points to larger zones of iconic (religious) and interpretative distress, the dislocation of Old World standards of faith and of Old World art, not least because of the dubious reliability of "the art critic" who is Felix Young. Thus Barth's critical strategy is anticipated, to a certain extent, in the sophisticated perspectives on Orientalism offered by James and, more malignly, by Poe.

The arabesque, however, also situates itself in a field that is both equivocal and historically determined, beginning on the surface with the American and French revolutions, but taking on a burden of symbolism for which, in its lightness, it is ill prepared, for which the hieroglyph and/or the grotesque must do compensatory labor. It has the aesthetic function of elaborating the anthropological possibilities of the *novus ordo saeclorum* and may thus be linked with a theosophical mathematics, especially, that of Sir Thomas Browne and Jacob Böhme. But the more interesting, if not entirely verifiable, claim I would make is that the arabesque (and the grotesque) reflect or represent the calculus by which the revolutionary citizen-subject, at least in the New World, would liberate him- or herself from the prior constraints (inhibitions) of religion and art by establishing a set of routines and/or manners with which to regulate and legitimate the liberated (not exactly liberal), commercial universe, of advertising, as James obliquely suggests, which was born between 1793 and 1840, which has terror, so to speak, at either end, or at its edges, from the French Revolution to the tales of Poe. In order to give this commercial universe (as capitalism—the science of money and its application to labor) its autonomy and legitimacy, these routines and/or manners had to be separated from the codes of art and religion and reconstituted on the sole principle of that which would serve the *interests* of capital, of work and...leisure.[23] What separates the liberal, bourgeois nineteenth from previous centuries is not the Industrial Age alone; it is the organizing of political and academic fans into bases of consensus, fraternal groups or clubs, and the gradual transference of attention from the atom of sacred devotion (fear of God), still within the context of religious institutions, to the molecule of political *devotio* (self-sacrifice) on the level of fantastic and secular terror (fear of becoming other than bourgeois, homeless and thus *sauvage* et al. in *this* world). In order for science and capital acquisition to become legitimated, to take the place formerly assigned to religion and art from antiquity to the Renaissance, the "new mythology" of Romanticism, above all in its quest of a delimitation of subjecthood, would have to be appropriated and/or assimilated. The domain of that assimilation would not be a church or a museum; it would, in America, be out-of-doors, on a field of play, where the "Super Subject," *qua* ballplayer in association with other similar ballplayers—according to the myth of leisure-time activity—would never age, natural processes sublimated, and aging itself demonized to the extent that it would be placed entirely off the Self-mythologizing ball-field. The American work-place would thus be prepared for a molecular, "sanitized" Super-Subject, a Fan who puts *Liber* (Dionysus) into liberty—moving from East to West and then back to the Orient, from the Brooklyn of Ebbetts Field to L. A.'s Chávez ravine to Tokyo, freed from obligation to ethnicity, community, and the narratives of elders, whose office- and factory-skills are honed off-hours in a place where only the young may play, where seasons would be remembered, as the sporting equivalent of history, in a litany of statistics and records, E.R.A.'s and batting averages.[24] Baseball, in its theorization, a coming-into-view like the sun's at dawn, embodies the con-sensual *Geist* whose decussation appears anew each day, rampant on the perfect diamond, for itself and for us, the fans of several continents, of the universal "league." Equally, perhaps because the player/fan strides out *after* Hegel, it is a projection of *the next* or Nietzschean dawn in which it is not the superman who is Zarathustra, but a superman look-alike named "Babe" or "The Kid" who is always taking the first step onto a field of ambiguously real and imaginary play, where else, but in an East that has become like the West or "more West than the West," say, in Tokyo or Shanghai:

> Americans of all ages, all conditions, and all dispositions, constantly form associations...The Americans make associations to give entertainments, to found seminaries, to build inns, to construct churches, to diffuse books, to send missionaries to the antipodes; they found in this manner hospitals, prisons, and schools. If it be proposed to inculcate some truth, or to foster some feeling by the encouragement of a great example, they form a society.[25]

The Universal Fan: From Runge's "Zarathustra" to a Field of Dreams

Once the body becomes reconciled with the spirit, Man will come striding forth to stun the universe with his eminence. Who could dispute his legacy were he to embrace the morning star?   Evan Connell, *The Alchymist's Journal*

Oh Rookies, come along/ And hear m' sad song!/ Old age is the bane o' mankind/ So enjoy while ya may/ The fair spring day,/ Cause the blue season ain't far behind. Robert Coover, *The Universal Baseball Association*

Wahrlich hier ist mehr als Gold und Diamant. Novalis, *Fragmente* [Truly, there is more here than gold and diamond<s>.]

The North German Romantic Philipp Otto Runge painted not once, but twice what Browne would have called the "decussation" of morning: a bold yet ambiguously motivated arabesque whose central axis aligns the goddess Aurora in her descent to earth with a celestial lily above her head and an infant placed on the ground beneath her feet. In the tragically brief period of his painterly activity, Runge attracts an astounding number of devotees or "fans," among them Goethe and Schelling. Though Caspar David Friedrich is more famous, possibly because there is more of him in the museums, Runge meets the requirements outlined by Barth, not least because of that most amazingly "Oriental" of paintings, *The Dawn*, painted in 1808 and again in 1809, the year of Gogol's and Poe's birth, which forces us to look to the east, if not the East, in order to observe the coming of the sun. While it is true that there is a pattern of equivalent, four-cornered interest in the other two examples from *Der Tag* (*The Times of Day*), it is equally evident that all three of the original designs, together with their symbolic, aqueous and/or vegetative sinuosities, obey an intensely motivated axial symmetry, whose action inevitably moves the beholder's eye from the bottom to the top and from the top to the bottom of each picture, so that the beholder is forced to consider his or her own relation with what may be defined, for hieroglyphic purposes, as an open, unearthly, or "heavenly" space and the ground or *Grund* beneath. The definition of this space is made explicit in the second of the series, *Der Tag*, where it is occupied by "genial spirits" on the up- or down-spiral of incarnation, fairy-like or "cherubic" children surrounding a seated maternal figure. The upward, spring-like thrust of liberation, on the other hand, becomes concretized as a fountain in the first version of *Der Morgen* (*Morning*):

1. Philipp Otto Runge. *Der Morgen*. 1807. Drawing and engraving. Kunsthalle, Hamburg

Despite the fact that the pen and ink sketch seems to our 21st-century eyes only a pale preliminary stage of the painting to come, in its versions of 1808 and 1809, it comes to have a far more decisive impact upon the general public and the philosophy of Runge's time. This is no doubt due, in part, to the reproducibility of engraving and to its astrological, chemical, and theosophical significance, which places the four directions of fluid human generation under "a" or "the" star's influence, but also to the fact that it "plays" on mythic paradigms, pagan and Christian, in what can only be described as a bold, or, indeed, equivocal projection of a transcendent and entirely novel mythology. It seems that the painting would be "saved" for our eyes, or for a time in which various other cultural phenomena "after Romanticism" might catch up with it and serve, perhaps, as commentary on the spectacular vividness and verve of its symmetrically ordered representation of universal passion or joy, Bach's "eternal flame," Schiller's "schöner Götterfunken." A figural element common to both the sketch and the painting is the proliferation of "angeloid" figures in the context of a joy which steps forth from the Aether to "take us higher" or "further" in a universal series of worlds. In the sketch, the child-like figures are all alike or nearly so, as angels are thought to be; in the painting, however, the ones closer to the earth are identifiable (to us, at least, who no longer foreground the biblical context and think of children as "cherubic" in the sense of cute, pudgy, and utterly power-less, a transfer of biblical characterization into the key of "Romantic" sentimentality for which Runge and others inspired by Rousseau may be partly to blame) in their fleshiness as mutant zephyrs or fairy-like cherubs; the ones up in the sky are seraphs. Runge's emphasis is consistently placed upon a hidden or occult universe inhabited throughout by Muse-like or "genial spirits," a pananimism or pantheism inspired not by Spinoza, but by Schiller, Novalis, and Schlegel, among his contemporaries, by theosophical texts, and, though this is less likely, by the Moslem belief in three kinds of spirits, the good (angels of God), the bad (*genii* who serve Satan), and the ugly (*genii* made of smokeless fire). The arabesque is made subservient to this animist design, which we, as postmoderns, may think of as quaintly metaphysical or theosophically obscure, but which is nonetheless made everywhere perspicuous. And, no doubt, part of the purpose of Runge's fluid and astral symbolism is to render visible, through painterly artifice, the dynamic energy of cosmos-creating, ubiquitous desire, a desire crossing day and night, linking the great to the small, the macro- and the microcosm, the dead and the living. Analogous rampant figures of glad golden energy are found everywhere in the engravings and watercolors of his "Behmenist" English contemporary, Willliam Blake, and, as Runge makes clear in a brief manifesto, the underlying subject of both the sketch/engraving and the later painting is none other than "the boundaryless illumination of the universe." This is a project which, framing its arabesques and/or hieroglyphs at the height of Napoleonic power, gathers great numbers of fans in art galleries and journals from Berlin to Hamburg, who greet the "new mythology" of the dawn with a revolutionary, but also spiritual or otherworldy fervor in their eyes—a virtual fan-magnet.

But the sketch also represents at some paradigmatic level the *fons et origo* of youth, since the beginning of life has become synonomous with morning. The fountain of youth is made here into a universal principle springing into ecstatic existence without boundary, border, or historical referent. The finite and the infinite are subordinated to the mathematical ordering of the star or stars (*Sterne*, Sterne), the four become one molecular whole, which then becomes three, and culminates finally in a single astral signature (as in the Astralis of Novalis) again. Nine would appear to be the "highest" symbolic number (reminding us not only of America's pastime, but also of the "Nine Nights" of Blake's *Vala or the Four Zoas*). Here, we may say, animist spirits or sprites proliferate in the centrally placed vertical jet rising up out of and looming over the four smaller, almost semicircular fluid-like arcs. These smaller arcs rise and then fall, symbols of the subordination of physical matter to gravity (or time), while the central stem, shooting upward like water or vegetation, blossoms at the top in petals of renewed fecundity, as yet another well-populated arc is traced, surmounted by a three-fold figural group, finally topped by a star (of the East). Thus something more than the acquisitive dream of the Spanish Empire, both to sail to the Orient for its riches and to discover the fountain of youth, is projected—something more suggestive in its efflorescent splendor of Blake's verses concerning the American revolution and what he took to be the *end* of Empire. Thus what makes the engraving of *Morning* controversial in its time[26] is the frame or framing of philosophical content in the *Bild* or pictorial representation, or, rather, the disseminative impact of that content, revolutionary in its deixis and otherworldly or Böhmean in its implication for a heaven to be realized when Oriental distance becomes the Occidental here and now. Schelling's claim that it represents *him* or serves as a portrait of *his* philosophy is to be taken as one among many attempts to make the arabesque into the Oriental signature of a uniquely inspired Romantic "principle of the universe" scanned on one or more of its sublime "heights." In this sense, the cherub-populated arabesque mutates or spills over into the hieroglyph. The furor provoked by *Der Morgen*, in the first painted version of 1808 and the second of 1809, at the height of the Napoleonic ascendancy, is of a piece with that engendered by Friedrich's cult-like, even kitschy projection of the German *Tracht* of a bygone era, while the projected, fragmentary series *Der Tag* or *The Times of Day* can itself be seen as the attempt to represent, resolve, or reframe—in hieroglyphic, occult, or arabesque *saturation*—an answer to the question asked by the Sphinx, "answered" by him whose myth would launch psychoanalysis.

The fountain design is replaced in the oil paintings by a centrally placed running figure, that of the Roman goddess of the dawn, Aurora, called Eos by the Greeks, who, as equivocally re-presented, seems identifiable, yet not unambiguously readable, as Venus/Aphrodite or Mary, while the upper portion becomes at once more definite and "infinite" as an Aether defined by a pure shade of blue and populated by angels distributed symmetrically, some of whom play musical instruments. As it now exists (prior to digital restoration) the central aetherial space is bordered by two large portions of sky left blank by the painting's incomplete state; an American reader who is also a fan of baseball might be reminded, despite the iconographic impossibility, of "nothing so much as" homeplate by the pentagon of azure above Aurora's head left to us from Runge's original painting. Such a mistaken reading has a certain value, however, in that it "marks the spot" of the lily of celestial purity (scarcely visible here, but perspicuous on the Internet). The celestial spaces are filled with seraphs, divine beings who appear in the Bible can also be defined by reference to the inexact, equivocal science of angelology in its relation to a tree tending into the aether, pointing to the absolute, casting the universal spell of Love:

> That history is interwoven with the history of the Seraphim, who, indeed, were the first creators of the spell. Nevertheless, for the sake of clearness, it will be better to dispose first of the hallucination which so much hinders the true vision.The spell which was pronounced to serve the purposes of Love has now passed into other hands, and is used for the purposes of hatred. In dispelling it, for that reason, we shall prove ourselves truer followers of Rousseau than those who murder in his name.
>
> In the meanwhile one hint may be given.
>
> The last, uppermost shoot of the tree is the one that is the most sensitive. The strongest to endure the light, it is at the same time the weakest against material might. Such is the order of the Seraphim.[27]

The motivation of love is crucial to Runge's equivocal enterprise, both because of the theosophical implications of the seraphs and cherubim, and because there is another figure, located at the bottom of the painting, completely in the shadows, awaiting, as it were, the arrival of the illuminating pagan goddess: a human infant. Without the infant, the painting might be just another example of a somewhat overheated neoclassicism. With it, the painting treads on the ground of Christianity in what is at least a problematic, or, no doubt to some, sacrilegious manner. My reading wishes only to emphasize the eclecticism of the painting and its assigning of preeminence to the pagan goddess—equally and for some time to come, a figure of Woman emancipated—who is certainly other than "the" Virgin Mary, just as the unilluminated child is surely other than "the" Baby Jesus. At the same time, since Runge's project is the "boundaryless illumination of the universe," we will postulate that *this* dawn projects and makes a *secular* case for the divine quality of universal love and/or desire.

As we have said, this is a painting of the invisible, whose powers, like those of of heaven and hell, are not of this world. Yet they affect this world, while standing just outside or above our "playing fields," the symbolic medallion at the center of experience. To put it in terms an American or Tibetan Buddhist might understand, seraphs and cherubs, powerless in the material world, haunt the bleachers (where things are whitened in the sun) on either side of, above and below, the great diamond of enlightened existence—to the extent that, if Runge's painting represents the ultimate *state* of the arabesque, as conceived by Novalis and Schlegel, and adopted or appropriated by Schelling, it also inscribes in its visual text the hieroglyphic, occult signature of a transcendental "team" or "club" spirit of enlightenment, while making a prophetic *statement* about the geography of the Western imagination, and anticipating with utter sincerity, cannily or uncannily, the geometry and spatial arrangements of what would later

2. Philipp Otto Runge. *Der Morgen*. 1809. Final stage. Oil on canvas. Kunsthalle, Hamburg

become the "national pastime" in a transplanted Hesperia of European (especially German) immigrants, not soccer, but a fairy, fair, and/or fraternal play of bats and leathern spheres,[28] of rectangles and diamonds, where numbers matter more than in any other play or sport, and are, indeed, revered by the average person as statistics worthy of being recited *ad infinitum*: memorial verses with which to compare past and present seasons in terms of a secular *prose*. The difference between the sketch/engraving and the final painting, which seems like an altar-piece for the cosmic church of a *Naturphilosophie* whose games are played both at home and on an aetherial or astral plane, is striking. It is characterized, first, by the abandonment of the static arrangement of the "fountain of youth," with its fourfold curvilinear arcs (though the axial symmetry is preserved) for a splashy, seductive "machine" capable of impressing the viewer, as might be expected, with a gleam of Apollonian illumination or enlightenment, but also with a sense of Eos as pure, uninhibited Eros. Morning, in Runge's painting, is free (*liber*) enough to suggest Dionysian liberation or desublimation of instinct—absolutely apart from conventional religion, i.e., Western Christianity—on several levels. The carefully defined bordering of the sketch has given way to a design whose corners are occupied only by the symbolic black of night. Sky, sunrise, and earth below are painted with the greatest possible fidelity to pure values of color (the reader may verify this on the Internet), yet each area is also dominated by the seraphs. "Morning" is thus awash in the symbolism or several symbolisms of morning, of impassioned play, but also of thought or wisdom, at its Oriental in- or conception. Runge, indeed, according to his own explanatory epigraph, is going after something theo- and philosophically *more*: "Der Morgen ist die grenzenlose Erleuchtung des Universums" ["Morning is the boundaryless illumination of the universe"]. This may be contrasted with what Barth understands as the "denaturing" of context: "...that is, the attempt to represent the supernatural by abstracting natural forms into geometrical designs that reveal the mind of God. Into this rarefied void the observer also dissolves. Self disappears into the great Void...." (*FF*, 317). While this suggests spiritual advancement in Sufism, Mevlana, or Buddhism and the postmodern theory of the subject's disappearance, it also skips ahead to Schopenhauer, paying little or no attention to the Fichtean and Schellingian notion of an illumination of the universe through the direct intuition of the philosophic subject (genius), an idea inherited from the Enlightenment before it is made the more exotic stepchild of Asian mysticism and the blue flower of the Aether, Novalis' "qualitative potentialization of the Self," ("qualitative Potenzierung des Selbst") and "inneres Du." Symbolic mathesis and absolute subjectivity go "hand in hand"; one fits the other "like a glove" or "second skin," providing medium and message for the equivocal generation of Romanticism's fan-base.

What we see in Runge is the radiant overloading of *mythos*, a hypertrophy of Western and Oriental superstition whose excess will become ever more monstrously evident as the 19th century progresses from perspicuous systematizations of enlightenment to irrationalisms unpredictable in their chaotic pathogenesis. Here, a daughter strides forth "aus Elysium"; there, Zarathustra comes down from the mountains to experience a fateful *Untergang* amid "our gang," *arriving* and running *towards* the beholder.[29] The beholder is thus asked, in a certain sense, to greet the dawn as a second or higher self coming forward out of the picture-plane, accompanied by the seraphs arrayed in the deep, Mallarméan azure of outer space to the left and right above her head. Far from dissolving into the blue, the spectator, an "infant" until now, has no choice but to witness the egregiously radiant new mythological game represented by the Venusian form of Aurora, as a new or other, higher self, come to greet her or him confrontationally—a dramatization of the *Ur-teil* or originary division of the philosophical subject in the act of reflection. What matters here is not a monastic or ashram-centered *vita contemplativa*, but the virtuosic, spiraling, fraternal play of spirit and matter *down* on the playing field, observed also by Gabriel-like seraphs seemingly emitting contrails from their "sky-boxes" on high. The vir(t)us of theosophy and *Naturphilosophie* provides both pathogenetic content and context, as one can gather from Schiller's *Philosophische Briefe*—written from a theosophical perspective in order to present views which may be deemed, according to the "Vorerinnerung," either "false" or "true," depending upon the reader's point of view.[30] Opinions *like* those expressed in the letters of "Julius" may have prompted Runge's design (and, indeed, the epistolary form and inner dialogization of Schlegel's *Lucinde*). In the section entitled "Gott," the color symbolism of the "divine I" is delineated in terms more unambiguously mythic than those of Goethe's *Farbenlehre*. The hyperbolic universe of Schiller's letter-writer is animated by spirits and presided over by the transcendental ego:

> Wie sich im prismatischen Glase ein weißer Lichtstreif in sieben dunklere Strahlen spaltet, hat sich das göttliche Ich in zahllose empfindende Substanzen gebrochen. Wie sieben dunklere Strahlen in *einen* hellen Lichtstreif wieder zusammenschmelzen, würde aus der Vereinigung aller dieser Substanzen ein göttliches Wesen hervorgehen. Die vorhandene Form des Naturgebäudes ist das optische Glas, und alle Tätigkeiten der Geister nur ein unendliches Farbenspiel jenes einfachen göttlichen Strahles. Gefiel' es der Allmacht dereinst, dieses Prisma zu zerschlagen, so stürzte der Damm zwischen ihr und der Welt ein, alle Geister würden in *einem* Unendlichen untergehen, alle Akkorde in *einer* Harmonie in einander fließen, alle Bäche in *einem* Ozean aufhören.[31]

[As a white band of light divides itself in the prismatic glass into seven darker rays, the divine 'I' has broken itself into innumerable sensory substances. As seven darker rays again melt together into *one* bright band of light, a divine being would proceed from the union of all these substances. The present form taken by the edifice of nature is the optical glass, and all activities of the spirits are only an infinite play of colors derived from that simple, divine ray. If it at some time were the pleasure of the Almighty to shatter this prism, then the dam between it <the Almighty> and the world would crumble, all spirits would be submerged in *one*, infinite <spirit>, and all chords would intermingle with each other in *one* infinite harmony, all brooks end in *one* ocean.]

Schiller's apocalyptic tone, derived from a state of juvenescent mind some fifteen years prior, when he still signed himself "Éleve Schiller," nonetheless suggests the *Sturm-und-Drang*-like identity crisis of philosophy in the 1790s and beyond (especially in the early Hegel and Schelling), one in which elements of naturalism (science) and supernaturalism, theism and atheism are indiscriminately and publicly linked. The letter "to Raphael" on the colors of the universe is followed by a poetic text on love in which seraphs are specifically mentioned and a Kantian notion of categorical duty, as "sweet coercion," is expressed in a text (dating from 1782) that are anything but coldly Olympian:

> 'Tote Gruppen sind wir, wenn wir hassen,
> Götter, wenn wir liebend uns umfassen,
>   lechzen nach dem süssen Fesselzwang.
> Aufwärts durch die tausendfache Stufen
> zahlenloser Geister, die nicht schufen,
>   waltet göttlich dieser Drang.
>
> Arm in Arme, höher stets und höher
> vom Barbaren bis zum griech'schen Seher,
>   der sich an den letzten Seraph reiht,
> Wallen wir einmüt'gen Ringeltanzes,
> bis sich dort im Meer des ew'gen Glanzes
>   sterbend untertauchen Maß und Zeit....'

['We are dead groups when we hate,/ Gods, when we embrace each other lovingly,/ yearn for the sweet restraint of <those> shackles./ Ascending through the thousandfold steps/ of numberless spirits, which did not create/ this yearning rules divinely.

Arm in arms, always higher and higher,/ from the barbarian to the Greek seer,/ who places himself in the ranks of the last seraph,/ We billow in the unanimous ring-dance,/ until measure and time in death submerge/ in the sea of the eternal radiance.']

Aurora....and Venus...and Mary: in the equivocally hybrid conception is reflected a figure of emancipation whose emphasis is decidedly female, one belonging to the same transcendent, astro-physical ball-club as the "Déesse Raison" of the French Revolution, the Statue of Liberty, and the

Zarathustran starchild of *2001, A Space Odyssey*; she steps out of the East—Afghanistan or Baghdad, perhaps?—to face the beholder, who is in the West, or in "a" West, Germany, Europe as a whole, or America. She is one of several mythological paradigms for a philosophy that sees itself just now coming to light (with Fichte and Schelling) and, equally and at all times, for an egalitarian, philanthropic spirit freighted with the republicanism of the French and American revolutions. That is to say, the light of the new day—yellow, the color of primary, primitive intuition prior to its splitting into prismatic hues of reflection—can be taken, on the political level, as a *Geist* or spirit of fraternal organization supposed to awaken the people to action in terms of a self-creating interest *in this world*, to energize what is naively and in an almost child-like or child-worshiping sense,[32] taken in the West to be, above all, *secular* human progress, the heritage of the Enlightenment, a *novus ordo saeculorum*. Before it takes to the streets or to the conspiratorial athletic field, the club is an affair of Jacobins, debating societies, Freemasons, and civic associations. That is why Blake's "Glad Day," celebrating the release human energies, resembles in its anthropomorphism Runge's dawn and why, and at the end of the ninth and final night of *The Four Zoas* (1797), we read:

> The Sun arises from his dewy bed, & the fresh airs
> Play in his smiling beams giving the seeds of life to grow,
> And the fresh Earth beams forth ten thousand thousand springs of life.
> Urthona is arisen in his strength, no longer now
> Divided from Enitharmon, no longer the Spectre Los.
> Where is the Spectre of Prophecy? where the delusive Phantom?
> Departed: & Urthona rises from the ruinous Walls
> In all his ancient strength to form the golden armour of science
> For intellectual War. The war of swords departed now,
> The dark Religions are departed & sweet Science reigns.[33]

Were we to seek a sports analogy for this "up- and outward" arrangement of enlightening energy moving in a westerly or ponent direction, bringing a spirit of emancipated political association, a "new mythology" of equality and fraternity found not in a church or debating club, but on the field of baseball (a "sweeter" science, perhaps, than boxing, or a more "intellectual" kind of warfare)—to the extent that the Runge, unbeknownst to the painter, may be seen as stating something akin to the dream or unconscious schematization not only of Schellingian *Naturphilosophie* in the first decade of the 19th century, but also of the American pastime to be "invented" not by a Civil War hero calling himself "Doubleday" in the 1860s,[34] but as early as 1825,[35] if not earlier—where the focus of action is on the batter's attempt to liberate himself by hitting a ball into an inner or outer field, or, much more rarely, beyond the field of play entirely, into the stands or out of the naturally/artificially illuminated "park." Until the ball goes into the field, the action is altogether static and "feudal"—restricted, and sometimes excessively prolonged, we feel, to the drama that unfolds between pitcher, hitter, and catcher. Aurora, of a cosmic scale compared to the landscape in the distance, strides toward us, as toward the home plate of higher, intuitive knowledge:

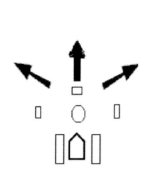

3. Vectors of potential action when the ball is hit beyond the infield diamond to the outfield.

4. Aurora emerging out of night, between the celestial lily and earthly "babe." Decussation of the occult diamond made spectacular.

If examined with the hermeneutic *Vorgriff* of looking for an occult symmetry, a procedure warranted by the problematics of a picture that wants nothing so much as to illustrate one or more theo-/philosophical texts hieroglyphically, a diamond- or lozenge-shaped figure emerges—whose bottom two lines are defined by the leading edges of the faces of the four spectating figures in the lower half of the frame and by the point where the stylized foot-like appendages of the airborne seraphs converge. Since they are bent over the ground, and are, indeed, foregrounded, appearing larger in perspective, we may call the lower two cherubs, homunculi, or fairies "groundskeepers," i.e., preparers of the *Grund* for a philosophical rebirth. Aurora, for all of the painting's symbolism of divine infancy, does not seem at all concerned with the half-lit baby on the ground, but brazenly "charges" toward the beholder, confronting him or her, making a spectacle of herself, as Dawn, in her rose-digited splendor, is wont to do.

But what or whose ground is it that they are keeping? In the Old Testament the cherubs are figures of divine power who, together with the seraphim, carry out the will of God. Herder in his text on the origin of language calls them "unbekannt und charakteristisch." According to *Zedler's Universal-Lexicon*, a standard 18th-century reference work, seraphs take on the name of "cherubs" when they are energized by divine purpose.[36] With Runge, however, we are no longer completely *in* the lexical universe of Zedler, based on the New and Old Testaments, nor are we yet entirely *out* of it. The secular throng of the polymorphously theistic "new mythology" assimilates East and West, Judeo-Christian and pagan elements, equally and eclectically, placing "boundaryless illumination" at the flashlit hieroglyphic/arabesque center and making cherubs mutate into homunculi-like figures preparing the ground for the cosmic Babe in a new dawn of shared values oriented around the communitarian philosophy of "for one and for all":

> Nun: wenn die Romantiker sich mit dem Mythos beschäftigt haben, so war ihnen vor allem um Folgendes zu tun: Um welche Art von gesellschaftlicher Handlung—so fragten sie sich—handelt es sich eigentlich bei der Mythen-Tradition? Und die Antwort darauf lautete: Mythen dienen, den Bestand und die Verfassung einer Gesellschaft aus einem obersten Wert zu beglaubigen. Man könnte das die kommunikative Funktion des Mythos nennen, weil sie auf das Verständigtsein der Gesellschaftsteilnehmer untereinander und auf die Einträchtigkeit ihrer Weltüberzeugungen abzielt. [37]
>
> [Now: when the Romantics occupied themselves with myth, it was above all a matter of the following: with what kind of social subject matter—so they asked themselves—is the mythic tradition actually concerned? And the answer to <this question> was: myths serve the purpose of affirming faith in the condition and constitution of a society on the basis of a supreme value. One could call this the communicative function of myth, because it aims toward the mutual understanding of the participants in a society among each other and toward the unity of their mundane convictions.]

The ground upon which the mutant cherubs stand, with the infant or cosmic child at its center, can thus be identified as a paradise-like, entirely new society, into which illuminating Aurora/Venus/Mary steps forth (an *Hervortreten* that is also a downward stepping or *Hinabtreten*, as with Zarathustra) to greet the beholder. This theoretical paradise is opened rather than closed by the angelic spirits above; the philosophical Adam and Eve are no longer sent out of the Garden, but welcomed into the New Eden by the primary yellow of day, a light that blazes everywhere—without boundary—throughout the material and spiritual worlds and will soon strike the face of the baby below. Ubiquitous though it may be, however, the

Dawn will spread its light with particular brilliance in a certain corner of the universe, in the utopian, partly theosophical, partly philosophical, climate of Europe's and Asia's erstwhile "fan" whose name is America, along the banks of the Susquehanna River, as Coleridge thought to do in his shortlived project of Pantisocracy, or as countless European immigrants did throughout the Midwest and Northeast.

But the infant in the shadows is only half of the story told, arabesquely or hieroglyphically, by the painting. A beholder might be forgiven if he or she remained focused on the rampant figure of the youthful goddess. who, indeed, is the focal point of attention. She, as we have said, represents sexual emancipation, liberty, and reason, the universal negation of medieval darkness. In that project she must arrive, finally in the Far West of North America. The American connection becomes cogent if we consider the painting as an allegory of the epochal shift in virtually every aspect of Western ideology, commerce, military science, and so on caused by the United States, for whom the game of baseball, beginning in the 19th century is emblematic. We may interpret Aurora as the "empowered I" of the runner who becomes the focus of attention on the basepaths, once he or she is allowed to move, in solitude, beyond the batter's box by hitting the ball into fair territory. If we think about the painting solely from the point of view of its shock-value or aesthetic impact (much more emphatic, to us, than the engraving which caused such a stir when first displayed in 1807), remembering too the lily, our "home plate" up in the sky, it is the subject/beholder who will be seen as the philosophic destination toward which this boldly illuminating "self as divine other" (a "potenziertes Selbst," in Novalis' terms) is running. "Home plate" is thus doubled— appearing up in the sky as a transcendent point of origin, but also serving as the mythic *telos* of the baserunner who is Aurora or Dawn. The beholder, then, is the other of the unillumined infant. The dawning light of day comes at or upon the grounded subject; it is up to him or her to create a new mythology of society, of the citizen who has become the bourgeois. The genii floating above, in the center, right, and left portions of the sky, can be seen as angelic or angeloid outfielders. The upstart *citoyen* has become not only the utopian child down on the field, but also the liberated fan for whom the sport of daylight, linked in his or her mind to and thus *representing* the abstract metropolis for which the ballplayer plays, New York, L.A., Philadelphia, Tokyo, Cuba, Santo Domingo, et al., exists, but not the local *civitas*, community, or *barrio*, the enthusiast who witnesses the coming out of the Orient of a new dawn of philosophic knowledge for him or her, ever running towards home plate out of the endlessly chaotic, teeming night of the *rus* and of medieval superstition. *Morgenröte* on the basepaths:

'Let the slave grinding at the mill run out into the field,
'Let him look into the heavens & laugh in the bright air;
'Let the inchained soul, shut up in darkness and in sighting,
'Whose face has never seen a smile in thirty weary years,
Rise and look out; his chains are loose; his dungeon-doors are open;
And let his wife and children return from the oppressor's scourge...

'For Empire is no more, and now the Lion & Wolf shall cease.'
(Plate 6 of *America*, *WB*, 198)

Cheers rising from the bleachers of baseball parks at the beginning of each spring in the New World, if not from the "nosebleed" sections of university lecture-halls. The quest for boundless knowledge is equally a dream of power; in the dark of night preceding the dawn, a scene whose channeling or spelling cannot be sketched but only staged, it is an umpire-like witch or *wyrd* who says "Fair is foul, and foul is fair," deciding fate and the outcome of the game played by day.

But Runge, here as elsewhere, "lends" himself to other fables and other truths.[38] In Coover's *The Universal Baseball Association*, it is the runner on the basebaths who, while subject to occult forces and unseen throws of the dice, is seen as the "traveling man" or Willy-Lomanesque archetype of American culture:

The streets, as always, were full of moving people, going going going, the endless jostling flow. They gave him somehow a vague and somber sense of fatality and closed circuits. Motion. The American scene. The rovin' gambler. Cowpoke and trainman. A travelin' man alwas longs for a home, cause a travelin' man is always alone. Out of the east into the north, push out to the west, then march through the south back home again: like a baserunner on the paths, alone in a hostile cosmos, the stars out there in their places, and him out there trying to dominate the world by stepping on it all. Probably suffered a sense of confinement there in the batter's box, felt the need to strike forth on a meaningful quest of some kind. Balls hurled down to him off the magic mound, regularly as the seasons: his limited seasons. Or rather: not to him, but just to earth, passive, faintly hostile, deprecatory, masked—while he interposed himself heroically to defy the holy condition...not knowing his defiance was only a part of it. [39]

The translation of religion and philosophy into the "mass" appeal of an arabesque art with hieroglyphic implications brings with it certain identifiable consequences with which we now live, in Europe as well as in the New Eden. American presidents participate in what has become a thoroughly secularized and ritualized hierophancy, throwing out the ball to initiate a new baseball season, and one begins to understand why political leaders are now coming to the fore who base their political aspirations almost solely upon media stardom and professional athletic experience. In

North America, the political *citoyen* has evolved from the subject into either "Player" or "Fan," and politics has become something akin to a "full fan-experience." Preceding being, politics will now be other or an Other, perhaps the ultimate team "sport," played out in the ancient confrontation between I and Other, my group and yours, Child and Father, to be experienced in the pharmaceutical embrace not of steroids, but of media spin and mass psychosis, in which the stadium has replaced the legislative assembly as the seat of "representation," scaling and rescaling, where real power is *exercised* over "teamed-up" minds and hearts, pitting one side of the color wheel against the other, "Reds" versus "Blues," in a color symbolism aimed at nothing so much as recriminatory payback and plutocratic resentment, dividing the primary yellow or white light of revolutionary solidarity[40] and substituting economic anarchy and Darwinian selection for an enlightened sense of community. Though the character Henry Waugh, simultaneously an "average Joe" and an omniscient "ruler of the universe" governed by dice-throws, suggests that the consensual fan-experience offers privileged access to the real, the *ens*—

'There were things about the game I liked. The crowds, for example. I felt like I was part of something there, you know, like in church, except is was more *real* than any church, and I joined in the score-keeping, the hollering, the eating of hot dogs and drinking of Cokes and beer, and for a while I even had the funny idea that ball stadiums and not European churches were the real American holy places.'

(*UBA*, 166)

—the narrative text dispels nostalgic preoccupations with a third strike:

Formulas for energy configurations where city boys came to see their country origins dramatized, some old lost fabric of unity...that never quite came off. (*UBA*, 166)

The dangerous and demagogic importation of politics, religion, and art "into the stadium" will not be lost on those with knowledge of political ideology in the 20th century: an irrational patterning of subjugation whose principles are "Western" (Machiavellian) and "Oriental" at once in their reliance upon the "bleachers," i.e., upon aesthetic scaling mechanisms, where anarchy disguises itself before the glazed eyes of Mr./Mrs. Average as the uncannily wired and/or weird spectacle of home, of "order."

Thus what separates Runge's *Times of Day* and, indeed, the German Romantics, including Schlegel, from the unworldliness of the Oriental textile is an emphasis upon the unstable trajectory or movement of transcendence, on the one hand, and, on the other, upon the problematic insurgency of subjective cognition, the attention lavished upon anthromorphic or androgynous figures in the *Kosmos* (Humboldt) as intuited, angels, emblematic children, and so on, and the abandonment of the abstract medallion (hinted at in the sketch), with its built-in flaws, for the myth of the perfected, rampant, eternally youthful subject (infant as father to the Faustian *Überfan*, the superwoman/man in touch with "spirits" above and below). This means that the batsman, *qua* Romantic ego, comes to approximate, or comes into problematic contact with, the divine at the node or contact-point of supreme intuition, where the knuckleball of the absolute, unpredictable as an electron, meets the bat of intuitive knowledge. Nowhere is such an intuited moment of transcendental operativity, the equivalent of a philosophic home-run, made clearer than in Schelling's youthful poetic exercise, "Die Epikuräisch[en] Glaubensbekenntnisse Heinz Widerporstens," written in the same *Knittelvers* (*Knittel* as a synonym for *Stab*, a staff or bat) that Goethe will employ with vastly different batsmanlike effect in *Faust*. The struggle between anxiety and inhibition, on the one hand, and emancipated desire on the other, collapses or rises into the philosophical One, as the "superhuman" subject claims a position formerly reserved for the supreme deity. If Ted Williams had written German poetry, thoughts were line-drives, and the "thousand eyes of the world" were all sitting in Fenway Park, his verses might have sounded like these:

> Ich bin der Gott, der sie im Busen hegt,
> Der Geist, der sich in Allem bewegt
> Vom ersten Ringen dunkler Kräfte
> Bis zum Erguß der ersten Lebensäfte,
> Wo Kraft in Kraft, und Stoff in Stoff verquillt,
> Die erste Blüt', die erste Knospe schwillt,
> Zum ersten Strahl von neu gebornem Licht,
> Das durch die Nacht wie zweite Schöpfung bricht
> Und aus den tausend Augen der Welt
> Den Himmel so Tag wie Nacht erhellt,
> Hinaus zu des Gedankens Jugendkraft,
> Wodurch Natur verjüngt sich selber schafft,
> In Eine Kraft, Ein Pulsschlag nur, Ein Leben,
> Ein Wechselspiel von Hemmen und von Streben.[41]

[I am the god who conjures them <haunted thoughts> up,/ The spirit that moves itself in everything/ From the first wrestling of dark powers/ To the pouring out of the first fluids of life,/ Where power merges into power, and material into material,/ The first bloom, the first bud swells,/ At the first ray of newborn light/ That breaks through the night like a second Creation/ And out of the thousand eyes of the world/ Enlightens the heavens by day and by night,/ Beyond <these> to the youthful power of thought,/ Through which nature, rejuvenated, creates itself,/ Into one power, a beating of a single pulse only, a life,/ A reciprocating play of repression and striving.]

Such is the pulsatile, problematic self-assertiveness of the hieroglyphically attuned game of East/West illumination called Romanticism, beginning in Novalis, Schlegel, and Runge, and culminating in a text that calls itself in a spirit of meta-Böhmean transcendence, *Morgenröte*. In Schlegel's *Lucinde*, "artificially constructed" chaos is conceived in the context of or upon the foundation of the passions which both serve and traverse the ego, not the least of which is a desire to fulfill a destiny of pleasure and pain through the error-prone experience of continually striving to achieve a middle point of stasis (the transcendental batting average) and to slide, in one or more senses, into home (the sexual implications of this are fully explored in Coover's novel). This life or season of irreverent "repression and striving" will become in the next more unpredictable, uncannier, and "stronger" in a spiritual as well as athletic sense. The *Urteil* or originary split of philosophic reflection is articulated in the dialogue of a higher (or major-league) *professional* self with a lower (or minor-league) one:

> Schon eilte ich, dir zu folgen, aber plötzlich hielt mich ein neuer Gedanke an, und ich sagte zu meinem Geiste: 'Unwürdiger, du kannst nicht einmal die kleinen Dissonanzen dieses mittelmäßigen Lebens ertragen, und du hältst dich schon fur ein höheres reif und würdig? Gehe hin, zu leiden und zu tun, was dein Beruf ist, und melde dich wieder, wenn deine Aufträge vollendet sind.' —Ist es nicht auch dir auffallend, wie alles auf dieser Erde nach der Mitte strebt, wie so ordentlich alles ist, wie so unbedeutend und kleinlich? So schien es mir stets; daher vermute ich—und ich habe dir diese Vermutung, wenn ich nicht irre, schon einmal mitgeteilt—, daß unser nachstes Dasein größer, im Guten wie im Schlechten kräftiger, wilder, kühner, ungeheurer sein wird.   (*L*, 104)

> [Already I hastened, in order to follows you, but suddenly a new thought held me, and I said to my <own> spirit: 'Unworthy one, you cannot even bear the small dissonances of this mediocre life, and you consider yourself ripe and worthy of a higher one? Go forth, to suffer and to do that which is your profession, and let yourself be heard again when your tasks are completed.' —Is it not obvious to you also that everything on this earth strives to achieve the middle, just as everything is as ordered as it is unmeaningful and trivial? So it seemed to me at all times; that is why I suppose—and I have communicated this supposition to you, if I am not mistaken, once already—, that our next existence will be greater <in magnitude>, in the Good and in the Bad, more powerful, wilder, bolder, uncannier.]

It is undeniable that this discourse moves into a dialectic of "higher" and "lower" selfhood comparable to the levels of complexity in a Mandelbrot fractal. But it is the "next life," in its ultimate or absolute asymmetry, beyond the systematizing congruencies of this one, that renders predictability problematic—in much the same way that the deterministic dicethrows of Henry Waugh in *The Universal Baseball Association* are a *device*, as textually decisive as Mallarmé's famous *coup de dés*, which, while symbolizing something cosmically larger, nonetheless "will never abolish chance" ("jamais n'abolira le hasard"). This would probably be something more than a tail supplementing the woven pattern or an imperfection meanst to ward off the evil eye. The full reverberation of Schlegel's phrase "in the Good and in the Bad" will be heard in Poe, in Baudelaire, and in Nietzsche's "Fröhliche Wissenschaft," in which the most successful artistic creation is said to come from the empty chalice of delight, where the bitter and sweet drops run *together* in the "happy science" of *Leidenschaft*. Certainly, this deeper mingling of passions finds an analogue in the careers and *amor fati* of hitters and pitchers alike in the cycle of baseball's eternal return, from day to day and year to year. Off the playing field it will be heard, in 20th-century ears attuned to the irrational, in the dithyrambs of the superman Zarathustra and in the denatured, uncanny, "Marsyan" music of Scriabin. On the eve of World War I, or in its aftermath, the music of these texts reverberates and eddies outward like the unpredictable swallow-tail of Thomian catastrophe, a less mappable state of chaos. If, as Barth suggests (*FF*, 315), "the pattern is the subject matter" in Schlegel, it is not the only subject matter, or it is a pattern in which the figures of. Nietzsche, Freud, and Heidegger are also discernible within the "framework" of the uncanny. These matters "come to a head" in the hermeneutic uncertainties informing the conclusion of Poe's *Narrative of A. Gordon Pym*, the text with which Barth might have sought to build a fractal bridge between Schlegel's *Lucinde* and the postmoderns, where the hieroglyph asserts its incommensurable preeminence with respect to the *literary* text in its proximity to the figural—leaving the perspicuous geometries of Mandelbrot and the centrally fielded medallion of the Oriental rug, as it were, stranded on first.[42]

Quincunx Redux: Teaming Up on Chaos

In the Calcutta edition of the first two hundred nights, the ass is made to quote verses to the bull. 'Hast thou not, he asks him, heard the poet say:—I occupy myself every day and night in anxious service of him in whose prosperity I have no enjoyment:/ Like the bleacher who blackens his face in the sun, while he watches the whitening of the clothes of others. '

> *The Arabian Nights*, note by Lane, appended
> to his translation

The Moslem and Old Testament taboo against anthropomorphic depiction is well-known. Though the textiles themselves can be dated back to a pre-Islamic period, as Barth suggests, the emphasis upon abstractness in the

Oriental rug means that figural representation of the human form is subordinate to the woven pattern and almost always missing altogether. Thus the rampant, mutant angelology of Runge's *Der Morgen*, in its absolute fusion of self and universe, militates against an interpretation suggesting a direct link between the Romantic arabesque and a postmodernism in which the absolute sovereignty or universe-determining nature of the emancipated subject, in art, above all, is denied, while the abstractness and chaos-like infinity represented either by the Mandelbrot fractal or the Oriental rug is affirmed. But the Oriental assertiveness of *The Times of Day* and its distribution of and population by seraphs and mutant cherubs differs also from the Persian textile and the paradigmatic decussation or play involved in another sport, basketball. In basketball, though the rules obviously restrict play to the axis of the court and the baskets at either end, the actual passing of the ball from player to player involves a five-fold or quincunxial arrangement similar to that which Barth sees in the fractal and Persian rug (see illustration below). As in hockey and soccer, the action in basketball is more fragmented, disorganized ("chaotic"), and exciting, some would say, than in baseball because the ball can be effectively played in any diagonal direction by means of a throw from the active ball-handler (A) to a potential ball-handler (P). The intensity of action "flows" more freely, without baseball's characteristic alternation between stasis (regulated now by the shot-clock) and frantic action. Thus is defined a dynamic, ever-changing, yet ever-the-same quincunx, whose purpose it is to enable the asymmetry of a transcendent "shot" (TS):

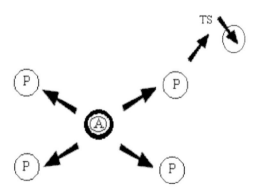

5. Diagram representing possible vectors of
play in basketball.

Sir Thomas Browne's claim for the theosophical significance of the number five is one that simply cannot be made for basketball with anything like the degree of hypothetical cogency that inheres in baseball's symmetries. The number nine is closer to the Pythagorean ideal of ten (two times five) than five. Baseball has no prescribed time limit, as basketball does, and tie ball-games seem to "Scheherazadize" the play as if by some enchanting spell, captivating or boring the fans seemingly *ad infinitum*. In baseball, the action, when there is any, moves always up and away, toward the inner or outer field, as it does in the Runge. Because it is played outdoors (or ws so until the advent of domed stadiums) one could confront the cosmic significance of the blue (aether) and the green (natural as opposed to artificial) grass, watching the gold of baseball's day fade into the blueblack inkiness of night. In baseball everything depends upon overcoming the terror involved in what is the most difficult feat in sports: hitting the ball into one of the fields to the left and right of the pitcher, a wedge defined by the basepaths. This is Runge-like in the sense that the trajectory is, more often than not, arching rather than linear (in a line-drive) and that the energy of the batsman propels the ball always away from home-plate into the field (unless he fouls out). As in Runge, to hit the ball to the out- or upper field is to be "almost home," in an otherworldy or transcendental sense. By propelling the ball into a fair rather than foul portion of the field, the batsman, in a sense, exits the limitation of anterior experiential time (where he is boxed in) and projects his hit into an exalted, indeterminate, yet not altogether chaotic future, hoping that it will turn into the "best of all possible" baseball worlds, a home run. The projectile as it leaves the bat completes a sentence begun in the kinetic, sometimes chaotic unpredictability of the pitch. Or, in a different mythological sense, the batter seeks to answer the pitcher's eternal Sphinx question, an interrogation of what it is to be human during the progressive innings of day.[43] And, in spectator- or beholder-like fashion, the batter occasionally observes his statement as it arcs up and outward into an azure infinite or the sullen, sunless darkness of outer space. Thus baseball, at times, combines passion with an element of reflection, something found only rarely in basketball. On the other hand, basketball, it seems, allows the individual star to shine more brightly, to be a "stand-out" when he happens to be Michael Jordan or one of the other greats. That is, in basketball more than in baseball, it is possible for one truly outstanding player to revolutionize the way we think or imagine the sport, in terms of its universe of possibilities. The Zarathustras of baseball, Babe Ruth or Jackie Robinson, are rare comets, indeed.

Though the records of basketball in past seasons can be researched, baseball seems designed to be a game where history matters crucially to the present, and star players measure themselves against the exemplary records of the past. Once known, these must be interrogated by everyone interested in the sport, from child to journalist, or made a proper field of encylopedic inquiry. Baseball, in its denatured infinitization of the subject, as eternal youth, but also in terms of the fandom of Mr./Mrs. Average, Heidegger's "they" (*das Man*), is open on all sides, infinitely, infinitesimally, to statistics in ways that basketball is not. At the same time, because it is the "national pastime," we remember the scandals of the past as if they were part of family romance; novelists like Malamud remind us of darker edges of culpability enfolding the game, negating the Boy Scout mystique of the citizen become bleached-white bourgeois subject. The Black Sox scandal of 1919, modern-day gambling, and steroid use may not be flaws built into the pastoral pattern, but they suggest contamination by the cultural context—an unraveling of *mores* and ethics in the world beyond the field, or in that part of the culture that decides what the public wants or, more importantly, what kinds of heroes—continuing elaborations of the *Geist* of baseball through an *Übermensch* or Super-Subject—it will pay to see and, just as importantly, to identify with through the group psychology of team jerseys and the like. As Freud suggests, we are obliged to contextualize, whether we wish to or not; abstract patterns or normative "case histories" betray the scientifically observed, locally complex chaoses that created them. And finally, because of the infinite possibilites of record-keeping and play, baseball may well be a fitter subject for romance and fiction because it is more dreamily ironic than basketball. As Friedrich Schlegel suggests, "irony is the clear consciousness of eternal agility, of an infinitely teeming chaos" (*FF*, 320). And, as Browne reminds us, chaos is the child of night:

> Night, which pagan mythology could make the daughter of Chaos, affords no advantage to the description of order, although no lower than that mass can we derive its genealogy. All things begin in order, so shall they end, and so shall they begin again, according to the ordainer of order and mystical mathematics in the City of Heaven.
> ...the huntsmen are up in America, and they are already past their first sleep in Persia....(*GC*, 107)

One hundred years after Runge paints *Morning*, Sigmund Freud visits the cityscape of an alternative, denatured universe called "Dreamland" on Coney Island, near New York City, touring a world, like heaven and hell, from which night has been banished, and artificial light glows more brightly than a thousand *Morgenrötes*. The Steeplechase celebrates the physiognomy of a smile more grotesque than any flute-player's cheeks, while Luna Park, from which straight lines have been banished, represents the American paroxysm of the arabesque, a site of ephemeral, artificial, pleasurable chaos given over to the curved empire of the amusement-park id—like something out of Prospero's palace in Poe's tale, "The Masque of the Red Death":

...it was his own guiding hand which had given character to the masqueraders. Be sure they were grotesque. There were much glint and glitter and piquancy and phantasm—much of what has been since seen in 'Hernani.' There were arabesque figures with unsuited limbs and appointments. There were delirious fancies such as the madman fashions. There was mch of the beautiful, much of the wanton, much of the *bizarre*, something of the terrible, and not a little of that which might have excited disgust. To and fro in the seven chambers there stalked, in fact, a multitude of dreams. [44]

In Russia, at very nearly the same time (1906–1915) Scriabin is writing what might serve as incidental music for Prince Prospero, piano sonatas abandoning the "home plate" of tonality altogether, ending the final Romantic phase of the arabesque (exemplified by Liszt), and beginning the process of art's mathematically denatured assault on the absolute.[45]

Hooked on Arabesque: Satire as Force and Farce in Poe and Gogol

...*струна звенит в тумане.*
[...*a musical string twangs in the mist.*]   Gogol, *Diary of a Madman*

...*he became his admirers.*   W. H. Auden, "In Memory of W. B. Yeats"

Poe may be seen either as a partial *Aufhebung* or as a seraphic imp of the perverse ("Israfel") haunting the Germanism of Schlegel and Runge. This means that, instead of lining up with the Boston "team" (Longfellow, Fuller, et al.) Poe's studied dissidence exorcises the spell of Romantic group identification which at the turn of the century is making cult-figures out of Schiller and Napoleon, on the one hand, while, on the other, elevating European letters to cult status in America. If meta-fiction in the latter 20th and early 21st centuries cannot endure the anachronism of being linked genealogically to Poe, it must at least acknowledge its debt to the precursor. Nowhere does this statement receive greater validation than in a text which goes undiscussed by Barth, but which might have shed additional light on the fractal or non-fractal denaturing of fiction. The satirical unreliability of narrative viewpoint in Poe's "The Thousand-and-Second Tale of Scheherazade" (1845) is informed by its own resident form of scholarly impishness, and by a sense of the text, as book, and bookish equivocation, a sign of the indecisive, preening vanity of modern scholar- and authorship.[46] In Poe's tale, as in many of his others, we sense the reverberation of that unbeauteous, Marsyas-like sound or *tone* alluded to earlier. The *fons et origo* of farce in this case lies in a disgust that is at once bordered and tortured by the fashionable Orientalizing of the early 1840s; what was taken in the generation of Schlegel and Runge most seriously as theosophical algebra becomes grist for Poe's all-American satire (a first-person mock on homegrown *docta ignorantia*), an unpronounceable "mill of particulars":

> Having had occasion, lately, in the course of some Oriental investigations, to consult the *Tellmenow Isitsöorrnoi*, a work which (like the Zohar of Simeon Jochaides) is scarcely known at all, even in Europe, and which has never been quote, to my knowledge, by any American—if we except, perhaps, the author of the 'Curiosities of American Literature;'—having had occasion, I say to turn over some pages of the first-mentioned work....   (*PT*, 787)

Thus begins the narrative of Poe's "extra" Arabian tale, which projects its story as a thinly veiled enumeration of modern technological "wonders," such as chicken incubators, calculating machines, mechanical chess-players, and the "electro-telegraph," larding the marginal subtext with footnotes on telescopes, the speed of light, and up-to-date observations on long ago extinguished stars. This encyclopedic subtext, its open window on the infinite, links Poe to Jean Paul, Sterne, and other Romantic theorists of the arabesque—in its disfigured or grotesque aspect. To Scheherazade's recitation of the wonders of newfangled commercial gadgetry, the Baghdad "king" invariably remarks, "Absurd!" or "Ridiculous!" To be sure, we soon forget that the ironic tale is told within the framing fiction of philological annotation on an "ancient" text; and are thus invited—so it seems—into the domain of meta-fiction. But what is unique to Poe, and destructive of any semblance of narrative mystification, is the fact that allusions to American and European inventions are transparently, "prosaically," labeled as "Oriental," that the meta-fiction is itself flimsy, self-deconstructing or ironizing, and disconcertingly *flat*. As soon as the East becomes the West, in Poe's malignly transformational grammar, abetted by the underwriting of footnotes—a matter of literary intonation rather than scopic delight—it turns into a hardware catalogue. The Oriental pattern (and the illusion of scholarly erudition behind it) finds itself not so much replaced by the matter-of-fact, Swiftian tone of what we might call Poe's perverse "Newspaperese," as undermined by a tenor of extraordinary ordinariness:

> 'Among this nation of necromancers there was also one who had in his veins the blood of the salamander; for he made no scruple of sitting down to smoke his *chibouc* in a red-hot oven until his dinner was thoroughly roasted upon its floor. Another had the faculty of converting the on metals into gold, without even looking at them in the process.' (*PT*, 802)

There is thus no way to extricate a pattern or medallion-like figure from the journalistic aversion of the tale or to tell frame from content. Poe's text, even in the ridiculous scholarly armature, "runs away," in a sense, from the mesmerizing recital of *The Arabian Nights*, never achieving the level of the arabesque *figura*, of the beautiful. The illusion is shattered, and the distance between truth and fiction collapsed, at the level of schizoid equivocation or *vertige* at the syntactical level, from sentence to sentence, and at the lexical, in matters of word-choice. The ultimate joke or scherzo movement of the text is provided by the word "crotchet," which has many meanings deriving from the French *crochet*: a hook, including a hook-shaped instrument used in barbarous 18th-century obstetrics, a musical note with half the value of a minim, in the shape of a stem with a round black head, a square bracket in typography, but which receives an extra-lexical definition from "Scheherazade" herself: "One of the evil genii who are perpetually upon the watch to inflict ill...." (*PT*, 804). It is this evil genius, related to but surpassing the meaning of crotchet as a "flight of whimsy" or "perverse conceit" that has "put it into the heads" of "accomplished ladies" that a certain protuberance or hump (translatable in terms of contemporary fashion as a hoop skirt) below the small of the back is a thing of beauty. Hearing of this invention, the king cries, "Stop!" and has Scheherazade killed. But the word "crotchet," in English, which we can now read, on the one hand, as a typographical reduction of the human head, in its most abbreviated or minimalized form, is also another form of the word "crocket," a curl placed in the hair, but also a bud- or leaf-shaped ornamentation, i.e., the sign or signature of the arabesque upon the text at its most mad or maddening point. The lightness or inconsequentiality of the arabesque surfaces in the whimsy of the crotchet or mental disposition that engenders the hooped skirt and in the joke on literature or "exit into nothingness" provided by Scheherazade's death. Nevertheless the "passional," perverse sign of Poe's own voice as a writer, struggling to break free of the "mass appeal" of the Scheherazade frame itself—turned against the adulation for things Oriental that Lane's translation had aroused—shows itself in the miniature theatre of cruelty by which Poe's tale, no longer being told by Scheherazade, ends. This drama is double-edged, however, since Poe, while not exactly on Scheherazade's side, at least appreciates the vengeance she, as a storyteller "cut off in the prime," wreaks upon her incredulous auditor. The reading public's own king- or caliph-like satisfaction is experienced at the cost of what is absolute terror, *for her*—in the moment immediately preceding execution, when the words "great consolation" bring the chill of Swift-like irony:

She derived, however, great consolation, (during the tightening of the bowstring) from the reflection that much of the history remained still untold, and that the petulance of the brute of a husband had reaped for him a most righteous reward, in depriving him of many inconceivable adventures. (*PT*, 804)

With Scheherazade's premature punishment dies an entire literature; the arabesque-like joke of an ending collapses the *"meta"* of this meta-fiction, the tomorrow of storytelling. Poe's Scheherazade-like vengeance upon the brutish public, Oriental groupies avid in 1845 for "one more" Arabian fiction, is complete.

As Barth indicates, and Görres also suggests, the arabesque seems to function well when concerned with levity or humor. But Poe writes in his introduction to *Tales of the Grotesque and Arabesque* that the critics have remarked on the arabesque element in his *serious* tales, which he himself does not term grotesque, but which he instead links to "Germanism and gloom." Görres, uncomfortable with the term arabesque, as applied to Runge, never mentions the grotesque, but identifies the art of the painter with the higher (philosophical and/or theosophical) aspirations of hieroglyphic symbolism. In other words, if Runge had been "merely" concerned with the arabesque, he would have never been taken seriously by Schelling or aroused a furor when his works became known to the public. Likewise, Poe will adopt the hieroglyphic, especially in *The Narrative of A. Gordon Pym,* as "his own," a device or symbol of a serious nature allied with a deeper problematics of subjectivity, repression, and representation. For now, in 1840, while Lane is publishing his expurgated translation of *The Arabian Nights,* it is sufficient to note how the "game" of arabesque and grotesque is one that Poe insists he may never play again, how it is subordinated to something altogether different and far more "serious," the legitimation of terror as a literary subject, and the equivocation of an authorial subject ever in search of himself:

The epithets 'Grotesque' and 'Arabesque' will be found to indicate with sufficient precision the prevalent tenor of the tales here published. But from the fact that, during a period of some two or three years, I have written five-and-twenty short stories whose general character may be so briefly defined, it cannot be fairly inferred—at all events it is not truly inferred—that I have, for this species of writing, any inordinate, or indeed any peculiar taste or prepossession. I may have written with an eye to this republication in volume form, and may, therefore, have desired to preserve, as far as a certain point, a certain unity of design. This is, indeed, the fact, and it may even happen that, in this manner, I shall never compose anything again. I speak of these things here, because I am led to think it is this prevalence of the 'Arabesque' in my serious tales, which has induced one or more critics to tax me, in all friendliness, with what they have been please to term 'Germanism' and gloom. The charge is in bad taste, and the grounds of the accusation have not been sufficiently considered. Let us admit, for the moment, that the 'phantasy-pieces' now given *are* Germanic, or what not. Then Germanism is 'the vein' for the time being. To morrow I may be anything but German, as yesterday I was everything else. These many pieces are yet one book. My friends would be quite as wise in taxing an astronomer with too much astronomy, or an ethical author with treating too largely of morals. But the truth is that, with a single exception, there is no one of these stories in which the scholar should recognise the distinctive species of that species of pseudo-horror which we are taught to call Germanic, for no better reason than that some of the secondary names of German literature have become identified with its folly. If in many of my productions terror has been the thesis, I maintain that terror is not of Germany, but of the soul,—that I have deduced this terror only from its legitimate sources, and urged it only to its legitimate results.[47]

Poe's divergences of opinion, in terms of what he and others consider to be the unspecifiable genre of his texts, or what he himself "is" from day to day, begins to suggest the terrain of postmodern metafiction, while the "floating" predication—yesterday pseudo-horror, tomorrow the real thing—hints not at lability or schizophrenia, where one is sure, in a clinically unfortunate sense, that one is Napoleon, for example, but at the flight from solid identification *by the other*, an attempt to remain masked, undefinable, and thus in *absolute* control, say, of one's own style and self-definition. Poe's equivocation, his prickly abrasive- and evasiveness, marked by twists of sentence structure and the use of asides in subjunctive mood, comes to an abrupt halt, however, when, beyond the labels "Arabesque," "Grotesque," and "Germanism," the subject of terror is broached. Terror, for Poe, has a legitimation or entire legal process surrounding it, and it is here that the authorial subject, as the one who sees terror through, so to speak, to the end, tears off the mask of evasion. "Tenor," the prevalence of a certain thematic or motivic *tone*, was the alpha of the discussion; terror is its omega—the moment just before Scheherazade's execution, a moment to be savored and returned to as the end of fiction and the morning of metafiction in America.

To be sure, the arabesque, at least as a title to be placed at the head of a page or in a table of contents, is an equivocal phenomenon which reverberates between Germany and America. The descent of the arabesque into the grotesque—in Gogol's "Diary of a Madman"—is marked by a terror which seems on the surface like Poe's, but which distances itself from Gothic gloom or "Germanism" through an even greater emphasis upon comedy and farce. Gogol's inimitable style demands transcendence of the past of Russian fiction, of genre, and of literature, or literariness, as understood *prior* to his own writing. In a passage reminiscent of Jean Paul's Luftschiffer Gianozzo, Gogol's first-person, "mad" diarist takes the Kantian *Ur-teil* to a schizophrenic *ultima thule* or point of no return; the terror of the "hunted man" is scanned at an ironic, melodramatic distance, becoming a matter of "clinical" interest for the reader. It is Gogol's style, carefully and parodically seeded with "Romantic" details, that is the "cold water" poured on the "hot head" of the madman's melodrama. After a demented carriage ride "out of this world," one that makes a mockery of flying carpets and balloon-flights into the aether while taking the wind out of Baudelaire's nearly contemporary "n'importe où, pourvu qu'il soit hors du monde," the exalted subject of Runge and Schelling exits into a nosological *hors du monde*, the otherworldliness of the agonized or schizophrenic patient, one that is not without a certain grandeur in its *furor*—the text itself must be reckoned among the greatest in Russian literature—a beauty of grotesque description far more breathtaking in the original than in any translation because of the grainy musicality of the Russian vowels, as it moves from a tone of indignation to one of interrogation and, finally, of mock-Romantic despair, demystifying transcendence between the semicoloned throbbings of a headache and a *Kopfgeburt*. At the same time, it leaves us with the vivid impression of something both precarious and precocious in its conceitfulness:

Нет, я больше не имею сил терпеть. Боже! что они делают со мною! Они льют мне на голову холодную воду! Они не внемлют, не видят, не слушают меня. Что я сделал им? За что они мучат меня? Чего хотят они отменя, бедного? Что могу дать я им? Я неичего не имею. Я не в силах. Я не могу вынести всех муж их, голова горит моя, и все кружится предо мною. Спасите мне! возьмите меня! даите мне тройку быстрых, как вихорь, коней! Садись мой ямщик, звени, мой колокольчик всвейтеся, кони и несите меня с етого света! Далее, далее, чтобы не видно было ничего, иничего. Вон небо клубится передо мною; звездочка сверкает вдали; лес несется с темными деревьями и месяцем; сизый туман стелется под ногами; струна звенит в туман; с одной стороны море; с другой Йталия; вон и русские избы виднеюут. Дом ли томой синеет вдали? Мать ли моя сидит перед окном? Матушка, спаси твоего бедного сына! урони слезинку на его больную головушку! посмотряи как мучат они его! прижми ко груди своей бедного сиротку! ему нет место на свете! До гонят Матушка пожалей о своем больном дитятка!...А знаете ли что у алжирского бея под самым носом шишка?[48]

[No, I have not the strength to bear this any longer. God, the things they are doing to me! They pour cold water upon my head! They do not heed me, nor see me, nor listen to me. What have I done to them? Why do they torture me? I have nothing. My strength is gone, I cannot endure all this torture. My head is aflame, and everything spins before my eyes. Save me, someone! Take me away. Give me three steeds, steeds as fast as the whirling wind! Seat yourself, driver, ring out, little harness bell, wing your way up, steeds, and rush me out of this world. On and on, so that nothing be seen of it, nothing. Yonder the sky wheels its clouds; a tiny star glitters afar; a forest sweeps by with its dark trees, and the moon comes in its wake; a silvergrey mist swims below; a musical string twangs in the mist; there is the sea on one hand, there is Italy on the other; and now Russian peasant huts can be discerned. Is that my home looming blue in the distance? Is that my mother sitting there at her window? Mother dear, save your poor soul! Shed a tear upon his aching head. See, how they torture him. Press the poor orphan to your heart. There is no place for him in the whole wide world! He is a hunted creature. Mother dear, take pity on your sick little child...And by the way, gentlemen, do you know that the Bey of Algiers has a round lump growing right under his nose?[49]]

What, specifically, is "arabesque" in Gogol—and how does it relate to Mandelbrot and postmodernism? We would not be completely wrong, given the interchangeability of the two terms, to define the Gogolian arabesque as a comedically grotesque attention to narrative detail, large and small, as a reflection or refraction of narrated consciousness. A Rabelaisian or Swiftian linkage in the stream of a single discourse of the microcosmic to the macrocosmic scale provides a double-edged, equivocal narrative sword: on the one hand, the reader may perceive a divine mind troubled by the least leaf that falls; on the other, a demented, hyper-inclusive intelligence that connects an inner or "Romantic" predicament to the nose of the Bey of Algiers, for example. Gogol's supreme aesthetic merit, that of noticing things in their cosmic particularity, can and usually does, in the arabesque mode, devolve into schizophrenic observations, on the part of a "hothouse" mind, of the "interrelatedness" of everything under the sun. Nabokov, in a classic study,[50] discerns, an impressionistic sensitivity to color on the part of Gogol himself, one that is able to depict "...the moving pattern of light and shade on the ground under trees or the tricks of color played by sunlight with leaves" (*NG*, 87). Thus is supplied that element of keen, first-hand observation which shocked Russian readers who had been left "purblind" by previous literature. Taken to a fantastic extreme, in postmodernism, one has a Gogolian impressionism without depth of field or feeling, the sense that everything, past, present, and future being "up for grabs" in the deranged or manic sensorium of the indiscriminately perceiving "host" or narrator. One is "hooked" on impressions in their chaotic scintillation or symmetry. The excessive, comedically accentuated attention to detail can be seen as one among a number of arabesque elements in Gogol's fiction: 1) marginal insertions, asides, digressions of an all-knowing narrator (as in Diderot and Jean Paul), 2) concern with detail, on the one hand a sign of realism or of a preoccupation with the objectivity of the real world, on the other, the mark of a style which prefers to lose itself in the *detour*: to become distracted by random, seemingly trivial details, 3) a dream-like reprojection of reality, bordering upon and at times descending into fits of madness, 4) irony and laughter.[51] Thus, in Gogol, the transcendental homelessness of Romanticism is translated into something altogether disruptive, comedic, and grotesque, as an infernal, farcical helplessness. Such a depiction of interpenetrating order and chaos, a constellation of vanity and despair representing *Leidenschaft* at the antipodes of sane and insane experience, it need only be noted in passing, lies beyond the capacity of perspicuous mapping to express.

A final remark. Poe's tale entitled "Lionizing" takes the levity of the arabesque, punningly, in terms of noses and nosology, beyond even a Gogolian frontier, indicting the egocentrism of the modern scholarly world—"only too saracastically"—as mental illness. Absent is Gogol's impressionism; we are left instead with a sense of *vertige* on the edge of a *virtual* precipice, scannning an abyss where the lunatic rules by the numbers, by the egregious juxtaposition of true and false articles of pedantic faith. In "Lionizing" there is no story; there is rather a sense of the absurdity underlying much of what goes under the name of narcissistic bookishness, an alphabetical parading of triumphant *doctes idiots* at a dinner presided over by the Prince of Wales, a potentate among erudite fools. Not least of the troubling aspects of this diabolical ("arabesque") parade of *grotesqueries* is the framing pronoun "we" and the subtly powerful, Swiftian insinuation that this is "our" world, that the characters assembled here are not *isolatos* like Gogol's Madman, but sought after by an adoring public, a perennially adolescent and fulsome fan-base:

> We were all lions and recherchés.
> There was a modern Platonist....
> There was a human-perfectibility man...
> There was Sir Positive Paradox...
> There was Æstheticus Ethix...
> There was the President of the Fum-Fudge University...
> There was Delphinus Polyglott. He told us what had become of the eighty-three lost tragedies of Æschylus; of the fifty-four orations of Isæus; of the three hundred and ninety-one speeches of Lysias; of the hundred and eighty treatises of Theophrastus; of the eighth book of the conic sections of Apollonius; of Pindar's hymns and dithyrambics; and of the five and forty tragedies of Homer Junior... (*PT*, 214–215)

These are listed before the first-person narrator chimes in with a pathological, Monty-Python-like stutter of narcissistic self-reference:

> There was myself. I spoke of myself;—of myself, of myself, of myself;—of Nosology, of my pamphlet, and of myself. I turned up my nose, and I spoke of myself.   (*PT*, 215–216)

"I," that is, placed in the center, at the medallion-like heart of lionizing, popular adulation, or fan appeal, turns out—with his little book on noses or diseases or both—to be the most snobbish, least reliable and praiseworthy of those gathered for the purpose of mutual admiration. A caricatured sensibility is no longer something outside the text, but woven and/or stuttered into the very fabric of its telling.

Barth's discussion of the "formal properties" of the Persian rug prompts parenthetical mention of *Lucinde* and Poe's *Narrative of Arthur Gordon Pym of NANTUCKET* (*FF*, 313), but these properties, of "pure" mathesis, fractal geometry, et al., cannot properly (in and of themselves) account for that which constitutes the uniqueness either of Schlegel's doubly voiced text or a complexity which is of an entirely different order of hieroglyphic complexity. It seems that we are left, precisely in *The Narrative of A. Gordon Pym*, with an uncertainty principle, of Poeish rather than Heisenbergian origin, in which "we," together with the "gestalt" become problematized, as soon as the Runge-like "representation of a human figure" occurs in nature. It is no longer possible to pose the difference between naturing or denaturing as a perspicuous dichotomy:

> ...Pym's and Peters' uncertainty about whether the markings are natural or man-made reflects a deeper uncertainty inherent in the very opposition between nature and art— a constitutive uncertainty that the markings in the chasm are intended to exhibit. Though the hieroglyphic figure on the wall evokes a language whose characters are necessarily natural shapes rather than arbitrary, man-made signs, the very fact that the hieroglyph in this case is the representation of a human figure tends to make the 'natural/man-made' distinction problematic. For it suggests, on the one hand, that since man is as naturally occurring an object as trees or rocks or rivers, his arbitrary designs, the traces of human movements, are just as much natural shapes as are leaves or fissures or erosions; and it suggests, on the other hand, that the concept of the 'natural,' as a function of the differential opposition 'natural/man-made,' is itself something man-made. [52]

Already here, one begins to perceive the strategy of such writers of postmodern fiction as Mitchell and Murakami, who leave us in continual doubt as to the boundaries separating the natural from the artificial— boundaries which are becoming progressively more obscure as the 21st century progresses The basis for such doubt resides in the ambivalently "artificial" nature of the hieroglyphic sign, which dwells in "two worlds," one real and one made-up or disposed by intelligent human agency. An ability to see the hieroglyph in nature assumes that nature is intelligent or in some way leaves signs for us. But to make such an assumption, we must first be disposed, by our second "nature," to think hermeneutically or cryptologically. That is why, especially in Murakami, the fractal stratifications of the text are strewn with patterns which "must be read," but which refuse to be read or are readable only after considerable hermeneutic effort, when we suspend our dogmatic belief in the dichotomy of "natural versus artificial." Something of the same sort is being suggested in the love fantasy of Runge's *Morning*, except that the "boundaryless illumination of the universe" reveals its debt to a Kantian (and Schellingian) Enlightenment where subjectivity reflects/refracts itself in the absolute medium of art. At the same time, back in the "real" world, the cryptological becomes an obsession, on the part of the financial and political security-state, with cybernetic fencing, where nothing matters so much as keeping the other, gold-bugger, hacker or terrorist, on the other side of the firewall:

'In the present case—indeed in all cases of secret writing—the first question regards the language of the cipher; for the principles of solution, so far, especially, as the more simple ciphers are concerned, depend upon and are varied by, the genius of the particular idiom. In general there is no alternative but experiment (directed by probability) of every tongue known to him who attempts the solution, until the true one be attained.' [53]

Poe's fascination with cryptography and hieroglyphics, as intense but aligned more with a Wagnerian twilight than a Rungean dawn, anticipates the wars for "total control" waged by those in possession of the latest digital gadgetry:

The technological and the cryptological are the parallel fast tracks along which the tech-no-future unrolls. Germany (in the twenties and thirties) and California (to this day) are the two fronts of total (suicidal) war installed within the group between self and other. (*CC*, 151).

This is the post-Poe, postmodern cyber-reality with which we shall be dealing, no doubt, for the rest of this century—no longer a medallion at the center, but an asymmetrical strife (Eris) waged between competitive hieroglyph-making strategies dividing self and other, fractionalized rather than fractal groups and groupies occupying digital space on a nearly infinite number of borders or cyber-shores.

Zarathustra and *das Man*

'What does it take to do the super thing, the thing that makes you bigger than life?'
"Devo"

For whatever reason, Barth's discussion of the Romantic arabesque studiously avoids mention of the word "passion," except on the last page, where "impassioned" appears as an adjective modifying Romanticism. This is understandable, given the postmodern disdain for affect, but, once again, it seems to make things a little too easy or perspicuously self-evident. Indeed, what seems to have mattered to contemporary readers of *Lucinde* was the insult done to the audience: its capacity to shock and awe simultaneously—a programmatic, problematic transcendence of values esteemed by the well-regulated *citoyen-bourgeois*: the championing of extramarital freedom and a Marsyas-like striving "to be the best." To omit mention of the context of reader-reception the the "new mythology" of Romanticism is to wall off the very universe for which the text was intended, to make the text into something "outside," into an item of decor, rather than to perceive the renovative patterning of society according to an overarching, "new" principle to be inculcated in the absence of aristocracy and religious dogma.

Down from the mountains overlooking bazaars where women have always done the weaving of rugs comes Zarathustra, a "Player" full of passion for the game (of life) and a zeal for perfection. As spectator to his descent we observe the figure of the fan, who is simultaneously "das Man" of Heidegger—who, we might say, is of an entirely different scale than the *Übermensch*, without whom the superwoman/man can certainly exist, but only in the darkness preceding the dawn, without the glitz that attends the sun's gladdened, golden arrival. Mr./Ms. Average *(das Man)*, no longer the Romantic subject of knowledge, provides a "fan-base" for the *Übermensch* who strides on game day into "the Valley," the corporate-sponsored sports stadium, which now bears the logo(s) of something which builds each fan into a much sought-after, supraindividual (data) base, the multinational "super-thing"—a dim, entirely primitive, selfishly motivated Player foreshadowing, *perhaps*, Kant's ideal world-state. *Das Man*, mutated into the Full Fan, is not other than the consumer "(data) base," without whom the full fan-experience provided by the multinational Player/Super-Subject is unthinkable. It is of a Zarathustran scale compared to the puny individual; only by becoming "super-sized," one with the post-Romantic's Full Fan-Experience, by consuming the product and wearing the cap and/or jersey, can the fan(atic) ally him- or herself with the "super thing" (juiced on steroids or not) that has just now arrived in the Valley. The transvaluation of values is complete, only *das Man* is the last to know. Digitalized or not, the neutered Fan-Man/Woman still thinks he or she is living in the 19th or 20th century, pretending that what is being witnessed down on the field, in the universal, boundaryless Valley, is just a game and not something more serious, like lionizing, narcissism, or money. The super-sized, fanatical, irrational present—with what it so obviously and ominously portends for a future already staging a rerun of near and more remote pasts (of 1930s Berlin, of 1970s Santiago, or of ancient Rome) without knowing it—lies with all of its clues out in the open, in front of the spectator. But the obvious is simultaneously the most hieroglyphically obscure to *das Man*, who fathoms, in his/her pre-judicial fan heart if not in his/her brain, that survival depends upon consenting to the Orwellian displacement of altruistic consciousness, a jocular demonizing of the other as evil ("double plus ungood"), and demagogic ignorance, a political calculus of unknowing based upon a more primitive *Ur-teil* separating each fan listed in the Corporate Player's data-base from the "out-of-bounds," the im-proper, the alien. What begins as the Romantics' boundaryless illumination of the universe becomes the "decussation" of the terrorized present, not so much denatured as given over to an averageness seen to exist at the heart of things: the empire of earned runs, on-base success, and strikeout failure, for which the full fan-experiencer never takes responsibility:

> The they has its own ways to be. The tendency of being-with, which we called distantiality is based on the fact that being-with-one-another as such creates averageness. it is an existential character of the they. In its being, the they is essentially concerned with averageness. Thus, the they maintains itself factically in the averageness of what is proper, what is allowed, and what is not. Of what is granted success and what is not...
> The they is everywhere, but in such a way that it has always already stolen away when Da-sein presses for a decision. However, because the they presents every judgment and decision as its own, it takes the responsibility of Da-sein away from it. The they can, as it were, manage to have 'them' constantly invoking it. It can most easily be responsible for everything, because no one has to vouch for anything. The they always 'did it,' and yet it can be said that 'no one' did it. In the everydayness of Da-sein, most things happen in such a way that we must say 'no one did it.'[54]

Yet this too is old news, of a sort, because it does not diminish the still vivid and valid Kantian vision of a world brought under the rule of reason, an imperative long neglected by the greed-driven West and piously ruthless East, without which there is no hope for the future. Here, the corporate Super-Subject down on the field must play a part and may at some time in the future be ready to do so, whether as Player or Fan—as self-interest gradually becomes (or is forced to become) universally enlightened and ethically responsible. The question is only whether such a truly enlightened self-interest, worthy of Runge's hieroglyphic vision of "the boundaryless illumination of the universe, can overtake, for more than a decade or two, the demagogic appeal to the wrong passions, to a lower rather than a higher Self, of those speaking in the stadium about differences separating "us" (*das Man*) from "them" (the Other), "the proper" from "the improper." *Das Man* ought to seize the future as well as the present as something for which the bleachers should, on the one hand, take unpanicked local responsibility, i.e., refusing vociferously to accept a future encrypted by a Sphinx of Self-absorption, the globalized corporate Super-Subject. This would entail the risk of a task which has, over the whole history of the full fan-experience from ancient Rome to Berlin to Dallas, proven impossible for *das Man*, the Fan, the Player, and Aurora, the mastering of the irrational (aesthetic) impulses structuring the political unconscious (on billboards, TV, and video screens), as it is rescaled/retailed in front of us and retooled behind our backs. Here is where we most need to be most active hermeneutically and to make our readings the subject of fully interactive, un-gamelike, and intricate experiences of analysis—touching rather than stepping on all the bases.

On the other hand, if we are students of Nietzsche, our affirmation can only take the form of a laughter in which all responsibility (and multicultural guilt) is, or should be, forgotten in the interest of Aurora's early light, a lighter *pas de deux* into a future that does not yet exist.

Chaos on the Installment Plan: The Meta-Fiction of Mitchell and Murakami

These concluding remarks on recent meta-fictional texts will proceed from the observation that the "Muse" of recent meta-fiction is not Schlegel or even Nietzsche, but Poe and, above all, Kafka. This will come as no surprise to readers of Haruki Murakami's latest novel *Kafka on the Shore*,[55] where the text acknowledges its debt to Scheherazade on many levels: the protagonist "Kafka" at one point actually reads *The Arabian Nights*. "I'm alone inside the world of the story," he says.[56] In these solipsistic circumstances, as Barth suggests in the context of Schlegel (*FF*, 315), "the pattern is the subject matter," and the reader is confronted with a near-characterless void where reality and dreams are seen as adjunct, borderless territories, the living can become ghosts, the dead haunt flesh and blood, the precursor text inhabits the current one, either as "Kafka" or as "Colonel Sanders." Worlds and cultures collide, while the veil of *maya* separating substance from appearance becomes ever thinner. The hero, whose goal it is to avoid an Oedipus-like fate, nevertheless sees his mother everywhere, in young as well as in older women, because the girl within lies concealed beneath the appearance of a woman in middle age.

Mitchell's *Ghostwritten*, on the other hand, moves from chapter to chapter through seven "locations," from Okinawa to London, via Tokyo, Hong Kong, "Holy Mountain," and Mongolia, before the final two chapters, "Night Train" and "Underground," move the first-person narrator and reader toward the consummation of some vaguely defined terroristic attack on a subway. But it is not as if these are projected as three- or four-dimensional, discrete worlds, with anything like the attention to arabesque or grotesque detail, say, of Poe or Gogol. What makes Tokyo, for example, distinct from other urban settings is the attention that the narrator lavishes on finding more or less exotic jazz records; the serial nature or routinization of the experience of finding the record and categorizing its rarity matters more than the music itself, which might prove affirming or liberating to subjective consciousness. The postmodernist taboo against affect, as noted by Jameson, is registered disconcertingly here, since the inner life of the protagonist remains a blank. For a reader who also happens to be a fan or aficionado of jazz, it is the feel of a solo or the "soul" of it that matters, but Mitchell at no point discloses what makes a given record, say, by Mal Waldron, aesthetically discrete from one by Lester Young. What exactly is a "Mal Waldron time of day" (*G*, 40)? We know or think we know what makes the terrorist "I" tick, but we have no clue as to how it relates to jazz. Such asides need not take an old-fashioned, "discursive" turn. They might be fragments or multifaceted incantations in the mode of Gertrude Stein, for example, or ironically accentuated, rhapsodic "spells."[57] Mitchell can serve as a kind of test-case not only for Hayles's "denaturing of context," but also for an emptying out of content coordinate with postmodernism's eschewal of "lived experience." In *Ghostwritten* the open universe of the Romantics, and especially the subject-centered, literary-artistic absolute of Runge and Schelling, falls victim to group psychosis and the kind of feedback looping which Barth, following Hayles, considers one among a number of prominent features in postmodern fiction (*FF*, 333)—to cosmic claustrophobia. The output of chapter A not only becomes part of the input of chapter Z; chapter A *determines* chapter Z in a system that is closed to affect (while still open to the random, interferential noise of the "stupid" other), to experiences that are not artificially induced and thus programmed in advance by records, movies, religious cults, chemical stimulus-response mechanisms and the like. Yet the reader at times feels the pressure of the uncanny or the disorientation of surprise, as when the character "Neal" perches his Rolex on a dragon and swims underwater, looking up at the bottom of wavelets in a Hong Kong fountain (*G*, 99). But his sudden empowerment and immortality are seen as delusive, yet another symptom of mental breakdown. History may be a demon to be exorcized through unicorns and jazz. But the paradigm of the liberated slave running out onto the field in the first inning of each new day is replaced by that of the bee-man, a "team-player," jostling for position but losing status as a cult-inspired "Übermensch" in the hive of a subway-car beneath the Empire State building. If *Ghostwritten's* cataclysmic "boxed-in-ness," ignores the imperative of a philosophical-literary *satura* at liberty to calls the genre or *Genrehaftigkeit* of the novelistic text into question, it internationalizes the Novalis-like quest for a second or "potentialized" inner self. By celebrating a *Bridge of San Luis Rey* variety of cosmic coincidence, it alters the arabesque, as conceived by Nietzsche: "To affirm is not to take responsibility for, to take on the burden of what is, but to set free what lives."[58] Indeed, the motivation of responsibility weighs heavily on the slave-like consciousness of *das Man* who is the neutered narrator, adding to the overall impression of a claustrophobia at odds with the moment or momentum of the Nietzschean and Rungean Aurora.

For Murakami, on the other hand, the Japanese translator of Fitzgerald, passion matters differently, insofar as it triggers curiosity, motivates research, and occasions discovery, albeit fractally or in mirror-like shards of digitalized consciousness, for example, when the narrator "Kafka" asks to hear (*KS*, 203) "Kafka on the Shore" as a record, not a CD, "...to hear how it originally sounded," then finds in it "something urgent and serious" (*KS*, 225), and finally studies the sheet music and lyrics themselves:

> *The drowning girls' fingers*
> *Search for the entrance stone, and more.*
> *Lifting the hem of her dress*
> *She gazes—*
> *At Kafka on the shore.* (*KS*, 232)

Rather than feeling himself subject to chance operations, "Kafka" senses disparate worlds of chaos closing in upon him, because random dots or bytes of information connect the past, especially that of his father and mother, to the present. The result is a fascination not different from the experience of reading *The Arabian Nights* or Kafka himself.

Self-negating unity with the great Void may be what the first-person terrorist-narrator in *Ghostwritten* is seeking, as he considers himself in various Zarathustra-like ways to be above "the great unwashed" who are less enlightened, i.e., everyday straphangers. But his "Enlightenment" is anything but all-inclusive and "boundaryless." Group identification is what this text is "all about," followed to its predictable, irrational outcome, conspiratorial apocalypse. The irony of the narrator's situation is that he has not arrived on the astral plane, but is now below, in a kind of hallucinatory "night of the living dead," where even team "strength" finds itself blocked:

> *Move! The unclean are dazzling you!* Empty yourself of self, and you may slip through where even a scream could not. A sailor blocks me. A sailor down here? Surely, this heaving coffin is the opposite of the sea? A glossy booklet is splayed against his uniform. The spine is warped and cracking. *Petersburg, City of Masterworks.* An icing-sugar palace, a promenade, a river spanned by graceful bridges. What stops this train collapsing under its own mass? Who stops the world? This is my stop. I explain to the unclean I am stepping on. *I get off here.*

> The unclean reply as one. *Move down the compartment.*
> I try to block them as they block me, and seek out their weakness. [59]

Rather than contemplating the night-sky prior to dawn and gaining a Super-Subject's sense of universal illumination and of mythically scaled, eternally youthful desire, the essence of Runge's hieroglyph, the narrator, like the immured victim in Poe's "The Cask of Amontillado," finds himself spiritually asphyxiated by the other. In the randomness of his thoughts, he falls prey to chaos, becoming a mere tissue of subway sensations. There may be a fractal logic in the extreme attention to detail, but it reveals a misguided conception of the irrecuperable tawdriness and obsoleteness of the "Not-I" in the crowded subway-car—everyone, that is, who does not belong to the "cool group" to which the first-person narrator belongs:

> Adrenalin swirls through my bloodstream like cream in coffee. One more meter closer to life. A vinyl shopping bag falls down from a rack. It bulges with a crayon-colored web that a computer might have doodled: *The London Underground.* I elbow it out of my face. *I get off here.* The fire in the hearth is the color of fellowship. Their smiles are warm and gluey as *Auld Lang Syne.* On the label of Kilmagoon whisky is an island old as the world.
> And I can go no further. A mere meter away, but with more unclean being crammed on. I am stuck fast as a bee in amber. I watch the light on the waves, and sink, my arm flailing out towards the exit thought the rest of me has given up fighting.
>
> (*G*, 425)

A rush of adrenalin alienates the traditional aesthetic response, limiting the horizon of reference to an all-too-predictable behaviorist twostep:

> I don't care who or what I'm trampling over as I reel myself in. With strength I never knew I possessed I prise open the doors to a fist-wide crack. I hear a grunt of panic. It's me. I shove my arm through...The guard glares at me, mouthing, *That is forbidden,* but the sound is lost. Will he try to shove me back into the zombie wagon? The fear is lost. I've fallen forwards and headbutted the Empire State Building, circled by an albino bat, scattering words and stars through the night. *Spend the night with Bat Segundo on 97.8 FM.*   (*G*, 425–426)

Amid the depiction of varying states of numbness and insensitivity, we have the sense of being locked with the narrator not only in a St. Petersburg ice palace, but in a lurching subterranean charnel- or ice-house, suggesting the metaphor Hazlitt applied to *Venus and Adonis* and *The Rape of Lucrece.*

These brief takes on multiple personalities in Mitchell and Murakami bring us back to Barth's use of the personal pronoun "our." One is unsure of the sense(s) of possession being expressed in the phrase "our man Schlegel" (*FF*, 287). If it means that Schlegel, together with Novalis, Poe, Gogol,

Nietzsche, Scriabin, and Freud—exhibiting a Marsyas-like difference residing in the infinite capacity of the sign or key signature for disfiguration and thus for unpredictable, "Heisenbergian" or "Brownian" shifts of modality, whose traces can only be perceived as coming before or after, but never "presented" or "presenced," can be reduced to perspicuous and mappable symmetries "within viewing range" of Persian rugs and the Mandelbrot fractal, then the "our" seems exaggerated. If, on the other hand, the "our" applies more to meta-fiction, say, that of David Mitchell, then the adjective is well-applied, since it exhibits a kind of "fearful symmetry" at its heart—seen through either end of a time-traveling telescope in *Ghostwritten* (or *Chaos*)—which lends itself to repetitions from one level of complexity to the next. In Murakami, however, the symmetry is still there, especially between war memories and the apocalyptic revelations of the present moment; things as well as persons "metamorphose." In a passage which seems designed with Runge's seraphs and their contrails in mind, but is responding "merely" to the hieroglyphic quality of birds flying through the sky, Mr. Wind-up Bird notices that his talisman-like bat has disappeared:

> I sat on the well curb my hands into my coat pockets, and surveyed my surroundings once again. It felt as if a cold rain or snow might begin falling at any time. There was no wind, but the air had a deep chill to it. A flock of little birds raced back and forth across the sky in a complex painting a coded hieroglyph up there, and then with a rush they were gone. Soon I heard the low rumble of a jet, but the plane stayed invisible above the thick layer of clouds. On such a dark, overcast day, I could go into the well without worrying that the sunlight would hurt my eyes when I came out.
> ...Where has they taken the bird sculpture that used to be in this yard? Was it decorating another yard now, still urged on by an endless, pointless impulse to soar into the sky? Or had it been discarded as trash when the Miyawaki's house was demolished last summer? I recalled the place fondly. Without the sculpture of the bird, I felt, the yeard had lost a subtle balance.
> When I ran out of thoughts, after eleven, I climbed down the steel ladder into the well. I set foot on the well bottom and took a few deep breaths, as always, checking the air. It was the same as ever, smelling somewhat of mold but breathable. I felt for where the bat where I had left it proped against the wall. *It was not there. It was not anywhere.* It had disappeared. Completely. Without a trace. (*WBC*, 549)

Amid meditations on *The Thieving Magpie* as performed by Abbado and Toscanini, just as everything seems to be changing for good with his own death, Mr. Wind-up Bird finds his own chronicle in a computer.

What Murakami seems to understand is the peculiar and unique anguish a name such as "Kafka" occasions, beyond in any one context, a distress in and of the iconic name, on the one hand, in its ironic nearness to and difference from the Czech word *kafka*, a magpie or small bird, and, on the other, in its nominal proximity to altered, unnatural states of (post) modernist being. Such parasitizing or grafting upon the name goes "hand in hand" with a certain Poe-like (ir-)reverence—a "fearing again" and "being seized by" coupled with a ferocity of style ranged against what Mary Wollstonecraft presciently called the "ferocity of fear"—which serves as one of postmodernism's aesthetic merits.[59] Such ferocity[60] seems as Mailerian as it is Wordsworthian :

> Good style is the record of such powerful emotion reaching the surface of the page through the conscious nets of restraint, caution, tact, elegance, taste, even inhibition—if the inhibition is not without dishonor.[61]

If one comes to it from a reading of the arabesque fictions privileged by Barth, the glaring defect of much postmodern metafiction is that it fails to live up to the burden or task of a laughter situated at the heart of satire's *castigat ridendo mores* and Nietzsche's *Fröhliche Wissenschaft*. In this respect, Coover and Grass are closer to a hilarity identified with the Romantics' assault on the absolute and even to the grotesque intrusion of *docta ignorantia* and gallows humor informing Poe's metafictional *Urtext*, "The Thousand-and-Second Tale of Scheherazade." Again, the exception seems to be Murakami's character named "Colonel Sanders" in *Kafka on the Shore*—who discusses the Japanese nature of divinity with a pimp in a mildly ironic cross-cultural take on the much-debated "death of God" announced by the Romantics and given programmatic status in Nietzsche. In the final translation or transfiguration, God goes out to the soccer stadium and puts on shorts, becoming a referee:

> Colonel Sanders folded his arms and stared straight at Hoshino. 'What is God?'
> The question threw Hoshino for a moment.
> Colonel Sanders pressed him further. 'What does God look like, and what can He do?'
> 'Don't ask *me*. God's *God*. He's everywhere, watching what we do, judging whether it's good or bad.'
> 'Sounds like a soccer referee.'
> 'Sort of, I guess.'
> 'So God wears shorts, has a whistle sticking out of His mouth, and keeps an eye on the clock?'
> 'You know that's not what I mean,' Hoshino said.
> 'Are the Japanese God and the foreign God relatives, or maybe enemies?'
> 'How should I know?'
> 'Listen—God only exists in people's minds. Especially in Japan. God's always been kind of a flexible concept. Look at what happened after the war. Douglas MacArthur ordered the divine emperor to quit being God, and he did, making a speech saying that he was just an ordinary person. So after 1946 he wasn't God anymore. That's what the Japanese gods are like—they can be tweaked and adjusted. Some American chomping on a cheap pipe gives the order and presto change-o—

God's no longer God. A very postmodern kind of thing. If you think God's there, He is. If you don't, he isn't. And if that's what God's like, I wouldn't worry about it.'

(*KS*, 265)

The American accent—linked to a "full fan-experience" translated from the soccer-playing West to Japan—placed upon transcendence suggests a surreal otherness compatible with a hilarity in which the hieroglyph is negated and preserved by being made thoroughly profane. Not only Japan, but God must surrender to MacArthur and the translation of the full fan-experience into the sky of Browne's theosophical decussation, the chiasmic "X," continues to mark the algebraic spot of (wo)man or Heidegger's *das Man* in her/his communication with the celestial, but of which *Man*, the one whose mathesis maps everything in nature or the one whose multiple discourses are resolvable only into the layering of multiple (multicultural) realities and replicated dreams? We touch the sky with E(r)os in Runge and build Babel-like towers to the heavens, but the once symmetrical quincunxes haunt us asymmetrically or in a "cropped, cramped, or distorted"[63] way, and the occult diamond remains often as not hidden "in plain sight" like a purloined letter or stolen bat. The flutter of a butterfly's wing in New York or Tokyo elicits an "I wouldn't worry about it" simultaneously deflecting the tenor of apocalyptic irreverence and ironically directing us to a point or *punctum* of ferocious levity where thinking can begin (again).

5. *"Tell me": Idiolect and the "Other Truth" in Padgett Powell, Faulkner, and Grass*

'I feel like a wet seed wild in the hot blind earth.'
"Dewey Dell," in *As I Lay Dying*

The work, the opus, does not belong to the field; it is the transformer of the field.
Jacques Derrida

Miteinandersprechen [ist] mit Weltdeutung angelegt.
[*Speaking to one another [is] intimated with the interpretation of the world.*]
Manfred Frank

The South Disfigured and Made Over

There are defects or deficits of culture which, while morally abhorrent, do not automatically render beauty suspect. Critics in the future may censure us for an ability to look up at the acropolis from an Athens street without thought of the slaves employed in building it or of the animal caracasses displayed in the market below. On the other hand, there is something more subtly and deeply disfiguring in the hideous institution of slavery, especially when it is part of our own culture and recent past. The beautiful mansions of the Old South, some of them diminutive Parthenons, seem somehow haunted by ancient evil, a malign otherness that lurks in the very foundations of the African-American heritage, whose vestiges are still evident in the headlines and in the street. Yet we are certainly "doing the right thing" by preserving those ambivalently hallowed halls. On the other hand, no one should deny that Southern letters and, *equally*, Southern music, i.e. jazz, the music of African-Americans who once tasted injustice on a daily basis, constitutes the better part of our best cultural "product." One measure of aesthetic merit would be the sheer untranslatability of the text, paralleled by the non-existence of a score or chart demonstrating how the melody and the chords get "bent out of shape"—i.e., inflected—by a genius of jazz improvisation. No doubt, the degradation of slavery, combined with the experience of defeat, gives the South its tragic focus, suggesting a rich and colorful "Blues" vocabulary for depicting its more odious and amorous denizens. A writer like George Washington Cable seems aware of the cultural paradox that a certain disfigurement of language—expressed in what Randolph Bourne famously called "phonetic atrocities"—is, perhaps, the only instrument with which to reflect the dissonance of reconstruction Louisiana. Bourne's disparagement is just; we read Cable *for* the disfigurement and the leavening of a *muthos* or declamatory utterance where the South, projected in idiomatic, juvenile, or, at times, idiotic intonation, "rises again"—to the level of fish-story or tragic myth. In Cable, speech-acts are taken more seriously than in Rhett Butler's "Frankly, my dear, I don't give a damn"; they may have greater force as oratorical performances or as pearls fleshed out from hideous grains of phonetic "sand." The writer's task becomes one of transliterating or spelling out facts of speech at the level of the phoneme, thus not only casting mimetic shadows of that which is already past or never was (aesthetic effects of a bygone era equivalent to "Moon-Pies," beignets, a favorite restaurant in New Orleans or bar in Charleston), but also adverting to complex and tangled issues of race, exploitation, and violence "in the American grain."[1] In such a deixis of Old Dixie, pitted against the vulgarity and mass-marketed xenophobia of what currently passes for "country music," epigone of noble Bluegrass, the consonants and vowels can still be as exquisitely evocative and turned toward romance as the name "Elvis" (whose name reminds us of "the gentleman of Elvas," a survivor of De Soto's expedition to the Mississippi): Edisto, name of an actual river in South Carolina,[2] Grandissimes, Aurore Nancanou, Raoul Innerarity, Simons (pronounced "Simmons") Manigault, juxtaposed with those fictional embodiments of an atrocious *Plattenglisch*, Anse Bundren and Flem Snopes. The Southern writer's attention to names is of a Gogolian intensity; it is thus no surprise that the South produces a manual of prosody and vowel quantity, Sidney Lanier's *The Science of English Verse* (1880), where pains are taken to reproduce the language, as spoken, in accurate musical notation—a text which may have suggested to William Carlos Williams the basis for a uniquely American metric.

If the disfigurements of Southern history and language find their "natural" medium in fictional epic, they lend themselves equally well to the sometimes uncannier procedures of romance. While it is said that Henry James abandons the romance form after *The Europeans*, in some sense it remains his fictional medium of choice—at least in terms of providing a method for "working up the material"—when considered from the point of view of another Southern writer, William Gilmore Simms, the bard of Charleston and Barnwell, South Carolina. Without labeling the later fictions such, James almost always takes the route prescribed by Simms for a romance, like *The Yemassee*, in the 1830s: "...placing a human agent in hitherto untried situations, it exercises ingenuity in extricating him from them, while describing his feelings and his fortunes in his progress."[3] James, we know, is concerned with linguistic and other kinds of abrasion taken to a passional, though rarely physical, limit: the distressing of icons by which persons (characters) live, the eclipsing of standards, the failure or vindication of will, the emaciation of virtue, applied in the broadest sense of the word, by sordid facts of class, commerce, and decaying manners. In the *Bostonians* (1885–1886), he gives us a portrait of Basil Ransom that alludes to the music of Southern speech as something inseparable from ethnicity, from the fact of its being "almost African." James's refusal to "reproduce" or transliterate the "charming dialect"—anticipating Bourne's disparagement of "phonetic atrocities"—may well have given Cable and others an even greater incentive to try it themselves :

> He came, in fact, from Mississippi, and he spoke very perceptibly with the accent of that country. It is not in my power to reproduce by any combination of characters this charming dialect; but the initiated reader will have no difficulty in evoking the sound, which is to be associated in the present instance with nothing vulgar or vain. This lean, pale, sallow, shabby, striking young man, with his superior head, his sedentary shoulders, his expression of bright grimness and hard enthusiasm, his provincial, distinguished appearance, is, as a representative of his sex, the most important personage in my narrative; he played a very active part in the events I have undertaken in some degree to set forth. And yet the reader who likes a complete image, who desires to read with the senses as well as with the reason, is entreated not to forget that he prolonged his consonants and swallowed his vowels, that he was guilty of elisions and interpolations which were equally unexpected, and that his discourse was pervaded by something sultry and vast, something almost African in its rich, basking tone, something that suggested the teeming expanse of the cotton-field.[4]

The beauty of the "sultry and vast" is never compromised—on the surface. Yet a sensitive reader knows why, how, and with whom the cotton-fields are "teeming." James phrases the dilemma of the penurious gentleman brought up on the problematic ideals of the Old South in terms not of physical ungainliness or phonetic disfigurement, but of an inner impairment unable to cope with serpentine realities in the capital of a new sort of gamesmanship, New York City:

> He had been diligent, he had been ambitious, but he had not yet been successful. During the few weeks preceding the moment at which we meet him again, he had even begun to lose faith altogether in his earthly destiny. It became much of a question with him whether success in any form was written there; whether for a hungry young Mississippian, without means, without friends, wanting, too, in the highest energy, the wisdom of the serpent, personal arts and national prestige, the game of life was to be won in New York. He had been on the point of giving it up and returning to the home of his ancestors, where, as he heard from his mother, there was still just a sufficient supply of hot corn-cake to support existence.

To this brilliant, yet troubled and troubling surface, Cable and, a century later, Padgett Powell bring the inflection of declamatory idiolect, mainly Gullah,[5] in Powell's case, a method for representing the chaos, cake-like layering (in terms of history), or cake-centeredness of the South, by means of an oblong attention to manners and an equally pronounced discernment regarding acts of random or ritual violence. Powell, like Simms, James, and Faulkner, exploits romance for the purpose of resensing the past, nor is it accidental that the protagonist in *Edisto* focuses upon what he calls "the material," which in his case means the folklore and superstitious culture of the African-Americans in his own microcosmic South Carolina neighborhood, especially in the bar known as the "Baby Grand." His myth or *muthos*, like Faulkner's and James's, is parabolic in the sense that representation is given the impossible task not only of reflecting, but redeeming historical disfigurement *through* the material, of customs, manners, and speech. As in James, it is the material, once focused upon and translated, that is thus "saved" through the art of narration. In a different but related way, Zora Neale Hurston and, later on, Toni Morrison, in *The Song of Solomon*, preserve and mythologize African-American heritage; gifting us with the contemporary equivalent of a "new myth," recalling Grass's project of "gifting us," his readers, with the other or *an* other truth.

The Simms-James-Cable-Faulkner-Powell tradition in fiction is interesting also because it represents something rather different from texts that embody what has been termed "American hieroglyphics."[6] It seems important to demonstrate how Powell's *Edisto*, a text wholly and somewhat untranslatably "in the American grain," serves a polyphonic rather than a hieroglyphic aesthetic, in the sense of that other 19th century dominated by Melville, Poe, and Hawthorne, and to suggest how such an aesthetic may be especially valuable or "usable" in light of the increasingly polyglot nature of the United States. What is worth thinking about is that phonetically represented speech or speech "material," often that of African Americans, may well be as untranslatable as the *Stoff* of jazz, but that this untranslatability is of a different sort from that, say, of the hieroglyphs in the *Narrative of A. Gordon Pym*, which inscribe the enigmatic subject on an entirely different plane of *cognitive* unreliability and whose interpretation depends on a different entrance into the hermeneutic circle. With Cable's Cajuns or Powell's Theenie we are presented graphic cultural material that is jazz-like in its syncopated, *affective* idiosyncrasy, and—while the question must still be answered, "This part or that?"—there can be little doubt that what counts, as in Twain, is the declamatory material, *qua* performative, often lying speech—"something I just made up"—not the interpretative instance of the reader. Thus, while Daniel Ferrer argues that there is no subjective "there" in Faulkner, the evidence nonetheless exists— on the page—of a declamatory subjectivity larger than any single character, of a fabulous, even fabulously fake, Super-Subject with no particular claim to truth beyond a certain, vivid, even corny graininess on the well-heaped plate of reader receptivity. The *Sprachmaterial*, like folk superstition, clothing, or food, represents the particular yet universal *hic et nunc*, a Mississipian *vox* from a desert-like nowhere—which is nonetheless *sui generis*. There is no place like *this* no place in terms of its qualification or cultural "signature." Fictions of empowerment through language or counter-factual myth make Twain or Powell "more untranslatable" than their predecessors, forming the abyssal, yet scintillating reserve of that "other truth," a form of higher aesthetic *and* ethical knowledge, *gnoseologia superior*, in all its epic clarity, a clarity which deserves (*pace* Lukács) in several respects to be called "Homeric." In *As I Lay Dying*, an "other truth" of a different gnoseological (and/or gynecological) order is encountered, where multidiscursivity reflects a "delectable" undecidability which is neither hieroglyphic nor an unalloyed, verifiable representation of redneck truth, but a Mississippi at once other and uniquely Faulknerian.[7]

The Supernatural as Speech Material: Faulkner, Grass, Powell

Simms and Cable provide one context for the monological *and* polyphonic procedures employed by Powell. To find something comparable in world literature, we might look to Jean Toomer's *Cane* (1923), Miguel Angel Asturias' ground-breaking exploration of Guatemalan dialect in *El Señor Presidente* (1948), to the post-apocalyptic meta-English of Russell Hoban's *Riddley Walker* (1980), the novels of Faulkner and Grass, or to Ntozake Shange's brilliant *Liliane* (1994). Whatever ungainly phonetic traits Faulkner's hybrid Mississippian, Grass's Gdańsk (Danzig) dialect, and Powell's coastal Gullah may or may not have in common, the imperative of a certain *patois* informs texts written from a first-person (nonnaturalistic) point of view (fictive soliloquy). In the monological text the status of storytelling, *Dichtung*, with respect to *Wahrheit* or truth is demonstrated, just as there is often "a" truth, deemed historically noteworthy, balanced by the "other" veracity, which history has seen fit not to record and which is therefore made all the more fascinating by virtue of its obscurity.

In the case of the virtuosic *As I Lay Dying*, an American romance built upon the foundation of equivocal streams of narrated consciousness, the text is also polyphonic in conception, since it places in serial order speeches by the characters Cash, Darl, Jewel, Cora, Tull, Anse, Dewey Dell, Peabody, and Vardaman, who has the mind of a child, the Reverend Whitfield, and Addie. The reader finds him- or herself plunged at once into this labyrinth of names and declamations, "hearing" voices in a darkness of enunciation both private and public, as disorienting as the privileged fantasies of Simons Manigault, yet seeking communication with each other. The characters' declamations are woven in and around the death, burial, and "after-life" of the matriarch Addie Bundren. A red thread of intense mythic suggestiveness surfaces in the discourse of the one who, because he is "different," i.e., gifted with a sense of the supernatural, a projection of "magic realism" which is both idiot-like and locally inflected. Vardaman imagines he will meet his mother in the water because he has been told as much by his brother Cash, who fashions their mother's wooden casket with his bare hands, and because the river, identified with both the Styx and the Jordan, "keeps on rising" throughout the narrative—as if to lend credence to the old Blues standard "Forty Days and Forty Nights"—sweeping the bridge away and then threatening to drown the land itself. According to a text found in every (Protestant) Christian hymnal, "we," the living and the dead, will also "gather" at the River. Addie Bundren is thus guaranteed a "life" beyond this one, which to a manner or mode of thinking as mythopoetically sophisticated as it is childlike in enunciation, must therefore take on fish-like qualities:

> Cash is my brother. *But Jewel's mother is a horse, My mother is a fish. Darl says that when we come to the watee again I might see her and Dewey Dell said, She's in the box; how could she have got out? She got out through the holes I bored, into the water I said, and when we come to the water again I am going to see her. My mother is not in the box. My mother does not smell like that. My mother is a fish.*
> 'Those cakes will be in fine shape by the time we get to Jefferson,' Darl says.[8]

The Bundrens must take a cross-county journey, an unromantic, aboriginal *via dolorosa*, in the rain, to give their mother the burial she wished for—in town. The taller part of the fish-story—and the verification of Vardaman's sagely idiotic, half-empirical, half-biblical imaginings—comes "true" when the family has to cross a swollen, unbridged river, and the wagon, together with the coffin containing Addie Bundren, is overturned and swept away— leaving Vardaman to ask Cash, "You knew she is a fish, but you let her get away" (*AIL*, 144). If floodwaters motivate *As I Lay Dying* at the level of myth, it is necessary to know that an equally primitive or primordial food, corn-cakes, based on the indigenous maize of Native Americans, serves as a connection to the socioeconomic status of the Bundrens as underdogs (they hope to sell them in order to buy medicine to treat Cash's broken leg), to the agrarian roots of the South, and to a kind of nativist or indigenous take on Holy Communion.[9] The corn-cakes or corn-bread, as we now call it, provide more than an element of local color shared by James's diagnosis of the alienation and possible homecoming of Basil Ransom, who is also a Mississippian, the speech of an idiot in *As I Lay Dying*, and the "tall tales" of the truant schoolboy protagonist in *Edisto*. What one eats determines who one is, not only physically but culturally. The corn-cakes are the feminine South's peculiar inflection or idiomatic version (translation) of bread, the staff of life. Through it, the Bundrens, in all their epic obtuseness and fallenness, hope to "redeem" the wound of brother Cash.

As with Homeric epic and the texts of Faulkner and Powell, eating is fore-grounded in *The Flounder*. Conversely, the monologue of the exceptional underdog serves as an equivocal window on recent history; the case of the diminutive Oskar Matzerath offers a prominent example. Readers will know that the first-person narrator in *The Flounder* is granted immortality by a fish named Aua, the prehistoric earth-mother, a magic animal he has caught and whose life he has spared. not far from the ground upon which Danzig (or Gdańsk) will later enter into fallen history. It is part of Grass's narrative strategy that the text concerns itself more with cuisine, food, and the preparation of food, than with the recording of "how things actually were" on the stage of "standard" historical events. In a chapter of *The Flounder* (*Der Butt*) entitled "Woran ich mich nicht erinnern will" ("Of that which I do not want to remember"), the narrator avers that stories, "like these," are "dumb" or idiotic, especially the ones that deal with disfigurement and are partially about criminal acts, repressed guilt, nakedness, and punishment (presumably of Christ or someone innocent as Christ) by stoning:

> An das Wort zuviel, an ranziges Fett, an den Rumpf ohne Kopf: Mestwina. An den Weg nach Einsiedeln und zurück: den Stein in der Faust, in der Tasche. An jenen Freitag, den 4. März, als mein Griff in die Streikkasse freitags. An Eisblumen (deine) und meinen Atem. An mich, wie ich lief: den Töpfen davon, immer Geschichte bergab. An Vatertag neulich, und Himmelfahrt, natürlich war ich dabei. An Abwasch in Scherben, Fleisch unterschoben, die Schweden auf Hela, den Mond uber Zuckau, den Kerl hinterm Ginster, an das Schweigen, Jasagen taub. An das Fett und den Stein an das Fleisch und den Gott, an dumme Geschichten wie diese....[10]

> [Of the word too much, of rancid fat, of the trunk without a head: Mestvina. On the way to Einsieldeln and back: the stone in the fist, in the pocket. On that Friday, March 4th, as my reaching into the strikers' funds each Friday. Of ice-flowers (yours) and my breath. Of myself, how I ran: off from the flowerpots, always downhill from history. On Father's Day (recently), and on Ascension Day, naturally I was there. Of washing dishes in shards, meat put beneath, the Swedes on Hela, the moon over Zuckau, the fellow behind the broom, of saying no word, deaf affirmation. Of the fat and the stone <applied> to the flesh and God, of stupid stories like this one....]

Similarly, from the perspective of the twelve-year-old narrator in *Edisto*, who is not granted immortality by a fish, but who has enough wit and expertise to make history dance around the maypole of *his* self-empowered make-believe (as with the sails and painted siding of clipper-ships he imagines floating on the horizon), the simplest of acts, like baking a cake, will be connected to the guilt and criminality that hound Theenie, the Manigault's family housekeeper, to the "making" of a baby in the womb of Theenie's daughter who fled to New York, to fishing, and to a more generic fat lady who sits on buckets filled with still biting mullet. The text lavishes fine-grained attention upon the mental stubbornness of the "great old earthy philosopher," the Manigaults' African-American cook named "Theenie" (whose name is shadowed by the Greek goddess of wisdom, Athena); the cook's conceiving labor and carefulness become mythically projected *in her absence*, when she finds herself in "big" trouble with the "gubmen" (government) assisted by the process-server, her grandson, whose name is not "really" Taurus at all.

> It didn't take a genius to know it was big, not after I knew Theenie had been at the house and thrown down the laundry and wasn't back at her shack and had left my cake out there without her wax paper sealed to it like peritoneum—you know, she has a thing about freshness...And she could cook mullet brought in head down in a pickle bucket of pink fresh slime and worm goo, fry them and bounce those bones a little too, but when it comes to making something like a cake, which, considering its components (like water and flour and other powders), can't be too foul, at least not like mullet in a bucket sat on by a fat lady in the sun until they stopped biting—it comes to making a bakery-clean white thing like a cake and she's got to have fresh eggs, fresh real butter, sweet milk, and you can't even walk around the house while it cooks lest it fall, and she won't run the vacuum cleaner while it's in there either. She can only sit down with another Co'-Cola and a Stanback powder to virtually pray for it, and then it's out, it will have to cool, and nine times out of ten, before you can touch it, she has grafted to it wax paper set into the hot buttery sugary crust of the cake and welded there by a fusion of wax and cake.... [11]

But the purpose of the narration seems equally to get to the point where Simons can make up a *muthos* of his own, one based upon the grandeur and dignity of Theenie's labor, but which pays attention to the otherworldly or uncannily waxed exquisiteness of the thing she has created:

> ...and that cake you could throw in the ocean and it would float like a crab-pot marker for years, and the day it washed up on a beach and was found by an islander he could take it to his hut and with great-eyed delight peel off the wax paper with his skinning knife and devour the rich, golden flesh inside. And as soon as you slice up this memorial, this baby, and make your smacky fuss about how good it is, she starts making her fuss about how much trouble it is, and she's not making any more, she's too old, you're too old, too old for her to have to work that hard, why she *raised* you. (She raised two other sets of white kids before me. And she's not through until she hears they got married.) You smile and smack and smile away, she sitting at the kitchen table in her white uniform, hair bluing and legs swollen.... (*E*, 27)

The first-person narrator, at the end of the text, moves with his mother, "The Doctor," to Hilton Head, an oddly un-American place: "There's not a baseball diamond on the island," he says (*E*, 182).

The function of multidiscursivity in Powell, as before in Cable and Faulkner, is to re-present worlds of cruelty and beauty no longer in the making, but elaborated, through *acts* of speech, at a certain time in the past. In the opening of these worlds, we get a sense of something that is not merely "gone with the wind," like the clipper ships of the late 1850s and the Confederacy, but that has gone into the palimpsest-like, much overpainted bulwark of North American being—something analogous, despite obvious differences in time and space to the quality Walter Pater discerns in the Greeks and valorizes as the "romantic element in literature":

> ...that inexhaustible discontent, languor, and home-sickness, that endless regret, the chords of which ring all through our modern literature. It is to the romantic element in literature that those qualities belong...the Greek spirit, with its engaging naturalness, simple, chastened, debonair, τρυφῆς [delicate], ἀβρότατος [softest], χλιδῆς [charming], χαρίτων [of graces], ἱμέρου [of desire], πόθου πατήρ [of longing, the father] is itself the Sangrail of an endless pilgrimage.... [12]

The going or gone "material" of Powell and Faulkner—episodic "close-up shots" of *mutho*-logical idiots and children, Gullah, the Old Testament, the ante-bellum and post-Reconstruction South, corncakes and birthday cakes—finds an aesthetic rebirth in exotic otherness. The polyglot nature of reported or first-person speech indicates something "rich and strange" in its decadence and absenting—like an old photograph or vernacular Latin on its way to becoming a romance language. The declamatory excess of the text is necessarily caught up in the "internal dialogization" of all discourse:

> The living utterance, having taken meaning and shape at a particular historical moment in a socially specific environment, cannot fail to brush up against thousands of living dialogic threads, woven by socio-ideological consciousness around the given object [or referent] of an utterance; it cannot fail to become an active participant in social dialogue. (Bakhtin, *Dialogic* 276). Dialogism, the function of the inter-referential field, therefore refers to the moment when linguistic systems (be they related to a specific region, text, or identity) confront the dialogizing context of other systems (other dialects, other genres, other characters). The dialogical economy works in tension with the substitutive binary oppositions of signification and the referential-metonymic structures of diegesis, pointing instead to a plurality of ontologically or stylistically defined points of view in dialogic interaction within the single work. It structures the interstices between the perspectives of different characters, between generic forms (as in, for example, parody or travesty), between (inter)texts, between authorial voice and reader. Dialogue thus traverses the liminal barrier between linguistic 'identities' as they confront each other in context, or when they anticipate an other who will respond. [13]

The past becomes usable in declamatory otherness through the salience of individual performances in the diegesis, each with its own deictic purpose:

> 'She's got a double use for you , mister. If you cain' see that, why you scudgin' us all. Ever since Mr. M. left, it's been a trile with that Simons. Because iss onliess us here. He roundbunction, in trouble, fallin' out of *buses, ekk*setra. All she wont is somebody to keep him right. Even *she* know that. And Law know I do. I see enough of that in my own. Somebody got to hep that boy kotch up. He so far ahead he's *behine.* Yes, he is.' Her head nodding, in a rhythm like a small, gentle locomotive: her whole head rolling on the syllables: *Yessuh.*' (*E*, 33)

It is not the hieroglyphic quality of the unknowable, communicated in the unanswerable silence of the written sign, but the flow and rhythm of spoken language, in its idiosyncratic graininess or texture, measured out in slice-like performative episodes, that are foregrounded, both here and in similar passages. A foreign speaker of English would need a glossary, like that provided in the Losada edition of Asturias' *El Presidente*, to know that "Law" means "Lord"; "roundbunction" means "rambunctious"; "hep" is Gullah for "help," and "kotch" stands for "catch." "*Ekk*setra" not only mirrors a popular Latinate turn of speech for "other things of the same sort"; it stands in relation to "proper English," the kind taught at Cooper-Boyd Academy, as unlettered, vernacular Latin, say, in Petronius, once stood with respect to Ciceronian or Sallustian diction. It illustrates the quality, well-understood by Bakhtin and Voloshinov, for living languages, especially in the transition from a monoculture to a multiculture, to exhibit centrifugal tendencies, engendering idiomatic (ecstatic) variations of nomenclature, spelling, and grammar. In a time before dictionaries, say, in the 15th and 16th centuries, written texts constantly mirrored the inflected mutancy of vernacular enunciation with no particular regard for "standard" orthography, because Latin was the only language taken seriously in the professions of academe, law, and religion. In the Gullah inflection of Theenie, English becomes murdered *uncriminally*—as distinct from the level of legal malfeasance that Taurus is sent out to avenge—or "aired out," which is to say that the experience of reading, its "pleasure," as they say, is experienced in the unregulated, muscular or grainy flavor of represented speech, especially that of women, and of *ekk*setra—that which is "simple, chastened, and debonair," like the Nurse's declamations in *Romeo and Juliet*—and thus increased. While Gullah may be dying out, American English is already showing many signs of becoming enriched ("outsourced," linguistically) by its south-of-the-border inflection—a process that seems "above" or "outside" the laws designed to enforce national and linguistic boundaries.

First Person: The Unnatural Imperative of Declamation

The issue of direct first-person narration has been addressed by the American critic Seymour Chatman. Chatman at first questions the use of the term "soliloquy," familiar in drama, in describing fictional speech. But he then applies it in a limited and rather specific sense:

> Soliloquy is perhaps best used as a term to refer to nonnaturalistic or 'expressionistic' narratives in which the only informational source is that of characters formally presenting, explaining, and commenting upon things. These are formal declamations—not speech or thought in the ordinary sense but a stylized merging of the two. As with dramatic monologue and dialogue, the convention is that they have been 'heard' by someone and transformed into a written text. [14]

We may therefore speak of an infiltration of the dramatic soliloquy (*persona*) into epic or narrative diegesis. However, since the fictional word is immediately "distanced" from reality, subject to framing devices, scaling, irony, and so forth, narrative soliloquy may be considered among the least reliable or verifiable forms of that which is wholly "made up," i.e. fictional speech. Soliloquy provides a vehicle for the representation of subjectivity in its Athena/Theenie-like absenting, while the speech-material remains as the deictic trace of an exquisite goneness: a silhouetted personahood that is all grainy, flavorful mask. Out of the speaking shadow or mask comes virtuous or muscular (in the sense of "strong") speech. In this, it connects with the roots of myth or declamatory *muthos* in all oral cultures, past as well as present, where truth and falsehood (*ficta*, unreal, imagined, or dreamed things) are equivocal partners in the deixis of something rich, strange, and sunken. Readers often sense that they are privy to the extra-ordinary, that privileged information is being communicated—which, even if false, is nonetheless significant as a reflection of character and *partially* redemptive of fallen history and a guilt-ridden memory. *Huckleberry Finn* and Faulkner's *As I Lay Dying* reproject the past in mythic terms strongly influenced by authorial point of view—each premised on the declamatory instance of a speaker, but the "I" that is speaking is far closer to an excess (*DF*, 23) or overflow of mythic information than to any real river or stream of singular consciousness. The episodic "speechifying" of *Edisto* has the function of allowing Simons Manigault to state his case; it is the *muthos* of a child who, like Odysseus or Huck, first of all has to defend himself against a hostile outside world, whose oratorical "signifying" supports a verbal technique as psychologically subtle as any in epic. The *vox clamans in deserto* quality of declamation, part *vera historia*, part fish-story, puts the counter-historical "my" before or ahead of narrative, embracing the notion that performance is superior to reliability, that a certain latitude of discourse can at least reframe if not reinvent facticity. A century before, Cable's validation of idiolect, representing the slave and mulatto "as they actually talked," syllable by syllable, had paved the way for the elevation of lower-caste characters; Powell continues the tradition by raising the process-server "Taurus" to mythic status and painstakingly transliterating the "cooked" Gullah English of Theenie. The fact that soliloquy is "nonnaturalistic" means that it can and often will include lying, the primary survival strategy of underdogs like Odysseus and Brer Rabbit, of slaves and prisoners, and therefore of *muthos*. Simons Manigault qualifies as an underdog in the sense that children and many jazz-players are underdogs, "grasping at the possible" but often wondering about the impossible or various levels of actualization between fantasy and reality. Lies, and the devices that further them, are weapons in the hands of a gifted child with an overactive imagination; a telescope proves useful in getting rid of less "desirable" adult companions who may be employed by one's mother and in making a great deal, or another reality, out of nothing but clouds:

> Anyway, these cloud shapes start moving around in the view, irregular and flowing, about like when you press your eyelids. And none of them looks like a clipper ship, so I tell the coroner named Cud: 'I see clipper ships at 0—9—2.' Then go purple in my descriptions. Well, it worked like a charm. He was gone, as I recall, before the Doctor returned. And it occurred to me after that that it was a nifty little adult gauge, a feeler, that telescope.
> But this night was a hint different. The Empirin had my tongue like a grit of sand in an oyster of nonsense, and this stranger was no Cud going to hightail because of a little imagination in the family...
> 'Some fetching old Yankee Doodle, yessiree." He has not flinched. 'Here. You look.' I stepped back, careful to hold the telescope on line, nodded to it. 'Come on, hurry, they're at good speed.'...
> 'Tell me what you see.'
> He sighed and then he jerked the scope a half inch to the right and froze it. Looking back on it, this is where I place his biggest gamble, his shewdest moment.
> 'Tell me, what should I see?
> 'Clippers!' I exhaled. 'Wooden laminate masted rolling regular clippers!'
> He grunted and shuffled his feet.   (*E*, 18–19)

The "inner dialogization" of Simons' "adult-testing" words has as its intertext literary romance from Spenser to Faulkner, as well as Galileo's scientific *muthos* and the telescopic liberties of Romantics like Shelley. The beauty of the nonexistent clipper-ships may test prospective employees, all of whom are black, in their aptitude for "going along" with beautiful lies, but it also takes fanciful measure of the Southern past, opening up a window or perspective on a short-lived period of Atlantic trade between

Yankees and Southerners—whose flamboyance floats in the narrator's enterprising memory like a cloud, in which beauty and craftsmanship coexist, briefly, with commercial purpose. His dream is true, in the Homeric sense of the gates of horn, because it remembers a patch of history "with all the trimmings" of accurate nautical description, while it is false in its omissions, in that it seems to detach beauty from an unspoken, hideous, "other" economic context, slavery (an act of unconscious ethical erasure analogous to that performed by the North prior to the Civil War and by us as we glance upward toward the acropolis). The myth of the small boy is redemptive (more than that of *Gone with the Wind*), only because it serves a practical narrative purpose—as a test of empathy on the part of the dialogical partner who can only be African-American. The "lost fields" where the cotton grew are unredeemable, even by memory, but can be re-sensed—which amounts to something more than nostalgia because it is part of a psychologically validated strategy on the part of a highly intelligent, if also "flaky," problem child and because the virtuosic performance leads to a kind of truce between white boy and black man, representing distinct strata of economic privilege. Layering and flakiness are traits applicable to cakes, but also to "special" people and exquisite boats:

'The canvases are coarse,' I say. 'Shredded and hemp-flogged, wet, salt-stained, grand pieces of cotton representing the lost fields who bore them!'
'Yes,' the stranger said.
'Muslin!' I nearly shout. Who was testing who? 'Great flying manila, popping in the breath of Neptune. And the wood. Varnished hard and sleek, teak and oak. The grains are a study.'
'Check the hulls!'...
'And the paints, marine paints, coat on coat, voyage on voyage, haul, haul, dry haul diurnal and long. The colors are myriad and embattled, layered soldiers on the land it is their end to protect: blues, yellows, marine greens, and reds barnacled all over each other in their hopeless flaking mission. They've had it, bleached christening of some jack-leg lubber....' Where had my boats been painted?
'Savannah,' he said, still looking...
'I'm Simons,' I said. We shook hands.   (*E*, 20)

Powell's description of the paint on the clipper-ship hulls raises the stakes involved in translating the repressed past still higher. Slavery remains out of the picture, to be sure, but the weary "soldiering" of the paint suggests the exhaustion of the South at the end of the Civil War, on its own kind of "hopeless flaking mission," and an otherworldly transcendence of the distinction between material and spiritual—translating the entire apparatus of prejudicial cultural error, *ante-bellum mores*, and post-war separation of colors, through a blurring of the nautical color "line," into the "pure," literary otherness of romance, the opposite of an illiterate "white mythology." Obsessive whiteness, a "bleached christening," becomes a thing beclouding the unusable, unspoken past. For the moment, in a particular "now" of fictive childhood, when precocious Simons Manigault has cracked ribs and a sure-fire method for testing adults, a demonstration of racial harmony, a symbolic shaking of hands between white and "non-white," who will later be named "Taurus" by the boy but is only a stranger at this point, is still possible. At the end of the text, the brief interlude of intimacy, name-calling, and name-giving, between races will be over; cakes will no longer be baked by the house-maid Theenie, and Simons will be going to a different school. Thus everything about the world of Simons Manigault is either going or gone. But the question suggests itself: how does this ephemeral construct of truant juvenile declamation impress itself on readerly consciousness as something enduring, of its time and and beyond it, a deictic "something" which a critic may, without hesitation, label "classic" in its epic or tall-tale atrociousness?

But then "reality" is remarkable enough in *Edisto*, even without the embellishments of a partly reliable narrator on Empirin, a much-prescribed tranquillizer of the time, whose name seems apt as the drug of pain-killing choice in a pale-face *civitas* bent on seeing to it that the world is made safe for its copywrighted brand-names and product placements. There is the expectation on the part of the reader that "normal" speech will provide the background or the basis upon which "art" or artful estrangement will state its insurgent case. From the first sentence, truancy is the medium or method by which the world of the narrator is projected, from the moment he sets out on his "Assignment," while "in Bluffton on a truancy spree" (*E*, 3). Truancy or being "out of school," we realize, is a generic choice, as well, since it defines romance—or romance taken to a certain Romantic limit, where, as in Simms, Cable, or James, the unknightly protagonist is put into a predicament "experimentally," in order to see what will happen next. Truancy suggests an emancipation not sanctioned by the book of those well-schooled, or by orthodox versions of what English is supposed to be, sounding a note of dissonance against the narrator's upbringing, when he had books instead of toys (*E*, 5).

The wonder-full, exhilirating, sand-between-the-toes truancy represented in Powell's romance is open to disfigurement and celebrates its inelegant arrival with reference to adolescent sadomasochism. When a classical name is inscribed, it belongs to a gas-station owner named "Vergil," who has a pumpman (these are the days before "self-service only") named Clyde who removes his wooden leg from time to time, providing access to a world which, to the mind of a teenager, is worth talking about precisely because it is scary and causes him to grow pale and faint at the thought of it. The narrator's mother, a medical doctor, whom "the negroes call 'the Duchess' (*E*, 4), clearly intends for him to become a writer: "Truancy is no big deal to the Doctor anyway because it's the 'material' has her send me to public school" (*E*, 5). The rare and unexpected agrammaticality, where the relative pronoun drops out, alerts us to the fact that "the material" has little to do with formal education: it relates more to Jamesian possibilities at the Bluffton gas station, to the local African-American hangout, and the betweenness of the *patois* that is Gullah. For most of the narrative, Simons Manigault attends a local public school, "podunkus Bluffton Elementary," while the "Old Man," his father, wants him to go to Cooper Boyd Academy, a "college-prep academy for all future white doctors, lawyers, and architects in the low country" (*E*, 5)—where dialect and the dialectic of Southern history, as it was and continues to be, especially in terms of hues other than "pure" white, of racial mixing, will be suppressed.[15] The fact that Simons Manigault winds up attending a private school at the text's conclusion indicates that the period of tall-tale-telling truancy is over, and with it the romance of childhood, when races can still intermingle innocently and mythic possibilities loom on every horizon. Now he can be an athlete according to Vergil, who owns the gas station where Clyde, the attendant with a wooden leg (*EE*, 171–172) works, yet even here the superstitious discourse suggests another, less verifiable kind of "mixed breeding," since Simons sees himself as "half-Republican," carrying political genes inherited from his father, and half-Democrat on his mother's side. At the academy he considers himself an "out-breed" and thus somehow superior to the "inbreed" he might have been if his mother had married her first lover, a poet: "altogether socialist and taking dancing or piano lessons"—as if a career in the arts were somehow made impossible by the political persuasion of his actual father. The "pure" political union of two left-leaning parents might have resulted in offspring "signed," in Simons Manigault's juvenile mind, with an artsy effeminacy, the worst thing in the world to a precocious twelve- or thirteen-year-old boy. The reader is left to judge for her- or himself at how many levels of dramatic irony such eccentricity is meant to be taken.

Rich Names and Strange Characters : The Case for "Surprisingness"

Where one man of real merit succeeds, how many break down in the training; and even where success is won, how much less that success where talent...takes its natural position at the start, and stimulated to its utmost exercise, fights its way from its first strivings to its ultimate triumphs—each day a day of activity and every week a trial of skill and strength; putting all of law that is evolved from its practice, and forced to know something, at least, of what the books teach of it; and getting that larger and better knowledge of men which books cannot impart, and still more important self-knowledge, of which experience is the only schoolmaster.

Joseph G. Baldwin, *The Flush Times of Alabama and Mississippi*

The virtue of declamation in a first-person fictional text, especially one told by an idiot or neurotic child, is that it need not frame local places, persons, and things as coloristic moments somehow added on as a feature or element in a larger picture. The eccentric part thus asserts its validity in terms of a wholeness which can be considered in slice-like isolation from other equally salient episodes. Both myth (the Cyclops in his cave, the Minotaur) and romance subtend the motivation of "Taurus," the process-server in *Edisto*, who acquires his Latin name, presumably, from the constellation of the bull, but who implies or implicates an entire Southern literature of avenging "angels" of mixed race and thus excavates both conventional and unconventional mythic paradigms. Taurus is a "regular" monster only in the mind of the narrator who calls him by that name, excluding him from the more generic run of homicidal maniacs, and then qualifies him further, basing his aesthetic judgment upon qualities of skin texture and physique:

He don't ax-murder us or anything like that. Yet there is something arresting about this dude the moment you see him. He is shimmery as an islander's god and solid as a butcher. I consider him to be the thing that the Negroes are afraid of when they paint the doors and windows of their shacks purple or yellow. (*E*, 8)

But this is the same Taurus whom Simons "tests" with his telescope and "fish story" about the clipper-ships when the two first meet on a South Carolina beach. It is not as if the two moments could or ought to be synthesized in the larger figure of the whole text; rather, each has its own idiosyncratic importance within a sequence of episodes, like the cave of the Cyclops or Calypso's island in Homer. It is in the unproblematic salience with which details and isolated episodes "speak" to us as readers, that the text moves into a semiotic space which is one of tall-tale-telling, of local inflection (a Brechtian *gestus*) placed upon material history and myth—altogether like that of the Bundrens or Grass's narrator in *The Flounder*—and thus not coupled with those deeper enigmas of cultural trouble or subjective fate represented by textual inscrutabilities in Poe or Melville. Or it may be that the idiot and child in their idiosyncratic personahood represent the ultimate enigma, at least for an idealism that sees in language only the means to achieve a semantics of personality. Subjects and the language(s) they speak are indexed only in and by situational (pragmatic) contexts and derive their meaning from them:

> Der ihm [dem Subjekt] dadurch zugewiesene Index von Einzigartigkeit entzieht es aber zugleich dem epistemologischen Rahmen einer rücksichtslos idealisierten Semantik der Personalität. Es hat eine Identität weder durch körperliche Eigenschaften (die als Naturgegebenheiten a priori gar nicht semantisiert sind und den *Sinn*, unter denen sie sich einer Sprachgemeinschaft erschließen, erst aus individuellen Deutungen erwerben, diese dann aber nicht umgekehrt konditionieren können), noch durch die Stabilität der Bedeutung der Prädikate, die ihm (dem Individuum) zu verschiedenen Zeiten zugesprochen werden (auch sie modifizieren sich schritthaltend mit dem kontinuierlich sich transformierenden Weltdeutungssystem des Individuums).[16]
>
> [The index of uniqueness which is thereby ascribed to the subject excludes it at the same time from the epistemological frame of an indiscriminately idealized semantics of personality. It [the subject] has an identity neither through bodily traits (which as natural circumstances are not at all semanticized a priori and take on the *sense*, within which they reveal themselves to a linguistic community, only from individual interpretations, <circumstances> which then, however, cannot condition these <interpretations> in reverse), nor through the stability of the meaning of predicates, which can be ascribed to it (the individual) from time to time (they too modify themselves in such a way as to keep step with the continually self-transforming world-interpretation-system of the individual).]

What such a philosophically rigorous statement means in terms of literary context is that "Taurus," who escapes from the semantics of personality and conventional naming, can be considered a "beautiful monster" in the index of uniqueness, both grotesque and arabesque at once and in varying combinations, depending upon the adolescent wit and wisdom of Simons Manigault in his situationally-bound world-view. To seek for a mythic typology or Jungian archetype is to misunderstand the fundamentally eccentric role of naming in *Edisto*, and to limit the freedom the text permits itself to diverge from every history, fallen or otherwise, past, present, and future. That is why its *muthoi* or "true lies," can, in 2005, still bear down upon us, in our own particular hooking or angular preoccupation with things "arabesque." Simons is under no particular obligation to represent the "whole cake" of the truth (about how the Sea Islands are being bought up by land developers anxious to cash in on Boomer retirees and how they are displacing the native Gullah-speakers in order to build golf courses) or will embellish it by means of a flaky, freaky sort of Salingeresque jivetalk—overheard, perhaps, at the dinner table or in Jake's Baby Grand bar—about how the real estate developers are all "invading Arabs" : "...they've bought ten islands, we'll all be camel-tenders soon" (*E*, 6). But this is pure (or not so pure) riffing on the part of a white boy on *Empir*in, who needs an inimical, alien target, so that he can seem less freakish himself: "And besides playing the freak I can jive a little, too, like the Arab alarum I like to ring. 'If it wasn't for the *Marines* down the road, these Arabs'd do more than buy this place!'" (*E*, 10). The value of such juvenile performances, tendentious riffs on a paranoid, chauvinistic world-view now in evidence "more than ever," is that they examine in a textual funhouse mirror both the predations of land speculators and the mendacities of demagogues—a mindset which from one decade or century to the next markets the ideological seductions of permanent war.

The texture of speeches, lies, and half-truths constitutes a tapestry that is "rich" in the sense of permitting language to be read—in dramatic intonation and epic isolation—at the level of "pure" performance. The purity of enunciative performances by a Theenie or Addie Bundren preserves the negativity of the ephemeral, in intensely feminist or matriarchal accentuation, turning it against a commercial and political ethos which treats human beings as (wage-)slaves, mere means to ends, and, among other things, denies adequate health care to its poorest citizens. In James and Faulkner, the *muthos* of fiction takes over the role of "truth-teller" in a frock-coated, brass-buttoned world of commerce where the only serviceable truth is that of a Flem Snopes or Anse Bundren: the tawdry certainty of "what works for me." The surprising, skewed clarity of that which Simons Manigault makes up does not indict the society in which he must grow up; rather, it reveals the possibility of sensing things and persons anew, in a community of wounded or strong persons who speak a unique *patois*, each of whom is an episodic Sea Island in and of him- or herself, refusing to become part of the mainland, to be "incorporated."

As to what constitutes a "true" folk-tale, we may be left in a state of meta-historical uncertainty and consternation. This is true for the multidiscursive text, where it is speaking or telling that matters more than philological rigor, especially when one of the discursive performers is either a truant, an idiot, or an idiot savant. In a chapter of *The Flounder* entitled "The Other Truth" Grass spins a tale from the margins of Romantic literary and art history, bringing together Clemens Brentano, Achim von Arnim, Jacob and Wilhelm Grimm, and the painter Philipp Otto Runge in a forest on the outskirts of Gdańsk/Danzig. This portion of the narrative highlights the difference between the "acceptable" or authorized version of a fish-tale told to Runge by an old woman, the text that will appear in *Grimms' Fairy Tales*, and the "true," but more dangerous and apocalyptic version, which is burned under ritual circumstances as though it possessed supernatural powers—a text which might have been the fictive "source" for Grass's novel, but, in any case, was for centuries an integral part of the insular and vibrant seacoast sub- or counter-culture of Rügen:

> Denn was ein altes Weib im Sommer 1805 dem Maler zusätzlich in die Feder schwatzte, wurde zwischen Rehwiese und Waldteich bei Vollmond verbrannt. So wollten die Herren die patriarchalische Ordnung schützen. Deshalb brachten die Brüder Grimm nur die eine Rügener Niederschrift 'Von dem Fischer un syne Frau' auf dem Märchenmarkt. Seitdem ist des Fischers Frau Ilsebill sprichwörtlich ein zänkisches Miststück, das immer mehr haben, besitzen, beherrschen will. Und der Butt, den der Fischer gefangen und wieder freigesetzt hat, muß liefern und liefern....
>
> (*B*, 23)
>
> [For that which an old woman in the summer of 1805 blabbed supplementally into the pen <of> the painter, was burned between deer-meadow and forest-pond by the light of a full moon. That is how the men protect the patriarchal order. This is the reason the brothers Grimm put only the one manuscript from Rügen 'On the fisherman an' he wife' on the fairy-tale market. From that time forward the fisherman's wife Ilsebill was, proverbially a quarrelsome pile of manure who only wants to have more, possess more, dominate more. And the flounder, which the fishermen caught and again set free, must provide and provide....]

Yet the power of the original text is such that parts of its truth continue to live on in the oral tradition, a tradition founded not on literature of the mainland, especially not the Lower Saxon interior of Germany, but on "unbeautiful words," a saltier, locally inflected agrammaticality and phonetic graininess. The part that is still quotable (and, as we say in the southern part of America, "sticks in the craw" or throat of the patriarchy) concerns women's ability to resist male domination:

> Der Butt sagt, er habe nur das Erzählbare eines komplizierten, weil Jahrtausende währenden Vorgangs, der sich trotz gelegentlicher Auswüchse, zum Wohle der Menschheit vollzogen habe, in einfache Worte gefaßt und dem Volksmund überliefert...Immerhin sei die volkstümliche Mär bis heutzutage zitierfähig geblieben. Sogleich gab der Butt ein Beispiel: "Myne Frau de Ilsebill—will nich so, as ik woll will.'
>
> (*B*, 47)
>
> [The flounder says, he put into simple words and transmitted to oral tradition only that which could be made into a story about a process which was complicated because it took thousands of years. <This process> was one that had taken place, despite occasional divergences, to the benefit of mankind...Nonetheless <despite the destruction of the original manuscript dictated to Runge> the fairy-tale of folk tradition has remained quotable up to the present day. The flounder immediately gave an example: 'Me wife Ilsebill—don' wan' what I want.'[17]]

Atrocity's Unbeauteous Community

It is part of our thesis that "phonetic atrocities" and "the other truth" of the alternative Grimm's fairy-tale or romantic truant serve as mimetic, grainy antidotes to the violence of history, restoring it not to innocence but to an aesthetic *gnoseologia superior*. In order to better understand the pedigree of Simons Manigault's *muthos*, in terms of its peculiar regard for Taurus, we must move back to the time when "phonetic atrocities" were first being attempted in American literature, to Cable's *Grandissimes*. The abrasion or fragmentation of language, in this case, tracks the depiction of violent acts done in the name of slavery, while at the same time also creating a space of divergence and conversation which, in effect, "makes over" or displaces both the victim and the victimizer :

> Bras-Coupé, they said, had been, in Africa, and under another name, a prince among his people. In a certain war of conquest, to which he had been driven by *ennui*, he was captured, stripped of his royalty, marched down upon the beach of the Atlantic, and, attired as a true son of Adam, with two goodly arms intact, became a commodity.[18]

Thus, in a slave ship, Bras-Coupé comes to what Cable terms, with the gem of a culinary phrase many a writer would "die for" and which has lost none of its idiomatic brilliance or relevance, in a language, once again, built from the ground or *Grund* of the materiality of food, upward, "the buttered side of the world." In the New World to which Bras-Coupé is introduced, violence can, at times, beget intelligence or require a language with which to communicate with its victims. When Bras-Coupé refuses to work in the cotton fields, he hits the overseer with the back of a hoe, and physically attacks several other slaves. For these offenses against plantation order, he is taken out to be whipped. But the overseer—who is anything but a Simon Legree—recognizing a certain extraordinary quality in Bras-Coupé, has the strategic intelligence to understand that language in this case is to be preferred to whipping. He seeks out a translator to converse with the recalcitrant former African prince. A number of candidates are consulted, and their reluctance to serve as go-betweens constitutes an unexpectedly comedic twist to the tale of the physical violence inflicted on Bras-Coupé— as if Cable wanted to show the intersubjective nature of resistance to the pressure of "doing a favor for the boss," a delaying tactic among those who are least powerful, not as a mere burnt-cork-faced minstrel "turn," but as a sign of intelligence working at the level of the collective unconscious within a polyglot community and passed on from one slave to the other. Clemence passes by, saying she cannot (because she has a fresh memory of being pushed into a ditch by Bras-Coupé). She recommends Agricole, who says, *"Mo pas capable! Mo pas capable!* (I cannot! I cannot!) Ya, ya, ya! 'oir Miché Agricole Fusilier! ouala yune bon monture, oui!"*—which was to signify that Agricola could interpret the very Papa Lébat" (*G*, 173). Refusing to provide the services of translator for "a negro," Agricola suggests Palmyre Philosophe:

> And she went to the don's plantation as interpreter, followed by Agricole's prayer to Fate that she might in some way be overtaken by disaster. The two hated each other with all the strength they had. He knew not only her pride, but her passion for Honoré. He hated her, also for her intelligence, for the high favor in which she stood with her mistress and her invincible spirit, which was more offensively patent to him than to others, since he was himself the chief object of her silent detestation. (*G*, 173)

Palmyre, named for an ancient city-state ruled by proud Zenobia, a famous queen who rebels unsuccessfully against Roman rule, not only translates for the overseer; she "tames" Bras-Coupé and reintegrates him into the slave community. The two fall in love, so it seems, and are betrothed to each other—that is, if the act of betrothal itself is not a strategy on the part of Palmyre to wreak vengeance upon Agricola. Yet another act of violence, this time at the wedding party, intrudes itself upon the marriage festivities, as a drunken Bras-Coupé disrespectfully demands more wine from his Spanish-speaking master, then strikes Don José before being disciplined for insubordination. In a "hurricane" that lends a chiaroscuro and/or melodramatic intensity to the garish nuptials, Bras-Coupé escapes to the swampy woods, whose description is at least half of what the narrative seems to be about, a richness and strangeness in nature which is, in its very capacity for incorporating both otherworldly beauty and carnal cruelty, the only possible setting for this lurching tale of slavery:

> Endless colonnades of cypresses; long-motionless drapings of gray moss; broad sheets of noisome waters, pitchy black, resting on bottomless ooze; cypress knees studding the surface; patches of floating green, gleaming brilliantly here and there; yonder where the sunbeams wedge themselves in, constellations of water-lilies, the many-hued iris, and a multitude of flowers that no man had named; here, too, serpents great and small, of wonderful colorings, and the dull and loathsome moccasin sliding warily off the dead tree; in dimmer recesses the cow alligator, with her nest hard by; turtles a century old; owls and bats, racoons, opossums, rats, centipedes and creatures of like vileness; great vines of beautiful leaf and scarlet fruit in deadly clusters; maddening mosquitoes, parasitic insects, gorgeous dragon-flies and pretty water-lizards; the blue heron, the snowy crane, the red-bird, the moss-bird, the night-hawk and the chuckwill's widow; a solemn stillness and stifled air only now and then disturbed by the call or whir of the summer duck, the dismal ventriloquous note of the rain-crow, or the splash of a dead branch falling into the clear but lifeless bayou. (*G*, 181–182)

As readers, we may be glad that Cable has ignored Poe's advice to American writers that they should omit depictions of American scenery and "quaint" characters in other to concentrate on a writing that is not subservient to the Audubon aesthetic. At the same time, however, there is a broader ethical condition being adumbrated by the bayou landscape; the condition of master and slave, of hunter and hunted, is not limited to this half-submerged Louisianan terrain, but replicated wherever power asserts itself. Bras-Coupé , the African slave, is made, at least for the moment, into an epic hero on the level of a homeless Odysseus:

> Many a wretch in his native wilderness has Bras-Coupé himself, in palmier days, driven to just such an existence.... (*G*, 182)

We remember that, only a paragraph or two before, nature was intruding on the wedding party in the form of a thunderstorm, telegraphing the violent and rather predictable complications to come. In a sense, it is Cable, with a supernaturally keen sense of realism in character motivation and language, but with no particular gift for or interest in verisimilitude of plot, who is the ventriloquist, making nature and character say what he wants them to say, so to speak, behind their back. It is the monological or ethical impulse in Cable, working against the polyphonic, multidiscursive "phonetic atrocities," which constitutes an area of considerable aesthetic interest.

In Faulkner, working within the multidiscursivity of first-person narrative, but also subtly undermining it by hybridizing declamatory utterance with a "narrative agency" (*DF*, 31) interested in a unified, "delectable" myth, the storm is not made an accessory to plot manipulation, but becomes the plot itself, into which the family of the Bundrens, together with the coffin containing the mother, is "poured." Generically romantic plot complications are thus transformed by being subordinated to the mythic paradigm of the flood, and the gnoseological/gynecological "other truth," whose place is unassignable because its "word" is situated in an emptiness or void between characterology (declamation) and narrative instance. How full or empty this void "really" is depends upon our readerly thirst for cognitive or referential certainty; if we want the deformed South, in graphic or pictographic immediacy, then it is missing from the frame. If, on the other hand, we desire a disfigured South made over, refashioned in the graininess of the exquisite phoneme, then there is "meat" enough for us in the motivation of its well-engineered speakers.

The Other Truth: Powell and the Lesson of the Three Poes

It was the hour at which young ladies should come out for an airing and roll past a hedge of pedestrians, holding their parasols askance. Henry James, *The Europeans*

And I think all that carrying on on my part necessitated some immediate investment consultations, changed the curve of custody junkets, invigorated faculty parties, sweetened my last hours at Jake's Baby Grand, for I knew a chapter was closing, and imperiled, of course, my friendship with the process server I got to even name like he was a character in those novels I was supposed to write.
Padgett Powell, *Edisto*

Language in Padgett Powell's *Edisto*, as in Faulkner and Grass, undergoes stunning sea-changes, whereby it is reinvigorated, but also caked, "cooked," and/or imperiled by a re-sensed, at times surreal, decentering on the part of a first-person narrator. In particular syntactical combinations there is a surface worthy of the master who is James, but also, without stretching things too much, it is possible also to discern a kind of Sallustian intensity and focus mingled with the dissonant rambunctiousness of a solo by Coltrane in his final, "difficult" phase. Powell has assimilated James's aesthetic of the exquisite, gone moment or chapter, together with a tone (as above) of imperilment and loss, of vehicles rolling or sailing away along ancient roads and coastlines. The lesson of the master is that to re-present ("paint") the ephemeral is to transcend the ephemeral, to "work up" the world's surface is to explore its depth.[19] The Gogolian aspect of naming, as well as the "phonetic atrocity game," derived from Cable, play their part in an eternizing strategy which may not consider the preserved neighborhoods of Savannah or Charleston to be the aesthetic equivalent of ancient Athens or Rome, but which nonetheless views unpaved or roughshod Southern locales (prior to gentrification) and language artifacts with the kind of reverence archeologists bestow on precious scraps from the garbage heaps and winding-sheets of antiquity.

But it may be possible to better understand the multidiscursive, epic deixis of Powell when it is seen apart from a native tradition with Simms at one end and Faulkner at the other and set against the method of and lesson taught by the Southern writer who is Edgar Allan Poe, or a critical trio of Poes, that of William Carlos Williams,[20] the *local*, though hardly provincial Poe, that of Edward Dahlberg,[21] the tragic Poe who also places women at the heart of things, and that of John Irwin, the hieroglyphic Poe, who, of the three, seems, on the surface at least, as we have seen, to be the most distant from Powell's inflected or epic multidiscursivity.

The "local Poe" of William Carlos Williams is the one we have been examining, in its modernist inflection, at some length thus far, one "intimately shaped by his locality and time" (*AG*, 216). This is the Poe that does *not* bear translation, say, into French, or into the grotesque misprisions by which his reputation has been seized, but that Baudelaire nonetheless had a sense of as the *sauvage or enfant terrible* antithesis of what passed for bourgeois or provincial letters in the America (and Europe) of the 1840s. Williams discerns in Poe's style, at the level of syntax, grammar, and diction, the desire to "clear the ground" of a sophistication affecting or infecting the supposedly literate north of Lowell and Longfellow, a desire, to quote Williams's carefully chosen word, to become "juvenescent"—the use of an inchoative suffix derived from Latin "-esco" denoting the process of becoming young again in a literary world that had become prematurely, superficially "old." Powell's Simons Manigault is a deixis of this juvenescent strain in Poe. On the other hand, "local" in Poe means everything other than a postcard-like depiction of the natural beauty of the American continent. Nor is it the arabesque surface, a series of "bizarre designs" (*AG*, 219), that matters. Rather, words, for Poe are "figures" that must be reduced to their most elementary properties *for him* or in *his* telling while the particles of language must be made "clear as sand" (*AG*, 221). Thus, though Williams does not say as much, there is a monological or grainy impetus behind Poe's texts, to "detach a 'method' from the smear of common usage' (*AG*, 221) as found in Lowell or Longfellow. Again, what unites Poe and the point of view of Powell's narrator, a point of view common among juveniles, but almost never expressed articulately let alone artistically, is a refusal to "go along with" the hypnosis-like bleaching of reality as conceived by adults used to narcissistic self-aggrandizing. Hence the claim that what Simons Manigault is "up to" is something bizarre, abnormal, or strange, instead of something altogether local in its particularity, idiosyncratic in its clarity, and memorably or quotably *sui generis*. And it is this quality of an inchoate, untranslatable juvenescence which may be seen to work against the hieroglyphic tendency in Poe himself (it is one of those "beautiful contradictions," as the poet says) , and which, *a fortiori*, informs the truant worlds of Simons Manigault.

Dahlberg, on the other hand, focuses on Poe's somewhat surprising aggravations and solicitudes:

> Poe's intemperate criticism of those male amateur Parnassians of his own day was wholly accurate; his wayward praise of female authors, however, was profuse gallantry.
>   The 'Marginalia' and 'Literati' were impudent diatribes on Whittier, Emerson, Bryant, Lowell, the 'Quacks of Helicon,' astrological fakirs with asses' blood—'Mr. Longfellow and other Plagiarists.'
>   ...The moody ciphers of lady-poets, however, were sibylline sighs.

Edgar Poe's cavalier reviews of female authors were surreptitious valentines. In each critical tribute 'the seraph-harper, Israfel' was wooing an unknown heart.
(*CTB*, 140–141)

Dahlberg's text may remind us that the strongest, most idiomatically "virtuous" characters in *Edisto* are matriarchs and that the romance is, in effect, a series of not-so-sibylline "sighs" pointed in the direction of the narrator's mother and, above, all, the now vanished Theenie. There is no explicit disparagement of "normal" Anglo-Saxons and WASP types, the ones who force their children to attend private schools or hold memberships in clubs of an exclusive racial or sexual persuasion. The whites simply have few, if any, stories to tell; they refuse to go along with or understand the kaleidoscopic visions seen through the end of Simons's telescope, and they do not tolerate truancy. Poe's overweening fondness for female angels is balanced in Powell, however, by the centrality of the narrator's friendship with Taurus.

Irwin's take on Poe as the representative of something he calls "American hieroglyphics" takes into full account a cognitive dissonance arising from the potential interpretations of enigmatic signs. Such dissonance is emblematic of how we think about literature, or how we may choose to think about it, especially as it affects us as readers, while declamation and idiolect are about cultural performance, what speakers do in situations where lying is a necessary and highly refined art, when they are children, prisoners, slaves, outcasts, or losers of one sort or another. Equally, if not more importantly, Poe's major text, the one that has elicited the greatest comment both from Irwin and other contemporary readers, is a narrative of exploration, in which the translation of foreign words and alien pictographs "for the first time," at the level of plot, and "always again," as if for the first time, on the part of the reader, in terms of a "being-seized by," plays the crucial cognitive or re-cognitive role:

> Any decision that we make in this case [that of reading the "natural" glyphs or script in *The Narrative of A. Gordon Pym*] will be more a matter of will than knowledge, of temperament than enlightenment...Pym's nonrecognition of spatial doubling at the abyss is consistent with his earlier nonrecognition of temporal doubling in the repeated scenario of symbolic death and rebirth. What Pym fails to recognize is that in terms of both space and time the self is an essentially repetitive entity and thus incompatible with a nonrepetitive finality that dissolves symbolic (that is, doubled) re-presentation, or re-cognition. (*AH*, 234)

In myth, the nonrepetitive finality of death is often denied. In the "other truth" of fiction, however, history is denied through the perdurability of the name, at the level of the emotion-laden phoneme, and the monological speech-performance takes on the quality of an art which is projected as existing beyond time, even though it is founded, in part, upon the deixis of a *hic et nunc*. Speech, in effect, becomes like a spontaneous, surprise-laden dance of words, which is something other than a scripted text existing either in nature or in a book. The nonrepetitive finality of death, since it cannot be negated, is suspended in the telescopic view of that which *may* have been and rises again, for the moment of make-believe, in the lying speech of the *I* that re-cognizes *it*, in a first time that is indelibly inscribed—"graphed" and grasped—in grains of speech.

The hieroglyph may grow out of or lean upon the Romantic theory of mythic (narratological) beauty:

> Und was ist jede schöne Mythologie anders als ein hieroglyphischer Ausdruck der umgebenden Natur in dieser Verklärung von Phantasie und Liebe?[22]
> [And what is every beautiful mythology but a hieroglyphic expression of surrounding nature in this transfiguration of fantasy and love?]

Poe turns the hieroglyph against readerly expectation (a form of revenge against all-knowing complacency) and the beauty of perspicuous endings, glimpsing the abyss. Literature is still "*belles lettres*," and the hieroglyph is its only weapon. In modernism, however, ugliness and atrocity, in the form of a phonetically spelled Creole or Gullah, for example, become weapons of the "other truth" in which nothing is as beautiful as the exotic atrocity and phonetic disgrace of an "unschöne Mythologie" reflected in "*ekk*setra" and simple food, such as corn-cakes.

With the literary lesson of the three Poes and their relevance to Powell in mind, we return to the "original" story of how America was first explored, then exploited by Spanish *caballeros*—an historical lesson, perhaps, in how *not* to do things. The oral narratives taken from survivors of the expedition state that when De Soto explored the interior of Florida and Alabama, he found a thriving civilization with a distinctive and rich indigenous culture based on fishing, hunting, and agriculture, one superior in many respects to that of the Europeans. Friendly relations between native and Spanish conqueror, however, more often than not gave way to a centaur-like intemperateness and the bestial facticity of violence. The conquistadors have gone, and whole provinces of the Carolinas, such as Cofitachequi, no longer exist, but the Indian names[23] that are not from India—Apalachee, Mobile, Talapoosa, Loxahatchee, Mississippi, remain—as that which once greeted European culture at its coming and will survive, much as the Spanish horses lived on as wild appaloosas, after non-indigenous languages and customs have vanished and been replaced by more muscular, metropolitan Aztláns of the future, :

In the De Soto narratives, fishing is primarily referenced in the Apalachee country of northern Florida, where there was said to be good fishing near the sea and in ponds all year round, and the Mississippi River region. In the latter area, fish were among presents sent by native chiefs. A rock fish weir was reported for catching rays in the Gulf. Nets and fishhooks were also reported.

The Gentleman of Elvas mentioned a kind of fish (probably catfish) taken in the Mississippi River and its tributaries near the mouth of the Arkansas:

'There was a fish called 'bagre,' a third of which was head; and it had large spines like a sharp shoemaker's awl at either side of its throat and along the sides. Those of them which were in the water were as large as a 'pico.' In the river, there were some of one hundred and one hundred and fifty pounds. Many of them were caught with the hook.' [24]

For Grass, who places *The Flounder* in the gaping mouth of "another truth" and traces fishing legends from the the Neolithic birth of thought into the medieval and modern periods, the way one spells a city's name is less important than the space of naming, the old "hook-work," and the food that characterizes two distinct cultures whose languages may be traced to some regional dialect of German or to one of the Lekhitic group—Polish and the various Kashubian dialects (remnants of an older Pomeranian language):

Mein Giotheschantz, Gidanie, Gdancyk, Danczik, Dantzig, Danzig, Gdańsk: von Anfang an umstritten. Wir pomorschen Fischer und Korbflechter blieben im Schutze der Burg auf dem alten Hakelwerk und aßen wie immer schon Grütze zu Fisch und Fisch zu Grütze, während die zumeist niedersächsischen Neusiedler, die Jordan Hovele, Johann Rapesilver, Hinrich Pape, Ludwig Skröver, Konrad Slichting und ähnlich hießen, als Handwerker und Händler hinter den Stadtmauern wohnten und Schweinswürste zu dicken Bohnen aßen.   (*B*, 113).

[My Giotheschantz, Gidanie, Gdancyk, Danczik, Dantzig, Danzig, Gdańsk: fought over from the beginning. We Pomeranian fishermen and basketweavers remained in the protection of the castle engaged in the old hook-work and ate groats with fish and fish with groats just as we always had, while the new settlers, mostly from Lower Saxony, the Jordan Hoveles, the Johann Rapesilvers, the Hinrich Papes, the Ludwig Skrövers, the Konrad Slichtings and all those like them, lived as craftsmen and traders behind the city-walls and ate sausages with fatty beans.]

The "I" of Grass appropriates the liberty to project itself in epic, first-person totalization upon all the aliased moments in a city's past, a glorification not of "great moments in history," but of names scattered about the graveyard that would otherwise be totally forgotten. The counter-historical "my" placed at the head of narrative discourse suggests that the "other reality" of performance is superior to the one learned about in school, that "a certain latitude of discourse can at least reframe if not reinvent facticity." The possessive pronoun, phonetic/grammatical atrocity, and the tale are wedded. "My mother is a fish," "Myne Frau de Ilsebill—will nich so, as ik woll will," "Mein Giotheschantz," "my toys," "my boats," "*Ekk*setra" (where the *my* is felt so forcefully that it need not be made explicit). There are only three apocalypses woven into the fabric of American history, the genocide performed upon native tribes and tribal nations, the slave trade, and the Civil War. In the history of American letters, only the latter two have been dealt with at all significantly in terms of the "other" reality and its multidiscursive fabulation. It remains to be seen how the "great American novel" of the Native American, which has yet to be written, will employ it.

The "other" reality need not be the exclusive province of anyone or of a particular ethnic voice in the multidiscursive, declamatory text. Perhaps the most exotic (and, at the same time, indigenous) case of doubling in which the other becomes only too real is the one in which Powell's alter ego Simons Manigault and a Southern boy of another time and place, pre-Civil-War Richmond, participate. Here we need not consult anything more than a marvelous, if somewhat dated, biography of Poe to discern similarities between them: an inordinate devotion to females (Dahlberg's Poe), a childhood spent with books, a love of tall tales, a taste for adventuresome and offbeat entertainment, and even a strange preoccupation with telescopes. Where precise knowledge of the other reality is lacking, the biographer is compelled to speculate upon or invent it, placing Poe—as a sort of North American embodiment of the "Individuelle–Allgemeine," the paradigmatic "Southern boy" of means—in the slave quarters, where he may experience communication as a form of ecstatic otherness:

> There he must have feasted upon corn-pone and listened while many a tale of Brer Rabbit and his ilk went round, while the ghosts, and 'hants' and spooks of an ignorant but imaginative and superstitious people walked with hair-raising effect, and songs with melancholy harmonies and strange rhythms beat themselves into his consciousness with their peculiar ecstasy and abandon which only children and... [slaves]... can experience. Here it was then, rather than upon some mythical journey to France or Russia, that he first laid the foundation for his weird imaginings and the strange 'new' cadences which he was to succeed in grafting upon the main tree of English poetry. Here, too, may have arisen the flair for the bizarre, and the concept that birds and animals were speaking characters, and that fear of graves and corpses and the paraphernalia of the charnel.[25]

As it might have been then, so it is in the impossible now of narration, in terms of a Gullah-speaking African-American house-servant named Theenie, whose irresistibly ecstatic affect, pitched at the level of vivid personahood and self-empowered alterity, resonates at the level of the phoneme:

> Somebody got to hep that boy kotch up. He so far ahead he's *behine*. Yes, he is.' Her head nodding, in a rhythm like a small, gentle locomotive: her whole head rolling on the syllables: *Yessuh*.' (*E*, 33)

Notes

Preliminaries

1. Erich Heller, *The Disinherited Mind* (Cleveland and New York: Meridian, 1969), 260.

Chapter One

1. See Noah Heringman, "Things And Sense in Two Lyrics Of Wordsworth," @ www. prometheus.cc.emory.edu (14 November 2004).
2. Jean Laplanche and J.-B. Pontalis. *Urphantasie. Phantasien über den Ursprung der Phantasie*, translated by Max Looser (Frankfurt/M.: 1992), 36. This is the German Translation of *Fantasme originaire. Fantasmes des origines. Origines du fantasme* (Paris: Hachette, 1985). References to this text will be indicated below by the abbreviation *U*. English translation by this writer.
3. See Jean Laplanche, "To Situate Sublimation," translated by Richard Miller, *October* 28 (Spring,1984), 26: "...we can posit the cohesive elements of a theory...not of sublimation but of sublimations." He bases this conclusion on an analysis of the complementary roles Played by violence and the quest for knowledge, as exemplified by the work of Da Vinci. References to this work will be indicated below by the abbreviation *TSS*.
4. "Nutting" (51–53) in *Poetical Works of Wordsworth,* edited by Thomas Hutchinson and Ernest de Selincourt (London: Oxford U. Press, 1960), 147. References to this text will be indicated below by the abbreviation *PW*.
5. William Wordsworth, *The Prelude or Growth of a Poet's Mind* (Text of 1805), edited by Ernest de Selincourt, revised by Stephen Gill (London: Oxford, 1970), 19. References to this text will be indicated below by the abbreviation *P*.
6. The Oedipal import of crossroads experiences for Wordsworth is discussed briefly by Alan Bewell in his *Wordsworth and the Enlightenment* (New Haven: Yale U. Press, 1989), 180. He also mentions the connection between "social outcasts and the damned" (witchcraft, gibbets, etc.) and the crossroads, but no one, as far as I can see, has read *The Prelude*, Book VI in this light, nor has it been treated as a touchstone of canonical interpretation. A "great" phobic link in the Wordsworthian unconscious, it seems to me, lies between the terror inspired by confrontations with British state authority at, near, or in the crossroads (capital punishment) and the French terror of the guillotine. The "siste viator" moment becomes a window opening on primal scenes, each testifying "from memory," and laden with a distinct premium of pleasure and/or displeasure.
7. Decades later, having become a poetic institution more or less aligned with the powers that be, Wordsworth (in "Sonnets upon the Punishment of Death") utilizes a highway metaphor adapted from what was fast becoming antequated practice, celebrating the way the State places fear of retribution in the hearts of would-be criminals and "plants well-measured terrors on the road/ Of wrongful acts" (viii, 4–5). In the 1790s his heart lay elsewhere;terror ruled across the Channel, and the road, together with what got "planted" In it, might still be contested. The crux-like nature or crossedness of what is done

"in" or "on the road" partakes of the antithetical sense of primal words, in Freud, and the doubleness of the shibboleth, as explicated by Derrida. Eros and Thanatos, joined to the binary rhythm of the heart, receive their share or due, precisely, at the crossroads, *e. g.,* in the archetypally suggestive Blues lyrics of the Mississippian genius Robert Johnson.

8. The 1800 "Preface" to *The Lyrical Ballads* poses the question of what constitutes a poetic text in a manner that goes, again, to the question of the origin of art; the pre- or pro-positioning of that question continues to affect poetry criticism today, especially in transatlantic debates between North American "yawpers" (revived in Pound's *Blast*) and more genteel and/or discreet arbiters of poetic taste. Wordsworth states a wish to "bring his language near to the language of men"—and thus bring about a radical renovation of poetic diction. Thus "...the pleasure which I have proposed to myself to impart...." will be "...very different from that which is supposed by many persons to be the proper art of poetry...." The "Preface" indicates how the pleasure of metre makes language less "real," thus tempering the naked immediacy of passion. Book VII of *The Prelude* reveals itself as contested generic or meta-generic ground, mountebank's trestle or side-show, where romance, pastoral, and drama jostle for preeminence, and quotations from Milton and Shakespeare surface briefly in the phenotext, only to become submerged in the carnivalesque-like welter of a deixis that makes reading "move along" to the next scene of qualitative this- or suchness, where "here" and "there," *hoc* and *illud* cross.

9. See Keith Hanley, "Wordsworth's Revolution in Poetic Language," *Romanticism on the Net* 9 (Feb., 1998) for an analysis of the *Lyrical Ballads* in the context of Kristeva's theory of the 19th-century transformation of literature.

10. Steven E. Jones reads the parallel passage in Book VII, where Wordsworth describes the hellish phantasmagoria and noise of Bartholomew Fair, including wax-works, as an ethical counter-satire to the scene of the rustic carnival at the beginning of Book VIII. Wordsworth may recall that St. Bartholomew's is where Protestants were executed under "bloody" Queen Mary. However that may be, my point here has to do with the power Wordsworth attempts to exert over a scene in *this* street, which looks beyond the ethical fact to the larger picture of England, of a present, past, and possible England, where the mind of the poet can assert totalizing, fanciful control—"as if the whole were one vast mill." In the context of "Romantic vagrancy," in general, one should also consider the ironic Roman *exemplum paupertatis* in Juvenal's third *Satire,* where it is homeless Jews who are squatters on urban precincts formerly reserved for the Muses. For many Romantics, the exiled or Wandering Jew symbolizes both the poet and art, in general.

11. On page 363 of his *Wordsworth's Poetry, 1787–1814* (New Haven: Yale U. Press, 6th printing, 1977), Geoffrey Hartman provides a comprehensive survey of critical opinion on the subject of visual imagination and its fluctuating appreciation in the later 18th century. References to Hartman's text will be indicated below by the abbreviation *WP.*

12. The notion of totalization, a term used to describe cosmological pictures or models in the texts of indigenous cultures, is worked out with subtlety and sophisticated rigor by the anthropologist-turned-poet Nathaniel Tarn in his analysis of Blake. It can be applied, with modifications, to Wordsworth's strategy of geographic/geomantic mediation, focusing on the multi-dimensional interpenetration of *rus* and *urbs,* of heaven and earth: "Telescoping Albion and the Divine Imagination, as Blake I believe gives us license to do, let Albion stand for the state of a poet's mind at the outset of a creative act...The poet's mind will contain a world-model which might be partly or wholly unconscious (the sum of the life to date, the sum of the poems)...The significance of an Adam, or Albion, lies in the pretence on the part of art that its objects have a natural origin, that art Imitates life, or, indeed, *is* life...Operating between the initial total and the retotalization, the poem works as if it were passing from a 'real heraldry,' through a 'projective

heraldry' to a 'selective heraldry.'" Nathaniel Tarn, "The Heraldic Vision: A Cognitive Model for Comparative Aesthetics," in *Alcheringa/Ethnopoetics*, A First International Symposium, edited by Benamou and Rothenberg (Boston University, 1976), 30. As a practicing poet with an international reputation, like Wordsworth, Tarn valorizes totalization within a process of psychological reintegration and stylistic actualization—the actual work of creating poetic texts. A distinction needs to be made, however, between two kinds of telescopy. Unhappy with the Bible, Blake seems able to summon up or, literally, *draw* originary scenes at will (as if every day were spent close to one or more *Ur*-springs of myth and totalizing mythopoeia), while Wordsworth, in/as another kind of Albion, has to do hard hermeneutic and transferential work to "recollect" originary scenes as spots rather than sweeps of time. This totalizing power becomes clearer still when one reads the 1814 preface to *The Excursion*, where the entire poetic work is projected as a Gothic cathedral. Tarn's notion of totalization is another way of characterizing what Kenneth Johnston Refers to as a "conjunction" to which the mesocosmic consciousness of the poet returns again and again, which is also a ground of conned confrontation, a crossroads, or a cross marking "the" viatic spot. I privilege the "heterocosm" because of its Goethean associations and because it enables us to problematize Wordsworth's apostasy from history's lapsing, posteriority, and ponency in favor of a fideistic (self-) prepositioning. The turn cannot be categorized as simply another myth of the origin because, as I show below, it is embedded in primal/prime-time fantasy and in specific choices of diction and grammar.

13. E. P. Thomson notes how Blake alters the literary convention of the "country gentle-man" visiting the town in order to take in the lower-class sights and how Wordsworth remains *more or less* faithful to it or adapts it to his own purposes: "...the convention was, in some part, a countryman's convention, in some part, a class convention. From whichever aspect, plebeian London was seen from outside as a spectacle. Wordsworth was still able to draw upon this convention—although with significant shifts of emphasis—in *The Prelude*." See *Witness to the Beast* (New York: New Press, 1993), 190. References to This text will be indicated by the abbreviation *WB*. Does not one also sense in the poet's fanciful, quasi-grotesque, "I am a camera" take on the London thoroughfare a premonition of Gogol's *Nevsky Prospekt*?

14. No doubt, much of the striking force of this passage relies upon its registering of the "shock of the new." Laplanche is once again instructive: "We must therefore entertain the notion that the sexual instinct is not something that springs into being once and only once, but that, taking this Freudian theory as being valid, there is the human being (essentially, of course, but not solely, in the child) a capacity unceasingly to create the sexual, almost from the commencement of life, on the basis of external shocks, beginning with the *new*, of which the traumatic represents only the most striking paradigm," *TSS*, 23.

15. Marjorie Levinson, *Wordsworth's great period poems. Four Essays.* (Cambridge, England, Cambridge U. Press, 1986). 16. References to this text will be indicated below by the abbreviation *ML*.

16. In the notes to "A Highland Hut," Wordsworth, immediately after alluding to its fitness for romance and the "faery-land of Spenser..." (*PW*, 717) suggests that the scene of the poem "with all its beautiful colours" might make a good pantomime *transplanted* onto the London stage at Drury-Lane. Such a transfer of scene, of local colors re-presented theatrically in an urban setting, is a master-motive in Wordsworth—allied with The transfer or liberation of energy implied by a perpetual (inexplicit) reinvading of a distant or Goethean spring brought near through a process of intimation and/or

recuperation. One thinks of *The Maid of Buttermere*, a more prominent example. Panoramas, yet another crux-like form of representation, were all the rage in London, especially at Bartholomew Fair, in the 1790s. Given the matter of Annette Vallon, a most telling transplantation of scene occurs in "The Waggoner," where the title character, seemingly on one long "guilt trip," imagines the wife and child he has abandoned: "All care with Benjamin is gone/ A Caesar past the Rubicon:/ He thinks not of his long, long, strife:—/The Sailor, Man by nature gay,/Hath no resolves to throw away:/And he hath now forgot his Wife,/Hath quite forgotten her—/Or may be/Thinks her the luckiest soul on earth,/Within that warm and peaceful berth,/Under cover,/Terror over,/Sleeping by her sleeping Babe" (*PW*, 177). The "Or may be" demonstrates how little has, in fact, been forgotten by the sailor who has himself been as left high and dry as a derelict on the roads of the North country.

17. Much has been made in the secondary literature about counterpastoral and counter-counterpastoral as implied in Wordsworth's texts. I am reading them as pastorals in a Theocritean sense, in which the *urbs* is already implicated in the sophisticated subtext. Counter-satire in *The Prelude* or *The Excursion*, for example, takes us back beyond the limits of 18th-century moralizing or coterie pastoral to an "originary" *literary* scene of double entendre. See note 23 below on Lawall, who in his characterization of Theocritus provides us with a heuristic model for what I take to be the Wordsworthian heterocosm. At the same time, Wordsworth must have been aware of Robert Southey's *English Eclogues*, which commence with *The Old Mansion-House*, a poem in blank-verse (first published in the 1795 *Poems)* reflecting an abiding concern with venerable piles and hospitality. As in *The Retrospect* of 1794, Southey constantly associates the ups and downs of a mansion's career with the vicissitudes of human existence. Just as he could not utilize 18th-century satire as his model, Wordsworth could not help seeing the limitations of Southey's uniformly dull, third-person pastoral style (especially when compared to those past masters of blank verse, Shakespeare and Milton). The opening for *his* genius, that which Duncan Wu calls the *Ur*-Wordsworth, lay in an eclectic mix of styles and perspectives ("pastiche"), made available to him, in the first place, by the schoolmaster Muse William Taylor, M. A. Wu, in his *Wordsworth: An Inner Life* (Oxford: Blackwell, 2002), makes an interesting case for the notion of such a larval or pristine poet (prior to reshaping by Coleridge), examining Wordsworth's schoolboy notebooks, where translations of Vergil can be found a few pages away from the early effort, "The Vale of Esthewaite." Swiftly following upon the heels of that first Muse came the *other* William Taylor (1785–1836), known as "Godless Billy," a man with staunchly republican ideals whom Southey derided for "blemishes" of "Germanisms, Latinisms, and Greekisms." The smoky summits (*culmina*) of Vergil's rustic houses (*Eclogue* I, 82) are implanted in Wordsworth's pastoral imagination almost *ab ovo*.

18. Martin Heidegger. *Being and Time*, translated by Joan Stambaugh (Albany, N. Y.: State U. of New York, 1996), 33: "...But since discovery of the meaning of being and of the basic structures of Da-sein in general exhibits the horizon for every further ontological research into beings unlike Da-sein, the present hermeneutic is at the same time 'hermeneutics' in the sense that it works out the conditions of the possibility of every ontological investigation. Finally, once Da-sein has ontological priority over all other beings—as a being in the possibility of existence [*Existenz*]—hermeneutics, as the Interpretation of the being of Da-sein, receives a specific third and, philosophically understood, *primary* meaning of an analysis of the existentiality of existence. To the extent that this hermeneutic elaborates the historicity of Da-sein ontologically as the ontic condition of the possibility of the discipline of history, it contains the roots of what can be called 'hermeneutics' only in a derivative sense: the methodology of the historical

humanistic disciplines."

19. Jonathan Wordsworth, *William Wordsworth, The Borders of Vision* (Oxford, Clarendon 1984), 450.

20. In an article entitled "Locating Wordsworth: 'Tintern Abbey' and the Community with Nature" (*Romanticism Online*, 20 (November, 2000), David Miall not only traces with geographical accuracy the steps most likely taken by Wordsworth in 1790 when he first visited the environs of Tintern Abbey, but also cites the guide-books that were then available. Symonds Yat offers "steep woods and lofty cliffs" to the intrepid traveler, while "on the edge of Doward Hill to the west of Symonds Yat is King Arthur's Cave, mentioned by Ireland in his tour, probably an old mine."

21. Paul de Man, "Wordsworth and the Victorians," in *The Rhetoric of Romanticism* (New York: Columbia U. Press, 1984), 87.

22. Philippe Lacoue-Labarthe, "The Echo of the Subject," in *Typography*, ed. and translated by Christopher Fynsk (Cambridge, Mass.: Harvard, 1989), 179.

23. The pastoral mode provides Wordsworth with a "con-venient" rhetorical structure for dialogical discourses contrasting a past "golden age" with contemporary reality, for taking what Steven E. Jones terms a "higher road" elevated above the somewhat pedestrian conventions of 18th-century satire. See his *Satire and Romanticism* (New York: St. Martin's, 2000). Jones is particularly illuminating on the ways in which the poet avoids the Hogarthian procedures of Crabbe's *Village*, for example. Not least of the attractions afforded by pastoral coding is that it allows Wordsworth, with the shepherd as mouthpiece, to exploit dramatic monologue. In Theocritus, the inventor of pastoral, "...the scene...is not constantly rustic, although images of the countryside represent the more idealized life commonly known as 'pastoral.' This idealized countryside finally becomes...an inner landscape of the imagination; it is the mysterious world of poetic creation, a dreamland world of repose and spiritual integration—a refuge from man's tormenting emotions...the focus is upon human experience, its frustrations and utopian desires." Gilbert Lawall, *Theocritus' Coan Pastorals* (Washington: Center for Hellenic Studies, 1967), 5. In Wordsworth's precursor, Milton, pastoral takes an elliptical turn toward the elegiac, involving a sustained address to someone who has been slain or, like Lycidas, drowned. Hartman, in *WP*, acknowledges elements of Theocritean pastoral as the source for his own recuperation of the halted traveller motif and the epitaph (12), but does not engage with the possibility of a synoptically bucolic coding of entire passages, especially in *The Excursion*, for countersatiric effect, for example, through organic effacement.

24. Jonathan Wordsworth in his *Borders of Vision* (Oxford: Clarendon, 1984), 314 quotes Kenneth Johnston on Wordsworth as the embodiment of the borderer at another kind of crossroads: "The cumulative effect of all these details [in a 'Night-Piece'] is to intimate, almost invisibly, the conjunctive character of the vision. A man suddenly discovers Himself to be standing between heaven and earth, standing, moreover, as a link between them. The traveller does not simply apprehend or suffer the dualism, he is the dualism—without him it does not exist. The two spheres are brought together not so much by, as in, man; recognizing his mediate position, he defines his being." Hartman uses the term "mesocosm," but, given the crossed roads of material im*plant*ation and metamorphosis in Wordsworth—disembodiments where vegetation and quasi-religious relics are often Involved in crossings and crossedness—"heterocosm" seems marginally preferable.

25. Martin Heidegger, "Über den Ursprung des Kunstwerks," in *Holzwege* (Frankfurt/M.: Klostermann, fifth edition 1972), 13. References to this text will be indicated below by the abbreviation *H.* Residual traces of Heidegger's arguments concerning the death of art are discernible in Hartman's text "Goethe and Wordsworth" in *The Fate of Reading*

(Chicago: U. of Chicago Press, 1975), 179–200, especially when he suggests a difference between the two poets in their attitudes toward the daemonic, with a "freer" Goethe coming out seemingly "on top," because of an intrinsic *amor fati* in his attitude toward character. Wordsworth, by implication, less "character'd" or "free," i.e., more inhibited, plagued by doubts as to whether imaginative power is not already dead or obsolete (184), is seen as questioning the function of poetry and hence of art itself. Wordsworth is thus personally or intimately focused, in a pre-phenomeno*logical* sense, i.e., within a logic of sense and the senses, *tout court*, upon the predicament of modern art focused upon in Hegel and Heidegger. Hypotyposis or self-reconciliation involves a hermeneutics of the existentiality of existence. Subsequent references to this text will be indicated by the abbreviation *FR*.

26. Rather surprisingly, Heidegger fails to mention Goethe's famous threefold translation model in *Der Westöstliche Divan*. Is it because he is unwilling to involve himself in an explication that would lean on and thus compete with Goethe as an *Ur-Vater* pre-positioned before his own theory, as at the *fons et origo* of *Weltliteratur*? Is there also a certain anxiety to discuss a text that devotes itself to the Orient and thus to an exotic rather than to a native, i..e., belated or Hesperian source?

27. "Nachwort" to "Über den Ursprung des Kunstwerks," in *H*, 66.

28. William Wordsworth, "Celebrated Epitaphs Considered," from the Author's MSS, in *Prose Works of William Wordsworth*, edited by Rev. Alexander B. Grosart (London: Edward Moxon, 1876; rpt. New York: AMS Press, 1967), Vol. II, 65.

29. See my essay "Wanderers at the Spa: Baths as a Source of Cultural Ethos in Goethe and Others," in *Mythic Paradigms in Literature, Philosophy, and the Arts* (New York and Bern: Peter Lang, 2004), 323–331.

30. Northrop Frye, "New Directions from Old," in *Myth and Myth-Making* (New York: Braziller, 1960), 130.

31. See Avital Ronell, *Dictations: On Haunted Writing* (Lincoln, Nebraska: U. of Nebraska, 1986), 6–19 for a discussion of Goethe's own birthing trauma in the context of Freudian discourse.

32. I am using this noun from the adjective "surreptitious" in order to distinguish Wordsworth's projection of the organic process of disembodiment and post-pastoral (quasi-Ovidian) transformation from that most characteristic tendency on his part, which is that of attributing human qualities to inanimate objects. The latter finds its explicator in Immanuel Kant. As Daniel Dwyer remarks, "Perhaps no other philosopher emphasized and critiqued the metaphysical urge of the mind to 'spread itself on external objects' more systematically than Kant. In fact, Kant had a special word for this mental inclination: 'subreption' (*Erschleichung*). Subreption is a logical fallacy whereby one 'slips under' (*sub*: 'under,' and *repere*: 'creep, crawl') a phenomenon under the wrong category; in Kant's specific use of the term, something objective is mistaken for something subjective" (from a synopsis of his paper "Subreption in the *Kritik der Urteilskraft*: Kant's Critique of Naive Objectivism in Aesthetics"). Surreption has the same Latin roots as subreption. Surreption is the form subreption takes once the ego leaves the body it has been housed in; it is a thoroughly "out-of-body" agency aligned with the id (of nature) and set *beneath* the ego of the (paternal) other in a position of *supervening* abjectness or humility, much like that of a child destined to become father to the man. The category mistakes of subreption elevate both the imagination and nature (they are "all-exalting"), while surreption comes with connotations of a negative sublime, analogous to Hartman's *via naturaliter negativa*, and is seen in Wordsworth as the antidote to human pride and stateliness. Surreption, whose concrete referents are often "creepy, crawly" things, such as moss, mold, lizards, newts, and the poetic imagination,

adheres for obvious reasons to the literal etymology. Margaret's relic-like bowl, "green with moss of years," in *The Excursion* is an excellent device of surreption lodged within the larger scene of pastoral decline and de-reliction resampling and reaccentuating a Goethean *Ur*-spring. It is interesting to note that the mature Goethe almost never avails himself of subreption, while surreption is one of the most important bases of alchemical thinking and the doctrine of metamorphosis. Lastly, my "surreption" echoes, as well, the sense of subreption in medieval canon law, where it referred to the concealment of the truth in order to obtain ecclesiastical or royal dispensation.

33. As shown convincingly by Jonathan Wordsworth in *The Music of Humanity* (London: Nelson, 1969). References to this text will be indicated below by the abbreviation *MH*.

34. For better or worse, it is germane, if not particularly supportive of my study, that many of its concerns—the private versus public road, the Grail, the otherworldly female spirit, et al.—were anticipated in 1915 by the Anglo-American essayist, Richard Le Gallienne, father of the famous actress, in an essay entitled "Vanishing Roads." Reference is made to it here in order to excavate an episode in "smart-set" American taste and *Kultur-geschichte* just prior to the trauma of World War I, the Russian Revolution, and the Roaring Twenties. Le Gallienne's essay purveys some of the "sunken cultural goods" of Romanticism in a rotogravure-like way that alternately cloys and irritates, as the critic Lionel Johnson suggests (in Pound's telegraphing): "*Prettiness*, not beauty, which implies more imaginative thought and beauty than he possesses. Sensitive by temperament, and feels the *sentiment* of beautiful things, in art and life, not their *truth*. A persistent note of—not vulgarity, nor bad taste—but of unconscious familiarity in a bad sense. He belittles things by his touch." Ezra Pound, "Lionel Johnson," in *Literary Essays of Ezra Pound* (New York: New Directions, 1968), 365. Reading Le Gallienne on Wordsworth is worse than reading a vulgarized and unphilosophical imitator, say, of Heidegger on Hölderlin: one knows that the primary text has been read carefully and appreciated, one is grateful that attention has been paid, but there seems to be a process of homogenization at work which reduces everything, not to the discourse of ontology, but to the level of conversation and readerly edification while riding the rails on the way to work. Since poetic deixis thus finds itself buried or eradicated entirely, it is at least possible that appreciations like "The Vanishing Road" are signs of a decadent deviation from the sense and grandeur of the text itself. The glorification of the female as a kind of alien spirit of beauty to be scrutinized by the appreciative masculine gaze is particularly disconcerting. On the other hand, what kind of Hesperian culture is it (a century later) for which Wordsworth is not part of the active lounge-car vocabulary and the Richard Le Galliennes are either teaching in grammar school or preoccupied with overpriced cups of coffee and the daily pageant of stock quotes and sports scores?

35. This fragment (*Poetical Works*, V, 343) is quoted by John Beer in *Wordsworth and the Human Heart* (New York: Columbia U. Press, 1978), 80. References to this work will be indicated below by the abbreviation *WHH*.

36. Thomas De Quincey, "The English Mail Coach," in *Selected Writings of Thomas De Quincey*, edited by Philip Van Doren Stern (New York: Random House, 1937), 923. References to this text will be indicated below by the abbreviation *TDQ*.

37. On Wordsworth's "experiments" with the *prima materia* (a kind of mythicized, early Romantic genetic code) and disembodiment see the paper by Heringman reference in note 1: "The leitmotif for this talk is a phrase which is for me probably the most crucial one in the preface to *Lyrical Ballads*: 'incorporated with the beautiful and permanent forms of Nature.' This vision of rural life will be an important point of reference throughout my discussion of 'Three years she grew in sun and shower' and 'Resolution and Independence.' Both poems, besides being among the best-known of Wordsworth's

lyrics, also approach more literally than many others what it means for human beings to be incorporated with nature. In both, thorough incorporation with nature means thoroughgoing disembodiment in another sense. The subjects incorporated with nature here, by contrast with the more political 'Michael,' cannot be viewed as fully human agents, and become implicated instead in a recalcitrant materiality; they are experimental subjects being tested against an aesthetic concept." Professor Heringman finds interesting evidence supporting the notion that the Lucy of the Lucy poems is, in reality or experimental projection, a kind of homunculus. The experimental reforming/reformation of organic bodies (anatomical, political, et al.) is a—or perhaps *the*—Romantic project undertaken zealously in many countries, though, because of Wordsworth's and Coleridge's trip to Germany in 1798–1799, it seems more likely that they and artists like Runge are sharing a common philosophical dawn. Statements such as the following, applied by Robert Rosenblum in his *Modern Painting and the Northern Romantic Tradition: Friedrich to Rothko* (New York: Harper and Row, 1975) to Runge's mysticism, seem especially suggestive, given the Goethean constellation of the homunculus and the *Ur*-spring: "It is a primitive, untamed world dominated by a kind of magic plasm, and peered at in wonder by a Romantic who hopes to uncover the secret wellsprings of natural vitality" (53). Our clones are but replicas of ectoplasm that cover much of the same monstrous ground of "Germanic pseudo-horror" as *Faust* and Mary Shelley's *Frankenstein*.

38. J. W. Goethe, "Der Wandrer," in *Goethes Gedichte*, ed. Emil Staiger (Zürich: Manesse, 1949), II, 115. Goethe's sources may include Goldsmith's "The Traveller" of 1764 and *Satire 3* of Juvenal, where wandering *Judaei* are seen squatting on sacred ground formerly reserved for the Muses.

39. Taylor's translation is found in *MH*, 264–268.

40. As Beer notes in *WHH*, "Study of the state of trance struck further chords, prompting memories of occasions when he had temporarily felt himself initiated into a sense of the divine" (80). The famous "Bless'd the infant Babe" passage from the 1799 *Prelude* suggests also why the infant is linked to this other state or state of the Other, so unlike the autumnal *ratio* of an advanced or mature Industrial Age society: "In terms of Coleridge's theory, the power which was still known to the suckling baby as its natural habitat was also present in the universe at large, sometimes to be apprehended directly in trance-like moments of revelation—and especially available to the child who had been exposed to the forces of nature" (88).

41. Margaret, like many other Wordsworthian "subjects," is composite not only in the sense of having one or more living archetypes, but in that of blending into or with the material world. In her service to travelers she not only ladles out the water; she, in a sense, *is* the water, just as she also *is* the ruined cottage. The metamorphosis of things once functional is seen as the sign of an *Aufhebung* preserving and negating relic-like, substantial thinghood, translating it into an absolutely private/privative world of fealty/faith. Again, Heringman: "Paul de Man concludes, in a discussion through which I will briefly represent the ongoing debate about what kind of a 'thing' Lucy is (this being the second issue), that what is at issue in the distinction between phenomenality and materiality is ultimately the materiality of language itself. It will be evident that I am concerned, on the contrary, with the materiality of the natural world." Relics in their *Aufhebung* lend form or a formal quality to disembodiment; they are organic "extracts," serving as evidence of dehumanization and/or a humbling of mortal pride, but also rendering enchantment tangible, at least to those who have the "faith," be it in fairies, fairy-kings (Goethe's "Erlkönig"), or fairy-tale-like ideologies. They are conduits to or touchstones of the supernatural. The Celtic faith in fairies (*Ur*-typical homunculi) and in Arthur as a

(Catholic) fairy-king about to return and thus regain political legitimacy, with profound ramifications for terror and counter-terror in the early 16th century, is at least as vivid and enduring a part of the tradition as the belief that fairies are psycho-klepts out to steal human souls. On the other hand, it is clear that Wordsworth sensed the Celtic fairy-world also as negativity or absence, the substance of things hoped for, the evidence of things both seen and unseen. In some sense, Campbell's "pagan Celtic lore" is both a Wordsworthian resource and part of the native pastoral code injecting counter-historical difference into the fallen status quo: "The Celtic myths and legends are full of tales of the singers and harpers of the fairy hills whose music has the power to enchant and to move the world: to make men weep, to make men sleep, and to make men laugh. They appear mysteriously, from the Land of Eternal Youth, the Land within the Fairy Hills, the Land below Waves, and though taken to be human beings—odd and exceptional, indeed, yet as self-contained, after all, as you or I (at least, as we suppose ourselves to be)—they are not actually so, but open out behind, so to say, toward the universe." Joseph Campbell, *The Masks of Creative Mythology* (New York: Viking, sixth printing 1974), 200. But Wordsworth, certainly no Celtic singer or harper, despite the "Northern enchantment," builds his Gothic cathedral in ways that do not foreshadow a Yeats, for example. Though open front and behind to the universe, the many eccentric characters are *not* fairies; distanced in the balladic frame, recontextualized through surreption, their admonitions—often enunciated through third parties or natural signs—are like shadows of the *Tuatha Dé Danaan*, the Celtic gods of old. See the accompanying essay, "The Numinous and the Noumenal and Wordsworthian Deixis" for other remarks concerning Wordsworth's ambivalence regarding fairy lore. At the same time, in the "Advertisement" to *The Lyrical Ballads* of 1798, Wordsworth alludes to the past three centuries as a single, unified epoch in the history of the English language—from his perspective, the "modern" as opposed to the ancient and medieval periods. Thus in the mind of one who will later become a "cathedralizer" and poetic mediator of Bede's *Ecclesiastical History*, the year 1498, on the eve of the dissolution of the monasteries, becomes relevant to, if not wholly contemporaneous in the mind with, 1798. Among other things, such leaping, lapsing, anachronistic thinking serves to distance Wordsworth from primal scenes of that "other" year, 1793. The ambivalent relation between Wordsworth and the paternal text of Dugdale's *Monasticon* remains a subject for future research, as does the marginality of Horace Walpole's Gothicism as an eccentric precursor and early photography.

42. Recent scholarly texts include Kenneth Johnston, *Wordsworth and 'The Recluse'* (New Haven: Yale U. Press, 1984) and Alison Hickey, *Impure Conceits: Rhetoric and Ideology in Wordsworth's Excursion* (Palo Alto: Stanford U. Press, 1997). The Wanderer himself is often said to project a Taylor-like persona. See J. B. Owen's note on the speaker named "Matthew" in "Expostulation and Reply": "Commonly identified with William Taylor, Wordsworth's master at Hawkshead Grammar School; Mrs. Moorman, *Early Years*, p. 52, suggests that he is, rather, the packman who was Wordsworth's model for the Wanderer in *The Excursion*. Whichever identification may be correct, the mention of Esthwaite...indicates that Wordsworth is transferring the scene to the region of his schooldays, whether or not the debate was suggested by talk with Hazlitt. In the I. F. note to 'Matthew'...Wordsworth says that 'this Schoolmaster' was made up of several both of his class and men of other occupations.'" *Wordsworth and Colerige: Lyrical Ballads*, edited by J. B. Owen (second edition, Oxford: Oxford U. Press, 1980), 145–146. Writing to Professor Henry Reed of Philadelphia in 1843, Wordsworth states that "the character of the schoolmaster, had like the Wanderer in *The Excursion*, a solid foundation in fact and reality, but like him it was also in some degree a composition. I will not, and need not, call it an invention—it was no such thing." One can only agree with what Hickey

says in the work cited above: "*The Excursion* is a vast landscape of epitaphs...but such [literary] objects, and the truths they yield to those who invest their interpretive labor in them, are held in the balance as the spread of industrialism changes the face of the signifying landscape, raising the disturbing possibility that the entire epitaphic poem itself may mark the demise of the actual landscape in which epitaphs have borne meaning...An epitaph for epitaphs...[and] for a way of life..." (103–4).

43. Hartman identifies the Wanderer with the Red-Cross Knight of Spenser (*WP*, 306). By reading Margaret in the context of pastoral, I hope to show how Romance and pastoral are problematically intertwined, as they are in Book VII of *The Prelude*. In that generic undecidability and friction lies an important clue to Wordsworth's crepitant, crossed imagination.

44. Celeste Langan, in her important *Romantic Vagrancy: Wordsworth and the Simulation of Freedom* (Cambridge, England: Cambridge U. Press, 1995), reads the narrative of the Wanderer at this point somewhat differently. In her view, the effort taken by travelers to leap over the wall and penetrate the shrubbery indicates the therapeutic efficacy of taking the water-cure at the rural wellhead itself, rather than in urban apothecary shops that sell mineral-water to passive customers. As she says, the Wanderer merely "points out the *source*" of relief; he does not assist the wayfarer in getting to it or ladle out the water in the way Margaret does (245). References to this text will be indicated below by the abbreviation *RV*. I would argue that the effort and energy that the conversational "I" must expend to slake his thirst relates to the larger context of suddenly uninhibited vividness in which the Wanderer himself participates, that which makes him *feel* and *see* rather than think and reflect. The therapeutic efficacy of walking, which Langan delineates with subtlety and rigor, gains in cogency if considered in the light of a partly conscious, partly unconscious reintegration of the self into nature or into its own psychic processes through first-hand experience. That is why the entire sequence reads like a dream of the History–Subject speaking through selves, or like the reflux of psychohistory (passion, including sexual passion) poured into a vessel of dialogical displacement and/or auto-analytical transference.

45. William Shakespeare, *The Sonnets*, edited by Douglas Bush and Alfred Harbage. (New York: Penguin, 1989), 50. References to this text will be indicated below by the abbreviation *SS*.

46. Jonathan Wordsworth, in *MH*, makes a similar point about "thisness" in the text, noting how the Wanderer's continual emphasis upon the condition of the cottage now, in terms of its dilapidated relics and the encroachment of wildlife, differs from what it was then (89), a difference which underlines the hope that alternately inspired and tortured Margaret.

47. Hartman identifies this interest in pagan rites and the regeneration of Catholic belief as an offshoot of Spenserian or "Protestant Romance" (*WP*, 328).

48. As *MH* makes clear, "The Ruined Cottage" projects Margaret's former abode as an inhospitable or even hostile place, a *locus hostilis* rather than *amoenus*. Jonathan Wordsworth sees these as symbolic of what he terms "moral defeat." To be sure, they cancel out the humanitarian *virtus* of Margaret, in effect effacing her acts of kindness toward strangers, her "magic spell." The invasion of adders, toadstools, and other "low" forms of life resample the emblems of Renaissance melancholia, as seen in works by Dürer and Carpaccio, for example, but also conjures up the rhetoric of the 17th-century Levellers, who waged war on private property, among other things. For them, the postlapsarian world of *their* time had become filled with venomous spiritual and moral fauna; they sought an apocalyptic reversal of fortune through revolution, eventually becoming too radical even for Cromwell.

49. For a thorough discussion of Wordsworth's intimations of Horace and the Stoics see Richard Chauncey, *Wordsworth's Classical Undersong* (New York: St. Martin's, 2000). Horace remained the poet's "great favourite" in his later days.

50. Walter Pater, "Wordsworth," in *Appreciations* (London: Macmillan, reprint 1911), 42. References to this text, written in 1874, will be indicated below by the abbreviation *WP*. Of course, my own counter-turn toward Pater privileges a bygone aestheticism. The virtue of such a strategy is that it reconnects Wordsworth, in the final analysis, with the spirit of A Greece which Heidegger seeks in vain in the translation of *hypokeimenon* into Latin as *substantia*. One cannot, of course, simply "leap" to Greece via Pater, by a kind of organic or romantic faith, thus falling into the trap of a Heidegger who, in the wake of Hölderlin, communicates antiquity not as representational absence but as vivid essence. The virtue of such a leap, however, is that it brings to mind the quality of a vividness by which Wordsworth, subreptively or surreptitiously, links *his* thought to primitiveness and primordial nature. A vivid or vivifying principle is that which turns the mind around in its tracks as it tries to make sense of or re-sense the world: the "numinous" quality of even the commonest things, of that which is *zuhanden*. It can be linked to the notion of the uncanny in Heidegger, as that which exposes an unheard-of truth to the light of day. In his essay on Sir Thomas Browne, Pater performs the equally illuminating task of placing Wordsworth in the context of Browne and Jean Paul Richter, whose common interest lies in the immortality of the soul, noting that an ethical impulse lurks behind the interest in the after-life: that "the force of man's temperament" lies "in the management of opinion, their own or that of others...." (*WP*, 159). As I attempted to show in a very schematic way in *Mythic Paradigms*, the ethical element of culture or cultural ethos itself (as *religio medici*) may be seen as a substantial part of Goethe's take on antiquity and modernity in "Der Wandrer."

51. These lines, from a *Prelude* draft of 1799, are quoted by Beer in *WHH*, 89.

52. Walter Pater, "Wordsworth," in *Appreciations* (London: Macmillan, reprint 1911), 45–46.

53. Supercession or suppression of grief is, of course, the subject of the "Intimations Ode," where, amid intimations of immortality, the speaker picks up a strain familiar from Milton's great pastoral elegy, but then soothes or smooths the way toward a resurgence of hope: "We will grieve not, rather find/ Strength in what remains behind;/ In the primal sympathy/ Which having been must ever be;/ In the soothing thoughts that spring/ out of human suffering...." Such Miltonic *Entsagung*, a saying/signing-off to participatory affect and a birthing of anodyne thought, is one hallmark of Wordsworth's self-cure, of a quest for sublimity/sublimation.

54. Jones might say that he is ridding himself of a certain satiric manner, as the 18th century understood it. Expanding upon such a notion, I would argue that Wordsworth is making the satiric more cogent or urgent through pastoral coding, i.e., through the transformation of military or governmental shapes and hues into the visible, audible "first" language of natural identification. Such an expansion simply acknowledges the obvious: that Rousseau needs to be considered (again, as if for the first time) as one of the primary continental influences upon Wordsworth, as he was upon the early Goethe.

55. Jean Laplanche, *New Foundations for Psychoanalysis*, translated by David Macey (Oxford and Cambridge, Mass.: Blackwell, 1988), 161. References to this text will be indicated below by the abbreviation *NF*.

56. Langan, in *RV*, provides fascinating insight into the problematic of "frankness" in Rousseau: "When they identify themselves as lovers neither of truth nor of justice by their refusal of the circular [used by the author to advertise his address to the whole nation], Rousseau declares, 'This was the only *frank* speech I had had from a *French*

mouth in fifteen years' ('Voilà la seule parole *franche* que depuis quinze ans j'aye obtenue d'aucune bouche Française'). The 'archaic,' that is, "natural" or proper, name of the Frenchman is revealed (connotations of 'frank' as open, transparent, 'honest' are relevant here) at the moment when each interlocutor is reduced to 'presque aucun'— 'almost nobody' (55). Langan then notes how the private citizen, in the last stage of the social contract, where a *state of nature* once again prevails, is reduced to nothing—a status equivalent to that of the vagrant. Such a politico-economic dilemma/dialectic feeds into or underwrites the problematic of "embodiment" and disembodiment, especially where stately figures are reduced to dust or buried under the surface of the naturally regreened earth, and plays a certain role in Wordsworth's embedded coding of pastoral. The nothingness paradigm is tucked as well into that most Rousseauistic of statements in Book V of *The Prelude*: "Now this is hollow, 'tis a life of lies/ From the beginning, and in lies must end,/Forth bring him to the air of common sense, And, fresh and shewy as it is, the Corps/ Slips from us into powder. Vanity/That is his soul, there lives he, and there moves...." (350–355). Not least among the virtues of "frank" is that it rhymes with "blank" and "clank"—as if to assist the poetic project of representing openness in virtuous differentiation from deception, goneness in confrontation with politico-religious states of corrupt being and/or stasis, and residual noisings raised in inanimate protest against forces of cultural devastation. "Frank," "blank," and "clank" cluster around the obstreperous possibility of reading nihilation in much the same way that the caterpillar builds its cocoon over the golden bough, obscuring its glittering beauty. "Urworte" more deictic than Orphic, pivots of obsession and obsessiveness, obstreperous, unchooled, and unscholarly, like children on summer holiday—"blank," "clank," and "frank" are as monosyllabically "rude" as Taylor's translation of "Der Wandrer."

57. Geoffrey Hartman, "Wordsworth and Goethe in Literary History," in *The Fate of Reading* (Chicago: U. of Chicago Press, 1975), 179-200. References to this text will be indicated by the abbreviation *WG*.

58. I have been able to trace the critical literature on Goethe, Taylor, and Wordsworth back to Georg Herzfeld's *William Taylor von Norwich. Eine Studie über den Einfluss der neueren deutschen Litteratur in England* (Halle: M. Niemeyer, 1897), which is illuminating also on Taylor and Wieland, now reprinted and made available by Sändig Reprints in Liechtenstein, Otto Heller's "Goethe and Wordsworth," an extended note on *Faust* and *The Excursion* in *Modern Language Notes*, XIV (May, 1899), 262–265, Max J. Herzberg's "William Wordsworth and German Literature," *PMLA* XL (#2, June, 1925), 302–345, L. A. Willoughby, "The Image of the 'Wanderer' and the 'Hut' in Goethe's Poetry," *Études Germaniques*, July–Dec 1951, Jonathan Wordsworth, *The Music of Humanity* (New York and London: Nelson, 1969), which deals with the influence of Taylor on "The Ruined Cottage," and David Chandler, "Southey's 'German Sublimity' and Coleridge's 'Dutch Attempt'" in *Romanticism Online*, 32–33, Nov. 2003– Feb. 2004 @ www. erudit. org. revue/ron 2003. Of these, by far the most seminal is Wordsworth's study. It is the one Hartman disparages by his remark concerning a "Taylorized Goethe" that "will not do" (*FR*, 280), chiding the author for inattention to Spenser and Milton and too much regard for "local literary influences," such as Taylor. Critical studies of the cross-currents between German and English Romanticism are obviously too many to be included here. René Wellek's history of criticism has become a standard reference for students of comparative literature. It is Wellek who traced the English derivation of the concepts of Classicsm and Romanticism to Coleridge's lectures of 1811 and Taylor's notices of A. W. Schlegel and of Mme. de Staël's *De l'Allemagne*, which appeared in *The Edinburgh Review* in 1813–1814, shortly before his death. Wellek's *Concepts of Criticism* (published in 1963), however, seems to assign

organicism to the "dark backward and abysm" of an earlier 20th-century avant-garde (Croce, I. A. Richards, John Crowe Ransom, Allen Tate, among others) experiencing the Indian summer of Romanticism, an impression reinforced *viva voce* in a seminar held some time ago at Princeton. My discussion has no interest in returning Wordsworth criticism to myths of organic presence, but attempts to lay the ground-work for a *strategic* retreat in the direction of literary-historical facts (such as Taylor's largely unacknowledged translation of "Der Wandrer" and Bürger's "Lenore") and a rereading of major texts in light of those facts, in order to further an ineluctable *saltus* to intimations concerning several *Ur*-scenes/springs and a *resensed* critique of Romantic totalization. In light of Professor Bromwich's discussion of the traumatic impetus to Wordsworth's imagination, it seems by no means misplaced to look for traces of Freudian substance both within and *beyond* the Goethean paradigm of organic effacement and surreption. Indeed, Professor Hartman's own statements regarding Wordsworth's "precarious mental journey" continually hint at such a reading: "The energy which is imagination does not substantialize as a single specter, an awful power rising from the mind's abyss. It blends with the semblance of a realm, a landscape of the colors of nature through which the poet moves as in a wakeful dream" (*WP*, 65). The only difficulty with this is that the mind's power, which is that of canceling the aesthetic and then reviving it, selectively, or in spots only, for the purpose of conferring power on the feeling intellect, partakes of an equally non-awful, innocent sublime located in infancy and youth, the "trance" of childhood whose intimations Wordsworth is so careful to trace in *The Prelude* and elsewhere. This less awful sublime is projected as being counter-historical and regenerative, though, in terms of psychoanalytical narrative (autobiography), it comes with its own set of neuroses and anxieties concerning the negotiation of an originary scene. These require successive and always precarious sublimations, as Laplanche suggests.

59. The famous essay "Beyond Formalism" (in *Velocities of Change*, ed. Richard Macksey (Baltimore, Johns Hopkins U. Press, 1973, 103–117) illustrates how sensitive Hartman can be to primal sources of being, as reflected in the literary text, accusing Poulet of ignoring substance in his commentary on Henry James: "A difficulty of *representation*, however, is not yet a difficulty of *being*. Poulet either assumes or does not make the connection. He writes as if everything were a procedural rather than substantive matter...." (*Velocities*, 114–115). This hits the mark, in my view, especially where James is concerned—who, better than any except Hawthorne, perhaps, knew that *Kern* and *Schale* were one, that the working-up of surface was the ideal way to project depth. Nonetheless, Hartman, followed by most if not all contemporary critics on both sides of the Atlantic, makes his own critical investment in the epitaph, which in turn is over-shadowed by the antecedent Heideggerian argument concerning the untranslatability of the Greek *hypokeimenon* into Latin as *substantia* and the continually deferred death of art, begging the question, just as Heidegger does, of the wellspring or origin of the *Kunstwerk* itself, of a halting by the wayside *and* a counter-turn through which the truth of art, as the *Ungeheuer*, is approximated through "unconscious intercourse," effacement, and organic surreption in the "state" of nature.

60. This should not be confused with the triadic structure of interpretation suggested by another "Yale critic." In his essay, "The Rhetoric of Blindness," Paul de Man notes how the texts of "non-blinded" authors such as Rousseau demand a triadic reading in which the critic reverses the field of traditional interpretation between the writer and his first or blinded readers in order to resample the "original insight." See *Blindness and Insight: Essays in the Rhetoric of Contemporary Criticism*, (second edition revised, Minneapolis: U. of Minnesota Press, 1983), 147. Hartman's structure, on the other hand, seems self-

critically designed to be "purely," but certainly not naively, literary-historical. By choosing to compare Goethe and Wordsworth *in terms of this particular triangle*, it nonetheless demonstrates a form of no doubt well-considered hermeneutic blindness, from which spring many incontrovertible insights. My commentary evokes an antecedent or slightly antiquated reading, the pitfalls and implications of which Hartman avoids when he privileges texts involving the "Northern enchantment" (Percy's) rather than those whose subtext is the "Southern enchantment," a Goethean topocosm and one or more journeys to Italys of the mind, whose fascination lies with Vergilian and Ovidian wellsprings. Goethe, by effacing the epitaphic inscription of *pietas*, unfolds a powerful organicism (coupled with the pleasured child/genius) rife with implications for Wordsworthian poetic logic, the recycling of anxieties associated with the French Revolution, Annette, and the public way, a transition from civil disobedience to the monastic *disciplina* of secluded tranquillity. To be reminded of the terror and pathos Wordsworth was fleeing, one should listen to Schubert's setting of "Der Erlkönig," as sung by Kirstin Flagstad. Here, the enchanting Wagnerian "fire," as remarkable as that which burns within, more than makes up for the lack of vocal nuance.

61. See Emily Apter, "Radical Pastoral," a review of John Kinsella's *Peripheral Light: New and Selected Poems*, in the *Boston Review*, April/May 2004. She writes, "Kinsella mobilizes a great literary tradition of utopian ruralism that includes the Arcadian primitivism of Virgil's *Eclogues*, the Rousseauist egalitarian paradise of 'ten acres and a mule,' the bucolic homeopathy of George Sand, Honoré de Balzac, William Wordsworth, and Thomas Hardy, Marx's dystopic vision of "the idiocy of rural life," and Émile Zola's rendering of the violence of peasant labor in his flawed masterpiece *La Terre...* Reminiscent of the way in which the Romantics employed fearful symmetries to illuminate the signs of a self-aware Nature, the poems offer an uncannily sentient pastoral. Multiple orders of aliveness (from the human to the mineral) are non-hierarchically and collectively summoned, creating a naturalist intimism that refuses the subjectivist fallacy yet remediates the impersonality of Kinsella's narrative voice." It should only be added that the *faux*-topian limits of "radical pastoral" were defined recently with multiple layerings of deadness in a place called Cambodia. *Et in Arcadia....*

62. The site of that trauma is France, and, as Professor Bromwich indicates, the attractiveness of Tintern Abbey as a place has to do with its remoteness from what is for Wordsworth a contemporary political scene of guilt. See David Bromwich, *Disowned by Memory* (Chicago: U. of Chicago Press, 1998), 81–82: "...he stations himself in a place of symbolic interest: at this site of a medieval abbey, relic of a medieval life which survives only in fragments; as far inland as he can get in his native land and as far as possible from France." Bromwich also shows how Paris during the Terror reprojects the trance-like atmosphere, knocking at the gate, *et al.* in *Macbeth*—with Wordsworth feeling complicit in the violence and thus being haunted by it. Traces of Macbeth, especially the "Out out, brief candle...." speech can be found elsewhere, especially in *The Excursion*.

63. Geoffrey H. Hartman, "Trauma within the limits of literature" (June 2002) in *Newsletter* 2 @ www.traumaresearch.net/fr_net.htm" (25 January 2005).

64. Wordsworth's own comments on the sonnet suggest its useful ability to "confer" upon us intellectual powers which we might not otherwise have known we possessed, powers which enable the imagination to transcend an empirically given psychological or sociohistorical situation. The word "conferring" is used by Professor Hartman in *The Unmediated Vision* (New York: Harcourt, Brace, 1966), 179. This is also the hetero-cosmic premise of much that Goethe wrote—aside from meteorological observations and scientific investigations—after *Die Leiden des jungen Werther*.

65. The reader will recognize a formula (modified here to include things seen) for Christian

faith and hope made famous in Hebrews 11, verse 1. The King James version, "Now faith is the substance of things hoped for, the evidence of things not seen" (῎Εστιν δε πίστις ἐλπιζομένων ὑποςτάσις, πραγμάτων ἐλεγχος οὐ βλεπομένων) translates *elenchos* with the legal word "evidence," but omits other definitions available in a good Greek dictionary (giving evidence of Heidegger's claim that translation has made us lose the ground upon which the Greeks stood), i.e., "means of testing," "trial," "test," Latin *argumentum*, "disproval," "refutation"—all of which indicate a confrontational seizure by faith, its implantation and testing in the well-lit agora or on the well-traveled road. If we, in turn, mistranslate *pistis* as *fides*, it is with the hermeneutic *Vorgriff* of evoking Wordsworth's keeping of faith with an English *substance* existing outside history, invisible and hoped for, in a heterocosm of utopian projection or in a Rousseau-inspired state of nature. Wordsworth's agoraphobic argument begins at the ground- or *Grund* level in the (dis)embodiments of surreptition.

66. Jean-Luc Nancy, *The Experience of Freedom*, translated by Bridget McDonald (Palo Alto: Stanford U. Press, 1993), 18.

Chapter Two

1. Thomas De Quincey, *Selected Writings of Thomas De Quincey*, edited by Philip Van Doren Stern (New York: Random House, 1937), 1099–1101.

2. William Wordsworth, *The Prelude or Growth of a Poet's Mind* (Text of 1805), edited by Ernest de Selincourt, revised by Stephen Gill (London: Oxford, 1970), XII, 309–312. Subsequent references to this text will be indicated in abbreviated form as *Prelude*, 1805.

3. Henri Bergson, *The Two Sources of Religion and Morality*, translated by R. Ashley Audra and Cloudesley Brereton with the assistance of W. Horsfall Carter (Garden City, N. Y.: Doubleday Anchor, 1954), 193.

4. Wordsworth identifies with *pius* Aeneas, positively and negatively, in scenes of transference and counter-transference. The identification is made all the more compelling by the medieval legend that Aeneas and the escaping Trojans visited England and by the Dido–Annette Vallon parallelism. It was Wordsworth's (and Dryden's) purpose to make Vergil accessible and thus understandable to speakers of contemporary English, but the project of translating the *Aeneid* proved shortlived. To observe yet another Englished Aeneas, in a state of dissonance with one or more *femmes fatales* and the *numina* under their control, among them Diana, the reader is directed to Purcell's opera, *Dido and Aeneas*: "Let Jove say what he may／ I'll stay, I'll stay."

5. William Wordsworth and Samuel Coleridge, *The Lyrical Ballads*, edited by W. J. B. Owen (Oxford: Oxford U. Press, second edition 1980), 45, lines 115–117. Subsequent references to this text will be indicated by the abbreviation *LB*.

6. Celeste Langan, in her study *Romantic Vagrancy* (Cambridge: Cambridge U. Press, 1995), 112 indicates that a Wordsworth source for "Goody Blake and Harry Gill" is Erasmus Darwin's *Zoonomia*. References to this text will be indicated below by the abbreviation *RV*.

7. Th e title of Wordsworth's poem reflects a familiar term of schoolboy derogation with no particular claim to clinical validity, but with that much greater juvenile *political force*—one that might have been heard even in a 20th-century school-bus or yard—without apparent allusion to the text of a Romantic poet. To take poetry out of school (or to make of waterfalls and goblins one's playmates) is to deliver the self from the effective reach of such epithets, a project that is like a secluding counterturn against the word or *wyrd* of the other, and thus Rousseau-like. "The Idiot Boy" is all about romantic truancy, from

school-boy taunts, from home, from sheltering female spirits, from responsibility. Only the women, Susan Gill and Betty Foy, worry; the Idiot Boy himself, unseen for most of the text, dwelling in offstage haunts, a *terra incognita* of elfin or savage imperturbability, is worriless. Unfortunately, he also *is* an imbecile. The tale concerns itself almost exclusively with what the women *think* has happened to him, phobic projections of witchcraft, of waterfalls and the sounds made by them. It is a tale *about* an idiot, full of intermittent bursts of sound and fury, focused on the dolt for whom the sun shines only at the end with an unnatural, unwarming light, who cannot say what he has experienced. One might speak here of a traumatic blanking-out or erasure of an 18th-century *Welt-anschauung* or paideuma and the putting-to-sleep of clinical reason. Bewell's emphasis on the priority of language over feeling seems crucial, but only if it is considered in tandem with the hilarious comedic effects inserted at the end of the ballad. These may well be seen in terms of a Brecht-like *gestus*, a "language of things," but also as the projection of a more robust, Rousseau-inspired state of pre-linguistic primitiveness.

8. Q. Horatius Flaccus, *Opera*, ed. D. R. Shackleton-Bailey (Tübingen: Teubner, 1995), 145. Epode 5, 49–54. Subsequent references to this work will be indicated by the abbreviation *HF*.

9. Georg Luck, in *Arcana Mundi* (Baltimore: Johns Hopkins U. Press, 1995), 29 describes the larger scene of *Epode* 5, where a group of witches led by Canidia prey upon a young boy in order to steal his liver, which they hope to use in perfecting a potent spell against a man they hate, named Varus. The boy, however, pronounces a terrible counter-curse upon them, turning the *numen*-invoking intention around. This scenario is, in some respects, like that of "The Danish Boy." Luck adds that "the spirits of those who die young or who die a violent death can turn into daemons of vengeance."

10. Geoffrey H. Hartman, "Trauma within the limits of literature" (June, 2002) in *Newsletter 2* @ www.traumaresearch.net/fr_net.htm"(25 January 2005).

11. One may see something similar in Nelly Sachs's judicious editing-out of any graphic depiction of *Einsatzgruppen* horrors, whose barking dogs can destroy a fabric of hope still in the cosmic weaving.

12. Duncan Wu stresses the Orpheus-like descents of the poet as magician in "Navigated by Magic: Wordsworth's Cambridge Sonnets," *The Review of English Studies*, New Series, Vol. 46, No. 183 (August, 1995), 352–365. Subsequent references to this text will be indicated by the abbreviation *NM*. Numinous silence will be considered below.

13. Charles Passage, note to line 7 of Epode 17, *The Complete Works of Horace*, translated and annotated by Charles Passage (New York: Ungar, 1983), 121.

14. Rudolf Dirk Schier, "The Experience of the Noumenal in Goethe and Wordsworth," *Comparative Literature*, Vol. 25, No. 1 (Winter, 1973), 37–59.

15. John Irwin, *American Hieroglyphics* (New Haven: Yale U. Press, 1980), 79.

16. The creation of a poetic idiom, a language of the individual, in *The Lyrical Ballads* runs the risk of being considered as "sheer idiocy" by an unadoring, less intelligent or ethically sensitive readership. As with Hölderlin in the project of translating Pindar, the imperative of the idiomatic, informed by pedagogical purpose, will be felt all the more vividly in terms of a message to the unseen other. Hazlitt addresses the odd choice of subject matter, vagrants, witches, blind beggars, and the like in Coleridge's and Wordsworth's "new-fangled 'metre ballad-mongering' scheme" and links it to Rousseau: "They took the same method...which Rousseau did in his prose paradoxes—of exciting attention by reversing the established standards of opinion, and estimation in the world. They were for bringing poetry back to its primitive sympathy and state of nature, as he was for bringing society back to the savage state: so that the only thing remarkable left in the world by this change, would be the persons who had produced it." William Hazlitt, "Lectures on the

Living Poets," in *Lectures on English Poets and The Spirit of the Age* (London: Dent, 1939), 163. Subsequent references to this text will be indicated by the abbreviation *LEP*. Almost every text in *The Lyrical Ballads* qualifies as a deixis and translation of the plight of the dispossessed and/or obsessed.

17. Geoffrey Hartman, *Wordsworth's Poetry, 1787–1814* (New Haven: Yale U. Press, 6th printing, 1977), 150. Subsequent references to this text will be indicated by the abbreviation *WP*.

18. Alan J. Bewell, in "Wordsworth's Primal Scene: Retrospective Tales of Idiots, Wild Children, and Savages," *ELH*, Vol. 50, No. 2 (Summer, 1983), 334, notes that the inability to formulate thoughts concerning somatic states of heat or cold is "proverbial" among imbeciles. Subsequent references to this text will be indicated by the abbreviation *WPS*. Many of the supernatural elements in "The Idiot Boy" are given a more macabre, yet powerfully feminist accentuation in Christina Rossetti's "Goblin Market" of 1859.

19. William Wordsworth, "Preface" [to *The Lyrical Ballads*] of 1800, in *LB*, 158.

20. Thomas Weiskel, *The Romantic Sublime*, (Baltimore, Johns Hopkins U. Press, 1976), 190. Subsequent references to this text will be indicated by the abbreviation *RS*.

21. For Saunderson's importance to the European Enlightenment see my essay "Via Speculativa" in *Paradox and Perspicacity: Horizons of Knowledge in the Literary Text* (Bern and New York: Peter Lang, 2004), 13f.

22. Edgar Allan Poe, "Some Account of Stonehenge, The Giant's Dance: A Druidical Ruin in England," in *Poetry and Tales*, edited by Patrick Quinn (New York: Library of America, 11th printing, 1984, 929–931.

23. Seth Benardete, *Socrates' Second Sailing* (Chicago: U. of Chicago Press, 1989), 173–174. References to this text will be indicated below by the abbreviation *SSS*.

24. Martin Heidegger, "Über den Ursprung des Kunstwerks," in *Holzwege* (Frankfurt/M.: Klostermann, fifth edition 1972), 43.

25. I refer here to de Man's "Foreword" to Carol Jacobs' *The Dissimulating Harmony*, collected in *Critical Writings, 1953–1978*, ed. Lindsay Waters (Minneapolis: U. of Minnesota Press, 1988), 223, where he explicitly links the necessity of a certain critical stuttering to the work of reading, especially there where the undecidability of the text becomes crucially apparent, where "literal designation" becomes an image, which is "never literal."

26. William Wordsworth, *The Excursion*, Book I, "The Wanderer," verses 1–20, in *Poetical Works of Wordsworth*, edited by Thomas Hutchinson and Ernest de Selincourt (London: Oxford U. Press, 1960), 591. Subsequent references to this text will be indicated by the abbreviation *W*. This particular passage also bears upon *An Evening Walk* (1798), when Wordsworth could still pull out all the stops of romance tradition and fairy-lore "with religious awe"—before sounding their death-knell: "The pomp is fled, and mute the wondrous strains..." The relevant lines from *The Ruined Cottage* are found in *MH*, 19.

27. On the prepositioning of thought see Andzrej Warminski, "Pre-positional By-play," *Glyph 3* (Baltimore: Johns Hopkins U. Press, 1978), 98–117. Subsequent references will be indicated by the abbreviation *PB*. Though this essay treats of examples (*Beispiele*) in philosophical thought, it may shed light on Wordsworth's excessive use of prepositional phrases. If, as Warminski suggests, "...the excess of *Beispiel* produces an unsublatable interiority and activity. And this excess, rather than coming anywhere from outside thought, is inscribed within thought itself, not as the 'nothing,' or 'the other,' the 'excess' of thought, but as the unthinkable nonthought whose thinking makes thought (im)possible" (114), then Wordsworth's excessive pre-positional phrasing reduces an exemplary (prime/primal/noontime) scene to the ensemble (*Gerüst*) of an unthinkable interiority which is nonetheless a thought—on its way elsewhere.

28. *Lesmosuné* is the technical term for an alleviation of pain effectuated by the Muses. Equally, as part of the mythic by-play to Artemis, it may lessen the pain of childbirth and, with sidelong reference to Socratic midwifery, the birth of thinking via "error, disappointment, and guilt."

29. See *RS*, 46, where Weiskel states that "the function of the sublime moment is to expose the cheat or subreption by which an object in nature invites awe and to redirect the awe to the subject himself. The sublime in fact subverts and dissolves *Schein* and all that it may stand for in the way of a hope of somehow realizing the unconditioned." My reading agrees entirely with the first sentence, but disagrees with the second, in the sense that I see that negativity of the sublime, which is, after all, conditioned by the over-whelmingness of nature, as producing something other than alienation, i.e., the "finer distance," which is "out there" on the moonlit, unconsumed branches, and reflected "in us" as an unconsumed fire, a Wordsworthian reprojection of the categorical imperative, a subjectivization of Mosaic law. That is what the words of Wordsworth, literally, say. However, we, as hermeneuts, then as now, we are free to place our credence or critical *fides* in whatever resensed meaning we may deduce from them. Such credence is conditioned by our position on the hermeneutic circle; its power or lack of power should not be reduced to the stammerings of the intense and unconditioned inane. If subreption is merely a cheat, and *Schein* is merely delusive appearance, we cannot redirect awe, but only pity, towards ourselves. Our pondering of the imponderable is worth considering, even if it only serves to reveal the process by which such error-prone projections come to a fire-like "light" in the cavern of subjective consciousness. "Fine," in the final analysis is *fine* in the sense that gold is fine and worthy of religious awe among the pre-Columbian inhabitants of the New World; it is not vulgar, cheap, or demagogic. A hope that is "somehow" can also exist, counterhistorically, "in *spite* of."

30. Reference is made here to Jean Starobinski's classic *La transparence et l'obstacle* (Paris, 1957) as modified (and/or intensified) by the readings of Paul de Man in *Allegories of Reading* (New Haven: Yale U. Press, 1979). The passage with which "The Excursion" opens tracks a number of dilemmas similar to those found in Rousseau, from the glaring intrusion of a daylit other and the seeking out of one or more oblique coverts to the necessity of further post-partum excursion.

31. Kenneth Johnston, *Wordsworth and 'The Recluse'* (New Haven: Yale U. Press, 1984), 273. Subsequent references to this text will be indicated by the abbreviation *J*.

32. The translation of *Erschweigen* is that of David Farrell Krell, in his marginal notes to Martin Heidegger, *Nietzsche* (San Francisco: Harper and Row, 1979–1987), II, 280–281.

Chapter Three

1. Hugh Kenner, *The Counterfeiters: An Historical Comedy* (New York: Doubleday, 1973). Subsequent references to this text will be indicated by the abbreviation *TC*.

2. *The Metaphysical Poets*, selected and edited by Dame Helen Gardner (Harmondsworth, England: Penguin, 1973–1974), 308.

3. What is surprising is that Kenner only tells half of the story concerning Johnson, who mixes blame with praise: "HAVING thus endeavoured to exhibit a general representation of the stile and sentiments of the metaphysical poets, it is now proper to examine particularly the works of Cowley, who was almost the last of that race, and undoubtedly the best." Samuel Johnson,"The Life of Abraham Cowley," from *The Penn State Archive of Samuel Johnson's Lives of the Poets*. Ed. Kathleen Nulton Kemmerer. (1 January 2005). Subsequent references to this source will be indicated by the abbreviation *PSA*.

Johnson also supplies this surprising and puzzling item of hearsay: "Milton is said to have declared that the three greatest English poets were Spenser, Shakespeare, and Cowley." Neither Kenner nor Gardner can account for such judgments.

4. The 20th-century critic who privileged surprise as an *ethical* criterion was Bakhtin. See the article "Bakhtin" by Gary Saul Morson and Caryl Emerson in *The Johns Hopkins Guide to Literary History and Criticism* (Baltimore: Johns Hopkins U., 1993), 63–68: "The recognition of each person's unfinalizability, the capacity for 'surprisingness,' is central to Bakhtin's ethics' (65). It is interesting that such a privileging occurs in the context of Bakhtin's criticism of the novel; the unpredictability of character is a hallmark of the *prose* epic. Thus, in terms of the fluctuation of his style and derivative enthusiasms, Cowley's unique surprise, surfaces not so much as a characteristic as an occasional flash of lightning against obscurity—his own and that which he projected onto Pindar, and occurs there where translation seeks, as *éclair age* or *Erleuchtung*, to improve on the original through metapoesis, to achieve the clarity of prose.

5. *The Cambridge History of English and American Literature* in 18 Volumes (1907–21). Volume VII. Cavalier and Puritan. Online version. (27 December 2004).

6. It seems essential to *Don Quixote's* purpose that the medieval romances it supposedly copies are deemed worthy of imitation only in the estimation of its demented protagonist. Cervantes makes us cognizant of the difference between simulacrum and original, between second- or third- and first-rate, almost from the opening page; the dramatic irony falls entirely on the head of Don Quixote himself, to our great delight and wonderment. But Cowley's project is other, in the sense that he sets out to clarify and amplify the precursor text, or to purvey the fiction that his is a more perspicuous language than that of the "obscure" Pindar. Cervantes, on the other hand, distances his reader progressively and with satiric certainty from the *Amadis of Gaul* template, so that we finally forget about it and remember only the novel that is *Don Quixote*. Had Cowley been Goethe, a similar purpose would have been achieved.

7. As Johnson notes in his *Preface to Cowley*, there is something Silver-Age and Petronian in Pindarizing: "This lax and lawless versification so much concealed the deficiencies of The barren, and flattered the laziness of the idle, that it immediately overspread our books of poetry; all the boys and girls caught the pleasing fashion, and they that could do nothing else could write like Pindar. The rights of antiquity were invaded, and disorder tried to break into the Latin: a poem on the Sheldonian Theatre, in which all kinds of verse are shaken together, is unhappily inserted in the *Musae Anglicanae*. Pindarism prevailed above half a century; but at last died gradually away, *and other imitations supply its place*" (emphasis mine).

8. Donald Davie's "Poetic Diction and Poetic Strength," in *The Augustan Age*, ed. Ian Watt (New York: Fawcett, 1968), 272–277, suggests an affinity between Cowley and John Denham in the latter's attempt to "rationalize" the strong conceits of Metaphysical poets such as Donne and Marvell. "Throughout the seventeenth century 'strong' or masculine' writing is associated with what modern critics have called the 'line of Wit,' and others, the 'marinist' or 'metaphysical' strain. But Pope and Johnson were right, I think, when they judged that Denham had saved the essential 'strength,' while disengaging it from the hyperbolical conceit" (273). In his "Life of Cowley," Johnson refers to Denham, Cowley, and Cleveland as inheritors of the Metaphysical school. References to this text will be indicated below by the abbreviation *AA*.

9. The *Characteristicks of men, manners, opinions, times*, published in 1711 and 1714, was for some time not easily obtainable in libraries. It is now available in the edition of Philip Ayres published by Oxford at the Clarendon Press (1999). I have used the fifth edition in three volumes (Birmingham, 1773). We think of the 18th century as the age of Johnson,

But it was equally that of Shaftesbury; and we would do well to engage again with the dialogical or dialectical currents of the era, as Dieckmann did at mid-century. Not least among the virtues of Shaftesbury's "Letter on Enthusiasm" is that it associates enthusiasm with melancholy and panic—and thus is Religion also *Panick*" (16). It is likely that the Pan-ic or Pan-ish element in Hamann, employed as a counter-Muse of criticism, was influenced by Shaftesbury's text. The latter also described the recently arrived French Protestants as "*too enthusiastic.*" They seem to want to be punished, he writes, but the English are too tolerant for this; they simply mock excessive enthusiasm, castigating it through raillery, the "Bart'lemy Fair method." This deprecation is followed by a distinction which will be seminal for the Romantics, where poetic inspiration is said to rely on "noble enthusiasm" (54). Shaftesbury ends by begging the toleration of his noble addressee, calling himself an "*Enthusiastick Friend.*" Goethe, on the other hand, refers in the *Divan* to texts in the Old Testament as "enthusiastisch."

10. Abraham Cowley, "The First Nemean Ode of Pindar," in *The Works of the English Poets With Prefaces, Biographical and Critical*, by Samuel Johnson, 58 volumes, vol. 1 (London: H. Hughs, 1779), 15–20.

11. I owe this reference to John T. Hamilton's erudite and illuminating *Soliciting Darkness: Pindar, Obscurity, and the Classical Tradition* (Cambridge, Mass.: Harvard U. Press, 2003), 56. References to this text will be indicated below by the abbreviation *SD*.

12. *Pindari Epinikia*, ed. Alexander Turyn (New York: Institute of Polish Arts and Sciences in America, 1944), 150, verses 69–73.

13. From the Tufts Perseus project: http://www.perseus.tufts.edu/cgi-bin/ptext?doc=Perseus: text:1999.01.0162 (28 December 2004).

14. As quoted in Benoit Mandelbrot, *The Practical Geometry of Nature* (New York: W. H. Freeman, 20th edition, augmented and updated, 2004), 9.

15. T. S. Eliot, "John Dryden," in *The Augustan Age*, ed. Ian Watt (New York: Fawcett, 1968), 201.

16. John Dryden, "Preface" to *Sylvae*, in *The Best of Dryden*, ed. Louis Bredfold (New York: Ronald Press, 1933), 499. Hereafter cited as *BD*.

17. Jean Baudrillard, "The Ecstasy of Communication," translated by John Johnston, in *The Anti-Aesthetic, Essays in Postmodern Culture*, ed. by Hal Foster (Seattle: Bay Press, 1983), 133.

18. From The Abraham Cowley Text and Image Archive, University of Virginia, website (29 December 2004).

19. After the literal and very brief echo of the *Second Olympian*, what one finds is actually a completely graceful rediscovery, conscious or unconscious, of the ground covered in the *Ninth Pythian*, whose subject matter is the surrender of Apollo to Eros and where a centaur, Chiron, is crucially involved. The *modus operandi* of "Meine Göttin" is utterly different from that of Goethe's quite literal translation of Pindar's *Fifth Olympian*. See Jonas Jølle, "Goethe's Translation of Pindar's *Fifth Olympian Ode*," *Goethe Yearbook*, X (Rochester, N. Y.: Camden House, 2001), 50–64. In the case of "Meine Göttin," Pindar seems to perform the function of an excuse-like launching-pad or cocoon from which the equestrian Cavalier-butterfly soars skyward.

20. Or he is "living in Pindar," as Hamilton suggests (*SD*, 237–248).

21. It is by no means certain which, if any, of the three translation models in the *West-Eastern Divan*, Goethe is entertaining here. He is certainly not being literal, nor is he writing prose. This leaves only the second option, where the translator evokes the sense of the original in his own metapoetic meaning or sense (*Sinn.*). An aristocratic facetiousness and Cavalier-like lightness of tone suggest Klopstock and Wieland as precursors rather than Cowley. The Philoctetes-like direness, which Hamilton notes in

Goethe's other experiments in Pindarism, is notably absent in "Die Göttin," as is the preoccupation with a cyclothymic, pain/pleasure dichotomy suggested by the alternation of light and dark (chiaroscuro)—until the darker, more tragically accentuated ending.

22. *Goethes Gedichte*, edited and annotated by Emil Staiger (Zurich: Manesse, 1949), II, 19–21.

23. The contents of the letter are cited in the notes to *Goethes Gedichte*, edited and annotated by Emil Staiger (Zurich: Manesse, 1949), II, 341.

24. See Goethe's letter to Herder of August, 1774, where he places himself in the role of a charioteer or *cybernos* whom Pindar is praising, as he attempts to control the four unwieldy horses in front of him by sheer virtuosity (*SD*, 237–239).

25. Rainer Nägele, *Echoes of Translation* (Baltimore: Johns Hopkins U. Press, 1997), 93. Subsequent references to this work will be indicated by the abbreviation *ET*.

26. The phrase "hyperbolic translation" is that of Douglas Robinson, as cited in *SD*, 301.

27. Friedrich Hölderlin, *Sämtliche Werke*, Kritische Textausgabe, ed. D. E. Sattler (Frankfurt/M.: Luchterhand, 1987), XV (Pindar), 298–300.

28. Philippe Lacoue-Labarthe, "Hölderlin and the Greeks," 247 in *Typography*, ed. C. Fynsk (Cambridge, Mass.: Harvard U. Press, 1989), 247.

29. *The Poems of Ossian*, translated by James Macpherson, Esq. (Boston: Philips, Sampson, 1853), 354–355.

30. Guggenheim Museum, descriptive brochure for the Barney exhibition, April 9, 2002, as published on the Internet (10 February, 2005). Subsequent references to this text will be indicated by the abbreviation *GM*.

31. David Farrell Krell, marginal notes to Martin Heidegger, *Nietzsche* (San Francisco: Harper and Row, 1979–1987), II, 280–281.

32. Soap smegma is made the object of serious mathematical study in Benoit Mandelbrot, *The Fractal Geometry of Nature* (New York: W. H. Freeman, updated and augmented edition, 2004), 176. My coining of the term "smegmatics" is meant to separate the aesthetic study of various liquid organic residues from Mandelbrot's altogether serious "smectics," the rigorous mathematical science of liquid crystal molecules in their tendency to slide or over the other, depending upon temperature and pressure conditions.

33. Choire Sicha, "The Art of the Fan," *New York Times*, section 2, page 2, January 2, 2005.

34. It seems that Poe was well-versed in the notion of "interested displeasure" on the part of the fickle reading public. See his text entitled "Lionizing."

35. Shaftesbury, "Miscellaneous Reflections, in *Characteristicks*, III (1714), 15–16.

36. Friedrich Nietzsche, *Morgenröte: Gedanken über die moralischen Vorurteile* (Munich: Goldmann, 1980), 81–82.

37. John Irwin, *American Hieroglyphics* (New Haven: Yale U. Press, 1980), 168.

38. David Mitchell, *Ghostwritten* (New York: Random House, 1999), 378.

Chapter Four

1. These are collected in John Barth, *Further Fridays* (New York: Little, Brown, 1995). References to this text, and to the two essays in question, "The Arabesque," 311–327, and "Chaos Theory, Postmod Science, Literary Model" 328–342, will be indicated by the abbreviation *FF*. Many of Professor Barth's remarks, as he readily admits, are based on the ground-breaking work of colleagues, most notably, Professors Michael Craig Hillman and G. R. Thompson.

2. Benoit Mandelbrot, *The Fractal Geometry of Nature* (San Francisco: Freeman, 1977), updated and augmented in Benoit Mandelbrot, *The Practical Geometry of Nature* (New

York: W. H. Freeman, 20th printing, 2004). References to this text will be indicated below by the abbreviation *PGN*.

3. Pasolini's R-rated film version, the product of a certain kind of "saintliness," seems informed by a desire to remain faithful to the uninhibited sexuality of the original text and a brilliant, if pederastic, zeal; its technicolor flair for the *in flagrante*, perhaps aimed, in part, at offending virgin Western eyes (it was filmed in 1974) or at least awakening the film-fan to an unexpurgated *Arabian Nights* freed from Victorian inhibition, is breathtakingly beautiful, at times. It does us the service of including some of the explicit parts that Lane deemed untranslatable, reminding us collaterally of the *scandal* once occasioned by the "anti-bourgeois" marital license of *Lucinde*. Pasolini, in his unabashed celebration of eroticism, suggests film-makers of the 1960s, such as Jack Smith and Kenneth Anger. For a definitive discussion of Pasolini see Philippe Lacoue-Labarthe, *Pasolini, une improvisation: d'une sainteté* (Bordeaux: William Blake & Co., 1995).

4. In *PGN*, Mandelbrot incorporates Brownian motion within his system as a "subordinand" (292). On the asymmetrical non-identity of nature from one degree of scale to the next see Nicholas Rescher, *Complexity* (New Brunswick and London: Transaction, 1998), 44: "To be sure, it could, in theory, possibly occur that just the same relationship-patterns simply from level to level—that the patterns of phenomena that we encounter at level $i+1$ simply are those already met with at level 1. (This is the functional equivalent at the nomic level of the recurrence of physical pattern at different levels of scale characterizing the 'fractal' structures made prominent by B. Mandelbrot.) However, this is a very special case that need not and will not obtain across the board. Science as we have it in all its branches indicates that there is no good reason to think that our world is fractal in the structure of its natural processes." So we have the predicament of a postmodern art which aspires to offer a sublime totalization or mapping of antecedent styles, yet cannot account for the full complexity of the universe except as the incorporation or crystallization of "two- or three-dimensional" sameness from one level of scale to the next, *in the absence of difference*; the fractal cannot account for nature "across the board," but nonetheless looks like or simulates infinity (symbolically) in the Oriental rug and in Romantic meta-fiction. The arabesque, as Poe's title suggests, requires the grotesque or is incomplete without a parallel universe where, as in the tales of Gogol or Poe himself, the beautiful and the monstrous, the rational (day) and the irrational (night), the mappable and the unmappable (an abyss of self-reflecton) coexist, when the flaw is not a matter of "the tail" or an almost invisible detail, but central to the tragic dilemma of the human and the dialogical unfolding of asymmetrical philosophical knowledge, both notably present in the Socratic "method" and in Schlegel's novel *Lucinde*. William Burroughs's "cut-up" method seems to have been, in part, one effort, among many, to include such in-determinacy in postmodern metafiction. The cascade-like representation of violence, for All its cartoon-like, cardboard-cutout two-dimensionality, has the virtue of reading "like" the chaotic state of affairs in the world in which we are living.

5. Haruki Murakami, *The Wind-Up Bird Chronicle*, translated by Jay Rubin (New York: Knopf, 1998), 42. Subsequent references to this text will be indicated by the abbreviation. *WBC*.

6. Discontinuous or Riemann space is specifically rejected as a mathematical model by Mandelbrot in *PGN*, 409.

7. These terms are borrowed from Clifford Geertz's *Islam Observed* (Chicago: U. of Chicago Press, 1973), 111–113, where aspects of the "force" and "scope" of Islam in Indonesia, for example, are compared to the "faith" practiced by American mobsters.

8. Immanuel Kant, "Perpetual Peace: A Philosophical Sketch," in *Kant, Selections*, ed. Lewis White Beck (New York: Macmillan, 1988), 440.

9. That the "new mythology" of Schlegel and Schelling begins in the rhetoric of philosophical and political liberation and ends in a reversion to a more or less doctrinaire religiosity, at least on the part of Schlegel, will come as a surprise to no one. As M. H. Abrams states, Schlegel "...looked to its imminent development out of a synthesis between the revolutionary inwardness of philosophical idealism and the revelations of contemporary science. Friedrich Schelling agreed that at the present moment 'each truly creative individual must invent a mythology for himself,' and saw in contemporary *Naturphilosophie* the adumbration of a universal mythology that would harmonize Greek myth and the seemingly antithetic claims of Christianity." M. H. Abrams, *Natural Supernaturalism* (New York: Norton, 1973), 67. The arabesque "Bild" or representation, part of the allegorical project of rendering the subject infinite, serves this larger philosophical purpose. In the greatest writers, such as Hölderlin, the harmony appears as an irrecuperable, Marsyas-like dissonance. If one takes the nature out of "natural supernaturalism" in a Haylesian reading, one can at least get to "first base" with postmodernist metafiction (and Poe), but it seems that one leaves Schlegel and Schelling, as it were, standing at the medallion-like "plate."

10. See John Hamilton, *Soliciting Darkness: Pindar, Obscurity, and the Classical Tradition* (Cambridge, Mass.: Harvard U. Press, 2003), 279f.

11. See the evaluation of Poe as a dandy and Rousseau-inspired *sauvage* in "Edgar Poe: sa vie et ses oeuvres" and "Notes novelles sur Edgar Poe." Nature, according to Baudelaire, creates nothing but "monsters." Yet these monsters are preferable to the so-called "civilized" members of polite society. Poe (like that other master of the grotesque and arabesque, never explicitly mentioned in the essays, Jean Paul) is said, because of his disaffiliation from bourgeois "civilization," to demonstrate prodigious or "monstrous" abilities and is even able, as the proverb goes, "to hear the grass growing." Such a sensory apparatus seems unnatural or uncanny only to the philistine; its encyclopedic keenness allows for extraordinary or even superhuman insights concerning the universe, the hieroglyph-like signatures of nature, and the *modi operandi* of criminals. From this milieu of heightened sensibility springs the detective story. On the other hand, at a distance of more than two generations from Schlegel and Runge, Baudelaire can claim that the arabesque and grotesque "repousse" or repel the human—something which is melodramatically true in Poe, but which is more philosophically complex in early Romanticism, because of an originary splitting centered on and traversing the human subject and the theory of the sublime.

12. See Patricia C. Smith, "Poe's Arabesque," from *Poe Studies*, vol. VII, no. 2, December 1974, 42–45 (subsequent references to this useful article are indicated by the abbreviation *PA*): "Both Robert Jacobs and Daniel Hoffman connect the words more closely with decorative art; both take 'grotesque' to refer to the monstrous details in Gothic designs and to corresponding elements in Poe's tales. Jacobs thinks 'arabesque' implies the total and beautiful pattern of a design or tale which may incorporate monstrous elements; Hoffman thinks the word refers to nonrepresentational Muslim designs, and hence is associated with Poe's desire to transcend the grossness of physical existence...In Poe's tales, the word 'grotesque' often appears in its extended sense of 'exaggerated' or 'out of place,' but the word 'arabesque' and descriptions of art forms which, though unnamed, are clearly arabesques are never used casually. Inevitably, the word is inserted in a passage to evoke the sense of impending death and to suggest that the nature of that death is some sort of dissolution into Unity...In 'The Philosophy of Furniture,' which appeared in *Burton's* in May 1840, Poe describes what he considers the ideal room, a chamber fit for a poet to inhabit. He is particular about all the decor, but most especially about the carpet, which he considers 'the soul of a room.' He deplores the

current fashions in carpets, including the Turkish, 'bedizzened out like a Riccaree Indian—all [column 2:] red chalk, yellow ochre, and cock's feathers.' The 'soul' of his room shall instead be adorned with arabesques. The giant mind, the mind of the poet fit to inhabit Poe's indoor Eden, is despotically ruled by visions of dissolution, and he quite appropriately wishes to surround himself in his at-home hours with the species of ornament most likely to induce the particularly stylized vision or dream which he seeks." In *FF* (288), Barth notes that the arabesque could be grotesque, on occasion, for example, when human heads spring forth from trellised vegetation, but finally reaches the verdict "in the language of Friedrich Schlegel" that the grotesque involves "chaos" as it is understood outside art and literary history, while the arabesque should be limited only to what Schlegel refers to as "an artificially constructed chaos." The grotesque is almost never a feature either of Schlegel's writing or of that most "arabesque" of paintings, Runge's *Der Morgen*. Rather, as shown by Ricarda Huch, a perceptive critic like Görres saw that "arabesque" was not the right term for what was being attempted. Rather, Romantic art was more concerned with a hermeneutic or hieroglyphic symbolism, in which would more would be left unstated than actually expressed. Thus the importance of the Romantic fragment. It should also be noted that it is Hazlitt who, I believe, first applies the word "hieroglyphic" in literary criticism, identifying it with Shakespeare's use of language.

13. Friedrich Schlegel, *Lucinde* (München: Goldmann, no date), 38. Subsequent references to this text will be indicated by the abbreviation *L*.
14. Mario Praz, *The Romantic Agony*, translated by Angus Davidson (London, 1933), 28–29.
15. Friedrich Schlegel, "Rede über die Mythologie," in *The Romantic Tradition in Germany*, edited by Ronald Taylor (London: Methuen, 1970), 169.
16. See the discussion of *generatio aequivoca*, especially with respect to Schlegel's *Athenaeum*, by Philippe Lacoue-Labarthe and Jean-Luc Nancy in *L'absolu littéraire* (Paris: Seuil, 1978), 420–425. To paraphrase their argument, satire, *satura*, or medley is not, in all rigor, a genre like lyric, epic, or drama. But since it combines all genres, it calls into question the notion of genre, as such, and thus opens itself, especially in the novel, to philosophy, criticism, art, music, et al. Literary medley or mélange "…mène jusqu'au bord extrême de ce qu'il mêle: le genre, la littérature, la philosophie. Il porterait au bord de ce qui défait ou interrompt l'opération, au bord de ce que l'on pourrait nommer, de manière délibérément équivoque, l'ab-solution de l'Absolu littéraire" (421). The Romantics are working, then, in their own paradoxical way, on the same alternately bordering and borderless "project" as Hegel: the auto-negation of literature and of art, in general, just as they were doing something altogether different or (as in the case of Novalis) diametrically opposed; the "Auflösung" of Schelling does not mean precisely what the "Aufhebung" of Hegel means, just as the novel of Schlegel does not entirely reflect the "Auflösung" of Schelling (420). The "arabesque" is the name Schegel assigns to such speculative literary-philosophical-scientific mingling of one genre with another between 1795 and 1815, and it is not accidental that he includes autobiography in the arabesque *generatio aequivoca*, beginning with the *Confessions* of Rousseau. For the Hölderlinian context of my argument see *ET*, 104
17. In Ricarda Huch, *Gesammelte Werke*, volume VI (Cologne and Berlin: Kiepenheuer & Witsch, 1969), 311ff.
18. Novalis, *Fragmente* (Stuttgart: Reclam, 1972), 146.
19. Sir Thomas Browne, *Hydrotaphia (Urn Burial) and The Garden of Cyrus*, ed. Frank Huntley (New York: Appleton-Century-Crofts, 1966), 99. References below to this text will be indicated by the abbreviation *GC*.

20. As the art historian Claude Keisch remarks, "...by 1802–3 Runge had already drawn Four compositions of *The Times of Day*, which were published in 1805 as engravings (a second edition appeared in 1807). The symmetrical, arabesquelike designs, symbolic down to the smallest detail, in which flowers, children, and rays of light all play an important role, reflect the philosophically based program that Runge conceived for a new universal landscape art. Runge abandoned his original intention of executing them as a room decoration. However, some years later—the outline engravings had in the meantime caused a great sensation—Runge went back to the compositions and designed, following an earlier plan, four monumental paintings, but his premature death prevented him from realizing this project. Runge had intended to exhibit these pictures in their own neo-Gothic shrine." His text is found in *The Romantic Spirit, German Drawings, 1780-1850, from the Nationalgalerie (Staatliche Museen, Berlin) and the Kupfer-stich-Kabinett (Staatliche Kunstsammlingen, Dresden), German Democratic Republic* (New York: The Pierpont Morgan Library and Oxford U. Press, 1988), 82. Subsequent references to this text will be indicated by the abbreviation *RS*. Nowhere is the ambitious scale of Runge's concept made clearer than in the evolution of his design from a domestic, middle-class interior to the sublimely Romantic estrangement of medieval religiosity, an evolution inspired, perhaps, by Goethe's meditations on the architecture of Strasbourg. The painter read the *Farbenlehre*, while Goethe studied Runge's work with great interest and was intending to install a "Runge room" in his house at Weimar, a project forestalled by the latter's death. Such architectonic thinking also lay at the heart of Wordsworth's vision of an all-inclusive Gothic cathedral of poetic texts, including not only *The Prelude* and *The Excursion*, but also smaller or occasional texts. The cathedral structure, while it too might claim to represent multifarious orders of complexity, from the lowest to the highest rung of cosmic scale, would seem to represent something quite different from the patterning of the Persian or Oriental rug—as different, say, as a baseball cap and a turban.

21. In the literal sense of "before the temple" and thus being excluded from the sacred circle. See the accompanying essay for a listing of the meanings and etymologies of words such as "fan" and "fantasy." See the accompanying essay "The Full Fan-Experience from Cowley to Barney" for pertinent lexical triangulations.

22. Henry James, *The Europeans* (Oxford and New York: Oxford U. Press, 1985), 8.

23. As Laurence Rickels points out in his admirable study *The Case of California* (Baltimore: Johns Hopkins U. Press, 1991), Freud mapped this terrain very well in *The Future of an Illusion* and in *Group Psychology and the Analysis of Ego*. References to this text will be indicated below by the abbreviation *CC*. As soon as the French Revolution dispensed with the Christian God, it set up a Festival of the Supreme Being and identified "it" with Reason. The need for religion could not be eliminated as easily as the monarchy. Rickels, follwoing Freud, shows how the politics of a state run by the citizen-bourgeois subject is ever more beholden to its "fan base" and how this base, especially in Germany and America, moves its group(ie) thinking in the direction of sadomasochistic impulses. If fractals can map crises in markets, the paroxysms of boom and bust, can we not link the arabesque to a conjoint psychic topography (claimed in advance by Poe)—say, any of the more recently exported, fan-based brands of imperial hubris and sadomasochism?

24. These particulars of the baseball myth are congruent with plot and motivic elements found in Coover's *Universal Baseball Association*. Even more, there is a Nietzschean *amor fati* at work in the "dicey" discourse of "the Prop.," aka Henry Waugh. On the other hand, it is Malamud who has given us the most insightful fictional record, to date, of what lies occulted *beneath* the rug-like or aleatory patterning of baseball, where the

flaw is not merely an incidental element, but perhaps the central or tragic ingredient informing biological decrepitude and corrosive economic pressures (giving the fans what they want).

25. Alexis de Tocqueville, *Democracy in America*, edited and abridged by Richard Hefner (New York: New American Library/Mentor, 1960), 200.

26. See, once again, Claude Keisch's commentary in *RS*, 83–84: "In 1825 Otto Speckter reproduced the design [of Runge's smaller, pen and ink version of *Morning* in a lithograph...The title with which the drawing entered the Berlin Kupferstichkabinett is significant. 'Allegorical Representation of Schelling's Philosophy. A Fairy Play.' This title appears to refer to conversations the art historian Carl Friedrich von Rumohr had with the philosopher Friedrich Wilhelm Joseph von Schelling, when Rumohr showed him the drawing in Munich early in 1808...Apparently, the drawing served, even more than as a practical working design for his painting, as advance pubļicity for it and for the exchange of ideas with those of a like mind."

27. Allen Upward, *The Divine Mystery* (Santa Barbara: Ross-Erikson, rpt. 1976), 345. References to this text will be indicated below by the abbreviation *DM*. From his theosophical perspective, Upward identifies the "evil spell" as humanistic materialism. From the hieroglyphic perspective of Runge, however, the seraphs supervise the emancipatory insurgency of a citizen-subject as a philosophically empowered batsman or entrpreneurial "player/operator." The difference in viewpoints may be "Nietzschean."

28. Now, in cyber-space, the full fan-experience takes the charming or enchanting shape of yet another universal baseball league, which puts Poe and numerous other literary-philosophical celebrities on fictitious teams. Needless to say, this is a uniquely American "new dawn" of adulation, wherein dead authors are given a kind of "Casey-at-the-bat" immortality, part of an all-American unwilllingness to accept the inevitability of death or to treat it as something more than a matter for intellectual-theoretical postulation. The dead celebrities are "systematized" in terms of the mental gymnastics of hypothetical leagues and thus memorialized and rendered harmless at once. At the same time, this website keeps its visitors up-to-date on the passing of celebrities such as Hunter Thompson, whose ghost, no doubt, will be similarly scouted and taught how to "play ball" at some point in the virtual future.

29. And in this emancipatory striding-forward uncannily anticipating Delacroix's *Liberty Leading the People, July 28, 1830*. Here, an entirely different "arabesque/grotesque" mélange of sublimity and vulgarity emerges—whose pathogenesis propels itself from the Olympian paradigm on a journalistic, i. e., equivocal and satirical, glide- or stride-path, with death rather than birth under the foot of the "love goddess" turned *citoyenne*.

30. The undecided, "quidam falsa...quidam vera" qualification suggests a reading of Augustine and/or of an Augustine filtered through Lessing.

31. Friedrich Schiller, "Philosophische Briefe," in *Sämtliche Werke*, V, "Erzählungen und theoretische Schriften," ed. Gerhard Fricke and Herbert Göpfert (Munich: Hanser, 4th edition, 1965), 352–353.

32. The mythic paradigm of the holy child can be traced to the earliest religions and is linked, as Runge apparently suggests, to the East (the Magi, Zoroastrianism, et al.) through astrology: "Monotheism has been a plant of slow growth. The heavenly King long remained a Child. He was reborn each year as the Divine Babe, and laid in the manger of the Bull. He was worshipped as the golden Calf. His strength was seen to wax and wane as he made his annual transit throught the Signs, from south to north and back again. To what could this be due but to the influence of the Signs? The elder Gods retained their secret might, and to their friendsip or enmity were attributed the son's birth and growth, his death and resurrection." Allen Upward, *The Divine Mystery* (Santa

Barbara: Ross-Erikson, rpt. 1976), 133. Upward's reference to children and plants in almost the same breath is uncanny, given the specific symbolism of Runge's painting.

33. William Blake, *Complete Writings*, edited by Geoffrey Keynes (New York: Oxford U. Press, 1988), 279. Subsequent references to this text will be indicated by the abbreviation *WB*. The affinity between Blake and Runge is further explored in Robert Rosenblum, *Modern Painting and the Northern Romantic Tradition: From Friedrich to Rothko* (New York: Harper and Row, 1975). Subsequent references to this text will be indicated by the abbreviation *MPNR*.

34. The urban legend of Doubleday's invention of baseball has been debunked, even at Cooperstown. What remains a little-known fact, however, is Doubleday's brief role as interim president of the American Theosophical Society, a philanthropic association guided by the principles of Madame Blavatsky's *Isis Unveiled* and directed in its day-to-day affairs, from Bombay, India, by Olcott. Doubleday was told to "keep up an active interest in all matters connected with the East and its mysteries and wisdom." For more on the connection between theosophy, the channeling of the dead, Germany, and America the reader should consult Laurence Rickels. Worth noting is the confluence of baseball and theosophy in the life and legend of Doubleday, while it is the seraphic emanations of Poe and Ruth that continue to haunt the consciousness of Baltimore. Meanwhile, back at the Internet clubhouse, a website for the intelligentsia calling itself "Cosmic Baseball" in 1997 advertised Edgar Allan Poe as a player on the "Eden Bohemians" of the Middle League and continues to hold a yearly world series in cyberspace.

35. "The July 13, 1825 edition of the 'Delhi (N.Y.) Gazette' (on microfilm) has a notice listing the names of nine men challenging any group in Delaware County to a game of baseball at the home of Edward B. Chace for $1 per game." This information is obtained From www.historybuff.com (20 February 2005), "Pre-1845 Baseball: Was Abner Doubleday Really the Originator?," by Tom Helgesen. A game of "baseball" is mentioned as far back as 1748 when "a Lady Hervey wrote a letter in which she describes family activities of Frederick, Prince of Wales. She refers to family members 'diverting themselves in baseball, a play all who are or have been schoolboys are well acquainted with.'" Knowledge of baseball seems to have been restricted to the English-speaking world; Runge's *Morning*, with its transcendentally energized geometry, emerges from a different branch of the theosophical tradition, one more Böhmean than Vedic, though diamond symbolism is consistently found in "Eastern mysticisms" from international Freemasonry to Buddhism.

36. *Zedler's Universal-Lexicon*, vol. 37, 325: "Den Nahmen der Cherubim scheinen sie [Seraphim] aber insbesondere zu erhalten, wenn von ihrer Behendigkeit oder Krafft die Rede ist, welche sie bey Vollziehung der göttlichen Befehle zeigen: Es lässet sich dieses auch einiger massen durch den Engel erläutern, welcher dort mit einem blossen hauenden Schwert vor das Paradiess gestellet wird, I Buch Mos. III. 24." ["The <seraphim> seem to receive the name cherubim, especially, when the subject of discourse is their agility or strength, which they demonstrate in the accomplishment of divine commands: This <circumstance> can be explained to some extent through the angel who is placed with a cutting sword in front of paradise. Genesis I. III. 24."]. *PA* cites an interesting 1827 review by Disraeli in which the unnaturalness of the grotesque and arabesque is seen as the sign of a postlapsarian apartness from God and the divine creation or as hallmarks of guilt: "Pleasant designs deviating from natural appearances, like 'a boy's head appearing out of a lily' in some garden of cherubic delights, serve no worthwhile purposes; the pleasurable may evidently be depicted in more natural ways. But the grotesque is justified when it makes us 'sensible of the terrors of a guilty mind.'" This is especially relevant to Runge's vegetative symbolism.

37. Manfred Frank, *Kaltes Herz, Unendliche Fahrt, Neue Mythologie. Motivuntersuchung zur Pathogenese der Modernen* (Frankfurt/M.: Suhrkamp, 1989), 96.

38. As he does most notably in Günter Grass's *The Flounder* (*Der Butt*). See the fifth essay of the present book. My discussion of Runge in the surprising context of baseball is meant to shed light only on the possibilities of interpretation itself, as it works through the complexities of the arabesque, the grotesque, and the hieroglyphic. Baseball, one might say, or the Idea of it, exists in a Romantic universe parallel to that of the Persian rug (but, one still may hope, not in its anti-universe), one which Runge, in particular, illuminates. The choice of baseball as a touchstone of interpretation is made in provocative divergence from Barth's privileging of the Persian rug. To my knowledge, Mandelbrot has not yet extended his equations to the national pastime, though he may well do so at some point in the future. Coover's dice-throwing protagonist Harry Waugh seems, however, too shrewdly conceived to be regarded only as the primitive or modernist prototype of such mathematical sophistication. Like Malamud, Coover has covered several unofficial, off-field bases.

39. Robert Coover, *The Universal Baseball Association, Inc. J. Henry Waugh Prop.* (New York: Penguin, 1971), 141. Subsequent references to this text will be indicated by the abbreviation *UBA*. Coover's text, first published in 1968, bears an epigraph from Kant's *Critique of Judgment*: "It is here not at all requisite for prove that such an *intellectus archetypus* is possible, but only that we are led to the Idea of it...." The intellectual and cultural foundation of *The Universal Baseball Association*, with metafictional allusions not only to Kant, but also to alchemy, can only begin to be "sketched" here. Taking a cue from the epigraph, I am suggesting only one or more apertures to baseball's "Idea."

40. In his seminal study, Rickels suggests many ways in which Germany and America "track together" in the symptomatology of mass psychosis and group identification. The rise of baseball, as secularized pastime, is contemporaneous with the suppression of instinct *beyond the ballpark* and the slipping of art from the status of cultural essence to that of accident, displacements accompanied by a pious jingoism (America as "God's own team") and the temperance movement. All that is left when mass replaces Mass is the "cool" group, team, or party with which one identifies (via a lapel-pin or sports jersey), to which one belongs or aspires to belong. Rickels shows how Freud recognized such phenomena: "Beginning in the 1920s Freud charted a genealogy of these group structures—from mass to mass to mass—which pushed only the relations of identification. From Christianity to America all the way back to primal-time programming, the only pleasure to be had belongs to the phantom projection which takes pleasure—but only in the group membership's lack of enjoyment. But this legacy of religion cannot be readily neutralized since its broadcasts of belief or public opinion have already been installed as part of the psychic apparatus" (*CC*, 153). The "winner/loser" mentality, in its sporting, phobic unwisdom, has a similar secular-psychological basis and can only spring from a polymorphously manipulated cultural unease.

41. Schelling's poetic text, "Die Epikuräisch[en] Glaubensbekenntnisse Heinz Widerporstens" is reprinted in Frank, *Eine Einführung in Schellings Naturphilosophie* (Frankfurt/M.: Suhrkamp, 1985), 103.

42. Barth mentions Poe's novel only in passing in his essays on chaos and the arabesque, but treats it at length in a paper delivered in the late 1980s, "'*Still Further South*': Some Notes on Poe's *Pym*." Here there is no mention of the mirrored abysses, and Barth bemoans the lack of those things which might be called hallmarks of 19th-century realism, a well-developed, "strong" central character and a "mainspring" of action. Notably absent, too, is any mention of the petroglyph inserted quite obviously in Poe's text, whose meaning, it seems to me, cannot be deduced from the perspicuously ordered,

decorative symmetry of the fractal and the Oriental rug, but may be pursued (non-exclusively) through a hermeneutics of figure, subject, and text, as de Man suggests.

43. The present and future in baseball are projected in terms of continuity with the past (as in the recently lifted curse of a cherubically powerful, numinous *Babe* Ruth). Basketball, on the other hand, seems more willing to accept the arrival of a Super-Subject/Player like Michael Jordan, who causes us to reassess completely what it means to play the game—or to rescale our sense of what is possible in it. His efforts to become a baseball player proved abortive for a number of reasons, but may have had something to do, at least theoretically, with the Zarathustran possibility of reinventing the game of basketball, on the one hand, and the impossibility of reinventing the national pastime, on the other. Malamud's *The Natural* observes the arrow-like flight of time connecting the sport's present with its past, but, in depicting a certain decadence and depraved excess associated with the national pastime, perceives as well the sun that is always setting on careers in the empire of baseball and other professional sports. Aurora and the only-too-Human fan are only "with us" at the beginning of the day; twilight brings out the owl (not only of Minerva) in us.

44. Edgar Allan Poe, *Poetry and Tales*, with notes by Patrick Quinn (New York: Library of America, 11th printing, 1984), 487–488. References to this edition will be indicated below by the abbreviation *PT*.

45. Especially in the Suprematists, but with signficant divergences among the Surrealists and Dadaists and in Picasso and De Kooning, to be sure. The line of mathematical abstraction in music is more easily discerned, while the complexities of the abstractness itself are daunting. See the paper by Scott Baker, Florida State University on Scriabin's Sonata No. 8, Op. 66 (1912–1913): "This paper explores using three distinct analytical approaches: motivic analysis, set-theoretical analysis, and Neo-Riemannian analysis. In the absence of functional tonality, the structure of the sonata will be elucidated primarily by investigating Scriabin's use of permutations of motivic cells and their temporal and harmonic relationships to one another. In addition to structural coherence, harmonic coherence will be shown through Scriabin's consistent use of certain pitch class sets (primarily of cardinalities 3, 4, or 5) that are subsets of referential collections established in the opening measures." "A Heterogeneous Analysis of the Eighth Piano Sonata, Op. 66 of Alexander Scriabin..." (January 5, 2005) In their arabesque-like, seemingly chaotic but also numerically definite qualities, these sonatas challenge many, if not all, of the West's assumptions concerning traditional or symmetrical sonata-form and motivic development, decomposing the subject. Scriabin's fractal, motivic, or "arabesque" cells Become ours to deal with, in the West, just as his "absolute" or Zarathustran music, in many ways yet another "last gasp" of Wagnerian tendencies, maps a terrain which, in its simultaneous adherence to Romantic universality and mathematical denaturing, lends itself to just the kind of Mandelbrotian analysis Barth recommends. See H. H. Stuckenschmidt, *Twentieth-Century Music*, translated by Richard Deveson (New York: McGraw-Hill, 1972), 16–21. György Ligeti's piano etudes and his concerto for piano and orchestra have extended the Mandelbrotian possibilities.

46. It is more than a matter of literary-historical coincidence that *The Tales of the Grotesque and Arabesque* (1840) and "The Thousand-and-Second Tale of Scheherazade" (1845) are published in the shadow of the Edward William Lane translation of *The Arabian Nights* (1838–1840). The American public wants to be entertained with "more" Arabian tales, and Poe, shadowed also by Longfellow and Washington Irving, sees himself compelled to play the role of a reluctant Scheherazade.

In the 18th century another fate awaited the translation of *The Arabian Nights*, first into the French of Antoine Galland's *Mille et une Nuits* (1704) and then into English (1704–

1717). What makes that tradition relevant to Poe and to our thesis is the *satirical* use to which *The Arabian Nights* is put, first in Voltaire and, at the end of the century, in an unpublished text of Horace Walpole, *Hieroglyphic Tales*. Eighteenth-century metafiction Inscribes itself from the beginning on the margins of *The Arabian Nights*, revealing usually a satirical edginess meant to outfox censorship or to blur generic distinctions. In the case of Walpole, who kept his supplemental tales private, the hieroglyphic element surfaces in the esoteric coding of names (Pissimissi) and situations, ribald plots, and a taste for the erudtely nonsensical. Poe could not have known of *The Hieroglyphic Tales*, but a number of stylistic similarities between them and the "Thousand-and-Second Tale of Scheherazade" can be discerned, especially in the Swift-like ridicule of academic scholarship. Walpole's *Tales* belong to an aristocratic, highly idiosyncratic or eccentric "full fan-experience" derived from 18th-century satire, while the hieroglyph in Poe's texts inscribes itself on radically different critical-journalistic, philosophical-psychological ground in terms of its read- and translatability. Satirical framing fictions may be the obverse of the widely received, sensationally "Gothic" aspects of Walpole's *Castle of Otranto*, where terror and cruelty are the order of the day. *The Hieroglyphic Tales*, read to a tiny female audience, and Poe's supplement also represent empowered females reacting to "Oriental" repression and the emancipation of instinct, subjects beyond the pale of academe and pious middle-class *mores*.

47. Edgar Allan Poe, "Preface" to *Tales of the Grotesque and Arabesque* (1840) in *PT*, 129.

48. Н. Б. Гоголь, *ПРОЗА · СТАТЬИ*, (Москва: СОВЕТСКАЯ РОССИЯ, 1977), 225.

49. The English translation appears at the front of Nabokov's study *Gogol*, (New York: New Directions, reprint 1961), no page.

50. Vladimir Nabokov, *Gogol*, (New York: New Directions, reprint 1961), 86–89.

51. These attributes are singled out as hallmarks of the arabesque, especially in Gogol, and discussed by Alain Salvatore in "Le problème de la *fin*, les *moyens*, et le rôle du diable dans la production artistique: le problème de l'art dans *Les Nouvelles de Petersbourg*" @ http://opus-all.paris.iufm.fr/tl/tl_gogol/art.htm (30 January, 2005).

52. John Irwin, *American Hieroglyphics* (New Haven: Yale U. Press, 1980), 168.

53. Edgar Allan Poe, "The Gold-Bug," *PT*, 587.

54. Martin Heidegger, *Being and Time*, translated by Joan Stambaugh (Albany: SUNY Press, 1996), 119–120.

55. Haruki Murakami, *Kafka on the Shore*, translated by Philip Gabriel (New York: Knopf, 2005). Subsequent references to this text will be indicated by the abbreviation *KS*.

56. The reader is referred to *CC*, 29, where Kafka is said to have "invented Amerika." Murakami's title seems to allude, bicoastally, to the Pacific shores of America and Japan, fractally mappable spaces where Kafka "translates well." Rickels text, from the early 1990s, can serve as a valuable introduction to the reading of Murakami—and vice versa.

57. Speaking as a "fan" of metafiction, I would argue that Mitchell's *Cloud Atlas* (New York: Random House, 2004) is a better "read" than *Ghostwritten*, not least because of the signature of identifiable styles and an ability to expatiate upon or "unpack" the full fan-experience of music, as in this passage, dazzling in its postmod dementia: "Dreamt I stood in a china-shop so crowded from floor to far-off ceiling with shelves of porcelain antiquities etc. that moving a muscle would cause several to fall off and smash to bits. Exactly what happened, but instead of a crashing noise, an august chord rang out, half-cello, half-celeste, D major (?), held for four beats. My wrist knocked a Ming vase affair off its pedestal—E-flat, whole string section, glorious, transcendent, angels wept. Deliberately now, smashed a figurine of an ox for the next note, then a milk-maid, then Saturday's Child—orgy of shrapnel filled the air, divine harmonies my head. Ah, such music!" (43). This Punk-like paroxysm of dream-violence is then trumped on the next

page by: "Had a view of an alley: downtrodden scriveners hurtling by like demisemi-quavers in a Beethoven *allegro*. Afraid of 'em? No, I'm afraid of *being* one. What value are education, breeding, and talent if one doesn't have a pot to piss in?"

58. Gilles Deleuze, *Nietzsche and Philosophy*, translated by Hugh Tomlinson (New York: Columbia U. Press, 1983), 185.

59. David Mitchell, *Ghostwritten* (New York: Random House, 1999), 424–425. References to this text will be indicated below by the abbreviation *G*.

60. The sense of looking backward, with a kind of reverential bewilderment, if not any more vivid emotion, surfaces in the "downtown" of plays by Richard Foreman, the photography of Cindy Sherman, the "sculptural" films of Matt Barney, and the music of David Byrne and Laurie Anderson, to name those with which I am somewhat familiar.

61. This is the word applied, in particular, by Irving Howe to African-Americans in their struggle for social justice and may be applied, more generally, to oppressed minorities and peoples throughout the world, so that the "boundaryless illuminaton" of the Romantics' Orient can shine also on their part of their universe. Ralph Ellison's debate with Howe focused, to a certain extent, on the "ferocity" and "pain" that informed Howe's perception of Richard Wright. I wish only to situate such an emotional subtext within the generic frame of arabesque *Leidenschaft* or passion. See the essay "The World and the Jug" in *Shadow and Act* (New York: Random House, 1953 and 1964), 107–143.

62. Norman Mailer, *Advertisements for Myself*, (New York: Putnam's/Signet, 1960), 257.

63. David Anfam uses these words to describe some of Runge's other work, most notably his portraits of children. Anfam suggests a similarity between their optical effects and certain paintings by Mark Rothko, but also notes that it is improbable that he or any Abstract Expressionist working in New York at the time had knowledge of Runge. See his catalogue raisonné *Mark Rothko* (London and New Haven: Yale U. Press, 1999), 79. Rosenblum notes (*MPNR*, 53) the nexus of children and plants in Runge (with echoes in Novalis), suggesting that it is part of the larger philosophical project of discovering a universal substance (the *en kai pan*) animating creation. In a later chapter (209–210) he links this to Barnett Newman's *Onement* series and to the Kabbala, noting how Rothko in 1946 termed artists wishing to jettison the orthodox academic tradition "Myth Makers."

Chapter Five

1. I refer here, with ambiguity, both to the title of William Carlos Williams's prose "snapshots" of a usable, if also nightmarish, American past, one that continues to traverse the present and future in ways we are scarcely aware of, and to Roland Barthes' *Camera Lucida*, a text on photography. The French tradition of literature in the phonetic vernacular goes back to Villon, as Raymond Queneau points out in the remarkable essay "Écrit en 1937," where literary French and the insistence upon orthography and gram-matical correctness are seen as examples of academic "vanity."

2. One wonders what "E-dis-to" once meant to native American ears. It is a beautiful name, rhyming with Callisto—she whom Hera turned into a bear because of a dalliance with Zeus. Mythic motivation seems to be seeded at the level of the the syllable, Olson's "king and pin of versification." *Edisto* as a text dialogues with Greek myth, the "Southern" literature of avenging mulattoes, modernism, postmodernism, and Grass's mythologizing of history in *The Flounder*, where the prehistoric "goddess" Aua gifts the narrator with immortality for his act of generosity. Many, if not most, of *Edisto*'s strong characters, Except for the narrator and Taurus, are women. An emphasis upon the fanciful inter-pretation of history, as seen through the eyes of a somewhat less than reliable narrator, is

shared by Powell and Grass, both writing from a coastal perspective and with uncommon or less common types of individual speech (idiolect) in mind.

3. William Gilmore Simms. *The Yemassee* (Boston: Houghton, Mifflin, 1961), 6. "The romance is of loftier origin than the Novel. It approximates the poem. It may be described as an amalgam of the two...The standards of the Romance—take such a story... as the Ivanhoe of Scott, or the Salathiel of Croly,—are very much those of the epic. It invests individuals with an absorbing interest—it hurries them rapidly through crowding and exacting events, in a narrow space of time—it requires the same unities of plan, of purpose, and harmony of part, and it seeks for its adventures among the wild and wonderful. It does not confine itself to what is known, or even what it is probable. It grasps at the possible; and, placing a human agent in hitherto untried situations, it exercises ingenuity in extricating him from them, while describing his feelings and his fortunes in his progress." Hawthorne's judgment on *The Yemassee* as an "*American romance*" (1853) and the evident rapture he experienced on reading it in his youth may well have caused James to take Simms's aesthetic seriously, up to and including the use of anachronisms. See *The Native Muse: Theories of American Literature*, ed. Richard Ruland (New York: Dutton, 1976), I, 378. One wonders, parenthetically, if the advertisers of West Virginia as "wild and wonderful" are aware of their debt to Simms.

4. E-text of *The Bostonians* from the Henry James Online website (10 February 2005).

5. The following information on Gullah is gleaned from the minutes of a recent conference on Southern dialects @ http://www.ecu.edu/english/tcr/22 (23 December 2004): "Michael Aceto delivered 'The Triangulation of Language Contact in the Anglophone Atlantic region: West Africa, the West Indies, and North America' at LAVIS III (Language Variety in the South): Historical and Contemporary Perspectives, University of Alabama in Tuscaloosa, April 16. Aceto examined 'linguistic and cultural links among the historical southern North American colonies/states, the Anglophone Caribbean, and West(ern) Africa.' He also discussed 'several competing theories about the directionality of influence among the following triangular points: 1) the general area of the east coast of North America; 2) the West Indies; and 3) West Africa, particularly the Guinea Coast. Some scholars suggest that the English-derived Creole languages of the Caribbean influenced the emergence of Gullah on the Sea Coast Islands of South Carolina and Georgia; others suggest Caribbean creoles influenced the emergence of Krio, a language of Sierra Leone spoken on the historic Upper Guinea Coast of West Africa.' According to Aceto, 'Some suggest Gullah influenced Krio; and yet others propose that the English-derived creoles of the Americas were significantly influenced by an early form of restructured English spoken somewhere on the Upper Guinea Coast/modern Sierra Leone (Hancock 1986, 1987) or the Lower Guinea Coast/modern Ghana (McWhorter 1997, Aceto 1999). Cassidy (1980, 1994) focused on the connections between Barbadian English and Gullah for understanding the possible historical relationships between an early form of Bajan (assumed to have had more creole-like features than are typically heard on the island today) and Gullah-speaking areas. Hancock (1980, 1986) suggests that Gullah (among other English-derived creoles of the Americas) was influenced by the formation of an early variety of Krio. Recently, Huber (fc.) has suggested that Gullah influenced the formation of Krio in Sierra Leone.'"

6. See John Irwin, *American Hieroglyphics* (New Haven: Yale U. Press, 1980). Subsequent references to this text will be indicated by the abbreviation *AH*. I cannot do justice here to the perspicacity and subtlety of Irwin's readings of Poe. I wish merely to suggest how 19th-century fiction and phonetically atrocious, mythically doubled modern and post-modern narratives take a non-hieroglyphic, declamatory turn. Issues of shadowing, irony, projection, and so forth remain, and the grainy quality of first-person speech is, in the

final if not first analysis, a matter of writing and reiteration.

To a certain extent, the Petronian, Dostoyevskyan, and/or (post)modernist insistence upon a vulgarly deformed, grammatically/phonetically pejorative *declamatio* elaborates itself in the same field of cultural transference as the derivation (ca. 1730) of the word "palaver," denoting worthless speech, from *palabra/parole/parable*. It is part of a vernacular milieu: of coffee houses, stock exchanges, and metapoetic fandom—reflecting, in short, the democratization of letters. Cable, Faulkner, and Powell seize upon "palaver" as their most precious resource, rescuing it from the moribundity of the aesthetic. The same may be said, *a fortiori*, of Wordsworth in the inaugurating text of poetic modernism, *The Lyrical Ballads*.

7. Daniel Ferrer, "In omnis iam vocabuli mortem," *The Oxford Literary Review*, vol. 5, 1 & 2, 21–36. Subsequent references to this text will be indicated by the abbreviation *DF*.

8. William Faulkner, *As I Lay Dying* (New York: Random House, 1957), 187. Subsequent references to this text will be indicated by the abbreviation *AIL*

9. Cornbread or corncake motivation subtends the larger totemic projection of the mother-fish as "food" for the consumption of her offspring. This aspect of communal cannibalism is well analyzed in *DF* (25ff) and supports the textual inscription of a transfer of supernatural (numinous) agency from the father to the mother.

10. Günter Grass, *Der Butt* (Frankfurt/M.: Fischer, 1979), 99–100. Subsequent references to this text will be indicated by the abbreviation *B*. All translations from the novel are by this writer.

11. Padgett Powell, *Edisto* (New York: Holt, Rinehart, Winston, 1985), 26–27. Subsequent references to this text will be indicated by the abbreviation *E*.

12. Walter Pater, "Wordsworth," in *Appreciations* (London: Macmillan, reprint 1911), 42.

13. Dino Felluga, "The Road Is Clear: Application," *Introductory Guide to Critical Theory*. ["http://www.sla.purdue.edu/academic/engl/theory/index.html"]. Purdue U. <http://www.purdue.edu/guidetotheory/narratology/applications/applicTheRoadisClear2.html> (12 December, 2004).

14. Seymour Chatman. *Story and Discourse: Narrative Structure in Fiction and Film* (Ithaca: Cornell U. Press, 1978), 181.

15. The narrator's mother thinks that Taurus, the process-server, is the grandson of "Theenie," and thus the son of her daughter, who has gone to New York, "which is Gomorrah to people here...Well, one look at him and you knew he was not *all* black, and that meant white people were involved, and one look at his blue summons and she knew the gubmen was involved, so it's major" (*E*, 25). Miscegenation looms large in Reconstruction romance, beginning with Joel Chandler's story "Where's Duncan?" and Cable's *The Grandissimes*, where characters such as Honoré Grandissime and Palmyre Philosoph are of mixed race. Faulkner's *Absalom! Absalom!* continues the tradition. See William Bedford Clark, "The Serpent of Lust in the Southern Garden," *The Southern Review*, vol. X, 4 (Autumn, 1974), 805–822. Clark's essay discusses the mulatto as alternating avenger and victim in Southern fiction, a motivation easily discernible at the level of the surface or phenotext of *Edisto*, since that is one of the roles—but by no means the largest—played by "Taurus." On the other hand, as Irwin reminds us in *AH*, it is Dirk Peters, a half-breed Indian, who saves Poe's Pym during the mutiny aboard the *Grampus*, while the Negro cook, a "perfect demon," slaughters the captive crew-members with an axe. We have a possible source here for Simons Manigault's default projection of Taurus as an "ax-murderer," while the cook, made more amenable to mercy because of his state of inebriation, suggests Cable's Bras-Coupé.

16. Manfred Frank, *Die Unhintergehbarkeit von Individualität* (Frankfurt/ M.: Suhrkamp, 1986), 122.

17. It is interesting to note in passing that the possibilites open to the English translator of Grass's Gdańsk/Danzig dialect are few: one can opt for some variation on a Scots-Irish brogue, Brooklynese, or the idiolect of Southerners, either lower-class whites or African-Americans. But Grass has been a thorn in the side of translators, even on his two native grounds, as indicated in Janina Gesche, "Geographische Realität und Fantasielandschaft," in *Das literarische und kulturelle Erbe von Danzig und Gdańsk* (Frankfurt/M.: Peter Lang, 2004), 35–46.

18. George Washington Cable, *The Grandissimes* (New York: Sagamore Press, 1957), 169. Subsequent references to this text will be indicated by the abbreviation *G*.

19. The recent celebration in Columbia, South Carolina, of the paintings of Jonathan Green—"Off the Wall and onto the Stage"—can be seen as part of the attempt to preserve the memory of Gullah culture and render it vivid to contemporary audiences through the nonverbal medium of dance. See the review by John Rockwell in *The New York Times*, pages B1 and B7, February 7, 2005.

20. William Carlos Williams, *In the American Grain* (New York; New Directions, 1956). Subsequent references to this text will be indicated by the abbreviation *AG*. What is significant about this Poe is that Williams inserts it as the coda in his collection of essays—so that we have the feeling that there is nothing beyond Poe or that Poe is where writers "in the American grain," after 1940, will be forced to look for inspiration. It seems strange that Williams, coming from an epic text calling itself *Paterson*, would not pay more attention to the declamatory, idiosyncratic *muthos* of Southern writers. Perhaps he saw that space already occupied by the giant form of Faulkner.

21. Edward Dahlberg, *Can These Bones Live* (Ann Arbor: U. of Michigan Press, 1967) and *Alms for Oblivion* (Minneapolis: U. of Minnesota Press, 1964). Subsequent references to the former will be indicated by the abbreviation *CTB*, to the latter by *AO*.

22. Friedrich Schlegel, "Rede über die Mythologie," in *The Romantic Tradition in Germany*, edited by Ronald Taylor (London: Methuen, 1970), 169.

23. North American Indians, like the Greeks, assigned a mythology to every brook, hill, and valley. White civilization, on the other hand, has had little regard, until recently, for the sacred individuality of places—unless they were the sites of famous battles of the Revolutionary or Civil War. Our scientific names do justice to classes, genera, and species, but not to the uniqueness of a particular tree, animal, or person. The very survival of Indian names suggests that our culture somehow lacks the aptitude for individuated naming or has left this region of the cerebral cortex, unlike the wilderness conquered by the acquisitive part, underdeveloped. The dominant Ango-Saxon culture has seen fit to bleach the names of its children and is now busily expunging the local reference of its sports stadiums, but, at least so far, has seen fit to leave the idio-syncratically distinctive Indian names of rivers alone. Again, African-Americans, especially, seem to understand the desirability of gifting children with culturally marked first names—Chaneequa, Booker, Latifah, and countless others. With incomparable micrological finesse and multicultural sensitivity, Henry James singles out one African person—Azarina—in *The Europeans*, giving us a sense of the name as a nucleus of native dignity and individuality among those who, as slaves, are forced by their owners to acquire Roman names such as Titus or Remus. A similar motivation seems to underlie Cable's use of the exquisite appellation "Palmyre Philosoph."

24. Text from "De Soto's Expedition" by Sylvia Flowers @ www. nps.gov.ocmu/ Desoto.htm (20 March, 2005).

25. Hervey Allen, *Israfel; The Life and Times of Edgar Allan Poe* (New York: Farrar and Rinehart, 1932), 50.

Bibliography

Primary Sources

The Arabian Nights' Entertainment–or the Thousand and One Nights. 9th–14th centuries C. E. Compilation in Arabic from Egyptian texts, 1835. Translated by Frederick Lane. 1838–1840. New York: Pickwick, 1927.

Arabian Nights' Entertainments. English translation of Galland's French version. 1704–1717. Edited by Robert L. Mack. Oxford: Oxford U. Press. 1998.

Barney, Matthew. *Cremaster 1.* 1995. Musical revue conceived and directed by Matthew Barney and performed on blue Astroturf at Bronco Stadium in Boise, Idaho, Barney's hometown.

———. *Cremaster 2.* 1999. Gothic Western conceived and directed by Matthew Barney. Sexual differentiation in the human embryo represented in the context of the lives of Harry Houdini and Gary Gilmore and the latter's execution.

———. *Cremaster 3.* 2002. Conceived and directed by Matthew Barney. Performed at and in the Chrysler Building, with narrative reference to its construction.

———. *Cremaster 4.* 1994. Mythic drama conceived and directed by Matthew Barney. Performed largely on the Isle of Man, with Barney impersonating a satyr based on the Loughton ram and with the Manx triskelion as an emblem. Motorcycle racing employed allegorically. Allusion to sexual embryogenesis as episodes of ascension and descension.

———. *Cremaster 5.* 1997. Conceived and directed by Matthew Barney. Endstage of Cremaster descension set as an opera in late 19th-century Budapest with Ursula Andress as Queen.

Baudrillard, Jean. "The Ecstasy of Communication." 1987. Translated by John Johnston. In *The Anti-Aesthetic, Essays in Postmodern Culture.* Edited by Hal Foster. Seattle: Bay Press, 1983. 126–133.

Bergson, Henri. *The Two Sources of Religion and Morality.* 1932. Translated by R. Ashley Audra and Cloudesley Brereton with the assistance of W. Horsfall Carter. Garden City, N. Y.: Doubleday Anchor, 1954.

Blake, William. *Complete Writings.* Edited by Geoffrey Keynes. New York: Oxford U. Press, 1988.

Browne, Sir Thomas. *Hydrotaphia (Urn Burial) and The Garden of Cyrus.* 1658. Edited by Frank Huntley. New York: Appleton-Century-Crofts, 1966.

Cable, George Washington. *The Grandissimes.* 1880. New York: Sagamore Press, 1957.

Coover, Robert. *The Universal Baseball Association, Inc. J. Henry Waugh Prop.* 1968. New York: Penguin, 1971.

238 *Bibliography*

"Cosmic Baseball" @ www. cosmicbaseball.com. (29 December 2004).

Cowley, Abraham. "The First Nemean Ode of Pindar." 1656. In *The Works of the English Poets With Prefaces, Biographical and Critical* by Samuel Johnson. 58 volumes. Vol. 1. London: H. Hughs, 1779. 15–20.

The Abraham Cowley Text and Image Archive, University of Virginia, website @ http://etextvirginia.edu/kinney/worksol.html (29 December 2004).

De Quincey, Thomas. "The English Mail Coach." 1849. *Selected Writings of Thomas De Quincey.* Edited by Philip Van Doren Stern. New York: Random House, 1937.

De Tocqueville, Alexis. *Democracy in America.* 1835 and 1840. Edited and abridged by Richard Hefner. New York: New American Library/Mentor, 1960.

Dryden, John. "Preface" to *Sylvae.* 1685. In *The Best of Dryden.* Edited by Louis Bredfold. New York: Ronald Press, 1933.

Faulkner, William. *As I Lay Dying.* 1930. New York: Random House, 1957.

Frank, Manfred *Die Unhintergehbarkeit von Individualität.* 1986. Frankfurt/M.: Suhrkamp, 1986.

Goethe, J. W. *Goethes Gedichte.* Edited by Emil Staiger in three volumes. Zürich: Manesse, 1949.

―――. *West-Östlicher Divan.* 1819. Goldmann: Frankfurt/M., no date.

Grass, Günter. *Der Butt.* 1977. Frankfurt/M.: Fischer, 1979.

Гогол, Н. Б. *ПРОЗА · СТАТЬИ.* Москва: СОВЕТСКАЯ РОССИЯ, 1977.

Heidegger. Martin. *Being and Time.* 1927. Translated by Joan Stambaugh. Albany, N. Y.: State U. of New York, 1996.

―――. *Nietzsche.* Volumes I–IV. A compilation of lectures and articles from the 1930s and 1940s. Translated with marginal notes by David Farrell Krell. San Francisco: Harper and Row, 1979–1987.

―――. "Über den Ursprung des Kunstwerks." 1935–1936. In *Holzwege* Frankfurt/M.: Klostermann, fifth edition 1972. 296–343.

The Complete Works of Horace. Translated and annotated by Charles Passage. New York: Ungar, 1983.

Q. Horatius Flaccus. *Opera.* Edited by D. R. Shackleton-Bailey. Tübingen: Teubner, 1995.

James, Henry. *The Europeans.* 1878. Oxford and New York: Oxford U. Press, 1985.

―――. *The Bostonians.* 1885. E-text from the Henry James Online website @ www.

2.new paltz.edu/~hathaway (10 February 2005).

Kant, Immanuel. "Perpetual Peace: A Philosophical Sketch." 1795. In *Kant, Selections.* Edited by Lewis White Beck. New York: Macmillan, 1988. 430–457.

Lacoue-Labarthe, Philippe. *Typography.* 1986. Edited and translated by Christopher Fynsk. Cambridge, Mass.: Harvard, 1989.

Lacoue-Labarthe, Philippe and Nancy, Jean-Luc. 1978. *L'absolu littéraire.* Paris: Seuil, 1978.

Liquid Sky. 1983. Directed by Slava Tsukerman from a screenplay by Slava Tsukerman and Anne Carlisle.

Mandelbrot, Benoit. *The Practical Geometry of Nature.* 1977. New York: W. H. Freeman, 20th edition, augmented and updated, 2004.

The Metaphysical Poets. Selected and edited by Dame Helen Gardner. Harmondsworth, England: Penguin, 1973–1974.

Les Mille et une nuits. Translated by Antoine Galland. 1704. Paris: Flammarion, 1965.

Mitchell, David. *Cloud Atlas.* 2004. New York: Random House, 2004

————. *Ghostwritten.* 1999. New York: Random House, 1999.

Murakami, Haruki. *Kafka on the Shore.* 2005. Translated by Philip Gabriel. New York: Knopf, 2005.

————. *The Wind-Up Bird Chronicle.* 1998. Translated by Jay Rubin. New York: Knopf, 1998.

Nancy, Jean-Luc. *The Experience of Freedom.* 1988. Translated by Bridget McDonald. Palo Alto: Stanford U. Press, 1993.

Nietzsche, Friedrich. *Morgenröte: Gedanken über die moralischen Vorurteile.* 1881. Munich: Goldmann, 1980.

Novalis. *Fragmente.* 1798–1801. Stuttgart: Reclam, 1972.

The Poems of Ossian. 1762. Translated by James Macpherson, Esq. Boston: Philips, Sampson, 1853.

Pasolini, Pier Paolo. *Il Fiore delle mille et una notte (Arabian Nights).* 1974. Screenplay by Piero Pasolini and Dacia Maraini. Adapted/translated from the literary text.

Pindar. *Nemean I.* Translated by T. K. Hubbard. Tufts Perseus project @ http://www.perseus.tufts.edu/cgi-bin/ptext?doc=Perseus:text:1999.01.0162 (28 December 2004).

Pindari Epinikia. Edited by Alexander Turyn. New York: Institute of Polish Arts and Sciences in America, 1944.

Poe, Edgar Allan. *Poetry and Tales.* Edited by Patrick Quinn. New York: Library of America, 11th printing, 1984.

Powell, Padgett. *Edisto.* 1983. New York: Holt, Rinehart, Winston, 1985.

Rescher, Nicholas. *Complexity.* 1998. New Brunswick and London: Transaction, 1998.

Philipp Otto Runges Briefwechsel mit Goethe. Edited by Hellmuth Freiherr von Maltzahn. Schriften der Goethe-Gesellschaft. 51. Band. Weimar, 1940.

Runge, Philipp Otto. *Die Tageszeiten (The Times of Day).* 1802–1803. Four compositional sketches.

——. *Die Tageszeiten (The Times of Day).* 1805. Engraved sketches.

——. *Der Morgen.* 1808. Oil painting. 10.9 cm. X 8.6 cm.

——. *Der Morgen.* 1808–1809. Oil painting surviving in large fragments. 152 cm. X 113 cm. in the restoration suggested by Almir and Delmar Mavignier and described in *Art* (German), October, 1998 and on the Internet @ www.mavignier.mal_run.htm (15 January 2005).

Schelling, F. W. J. "Die Epikuräisch[en] Glaubensbekenntnisse Heinz Widerporstens." 1798. In Manfred Frank, *Eine Einführung in Schellings Naturphilosophie.* Frankfurt/M.: Suhrkamp, 1985.

Schiller, Friedrich. "Philosophische Briefe." 1786. In *Sämtliche Werke*, V, "Erzählungen und theoretische Schriften." Edited by Gerhard Fricke and Herbert Göpfert. Munich: Hanser, 4th edition, 1965. 336–358.

Schlegel, Friedrich. *Lucinde.* 1799. Munich: Goldmann, no date.

——. "Rede über die Mythologie." 1800. In *The Romantic Tradition in Germany.* Edited by Ronald Taylor. London: Methuen, 1970. 165–171.

Shaftesbury, Lord. *Characteristicks of men, manners, opinions, times.* 1711 and 1714. Birmingham, fifth edition, 1773.

Shakespeare, William. *The Sonnets.* Edited by Douglas Bush and Alfred Harbage. New York: Penguin, 1989.

Simms, William Gilmore. *The Yemassee.* 1835. Boston: Houghton, Mifflin, 1961.

Walpole, Horace. *Hieroglyphic Tales.* 1766–1772. Edited by Thomas Christensen. San Francisco: Mercury House. 1993.

Williams, William Carlos. *In the American Grain.* 1925. New York; New Directions, 1956.

Wordsworth, William. "Celebrated Epitaphs Considered." Ca. 1810. From the Author's MSS. In *Prose Works of William Wordsworth.* Edited by Rev. Alexander B. Grosart. London: Edward Moxon, 1876; rpt. New York: AMS Press, 1967. Vol. II. 60–75.

————. *Poetical Works of Wordsworth.* Edited by Thomas Hutchinson and Ernest de Selincourt. London: Oxford U. Press, 1960.

————. *The Prelude or Growth of a Poet's Mind* (Text of 1799). In *Poetical Works,* vol. 2 (1799). Project Gutenberg e-text in the edition of William Knight (1896) @ http://www.gutenberg.org/dirs (28 November 2004).

————. *The Prelude or Growth of a Poet's Mind* (Text of 1805). Edited by Ernest de Selincourt, revised by Stephen Gill. London: Oxford, 1970.

Wordsworth, William and Coleridge, Samuel. *The Lyrical Ballads.* Edited by W. J. B. Owen. Oxford: Oxford U. Press, second edition 1980.

Secondary Sources

Abrams, M. H. *Natural Supernaturalism.* New York: Norton, 1973.

Allen, Hervey. *Israfel: The Life and Times of Edgar Allan Poe.* New York: Farrar and Rinehart, 1934.

Anfam, David. *Mark Rothko.* London and New Haven: Yale U. Press, 1999.

Apter, Emily. "Radical Pastoral," a review of John Kinsella's *Peripheral Light: New and Selected Poems.* In *The Boston Review,* April/May 2004.

Barth, John. *Further Fridays.* New York: Little, Brown, 1995.

Baseball/Literature/Culture: Essays, 1995-2001. Edited by Peter Carino. Jefferson, North Carolina: McFarland, 2003.

Baseball/Literature/Culture: Essays, 2002–2003. Edited by Peter Carino. Jefferson, North Carolina: McFarland, 2004.

Baudelaire, Charles. "Edgar Poe: sa vie et ses oeuvres" and "Notes nouvelles sur Edgar Poe." In Charles Baudelaire, *L'art romantique: littérature et musique.* Paris: Garnier-Flammarion, 1968. 111–148 and 175–192.

Beer, John. *Wordsworth and the Human Heart.* New York: Columbia U. Press, 1978.

Benardete, Seth. *Socrates' Second Sailing.* Chicago: U. of Chicago Press, 1989.

Bewell Alan. *Wordsworth and the Enlightenment.* New Haven: Yale U. Press, 1989.

Bewell, Alan J. "Wordsworth's Primal Scene: Retrospective Tales of Idiots, Wild Children, and Savages." *ELH*, Vol. 50, No. 2 (Summer, 1983). 321–346.

Bromwich, David. *Disowned by Memory.* Chicago, U. of Chicago Press, 1998.

Bueckling, Adrian. "Philipp Otto Runges Beziehungen zu Goethe. Rungehaus website @ www. usedom-exclusiv.de/fruejahr2003/runge2.htm (10 May 2005).

The Cambridge History of English and American Literature in 18 Volumes (1907–21). Volume VII. Cavalier and Puritan. Online version @ bartleby.com/cambridge/. (27 December 2004).

Campbell, Joseph. *The Masks of Creative Mythology.* New York: Viking, sixth printing 1974.

Chandler, David. "Southey's 'German Sublimity' and Coleridge's 'Dutch Attempt'" In *Romanticism Online*, 32–33, Nov. 2003–Feb. 2004 @ www. erudit. org. revue/ron 2003.

Chatman, Seymour. *Story and Discourse: Narrative Structure in Fiction and Film.* Ithaca: Cornell U. Press, 1978.

Chauncey, Richard. *Wordsworth's Classical Undersong.* New York: St. Martin's, 2000.

Clark, William Bedford. "The Serpent of Lust in the Southern Garden." *The Southern Review*, vol. X, 4 (Autumn, 1974). 805–822.

Clarke, Grahame. *Aspects of Prehistory.* Berkeley: U. of California Press, 1974.

Dahlberg, Edward. *Alms for Oblivion.* Minneapolis: U. of Minnesota Press, 1964.

Dahlberg, Edward. *Can These Bones Live.* Ann Arbor: U. of Michigan Press, 1967.

Davie, Donald. "Poetic Diction and Poetic Strength." In *The Augustan Age.* Edited by Ian Watt. New York: Fawcett, 1968. 272–277.

Deleuze, Gilles. *Nietzsche and Philosophy.* Translated by Hugh Tomlinson. New York: Columbia U. Press, 1983.

De Man, Paul. *Allegories of Reading.* New Haven: Yale U. Press, 1979.

De Man, Paul. *Blindness and Insight: Essays in the Rhetoric of Contemporary Criticism.* (Minneapolis: U. of Minnesota Press, second edition revised, 1983.

De Man, Paul. "Foreword" to Carol Jacobs' *The Dissimulating Harmony.* In *Critical Writings, 1953-1978.* Edited by Lindsay Waters. Minneapolis: U. of Minnesota Press, 1988. 218–223.

De Man, Paul. "Wordsworth and the Victorians." In *The Rhetoric of Romanticism.* New

York: Columbia U. Press, 1984. 83–92.

Eisenhauer, Robert. "Wanderers at the Spa: Baths as a Source of Cultural Ethos in Goethe and Others." In *Mythic Paradigms in Literature, Philosophy, and the Arts*. Bern and New York: Peter Lang, 2004. 323–331.

_____. *Paradox and Perspicacity: Horizons of Knowledge in the Literary Text*. Bern and New York: Peter Lang, 2004.

Eliot, T. S. "John Dryden." in *The Augustan Age*. Edited by Ian Watt. New York: Fawcett, 1968. 198–207

Felluga, Dino. "The Road Is Clear: Application." *Introductory Guide to Critical Theory* @ http: // www.sla.purdue.edu/academic/engl/theory/index.html. Purdue U. <http: // www. purdue. edu/ guidetotheory/narratology/ applications/ applicTheRoadisClear2.html> (12 December 2004).

Ferrer, Daniel. "In omnis iam vocabuli mortem: Representation of Absence: The Subject of Representation and Absence of the Subject in William Faulkner's *As I Lay Dying*." *The Oxford Literary Review*, vol. 5 (1982), 1 & 2. 21–36.

Flowers, Sylvia. "Desoto's Expedition" @ www. nps.gov.ocmu/Desoto.htm (20 March 2005).

Frank, Manfred. *Kaltes Herz, Unendliche Fahrt, Neue Mythologie. Motivuntersuchung zur Pathogenese der Modernen*. F./M.: Suhrkamp, 1989.

Frye, Northrop. "New Directions from Old." In *Myth and Myth-Making*. New York: Braziller, 1960. 113–131.

Geertz, Clifford. *Islam Observed*. Chicago: U. of Chicago Press, 1973.

Gesche, Janina. "Geographische Realität und Fantasielandschaft." In *Das literarische und kulturelle Erbe von Danzig und Gdańsk*. F./M.: Peter Lang, 2004. 35–46.

Grutzmacher, Kurt. *Novalis und Philipp Otto Runge. Die Zentralmotive und ihre Bedeutungssphäre, Die Blume—Das Kind—Das Licht*. Munich, 1964.

Guggenheim Museum, descriptive brochure for the Barney exhibition, April 9, 2002, as published on the Internet @ www.guggenheim.org/exhibitions/past_exhibitions/barney/ (10 February, 2005).

Hamilton, John T. *Soliciting Darkness: Pindar, Obscurity, and the Classical Tradition*. Cambridge, Mass.: Harvard U. Press, 2003.

Hanley, Keith. "Wordsworth's Revolution in Poetic Language." *Romanticism on the Net* 9 (Feb., 1998) @ www. erudit. org. revue/ron 98.

Hartman, Geoffrey. "Beyond Formalism." In *Velocities of Change*. Edited by Richard Macksey. Baltimore: Johns Hopkins U. Press, 1973. 103–117.

Hartman, Geoffrey. "Trauma within the limits of literature" (June 2002). In *Newsletter* 2 @ www.traumaresearch.net/fr_net.htm" (25 January 2005).

Hartman, Geoffrey. The *Unmediated Vision.* New York: Harcourt, Brace, 1966.

Hartman, Geoffrey. "Wordsworth and Goethe in Literary History." In *The Fate of Reading.* Chicago: U. of Chicago Press, 1975. 179–200,

Hartman, Geoffrey. *Wordsworth's Poetry, 1787–1814.* New Haven: Yale U. Press, 6th printing, 1977.

Hazlitt, William. "Lectures on the Living Poets." In *Lectures on English Poets and The Spirit of the Age.* London: Dent, 1939.

Heller, Erich. *The Disinherited Mind.* Cleveland and New York: Meridian, 1969.

Heller, Otto. "Goethe and Wordsworth." *Modern Language Notes*, XIV (May, 1899). 262–265.

Heringman, Noah. "Things And Sense in Two Lyrics Of Wordsworth." @ www. prometheus.cc.emory.edu (14 November 2004).

Herzberg, Max J. "William Wordsworth and German Literature." *PMLA* XL (#2, June, 1925. 302–345.

Herzfeld, Georg. *William Taylor von Norwich. Eine Studie über den Einfluss der neueren deutschen Litteratur in England.* Halle: M. Niemeyer, 1897.

Hickey, Alison. *Impure Conceits:Rhetoric and Ideology in Wordsworth's Excursion.* Palo Alto: Stanford U. Press, 1997.

Hölderlin, Friedrich. *Sämtliche Werke.* Kritische Textausgabe. Edited by D. E. Sattler. F./M.: Luchterhand, 1987. XV (Pindar).

Huch, Ricarda. *Gesammelte Werke.* Cologne and Berlin: Kiepenheuer & Witsch, 1969. Volume VI.

Irwin, John. *American Hieroglyphics.* New Haven: Yale U. Press, 1980.

Johnson, Samuel. "The Life of Abraham Cowley." From *The Penn State Archive of Samuel Johnson's Lives of the Poets.* Ed. Kathleen Nulton Kemmerer. (1 January 2005).

Johnston, Kenneth. *Wordsworth and 'The Recluse.'* New Haven: Yale U. Press, 1984.

Jølle, Jonas. "Goethe's Translation of Pindar's *Fifth Olympian Ode.*" *Goethe Yearbook* X. Rochester, N. Y.: Camden House, 2001. 50–64.

Jones, Steven E. *Satire and Romanticism.* New York: St. Martin's, 2000.

Keisch, Claude, and others. *The Romantic Spirit, German Drawings, 1780-1850, from the*

Nationalgalerie (Stattliche Museen, Berlin) and the Kupferstich-Kabinett (Staatliche Kunstsammlingen, Dresden), German Democratic Republic. New York: The Pierpont Morgan Library and Oxford U. Press, 1988.

Kenner, Hugh. *The Counterfeiters: An Historical Comedy.* New York: Doubleday, 1973.

Langan, Celeste. *Romantic Vagrancy: Wordsworth and the Simulation of Freedom.* Cambridge, England: Cambridge U. Press, 1995.

LAVIS III (Language Variety in the South): Historical and Contemporary Perspectives, University of Alabama in Tuscaloosa, April 16, 2004 @ http://www.ecu.edu/english/tcr/22 (23 December 2004).

Laplanche, Jean. *New Foundations for Psychoanalysis.* Translated by David Macey. Oxford and Cambridge, Mass.: Blackwell, 1988.

Laplanche, Jean. "To Situate Sublimation." Translated by Richard Miller. *October* 28 (Spring, 1984). 7–26.

Laplanche, Jean and Pontalis, J.-B. *Urphantasie. Phantasien über den Ursprung der Phantasie.* Translated by Max Looser. Frankfurt/M.: 1992.

Lawall, Gilbert. *Theocritus' Coan Pastorals.* Washington: Center for Hellenic Studies, 1967.

Le Gallienne, Richard. "Vanishing Roads." Project Gutenberg e-text @ www. gutenberg. org/etext/11675 (28 November 2004).

Levinson, Marjorie. *Wordsworth's great period poems. Four Essays.* Cambridge, England, Cambridge U. Press, 1986.

Luck, Georg. *Arcana Mundi.* Baltimore: Johns Hopkins U. Press, 1995.

Mailer, Norman. *Advertisements for Myself.* New York: Putnam's/Signet, 1960.

Miall, David. "Locating Wordsworth: 'Tintern Abbey' and the Community with Nature" (*Romanticism Online*, 20 (November, 2000) @ www. erudit. org. revue/ron 2000.

Morson, Gary Saul and Emerson, Caryl. "Bakhtin." In *The Johns Hopkins Guide to Literary History and Criticism.* Baltimore: Johns Hopkins U., 1993. 63–68.

Nabokov, Vladimir. *Gogol.* New York: New Directions, reprint 1961.

Nägele, Rainer. *Echoes of Translation.* Baltimore: Johns Hopkins U. Press, 1997.

The Native Muse: Theories of American Literature. Edited by Richard Ruland. New York: Dutton, 1976), I.

Pater, Walter. "Wordsworth." In *Appreciations.* London: Macmillan, reprint 1911.

Pound, Ezra. "Lionel Johnson." In *Literary Essays of Ezra Pound.* New York: New

Directions, 1968.

Praz, Mario. *The Romantic Agony.* Translated by Angus Davidson. London, 1933.

Queneau, Raymond. "Écrit en 1937." In *bâtons, chiffres et lettres.* Paris: NRF, 1965.

Rickels, Laurence. *The Case of California.* Baltimore: Johns Hopkins U. Press, 1991.

Rockwell John. "Off the Wall and onto the Stage." *The New York Times*, pages B1 and B7. February 7, 2005.

Ronell, Avital. *Dictations: On Haunted Writing.* Lincoln, Nebraska: U. of Nebraska, 1986.

Rosenblum, Robert. *Modern Painting and the Northern Romantic Tradition: From Friedrich to Rothko.* New York: Harper and Row. 1975.

Salvatore, Alain. "Le problème de la *fin*, les *moyens*, et le rôle du diable dans la production artistique: le problème de l'art dans *Les Nouvelles de Petersbourg*" @ http://opus-all.paris.iufm.fr/tl/tl_gogol/art.htm (30 January, 2005).

Schier, Rudolf Dirk. "The Experience of the Noumenal in Goethe and Wordsworth," *Comparative Literature*, Vol. 25, No. 1 (Winter, 1973). 37–59.

Sicha, Choire. "The Art of the Fan." *New York Times*, section 2, page 2, January 2, 2005.

Smith, Patricia C. "Poe's Arabesque." *Poe Studies*, vol. VII, no. 2 (December, 1974). 42–45.

Starobinski, Jean. *La transparence et l'obstacle.* Paris, 1957.

Stuckenschmidt, H. H. *Twentieth-Century Music.* Translated by Richard Deveson. New York: McGraw-Hill, 1972.

Tarn, Nathaniel. "The Heraldic Vision: A Cognitive Model for Comparative Aesthetics." In *Alcheringa/Ethnopoetics*, A First International Symposium, edited by Benamou and Rothenberg. Boston University, 1976.

Thompson, J. P. *Witness to the Beast.* New York: New Press, 1993.

Upward, Allen. *The Divine Mystery.* Santa Barbara: Ross-Erikson, rpt. 1976.

Warminski, Andzrej. "Pre-positional By-play." *Glyph 3.* Baltimore: Johns Hopkins U. Press, 1978. 98–117.

Weiskel, Thomas. *The Romantic Sublime.* Baltimore, Johns Hopkins U. Press, 1976.

Wellek, René. *Concepts of Criticism.* New Haven: Yale U. Press, 1963.

Willoughby, L. A. "The Image of the 'Wanderer' and the 'Hut' in Goethe's Poetry." In *Études Germaniques*, nos. 3–4, July–Dec 1951. 207–219.

Wordsworth, Jonathan. *The Music of Humanity.* London: Nelson, 1969.

Wordsworth, Jonathan. *William Wordsworth, The Borders of Vision* Oxford, Clarendon 1984.

Wu Duncan. "Navigated by Magic: Wordsworth's Cambridge Sonnets," *The Review of English Studies*, New Series, Vol. 46, No. 183 (August, 1995), 352–365.

Wu, Duncan. *Wordsworth: An Inner Life.* Oxford: Blackwell, 2002.

Zedler's Universal-Lexicon. @ http://mdz.bib-bvb.de/digbib/lexika/zedler (10 December 2004).

Index

[Explanatory note: a number of key terms appear in the index in **boldface** print. These are provided as an aid to those interested in a particular focus of discussion.]

Studies on Themes and Motifs in Literature

The series is designed to advance the publication of research pertaining to themes and motifs in literature. The studies cover cross-cultural patterns as well as the entire range of national literatures. They trace the development and use of themes and motifs over extended periods, elucidate the significance of specific themes or motifs for the formation of period styles, and analyze the unique structural function of themes and motifs. By examining themes or motifs in the work of an author or period, the studies point to the impulses authors received from literary tradition, the choices made, and the creative transformation of the cultural heritage. The series will include publications of colloquia and theoretical studies that contribute to a greater understanding of literature.

For additional information about this series or for the submission of manuscripts, please contact:

Dr. Heidi Burns
Peter Lang Publishing
P.O. Box 1246
Bel Air, MD 21014-1246

To order other books in this series, please contact our Customer Service Department:

800-770-LANG (within the U.S.)
212-647-7706 (outside the U.S.)
212-647-7707 FAX

Or browse online by series at:

www.peterlangusa.com